Also by Tim Weiner

Blank Check: The Pentagon's Black Budget

Legacy of Ashes: The History of the CIA

Enemies: A History of the FBI

ONE MAN AGAINST THE WORLD

President Richard M. Nixon, June 23, 1972—the day of the "smoking gun" tape

ONE MAN AGAINST THE WORLD

THE TRAGEDY OF RICHARD NIXON

Tim Weiner

HENRY HOLT AND COMPANY

NEW YORK

Henry Holt and Company, LLC
Publishers since 1866
175 Fifth Avenue
New York, New York 10010
www.henryholt.com

Henry Holt® and 🅗® are registered trademarks of Henry Holt and Company, LLC.

Library of Congress Cataloging-in-Publication Data

Weiner, Tim.
  One man against the world : the tragedy of Richard Nixon / Tim Weiner. — First
edition.
     pages cm
  ISBN 978-1-62779-083-3 (hardcover) — ISBN 978-1-62779-084-0 (e-book)
1. Nixon, Richard M. (Richard Milhous), 1913–1994. 2. Presidents—United States—
Biography. 3. United States—Politics and government—1969–1974. I. Title.
  E856.W425 2015
  973.924092—dc23
  [B]   2015012381

Henry Holt books are available for special promotions and premiums.
For details contact: Director, Special Markets.

Designed by Meryl Sussman Levavi

Printed in the United States of America

3 5 7 9 10 8 6 4

To Kate, Emma, and Ruby Doyle,

with everlasting love

Contents

ONE MAN AGAINST THE WORLD

Author's Note

Balzac once wrote that politicians are "monsters of self-possession." Yet while we may show this veneer on the outside, inside the turmoil becomes almost unbearable.

—Richard M. Nixon, *Six Crises*, 1962

RICHARD NIXON led the United States through a time of unbearable turmoil. He made war in pursuit of peace. He committed crimes in the name of the law. He tore the country apart while trying to unite it. He sabotaged his presidency by violating the Constitution. He destroyed himself and damaged the nation through deliberate acts of folly.

He vowed to bring the tragedy of Vietnam to an honorable end; he brought death and disgrace instead. He practiced geopolitics without subtlety; he preferred subterfuge and brutality. He dropped bombs and napalm without remorse; he believed they delivered a political message beyond blood and fire. He charted the course of the war without a strategy; he delivered victory to his adversaries.

His gravest decisions undermined his allies abroad. His grandest delusions armed his enemies at home. "I gave them a sword," he said after his downfall, "and they stuck it in."

That sword was a weapon he forged and sharpened himself. His conduct in office bent the Constitution to its breaking point. The truth was not in him; secrecy and deception were his touchstones.

Yet he had an undeniable greatness, an unsurpassed gift for the art of politics, an unquestionable desire to change the world. He wielded power like a Shakespearean king.

In his eyes, he stood above the law, and that was his fatal flaw, for he fell like a king fated to die in the final act of a tragedy. His arrogation of power created the criminal conduct that his White House counsel warned him was "a cancer within, close to the presidency, that's growing. It's growing daily."

This book is a history of Richard Nixon's anguished presidency. It concentrates on the intertwined issues of war and national security, because Nixon spent so many of his hours and so much of his power wrestling with those twin demons.

Nixon was the first president I remember vividly. I saw the anger in his eyes and I heard the anguish in his voice as he spoke to the nation about the war in Vietnam. His dark scowl, radiating from our black-and-white television, was an image as indelible as the bloody battles broadcast on the nightly news. I witnessed hundreds of thousands of citizens marching against the war in Washington, while I read that hundreds of American soldiers were dying every week. I talked with my parents about what I would do if drafted into battle. I gasped when National Guardsmen killed four kids at Kent State in Ohio during a protest against Nixon's invasion of Cambodia. It dawned on me that dissent could be dangerous, even in a democratic country.

Nixon's grasp on power began to slip soon after he won reelection in 1972 by a margin of almost eighteen million votes, the largest in American history. He was undone by the slow but steady revelation of "the White House horrors," in the immortal words of John N. Mitchell, Nixon's former attorney general and campaign manager, one among many once-honorable men who went to prison to protect the president. The Watergate break-in was only one of those horrors, and hardly the worst.

I was riveted by the televised congressional hearings that forced his closest aides to lie about the dirty tricks he had deployed to secure his overwhelming victory. I was transfixed by the intensity of the struggle as the White House battled Congress and the Supreme Court over the president's prerogatives. At first Nixon seemed to fight under the rule of law rather than the laws of war. Then he fired the attorney general and the special prosecutor in charge of the Watergate investigation; he would risk impeachment and ponder imprisonment rather than release his secret White House tapes. His days were numbered after that blunder. I recall the last throes of his doomed presidency, the pathos of his farewell to the nation.

Nixon has fascinated me ever since. I wrote about his command and control of the Central Intelligence Agency and the Federal Bureau of Investigation in two books, *Legacy of Ashes* and *Enemies.* As a reporter for the *New York Times*, I interviewed some of his right-hand men, among them Henry Kissinger, his national security adviser and secretary of state. I have discussed Nixon's legacy with the presidents who succeeded him, Gerald Ford and Jimmy Carter. I covered the continuing debate over the disgraced president's reputation and his rightful place in history. So I thought I knew something of the man when I began this work.

Then I dug into a treasure trove of top-secret records from the Nixon years, recently released from the vaults of the government of the United States. This book is based in great part on documents declassified between 2007 and 2014. I read them with a growing excitement. I felt like an archaeologist unearthing the palace of a lost empire.

Tens of thousands of files from his White House, his National Security Council, the CIA, the FBI, the State Department, the Pentagon, and the Joint Chiefs of Staff were newly unsealed. So were minutes of the secret White House committees that controlled military and intelligence operations under Nixon. The transcripts of federal grand jury testimony by Nixon himself, the only president ever compelled to answer questions under oath in a criminal case, were now public records. Hundreds of hours of his infamous tapes finally came out in 2013 and 2014, along with previously classified entries in the daily diary of Nixon's closest aide, H. R. Haldeman. Together, they ensure that every quotation and each citation herein is on the record: no blind quotes, no unnamed sources, and no hearsay statements.

We have laws governing the declassification of documents and freedom of information, and they endure despite all that has been done in the name of government secrecy in the United States. Without them, the acts that President Nixon hoped to conceal forever would remain state secrets.

What compelled him to commit crimes—secretly collecting campaign cash from foreign dictators and aspiring American ambassadors, wiretapping his loyal aides and distinguished diplomats as if they were foreign spies—and then conspire to conceal them? Why did he drive the nation deeper into Vietnam, at a cost of tens of thousands of American lives, only to accept a settlement no better than the one he could have signed on his first day in office? Why did he lie about his war plans to his secretary of defense and his secretary of state? What were the Watergate burglars seeking? Why did Nixon tape-record the evidence that proved his complicity in the cover-up? Why did he undertake the unconstitutional actions that led to his resignation?

Now we have answers, straight from the president and his closest aides. The story is richer and stranger than we ever knew.

For those who lived under Nixon, it is worse than you may recollect. For those too young to recall, it is worse than you can imagine.

"Always remember," Nixon said on the day he resigned, "others may hate you. But those who hate you don't win unless you hate them. And then you destroy yourself." This story is the tragedy of a man destroying himself.

CHAPTER ONE

"A great, bad man"

Richard Nixon saw himself as a great statesman, a giant for the ages, a general who could command the globe, a master of war, not merely the leader of the free world but *"the* world leader." Yet he was addicted to the gutter politics that ruined him. He was—as an English earl once said of the warlord Oliver Cromwell—"a great, bad man."

In Nixon's first State of the Union speech, he said that he was possessed by "an indefinable spirit—the lift of a driving dream which has made America, from its beginning, the hope of the world." He promised the American people "the best chance since World War II to enjoy a generation of uninterrupted peace."

But Richard Nixon was never at peace. A darker spirit animated him—malevolent and violent, driven by anger and an insatiable appetite for revenge. At his worst he stood on the brink of madness. He thought the world was against him. He saw enemies everywhere. His greatness became an arrogant grandeur.

By experience deeply suspicious, by instinct incurably deceptive, he was branded by an indelible epithet: Tricky Dick. No less a man than Martin Luther King Jr. saw a glimpse of the monster beneath the veneer the first time they met, when King was the rising leader of the civil rights movement. "Nixon has a genius for convincing one that he is sincere," King wrote in 1958. "If Richard Nixon is not sincere, he is the most dangerous man in America."

Nixon had that genius, a genuine conviction that he could change the world. He was also a most dangerous man.

He had vowed all his political life to fight communism; then he clinked glasses with the world's foremost Communist tyrants in China and Russia. He gambled on their good faith; he had hopes that they would help him out of Vietnam. He lost that bet. Had he won, he might have remade the political map of the planet. In the long run, at best America broke even after Nixon went to the capitals of world communism. He returned with treaties and statements signifying comity and coexistence, but these liaisons were fragile. They were political communiqués, not peace deals. Russia and China were our greatest foes then; they remain America's strongest opponents today.

Nixon was realistic about America's relations with them. "We are still dealing with governments that are basically hostile to us," he said in May 1971, each word recorded on tape. "Those Chinese are out to whip me." As for the Russians, he called their leaders gangsters. He predicted that mutual mistrust would prevail. "They particularly won't believe me," he said in the Oval Office that same spring. "You see, they really think I'm a tricky bastard. And they're right."

But Nixon wanted to give the American people what he had promised: an honorable end to the war in Vietnam. If he achieved that goal, he calculated that he could win reelection by a landslide so enormous that the landscape of American politics would be forever altered. And that was *why* Nixon went to China.

Nixon's geostrategic gambits were a great success with the majority of the American people. "Nixon went to China" remains a catchphrase for politics as the art of the possible. If America's cold warrior in chief could champion détente, easing tensions with the United States' nuclear-armed adversaries, then *anything* was possible.

* * *

The political and social crises Nixon faced still confront the country today. He faced them with his genius for appearing sincere.

Equal justice under law, words engraved on the entrance to the Supreme Court, was an elusive ideal. The civil rights laws of the 1960s were barely four years old. Nixon was given to making racist remarks in private; he tried with all his might to dismantle the new federal agencies designed to enforce racial equality and social justice. He supported desegregation in principle, because the Supreme Court demanded it, but in practice, and in detail, he resisted it.

Nixon confided in private that he would always favor the economic interests of corporations over the environment. But when Americans realized they were ruining the air they breathed and the water they drank, they marched in great numbers in the name of saving the earth. In response, Congress passed the strongest environmental laws in American history. To his credit, Nixon signed them, along with rules and regulations to enforce them. Yet he believed, as he said, that "the environment is not an issue that's worth a damn to us."

Nixon said time and again that he really *didn't* give a damn about the domestic issues of the day. He contended that the country could run itself without a president to watch over every picayune political problem. He embraced economic policies that were "in the long run . . . a catastrophe," in the words of George P. Shultz, his treasury secretary. Unemployment and inflation nearly tripled during the Nixon years; this led to the longest recession in four decades.

His clashes with the courts left lasting wounds on the American body politic. He had an abiding contempt for Congress, and he treated most of his Cabinet with cool disdain. His conferences with congressional leaders and Cabinet members and the National Security Council were show-and-tell sessions, not the time or place for policies to take shape. These full-dress meetings were shadow plays. He had reached his life-or-death resolutions before they convened.

Nixon would appear to hear out his most senior military, diplomatic, and intelligence chiefs. But he didn't want advice or counsel from the Pentagon or the CIA, where there were men who had devoted their lives to Vietnam since Americans first left footprints in the mud back in 1954. The sword of war and the shield of national security were his alone to wield.

"Nixon never trusted anybody," wrote Richard Helms, his CIA chieftain, one among the many leading figures of his administration who would face the prospect of prison for protecting the president from the consequences of his secrecy and deception. "He was constantly telling people that the Air Force in their bombings in Vietnam couldn't hit their ass with their hand, the State Department was just a bunch of pinstriped cocktail-drinking diplomats, the Agency couldn't come up with a winning victory in Vietnam."

The president's harangues went "on and on and on," Helms remembered. Nixon ranted: "They are dumb, they are stupid, they can't do this, and they can't do that." These same generals, spymasters, admirals, and ambassadors were America's point men in an increasingly impossible war. Nixon's lack of faith in them was immutable—and, ultimately, mutual.

This mistrust led him to deceive his Cabinet, the Congress, and the citizenry about the course of the war as he charted it. He saw himself as commander in chief not only of the army and the navy, as the Constitution says, but of all the American people. He was the leader of a worldwide battle where the future of the nation was at stake. His enemies abroad and his enemies at home, he felt, were conspiring to bring the United States to its knees.

Nixon believed to the marrow of his bones that the Soviets, the Chinese, the North Vietnamese, and the Cubans were secretly financing the American antiwar movement, which could mobilize a million marchers at a month's notice. These people were mainstream citizens, not mad bombers. Yet while Nixon was still getting his bearings as president, a small faction of the radical left, a few hundred people, broke away to form a revolutionary gang called the Weathermen. The marchers carried placards; the Weathermen preferred Molotov cocktails. They set off small bombs inside the Senate and the Pentagon; the FBI never caught the bombers. The Weathermen declared war on the government; Nixon called them terrorists. The response he demanded—a series of illegal break-ins and warrantless wiretaps—would result in the indictments of the leaders of the FBI, not the bombers they pursued.*

---

* Terrorism started showing its modern masked face in 1970. Arab radicals seized international flights and held Americans hostage. An Iraqi planted a car bomb at New York's Kennedy Airport; his target was the Israeli leader Golda Meir. American Zionists tried to kill Soviet diplomats in the United States. The Palestinian gang Black September murdered Israeli athletes at the 1972 Summer Olympics in Germany and assassinated the American ambassador in Sudan. Nixon set up the first presidential commission on terrorism in 1972. It met once; nothing came of it. Each crisis was addressed as it arose, without a policy or a strategy. The Weathermen killed no one but themselves, due to their incompetent bomb making and their persistent intake of psychedelic drugs.

Nixon insisted that the CIA and the FBI discover the sources of underground Communist support for American peace groups. Where was the evidence? His intelligence chiefs reported that none existed. Yet Nixon convinced himself that the capital was besieged by Americans who had formed enemy battalions financed by Moscow and Beijing and Hanoi and Havana. He saw the antiwar movement as the fifth column of international communism.

Washington became a combat zone when the radical left confronted Richard Nixon. Tear gas hurled by police against protesters wafted through the windows of the Justice Department headquarters, gagging Attorney General Mitchell. Army soldiers in full combat gear camped on the fourth floor of the Executive Office Building, next door to the White House, to protect the president from attack. The days of rage and fear passed for the protesters. But not for Nixon: he was scarred by a quarter century of political warfare against his enemies. He stayed on high alert.

* * *

Nixon saw the clashes he faced in Washington and around the world as a continuing constitutional crisis. He compared them to the Civil War, when President Abraham Lincoln suspended the law of habeas corpus, the ancient writ that allows anyone under arrest to appear before a court. Lincoln's act was unconstitutional, but he believed—and Nixon agreed—that there were times when a president had to break the law to save the nation.

"When the president does it, that means it is not illegal," Nixon insisted. "Actions which otherwise would be unconstitutional could become lawful if undertaken for the purpose of preserving the Constitution and the nation," he said. "This nation was torn apart in an ideological way by the war in Vietnam, as much as the Civil War tore apart the nation when Lincoln was president."

So no one could question Nixon's actions in the name of national security—not the courts, not the Congress, and certainly no citizen. And Nixon defined national security as far more than the powers of America's soldiers and spies to fight their enemies abroad. It included the powers of a secret police, the power to spy on American citizens, to break into their homes, to tap their telephones, to burglarize their offices, seeking evidence of sedition and treason. For Nixon, every American citizen and every elected official who opposed the war in Vietnam was an enemy, no less than a soldier of the army of North Vietnam, and he stood surrounded by foes left and right, the lone warrior.

Nixon believed that "it was 'me against the world,'" said Robert Finch, who served him for many years as a campaign manager, Cabinet officer, and presidential counselor.

The president, the pillar of national security, was undermined by his own political insecurity. Against all evidence that he would win an overwhelming reelection, he compulsively spied on his political opponents and sought secret cash contributions to shore up his campaign coffers. Against the law, he paid hush money to the crew of washed-up CIA and FBI agents arrested for the break-in at the Democratic National Committee headquarters in Washington. Against all logic, he wiretapped his loyal aides and compulsively tape-recorded his own complicity in the concomitant crimes, conspiracies, and cover-ups that destroyed him.

What drove him to political suicide? That was one secret Nixon hoped he might take to the grave.

* * *

He is buried next to the tiny wooden house where he was raised in Yorba Linda, California, amid what once were citrus groves coaxed from the dry land roughly forty miles southeast of Los Angeles, enclosed on the grounds of his presidential memorial and library. He was born more than a century ago, in 1913, on the eve of the First World War. Fewer than three hundred souls then inhabited Yorba Linda, most barely scraping by on what little the land could provide. Today it is a well-to-do suburb with landscaped lawns; the median household income exceeds one hundred twenty thousand dollars. One thing is unchanged: a railroad line runs through the heart of town, and as a child, Richard Nixon heard a locomotive's lonesome whistle, and he wondered if that train would carry him away and where it might take him.

"He hears the train go by at night and he dreams of faraway places where he'd like to go," Nixon said, in a rare invocation of his childhood memories. "It seems like an impossible dream."

He and his four brothers were named after British kings by a pious mother and a hot-tempered father with a sixth-grade education who barely made a go of it as a greengrocer. "He had a lemon ranch," Nixon remembered. "It was the poorest lemon ranch in California, I can assure you. He sold it before they found oil on it." Richard's childhood was unhappy. Two of his siblings died young. He strove with quiet desperation to escape the depths of the Depression, to invent a new life outside the dusty and desolate confines of his youth.

Twenty years old when President Franklin D. Roosevelt first took office in 1933, Nixon put himself through the local college in Whittier. He tried out for the football team, but was consigned to the bench as a water boy. He won a full scholarship to Duke University's law school by dint of hard work and ambition, but no great opportunity awaited him after his 1937 graduation. He sought positions at prestigious New York law firms, but received no offers. He applied to be an agent at the Federal Bureau of Investigation, but received no reply. Only one man, a twenty-seven-year-old assistant law professor at Duke named Kenneth Rush, saw the potential in Nixon. Rush advised his student to go back to California and get into politics.*

Nixon suffered another series of humiliations after returning home. He established a small law practice in Whittier, but writing wills and contracts bored him. His political aspirations were diminished. "The last thing my mother, a devout Quaker, wanted me to do was to go into the warfare of politics," Nixon recounted. (She dreamed he would become a missionary in Central America.) He courted the woman he would marry one day, Thelma "Pat" Ryan, but that day was long in coming.

She turned him down repeatedly when he asked for a first date; two years passed before his immediate attraction to her became mutual. They married in 1940 and their union lasted more than fifty years. Though she despised the darker side of politics, detested pressing the flesh on the campaign trail, and despaired at the pain her husband suffered in pursuit of power, she stayed with him in victory and defeat, stoic and steadfast in the solitary confinement of their marriage.

Commissioned as a navy lieutenant after Pearl Harbor, Richard Nixon served as a supply officer in the South Pacific, but never saw a moment of combat. When the war ended in 1945, he had no great

---

* This foresight proved fortuitous for both men. President Nixon returned the favor three decades later, by appointing Rush, a chemical company executive without experience in government, as the American ambassador to West Germany and then, by turns, deputy secretary of defense and deputy secretary of state.

prospects. Seven years later, he was on the way to the White House as the running mate of Dwight D. Eisenhower, America's greatest military hero.

* * *

Nixon's rise has few parallels in American politics. A member of a local Republican committee who knew Nixon from college urged him to run for Congress. Nixon challenged a popular Democratic incumbent in the November 1946 election. The contest coincided with the rising dawn of a great fear: that the Soviet Union would challenge Christian civilization in the United States, its spies and subversives burrowing into American institutions from college campuses to the chambers of the State Department and the corridors of the Pentagon.

Nixon ran as one of the first cold warriors. He fiercely attacked his opponent as the tool of Communist-controlled labor unions. He won handily. So did Republicans across the country: the party took control of both the Senate and the House for the first time in two decades.

By the time Nixon arrived in Washington, the war on communism was on in full. He sought and won membership on the newly revitalized House Un-American Activities Committee. Nixon and the committee's Republican staff would be supplied, in secret, with information from the FBI. That information, once Nixon grasped its significance, would soon propel him to power.

On March 26, 1947, the committee's members heard rare public testimony from the FBI director, J. Edgar Hoover, who already had run the Bureau for twenty-three years. He called upon them to summon "the zeal, the fervor, the persistence, and the industry to learn about this menace of Red fascism," and to beware "the liberal and the progressive who have been hoodwinked and duped into joining hands with the Communists."

Nixon took these words as his political credo. He and Hoover spoke one on one at the hearing's conclusion. They had an instant and instinctive meeting of the minds. The director urged Nixon to be on the lookout for Communist infiltration of the American government. Heeding Hoover, Nixon soon rose to nationwide fame hunting traitors and spies. Thus began an alliance that would last a quarter century. Nixon became a leading figure in the Cold War's culture of espionage and counterespionage, where bugging, break-ins, and wiretaps without warrants were weapons of political warfare. As president, Nixon would call Hoover "my closest friend in all of political life."

As the Cold War intensified and the Korean War erupted, Nixon won election to the U.S. Senate in 1950, catapulted upward by his relentless pursuit of Alger Hiss, a hunt for which Nixon received great acclaim and immense publicity. Hiss was a pillar of the Eastern Establishment, that congregation of well-raised, well-educated men who had ruled much of Washington for a generation; Nixon despised them by instinct. Hiss had been a standout at the State Department during World War II; he helped organize the Yalta Conference, where President Roosevelt, Prime Minister Winston Churchill, and Generalissimo Joseph Stalin met for the last time in the closing months of the war; he was a political architect of the blueprint for the United Nations.

When Nixon began hunting him, Hiss was running the Carnegie Endowment for International Peace. The endowment's chairman was John Foster Dulles, a Republican stalwart who would become President Eisenhower's secretary of state and, in time, a confidant to Richard Nixon.

The Hiss case was the first crisis by which Nixon defined his political life. The accusation that Alger Hiss had been a secret agent of the Soviet intelligence service seemed incredible. Nixon hunted him relentlessly, often ruthlessly, with the single-minded determination of a Hollywood homicide detective. He was convinced that the case involved "the security of the whole nation and the cause of free men everywhere."

Hiss faced one hostile witness, Whittaker Chambers (a *Time* magazine editor who had worked for the Soviet underground in the 1930s), and one deeply hidden shred of evidence that could condemn him as a spy. As a witness, in the judgment of J. Edgar Hoover, Chambers had three strikes against him: his past life as a Communist spy, his secret life as a homosexual, and his occasional mistruths under oath. The evidence of Chambers's espionage was too important a secret to reveal. And though Hiss had been mentioned under a code name in a Soviet intelligence communiqué decoded by the military intelligence service that evolved into today's National Security Agency, the existence of that service and its work could not be disclosed in open court.

Hiss never could be tried for espionage. So Nixon, in his own words, convicted him in the press. He set a perjury trap for Hiss. In sworn testimony, Nixon caught him in a series of seemingly evasive statements about the most obscure details of his relationship with Chambers. Then he used his allies among the corps of Washington reporters and his contacts in the FBI to smear Hiss in the newspapers. Hiss was indicted for perjury by a federal grand jury in December 1948 after denying under oath that he had given State Department documents to Chambers. The jury was hung. Hiss was convicted at a second trial in January 1950.

The publicity was priceless for Nixon. And he was right about Hiss. Soviet intelligence records released sixty years later established that Hiss had worked with the Communist underground before World War II. Chambers had lied to the grand jury, too, but without penalty. No prosecutor would take the political heat of a perjury case against Nixon's star witness.

"The Hiss case brought me national fame," Nixon wrote in *Six Crises*. "Two years after that, General Eisenhower introduced me as his running mate to the Republican National Convention as 'a man who has a special talent and an ability to ferret out any kind of subversive influence wherever it may be found, and the strength and persistence to get rid of it.'" By November 1952, still shy of forty, Nixon was Dwight D. Eisenhower's vice president. Six years later he decided to seek the presidency himself.

That was the sixth crisis.

Nixon believed to his dying day that Senator John F. Kennedy stole the 1960 presidential election from him. Nixon lost by 118,550 votes among 69 million cast. A shift of fewer than 14,000 votes in three crucial states could have given him a political victory in the Electoral College. In two of those states, Illinois and Texas—where powerful Democratic political machines were controlled by Chicago's mayor, Richard J. Daley, and Kennedy's running mate, Senator Lyndon B. Johnson—the Republicans claimed evidence of vote fraud.

Nixon was convinced that Kennedy's millions and political manipulations had provided the margin of victory. Nixon's supporters urged him to mount a legal challenge to the election. But he decided, after agonizing, that "even suggesting that the presidency itself could be stolen at the ballot box" would do "incalculable and lasting damage throughout the country."

He vowed he would not be outdone again. But he would suffer one final humiliation when he returned to his home state of California to run for governor in 1962. He lost convincingly, by nearly three times the number of voters who had opposed him for the presidency.

He had been up all night and he had been drinking when he conceded defeat. "For sixteen years, ever since the Hiss case, you've had a lot of—a lot of fun—that you've had an opportunity to attack me," he told the reporters gathered around him. "But as I leave you I want you to know—just think how much you're going to be missing. You won't have Nixon to kick around anymore, because, gentlemen, this is my last press conference."

After that, Nixon's daughter Tricia wrote, there was a terrible sadness in him, and the sadness went on for years.

CHAPTER TWO

"This is treason"

POLITICS WAS war for Richard Nixon, a war in which all was fair. He came back from defeat and exile by his force of will and his taste for vengeance. He won the presidency in 1968 after an act of treachery unparalleled in American politics.

Nixon left California after his "last press conference" and moved to New York, where he joined a Wall Street law firm. He brought the firm what remained of his political cachet and a handful of wealthy corporate clients who were longtime Nixon backers. The firm made him rich enough to afford a ten-room apartment on Fifth Avenue facing Central Park.

He did not make a political move until after President Kennedy was assassinated on November 22, 1963. In January 1964 a national poll by the Gallup organization showed Nixon resurrected as a potential presidential candidate. He appeared to lead the pack in his support among the party's rank and file. This news was a ray of light, but not enough to dissipate the darkness. Nixon did not think the time was ripe, and he was right. Lyndon B. Johnson, elevated to the White House from the doghouse of his vice presidency when Kennedy died, won an overwhelming victory in 1964.

Historians almost always describe Nixon's time of political exile as a wandering in the wilderness. Nixon wasn't wandering. He began ceaselessly cultivating future campaign supporters: corporate kingpins and foreign rulers, county chairmen and congressional leaders. He was blazing a trail back to power. "In those years in limbo," said William Watts, a future Nixon National Security Council aide, "he traveled around the world, and lined up delegates. His time in the U.S. was spent going to every graduation, bar mitzvah, christening ceremony for every Republican potential delegate that he could. He lined up votes all over the country. It was an incredible job that he did. The other side was that he traveled all over the world and met everybody."

Marshall Green was the American ambassador in Indonesia when Nixon came to visit the nation's military ruler in April 1967. "When Mr. Nixon and I called on President Suharto," said Ambassador Green, who became Nixon's State Department overseer for East Asia, "Mr. Nixon took down notes on key points they made and when we got back to my residence, we had a long conversation on events in Indonesia and the rest of East Asia, especially China. Our conversation was tape-recorded by Mr. Nixon, and when I asked him what he did with all these notes and tapes, he replied that he had them transcribed, filed and cross-filed for later reference."

By then it was becoming clear that Nixon would run once again for president, and that the key issue in the campaign would be the war in Vietnam.

* * *

The first months of 1968 were among the most brutal passages in American history. In February, more than 500 U.S. soldiers died in combat in a single week in Vietnam. In all, 16,592 Americans were killed and 87,388 wounded that year, along with 27,915 South Vietnamese killed and perhaps a quarter of a million military and civilian deaths among the enemy. On March 31, President Johnson announced that he would not run for reelection but would devote the rest of his presidency to seeking peace. Four days later, in April, came the assassination of Martin Luther King Jr. The streets of Washington burned with rage. Seventy percent of the people living in the nation's capital were black, and their anger turned to arson. Flying back from King's funeral in Atlanta, the president's entourage looked down upon a city in flames. In June the murder of Bobby Kennedy on the campaign trail left millions of Americans in despair. Nixon was not among them: Kennedy was the potential opponent he'd feared the most. Nixon swept all the 1968 Republican primaries and faced a fractured Democratic field after President Johnson announced he would leave the Oval Office. Vietnam had splintered the Democrats and poisoned Johnson's presidency from the moment he sent troops into battle back in 1965. The war and its political fallout crushed his hopes of creating the "Great Society," a nation where peace, justice, and equality might prevail.

"I was bound to be crucified either way I moved," LBJ told his biographer. "If I left the woman I really loved—the Great Society—in order to get involved in that bitch of a war on the other side of the world, then I would lose everything at home. . . . All my hopes to feed the hungry and shelter the homeless. All my dreams. . . . But if I left that war and let the Communists take over South Vietnam, then I would be seen as a coward and my nation would be seen as an appeaser and we would both find it impossible to accomplish anything for anybody anywhere on the entire globe." In his nightmares, he saw himself tied to the ground as a great mob ran at him screaming, "Traitor!"

Now 549,500 Americans were in Vietnam, and hundreds were dying every week at the hands of the Communists. The dead haunted Lyndon Johnson to the depths of his soul. The American death toll in Vietnam was approaching 30,000; three years of conflict had cost the United States roughly $330 billion in today's dollars. Polls showed that popular opinion had turned against the war policies of the White House; a majority of Americans thought that going into combat had been a mistake.

Yet Nixon rarely spoke of Vietnam as he secured the Republican nomination and as LBJ's vice president, Hubert H. Humphrey, emerged as his opponent, after a tumultuous Democratic convention featuring the Chicago police clubbing demonstrators. Nixon pledged a program for peace without saying what his plan might be. Then he flooded the airwaves with television ads depicting dead American soldiers. In public, he justified his evasions by saying he wanted to avoid interfering with peace negotiations begun in Paris between the United States and North Vietnam. In private, he aimed to make sure that there would be no peace deal without his foreknowledge.

* * *

On July 12, 1968, Nixon welcomed the ambassador of South Vietnam to his campaign suite at the Hotel Pierre in New York. In the elegant room that served as Nixon's base of operations, he and Ambassador Bui Diem spent ninety minutes talking about the war and the peace talks. Alongside Nixon sat his law partner and campaign manager, John N. Mitchell, who in his accustomed style puffed his pipe, listened intently, and said little. Mitchell was accompanied by the most famous Asian anticommunist in the United States, Anna Chennault, the widow of the aviator who had created the CIA's private air force, Air America, a linchpin for secret operations in the Vietnam War. Madame Chennault, born Chen Xiangmei, was an influential Washington lobbyist who cultivated an air of intrigue with a hint of danger; she was known as the Dragon Lady.

Nixon told the ambassador that Mitchell and Chennault would be his private liaisons to the embassy of South Vietnam. Nixon wanted Bui Diem to serve as his direct back channel to President Nguyen Van Thieu in Saigon. He wanted to make sure that a clear message was conveyed in private: whatever peace deal the Democrats were offering, South Vietnam would be far better served if the staunchly anticommunist Richard Nixon were in the White House.

Ambassador Diem left this meeting "increasingly attracted to the Republican side," he wrote thirty years later. Nixon made a convincing argument that he would be the man to settle the war on terms most favorable to America's allies in South Vietnam. And the ambassador was delighted with the offer of entrée to the court of the Dragon Lady. "As far as courting Republicans went, there were few places in Washington like Anna Chennault's penthouse apartment at the Watergate."

The courtship intensified as the election approached. "I am regularly in touch with the Nixon entourage," Ambassador Diem reported to President Thieu. Diem kept Mitchell closely apprised of Thieu's aversion to the peace talks in Paris.

* * *

Nixon's foreign intrigues extended to fund-raising. He raised thirty million dollars from Americans that summer and fall, more than any presidential candidate before him. But he also had secret sources of foreign money. Illegal and unreported funds started flowing into the campaign during September and October 1968. Nixon had learned through his associations with the CIA and the FBI during his years under Eisenhower that suitcases stuffed with cash were instruments of foreign policy for an American commander in chief. He now applied the methods of covert operations to obtaining campaign contributions.

One source of his clandestine cash was the military junta in Greece. Its leaders were pleased by Nixon's surprising choice of a running mate, the governor of Maryland, Spiro T. Agnew, born Spiros Anagnostopoulos, raised in the Greek Orthodox Church. The junta contributed $549,000 to the Nixon campaign through Thomas Pappas, a Boston businessman who ran the largest oil company in Greece. Pappas was a personal friend to Nixon and the colonels; he became known in the White House as "the Greek bearing gifts."

A coalition of right-wing leaders in Italy served as another source of covert contributions to Nixon. They kicked in hundreds of thousands of dollars through Pier Talenti, an Italian American industrialist with fascist tendencies and a vast family estate in Rome. Nixon himself instructed his chief of staff, H. R. Haldeman, to help handle "this contribution from the Italian." Nixon liked to reward his contributors when he could: as president, he personally approved millions of dollars in covert support to right-wing Italian politicians through the CIA and tens of millions in weapons sales to the Greek colonels through the Pentagon. American corporate executives who gave at least four million dollars to the campaign off the books knew whom to call when delivering their contributions: Rose Mary Woods, Nixon's personal secretary since 1951, fiercely loyal and famously tight-lipped. She made the appointment when the president of Phillips Petroleum personally delivered fifty thousand dollars in cash to Nixon at the candidate's Fifth Avenue apartment in New York City. She told Nixon about an off-the-record "seven-figure contribution" collected by Wiley Buchanan, a Texas millionaire who had served as Eisenhower's White House chief of protocol. And she privately recorded a fifteen-thousand-dollar donation from the former Cuban ambassador Nicolás Arroyo Márquez. "He was in Washington when Castro took over," she noted. "RN knows him."

The 1968 Nixon campaign also had the ability to tap wellsprings of cash whose ultimate source is still a mystery. Robert C. Hill, the Republican National Committee's foreign policy chairman, reported to the

Nixon campaign on September 29, 1968, that "RN's Committee in Mexico" had access to a cache controlled by Win Scott, the CIA's station chief in Mexico City since 1956. Scott had personal ties to Mexican presidents, the nation's security ministers, and wealthy Republicans with haciendas in Mexico. Hill said the station chief had "between three and five million dollars to play with." Hill had been Eisenhower's ambassador to Mexico; Nixon would make him ambassador to Spain. The millions remain untraceable. Four years after the 1968 election, campaign cash in Mexican banks would provide a link in the chain of events that began the agonies of Nixon's downfall.

* * *

These transactions were only one cog in the Nixon machine. The candidate's days were consumed with the ceaseless grind of politics: recording television ads, making stump speeches, calibrating the vote in every state. In early October, with the election a month away, Nixon held a solid lead in the polls. He knew of, and feared, only one thing that could derail him: a dramatic development in Vietnam. Vice President Humphrey's campaign had been hamstrung by his loyalties to Lyndon Johnson; antiwar liberals were loath to support him. But if Johnson stopped the bombing of North Vietnam, brokered a cease-fire, or brought a peace deal in the Paris talks, the Democratic nominee might garner millions of votes from war-weary Americans. A peace agreement could swing the election.

"Many Republican friends have contacted me and encouraged us to stand firm" against a bombing halt, Ambassador Diem reported to President Thieu on October 23. Thieu responded that South Vietnam might indeed oppose it; he believed that Nixon, the staunch anticommunist, would cut a better deal than any Democrat.

The National Security Agency, spying on America's allies as it had done since its creation, intercepted these cables in Saigon and reported their gist directly to President Johnson. The NSA and the FBI also monitored the embassy of South Vietnam in Washington, so LBJ knew what transpired in the telephone calls and diplomatic cables on both ends of the conversation.

But Nixon had his own spy in the White House, "someone in Johnson's innermost circle," in his words. The next day, the candidate learned without question that the United States had struck a secret pact with North Vietnam to stop the bombing and seek peace. The election was ten days away. "I immediately decided that the only way to prevent Johnson from totally undercutting my candidacy at the eleventh hour was for me to make public the fact that a bombing halt was imminent," Nixon wrote in his memoirs.

He went public on October 26 with a classic phrase of political language: he suggested that the pact might be "a cynical last-minute attempt by President Johnson to salvage the candidacy of Mr. Humphrey. This I do not believe." Those last five words were false.

Johnson and Nixon had hated each other since they first met as senators in 1951. Both were hardened veterans of political warfare. For this battle the president had more firepower (the NSA, the CIA, and the FBI), but Nixon had the guerrilla's edge of sabotage and sneak attacks.

On October 28 an NSA intercept from Saigon landed at the White House, direct from the agency's headquarters in Maryland. It quoted President Thieu word for word: "It appears Mr. Nixon will be elected as the next President, and he thinks it would be good to try to solve the important question of the political talks with the next President." The intercept was unambiguous: Nixon was in contact with Saigon, and he was trying to undermine the peace deal.

At dawn on October 29, Johnson read a memo from his national security adviser, Walt Whitman Rostow, quoting a Wall Street executive very close to Nixon. His inside information matched the NSA's intelligence reporting: "Nixon was playing the problem," trying to "incite Saigon to be difficult," sending a message to Thieu to hold out for a better deal in the next administration.

His fury mounting, the president ordered the FBI to place Anna Chennault under surveillance and to monitor the telephone lines of Ambassador Bui Diem at the embassy of South Vietnam.

The FBI immediately picked up their conversations. On October 30, Diem told the Dragon Lady to come see him immediately. The FBI's deputy director, Cartha "Deke" DeLoach, had the report in the president's hands within hours. After reading it, Johnson conveyed a clear warning to Nixon through the Republican leader of the Senate, Everett Dirksen of Illinois. LBJ advised, "He better keep Mrs. Chennault and all this crowd tied up for a few days."

On Thursday, October 31, Johnson announced a bombing halt. The national polling networks recorded an immediate and immense shift, measured in millions of votes, away from Nixon and toward Humphrey.

But Thieu had balked. He proclaimed that he would not go to the Paris peace conference alongside the Americans. He would not negotiate with the Communists. He would not accept any deal in the name of peace. He would not consider a coalition in pursuit of a cease-fire. Nor would he see the American ambassador or take his urgent calls. "South Vietnam is not a truck to be attached to a locomotive which will pull it wherever it likes," he told reporters in Saigon.

Peace was on hold.

* * *

LBJ, certain that a Nixon plot was afoot, telephoned his closest friend in the Senate, Richard Russell of Georgia, the longtime chairman of the Senate Armed Services Committee, on the day he announced the bombing halt, October 31. "The Republican nominee—our California friend—has been playing on the outskirts with our enemies and our friends," LBJ told the senator. "He's been doing it through rather subterranean sources. He has been saying to the allies that 'You're going to get sold out . . . You better not give away your liberty just a few hours before I can preserve it for you.' "

LBJ's top aides huddled on Saturday morning, November 2, to assess the situation. "It's clear as day!" said the deputy secretary of defense, Paul Nitze. "Thieu is scared that Humphrey & Democrats will force a coalition on him & the Republicans won't," read the minutes of their meeting. That night, the president had the proof in hand. Rostow sent an urgent teletype from the White House to the president at the LBJ Ranch in Texas. The FBI had overheard Chennault delivering "a message from her boss" to Ambassador Diem. The message was "Hold on. We are going to win."

The president was sure who the boss was: Richard Nixon.

"This is treason," said the president of the United States. "They're contacting a foreign power in the middle of a war." If not treason, it was a federal crime for a citizen to conduct private diplomacy with a foreign government against the interests of the United States.

"We know what Thieu is saying to them," LBJ rasped, his tobacco- and whiskey-cured voice thickened by a cold. "They ought to know that we know what they're doing. We know who they're talking to. I know what they're saying. . . . If Nixon keeps the South Vietnamese away from the conference, well, that's going to be his responsibility. If they don't want it on the front pages, they better quit it."

Nixon got the word from Republican allies in the Senate that LBJ was on to him. He telephoned the president at 1:54 p.m. on Sunday, November 3, and denied everything. "My God," Nixon said, "I would *never* do anything to encourage Saigon not to come to the table."

* * *

The Paris peace talks were scuttled. Philip Habib, a senior State Department diplomat at the peace table, thought that the war in Vietnam would have ended if Nixon had not sabotaged the talks.

"The deal was cooked. And then something happened. Somebody got to Thieu on behalf of Nixon and said, 'Don't agree, don't come to Paris,'" Habib, who went on to serve loyally under Nixon, recollected years later. "I'm convinced that, if Humphrey had won the election, the war would have been over much sooner."

Had the election been held that Sunday, Humphrey might well have won, as the polls reflected. But peace was no longer at hand. On Monday, November 4, preelection polls showed the pendulum of popular opinion swinging back to Nixon.

That afternoon, the president conferred with Secretary of State Dean Rusk, Secretary of Defense Clark Clifford, and National Security Adviser Walt Rostow. The voting booths would open in a matter of hours. The question was whether to reveal Nixon's treachery. The problem was twofold: the charge was explosive and the evidence secret. Could the nation handle the disclosure that Nixon was playing a double game with the lives of American soldiers? Or that the U.S. government was spying on the president of South Vietnam?

"I do not believe that any President can make any use of interceptions or telephone taps in any way that would involve politics," Rusk told the president. "The moment we cross over that divide we are in a different kind of society."

Nor could the electorate tolerate a last-minute political bombshell of this magnitude. If Nixon won, the revelation could destroy him before he was sworn into office.

"Some elements of the story are so shocking in their nature that I'm wondering whether it would be good for the country to disclose the story," Clifford said. "It could cast his whole administration under such doubts that I would think it would be inimical to our country's interests."

The president and his advisers kept their silence. Election Day came and went. Not until dawn the next day did the result become clear. Nixon had won by a margin of fewer than half a million votes, a narrow plurality, not a ringing majority: 43.4 percent of the vote to Humphrey's 42.7 percent, with the racist ex-governor of Alabama, George C. Wallace, putatively a Democrat, winning 13.5 percent. Not since 1912 had a president been elected with less of a popular mandate.

The price of victory was immeasurable. Nixon had scuttled the chance for peace in Vietnam in order to win.

The president confronted Nixon in a telephone call on November 8. "These messages started coming out from here that 'Johnson was going to have a bombing pause to try to elect Humphrey' and that they ought to hold out because 'Nixon will not sell you out,'" LBJ told the president-elect. "Now, that is the story, Dick. And it is a sordid story."

Nixon always maintained—apparently because J. Edgar Hoover suggested the possibility a few weeks later—that the president had eavesdropped on him personally in the last days of the campaign, with bugs or wiretaps. "We were tapped," he averred on his own White House tapes. "Johnson tapped us." Though it was not so, that would have made a far more sordid story, he believed.

All decided to keep the affair under seal in the name of national security.

Walt Rostow wrote the last chapter of the story in 1973, shortly after Nixon was reelected and Lyndon Johnson died. Rostow had smuggled out of the White House the key documents that told the tale. He had copies of the NSA's reports, the FBI wiretaps, and a cable from the CIA station in Saigon that directly quoted President Thieu saying "he had sent two secret emissaries to the U.S. to contact Richard Nixon" in response to Johnson's "betrayal."

Rostow placed the documents in a folder and wrote, "The 'X' Files," on the cover. He sent it to the LBJ Presidential Library, with a request that it remain secret for fifty years. Before he sealed it, he added some personal reflections in a postscript.

"I am inclined to believe the Republican operation in 1968 relates in two ways to the Watergate affair," he wrote. "First, the election of 1968 proved to be close and there was some reason for those involved on the Republican side to believe their enterprise with the South Vietnamese [provided] the margin of victory. Second, they got away with it." As Rostow concluded, "There were memories of how close an election could get and the possible utility of pressing to the limit—or beyond" in the pursuit of power.

A measure of deep bitterness remained in Nixon after his hour of triumph, over his suspicion of LBJ's spying and his unshakable belief that the bombing halt in Vietnam was a ploy to deny him the presidency. Nixon would always remember that his victory depended on deception, duplicity, and acts of dubious legality.

CHAPTER THREE

"He was surrounded by enemies"

Nixon's sense of siege started minutes after he was sworn into office on January 20, 1969, the president of a nation as deeply divided as it had been since the end of the Civil War.

The war at home began on Inauguration Day, said Tom Charles Huston, a young White House aide charged with intelligence gathering. When Nixon rode from the Capitol to the White House, he confronted thousands of "radical people that were throwing rocks," hurling obscenities at the president's black limousine, "screaming and carrying on." No president had ever arrived in office under a hail of garbage and curses, mocked by middle-finger salutes.

Nixon would have his vengeance; Huston would help him seek it. A former military intelligence officer, by the end of the year he had become Nixon's in-house consultant for domestic spying. When Nixon created the special investigative unit later known as the Plumbers, the group that carried out the president's orders for gathering intelligence on his political enemies, he looked for a leader. He said, "I really need a son-of-a-bitch like Huston who will work his butt off and do it dishonorably." But by then, he had a multitude of White House staffers willing and able to perform those tasks.

A generation of the American right arose with Nixon; through them, his influence resounds down the decades. A future president, George H. W. Bush, was his steadfast Republican National Committee chairman. Seven future secretaries of defense served Nixon, including Dick Cheney and Donald Rumsfeld, who labored mightily to destroy the foundations of Lyndon Johnson's Great Society, at Nixon's command. Six future secretaries of state came up through the Nixon White House; so did six directors and deputy directors of central intelligence.

The hard-right views of a young Justice Department attorney, William Rehnquist, caught Nixon's eye. Rehnquist would spend thirty-two years on the Supreme Court, nearly two decades as the chief justice, reshaping the law in Nixon's image, until he died in 2005. Nixon named Antonin Scalia as a successor to Rehnquist, as head of the Justice Department's Office of Legal Counsel—the first real taste of power for the man who has been the most consistently conservative voice in the Supreme Court for the past three decades. Every 5–4 Supreme Court ruling with their names on it—notably, *Bush v. Gore*, which handed the disputed 2000 election to the candidate who had lost by more than half a million votes—bears the trace of Nixon's fingerprints.

Yet three men, and only three, formed the core of Nixon's inner circle. Two went to prison for crimes committed on the president's behalf. The third won both the Nobel Peace Prize and condemnation as a war criminal.

* * *

Harry Robbins Haldeman had been at Nixon's side as an advance man in the 1960 presidential campaign; he had managed the disastrous 1962 California race; he had remained loyal throughout Nixon's years of exile. His devotion to the president was superhuman. He worked hundred-hour weeks. He served for 1,561 days as White House chief of staff; in that time, he was physically apart from Nixon for fewer than thirty of those days. Nixon spent more time with Haldeman than with his own wife. No president, and no king, ever had a more devoted servant.

Haldeman knew his man in intimate detail. He went on full alert when Nixon flagged, stayed sharp when Nixon had had one drink too many, executed the president's orders when Nixon lacked courage, and scuttled them when they lacked wisdom. Haldeman handled everything. He had a martial air of discipline and order that fitted his military brush cut and his stern and steely gaze. You had to go through him to get to the president. His loyalty was ironclad. But when Nixon let him go, firing him as the Watergate flood tides rose, Haldeman recalled, it was the first time the two men ever shook hands.

John Newton Mitchell had no experience in law enforcement when he became attorney general of the United States. But he had shown total discipline as Nixon's campaign manager. From their first meeting at Nixon's New York law firm, where Mitchell was a named partner, he became fiercely devoted to the man and his ambitions. He would do anything the president asked.

Mitchell was the unsmiling face of law and order in America, the national police chief. He became a symbol of the power of the government to suppress dissent. He believed that police and federal agents should be able to enter the homes of suspects without warning—"no-knock" laws, as they were known. He pushed for warrantless wiretaps, preventive detention, and other tactics associated with police states. In his most famous political pronouncement (a prophecy fulfilled), he predicted, "This country is going so far right you won't even recognize it."

Nixon wanted Mitchell to strike fear in liberals and leftists with subpoenas and indictments brought by federal prosecutors and grand juries at the command of the Justice Department. Like President Woodrow Wilson during World War I, Nixon sought to use conspiracy and sedition laws against his most vocal political opponents in the name of national security. One of Nixon's first orders to Attorney General Mitchell was to indict the best-known leaders of the antiwar and Black Power movements. They were tried on political charges that juries found unconvincing.

To crush Nixon's left-wing enemies, Mitchell needed the investigative powers of J. Edgar Hoover, director of the FBI since 1924. The Bureau was in theory subordinate to Mitchell. But "Attorneys General seldom directed Mr. Hoover," Nixon said. "It was difficult even for Presidents." His increasing inability to command and control Hoover created political frictions fundamental to the disasters that befell his presidency. Mitchell was a lawyer whose specialty was municipal bonds, not covert action. But Nixon trusted him deeply in the realm of secret operations; Mitchell had displayed utter discretion in the sabotage of the Paris peace talks. The president placed him on the National Security Council, which met in the cloistered basement office that served as the White House

Situation Room. The membership of the NSC and its six subcouncils included the director of central intelligence, the chairman of the Joint Chiefs of Staff, the deputy secretary of defense, and the undersecretary of state.

But they all would have one chairman: the national security adviser, Henry Kissinger. And Nixon wanted Mitchell to keep an eye on him, for he hardly knew Kissinger when he hired him.

Kissinger had met Nixon once, at a Christmas party in 1967; small talk with strangers was not Nixon's strong suit. But Kissinger had shown a talent for conspiracy in the crucial moment of the 1968 campaign. A politically ambitious Harvard professor, Kissinger was seeking high office in the next administration no matter who won. He was dealing with both parties, trading in the hardest political currency: secret information. He had two contacts among the American delegation at the Paris peace talks; they never dreamed that Kissinger would back-channel their conversations to Republican headquarters. On October 9, 1968, Kissinger called Mitchell with a report that LBJ would stop the bombing of North Vietnam and offer a cease-fire to the Communists. Kissinger's tip proved accurate; with that inside information, Nixon began to plan his counterstrategy to lure South Vietnam away from the peace talks.

Nixon decided to take Kissinger on board as national security adviser after a three-hour meeting at the president-elect's Pierre Hotel command post in December 1968. "I had a strong intuition about Henry Kissinger," Nixon wrote ten years later. "The combination was unlikely—the grocer's son from Whittier and the refugee from Hitler's Germany." But Nixon recognized something of a kindred spirit.

Nixon was the grand strategist, Kissinger the great tactician, and this working relationship between two strangers grew quickly and powerfully. Together they set out to destroy and re-create the foreign policy architecture of the United States, to break and remake the Pentagon and the State Department and the CIA, to bend and reshape the instruments of American power at their will. These were not figures of speech for Nixon and Kissinger, but the daily reality in their relationship.

Both men had clandestine minds. Both had a brittle brilliance. Both were talented liars; both saw that talent as crucial to diplomacy and politics. Both shared a sense that history was a tragedy.

Both wanted to change the world they had inherited from Presidents Johnson, Kennedy, Eisenhower, and Truman. Nixon and Kissinger ripped out the wiring mechanisms of power, destroyed structures that had served those four presidents since World War II, and created a system that placed the powers of statecraft in their hands and theirs alone. They overhauled the National Security Council system and usurped the powers of State and the Pentagon. Every important decision, and every document, on the foreign policy of the United States would henceforth flow to Kissinger as the NSC chairman. All power and all decisions regarding war, foreign policy, diplomacy, and covert operations would be concentrated in his hands.*

Then Kissinger would consult the president on the crises of the moment. Kissinger's aides joked that world-shaking decisions would go to Nixon with three options: (1) unconditional surrender, (2) nuclear war, or (3) Kissinger's recommendation. Nixon invariably chose option three. The intent was to immensely increase the power of the president to make life-and-death decisions in secret.

Nixon presented this radical reorganization over cocktails in Key Bis-

---

* To consolidate his power, Kissinger quickly tripled the NSC staff to thirty-four people. He created and chaired six NSC committees—the Senior Review Group, the Washington Special Actions Group, the Verification Panel, the 40 Committee, the Intelligence Committee, and the Defense Program Review Committee—which handled every major decision concerning the war in Indochina, CIA covert operations, coups, crises, potential conflagrations, and nuclear weapons policies. Kissinger demanded authority to review cables sent by the secretary of state to American embassies. He held private meetings with foreign heads of state and ambassadors. To grasp the scope of the power grab, it is important to remember that the post of national security adviser did not exist until 1961.

Kissinger set his own staff at war with one another. "Henry would have three different groups working on a problem," said John Holdridge, Kissinger's best China hand, later ambassador to Indonesia. "Not one of the members of those groups knew that the others were working on the same problem. That is the way he did it. It was a paranoiac way of doing things, which I hated. I detested it. . . . Henry is a brilliant man, but he is a shit when you really get down to it." Mark Pratt, who came to Kissinger's secret war councils as the State Department's expert on Laos and Cambodia, put it bluntly: "It's not that there is a U.S. Government. These are all fiefdoms spinning off from Henry Kissinger, who distributed them as grand duchies to his various minions, and then they would try to use the other structure and play them off one against the other. . . . Kissinger, of course, was very good in signaling both that he would do exactly what Nixon wanted and secondly in implying—even when it was not true—that he had just raised his own ideas with the President and the President supported them totally."

These interviews are taken from the Foreign Affairs Oral History series led by the Association for Diplomatic Studies and Training, an independent nonprofit based at the State Department's George P. Shultz National Foreign Affairs Training Center.

cayne, Florida, on December 28, 1968, to the men he had chosen to serve as the secretary of state, William Rogers, and the secretary of defense, Melvin Laird.

Bill Rogers, who had advised Nixon since the first Eisenhower campaign in 1952, and who had served Ike as attorney general, was a genial man and an honest broker, but not a diplomat or a strategist. Mel Laird, a Republican congressman since 1953, was equally affable, and he knew the intricacies and intrigues of Washington politics, but he was no commander. Nixon selected them for their weaknesses, not their strengths. Neither man could conceive what lay ahead in the world of political warfare that Nixon and Kissinger would create. The president would seek to make them figureheads, in charge of little beyond the edges of their desks.

"It was a bizarre way to run a government. I think we all knew it was bizarre. But this is how Nixon wanted it," said Peter Rodman, Kissinger's Soviet specialist at the NSC and a key Rumsfeld aide at the Pentagon after 9/11. "Nixon decided that he would rather do these things himself. He had Henry there to do it. Henry and he had an ideological affinity. They both looked at the world in the same way."

Nixon knew what he was doing: striving for greatness. And greatness could be won only on a global scale, by making war and peace with honor. He cared about law and order, he cared deeply about his own reelection, but above all he cared about the war. The war touched everything, at home and abroad, and if it went on, it would break him as it had broken Lyndon Johnson. He was so bold as to predict he could make peace in a matter of months. "There was an absolute conviction on Nixon's part that, by the fall of 1969, he would have Vietnam settled," Haldeman said.

To do so, he would have to concentrate all the powers of government in his hands.

Nixon was the first president in one hundred twenty years who confronted a Congress controlled by his political opponents. Democrats held the Senate 57–43 and the House 243–192. Thus, he decided, when it came to the conduct of the war, he would have to circumvent Congress.

Since the start of the Eisenhower era, the Supreme Court under Chief Justice Earl Warren had expanded civil liberties and curtailed police powers. So Nixon would have to find ways to bend or break the law to fight his enemies at home—or stack the court with conservatives. He was the only Republican president, save Eisenhower, since 1933. Thus, he believed, the State Department, the CIA, and even the Pentagon were riddled with a generation of liberals and leftists appointed by Democrats. These centers of power would have to be purged of enemies and replenished with allies.

Nixon thought that a permanent government, the Establishment—led by eastern elitists and Ivy League intellectuals, Kennedy men and Johnson loyalists—would fight him on every front. He foresaw their strategy. The liberals, working with their allies in Washington, would use the law to tie his hands in Vietnam. The leftists, working with like-minded friends at think tanks and universities, would organize massive demonstrations against the war. Increasingly frustrated with the powers of the Justice Department and the FBI to investigate and indict his enemies, Nixon soon conceived and executed eavesdropping and espionage operations that would be run by his most trusted aides at the White House.

* * *

Each of the three men in Nixon's innermost circle had a highly ambitious aide who gained great power through proximity to the president. Like their patrons, two of these three protégés would go to prison.

Kissinger's right-hand man was Alexander M. Haig, his military assistant at the National Security Council. Haig rose in rank from colonel to four-star general under Nixon without leading troops in combat. The White House was his battleground. He won his stars through tireless service; if a light burned in an office at 3:00 a.m., it was likely Haig's. By turns charming and mercurial, but consistently a martinet, Haig worshipped Gen. Douglas MacArthur, the vainglorious commander relieved for insubordination by President Truman during the Korean War. In 2007, Haig called him "the greatest military man I had ever met." Like his hero, Haig was a rarity in American history: a political general.

He had a unique way with words, a never-ending battle between politics and the English language. A classic example: "I'll have to caveat my response, Senator." *Caveat* is Latin for "let him beware." In English, it is a noun meaning "warning." In Haigspeak, it signaled he was saying something that might or might not be true.

Mitchell's contribution to the White House staff was another man who had his struggles with the truth: John Wesley Dean III, a thirty-one-year-old Justice Department lawyer whom the attorney general had relied on to conduct background briefings for reporters. Dean served as Nixon's legal counsel and liaison with federal law enforcers. His first assignment from Nixon was to order an IRS tax audit against *Scanlan's*, a short-lived satirical monthly magazine that had published a patently absurd article claiming that Vice President Agnew had a secret plan to repeal the Bill of Rights. Using the IRS as a political weapon was at best unethical, arguably a felony. Dean got it done. "I had clearly crossed the line for the first time, and it had been very easy to do," he said in 2006. "With hindsight, I can see that it was an abuse of presidential power."

Dean had replaced John D. Ehrlichman as the White House legal counsel; Ehrlichman was Haldeman's indispensable man. The two invariably were twinned in the eyes of the public and the press for their rhyming names, their unsmiling demeanors, their Teutonic bearing. But their roles and their characters were utterly different. Haldeman had far more clout as the White House chief of staff. Ehrlichman was not his counterpart in rank or influence. But they relied on each other to make the machinery of the White House hum.

They had been close friends for more than twenty years, since their days as undergraduates at UCLA after World War II. Haldeman had recruited Ehrlichman as an advance man for Nixon's 1960 presidential campaign, the thankless but vital role of planning and setting up rallies and speeches so a candidate's days and nights run without disasters.

Nixon himself had asked Ehrlichman to coordinate the advance work for 1968. Ehrlichman agreed—on one condition. He was "convinced that Nixon's drinking could cost him any chance of a return to public life." He had seen Nixon drunk during the 1960 and 1962 campaigns and the 1964 Republican convention, and he made him take the pledge: "If he wanted me to work for him he would lay off the booze."

Ehrlichman became the president's chief adviser on domestic policy, handling the problems the president found the least pressing, such as health care and welfare. His powers were thus limited during Nixon's first years in office by the president's lack of interest in the lives of the poor and the dispossessed. But he became essential in Nixon's campaign for reelection; he called himself the president's "house detective" in matters of political intrigue. The record reflects that Ehrlichman had daily access to Nixon, a privilege shared only by Kissinger and Haldeman; he met with the president on 1,005 occasions over the course of five years and three months. So he knew Nixon's mind as well as anyone. And he saw its dark side with clarity.

"From the first time he ran for office, as a young Congressman, he was engaged in combat," Ehrlichman said late in his life. "There were them and there was us; and he never ever saw it any differently. He was surrounded by enemies."

CHAPTER FOUR

"He will let them know
who is boss around here"

Nixon AGONIZED daily over how to use diplomacy and deception, bombast and bombs, in Vietnam. Grasping every detail of his war strategy was essential "to understand the situation, so he could make what he believed—in his heart—to be the right decision, because these were horrible decisions," Haldeman said. Each military maneuver was a search for a way to end the nightmare of Vietnam, an act of war intended to make peace. Each sought to change the tragic course of history. Each led to death and destruction.

"Go for the big play," Nixon always said, as if war were a football game. The big play was Nixon's plan for a way out of Vietnam—"to the extent he had a plan," said Winston Lord, Nixon's ranking National Security Council staffer, who became ambassador to China in 1985. Lord said that Nixon believed from the start that "he could use the Russians and maybe the Chinese to pressure Hanoi, to bring the war to an end by trying to improve relations with them, and cornering Vietnam in that way."

Nixon would use the art of diplomacy with Moscow and Beijing, and the art of war in Indochina, in a radically new way to create a rapprochement between the most powerful Communists on earth and the United States. The grand bargain would work if Nixon could persuade the leaders of China and Russia to help pursue peace in Vietnam.

This audacious stratagem began to take shape before the inauguration. The first moves were encoded messages woven into Nixon's inaugural address.

On January 2, 1969, after checking with J. Edgar Hoover, Kissinger met with Boris Sedov, officially counselor at the Soviet embassy in Washington but better known as a KGB spy. "Sedov said that the Soviet Union was very interested that the inaugural speech contain some reference to open channels of communication to Moscow," Kissinger told Nixon. "I said that all this would be easier if Moscow showed some cooperativeness on Vietnam." The KGB's proposal to ghostwrite a passage of the inaugural address gave Nixon the inspiration to send an equally subtle message to China. In 1967, Nixon had written an article for *Foreign Affairs* that touched on America's need to establish political and diplomatic relations with China. "There is no place on this planet for a billion of its potentially able people to live in angry isolation," he wrote.

Nixon's inaugural directly addressed Moscow with the words suggested by the spy Sedov: "Our lines of communication will be open." Then, aiming his words at Chairman Mao Tse-tung, Nixon repeated his "angry isolation" lines from *Foreign Affairs*. Mao noticed: on his orders, the Beijing *People's Daily* took the unprecedented step of printing the complete translated text of Nixon's inaugural on its front page. Nixon had told Kissinger about sending signals to Mao. Haig recounted, "In the second week of the administration, Henry came back from the Oval Office and said to me, 'Al, this madman wants to normalize our relations with China.' And he laughed. And I said, 'Oh, my God.'" It seemed inconceivable. And yet, when Nixon began a more direct approach to China later that year, he would find out that he was pushing on an open door.

But how to get the attention of the Soviets, and how to persuade them to help pursue peace in Vietnam? At his first National Security Council meeting, on January 25, 1969, Nixon suggested a carrot: talks on a nuclear weapons treaty. "This will be a great symbol," he announced. Kissinger proposed a big stick: the threat of a nuclear attack.

Kissinger had made his name with a 1957 treatise titled *Nuclear*

Weapons and Foreign Policy, a book often cited, if rarely read, by the high priests of Pentagon war planning. Its thesis was that nuclear weapons had a political and diplomatic utility: to coerce enemies. The challenge was translating their immense military power into coherent foreign policy. Now he put his theories into practice.

In the secretary of defense's dining room, on January 27, Kissinger and Laird discussed "military actions which might jar the North Vietnamese into being more forthcoming at the Paris talks." Kissinger proposed that the Joint Chiefs of Staff prepare a plan of nuclear brinkmanship, designed to convince the Soviets that President Nixon was ready to launch a nuclear attack against North Vietnam over the coming weeks. The idea was to startle Moscow and Hanoi into settling the war. "To preclude prolonged stalling tactics by the communists in Paris," the plan read, the United States would "create fear in the Hanoi leadership that the United States is preparing to undertake new highly damaging military actions"—including "actual or feigned technical escalation of war against North (nuclear)."

Nixon had asked his ranking generals, spies, and diplomats at that first National Security Council meeting, "What is the most effective way to bring the war to a conclusion?" No one at the table had any new ideas—except Kissinger. He proposed immense, prolonged, and unprecedented attacks by B-52 bombers against North Vietnam's encampments in Cambodia. The planning began immediately.

* * *

On February 11, 1969, Kissinger convened the NSC to weigh covert operations and secret bombing campaigns to help win the war.

The CIA had been shoring up President Thieu with cash payments designed to create the appearance of democracy in the Saigon government, some intended to support supposedly independent political parties. The secret subsidies, amounting to millions of dollars, had been flowing since 1965, and they would keep flowing under Nixon. Thieu, in power thanks to a rigged election, was at best dubious about democracy, the CIA reported, and he was putting a substantial amount of the Agency's cash in his pocket.

"Mr. Kissinger questioned if anyone in the United States really knows what a viable political structure in South Vietnam is," read the minutes of the covert action meeting. Yet the group kept the secret subsidies going on and on, in the enduring hope that democracy could be created with the CIA's dollars.

Kissinger quickly turned the discussion to the question of attacking North Vietnamese troops in their Cambodian sanctuaries along the border with South Vietnam. If it could not be done with guerrilla operations, he concluded, it would have to be done with bombs. The Joint Chiefs of Staff proposed an immense and sustained attack on targets in Cambodia. Nixon agreed. He had made up his mind earlier that day.

"I believe it is absolutely urgent if we are to make any kind of headway in Vietnam that we find new ways to increase the pressure militarily," Nixon had told Kissinger. Nixon wanted to launch the bombers immediately. But Secretary of Defense Laird and Secretary of State Rogers strongly opposed the attacks. Rogers thought that widening the war would create a diplomatic disaster. Laird argued that airpower alone would not change the course of the war. The United States already had dropped more bombs in Vietnam (2.8 million tons) than in World War II and Korea combined.

"The question that arises is not whether we should do more in South Vietnam," Laird told the president, "but rather whether we should do less."

After three weeks in office, Nixon had decided to do more, much more. But it would best be done in secret. He would henceforth work harder to keep his war plans hidden. Dissent would be suppressed by deception.

* * *

In these early days, the White House aides who served Nixon and Kissinger loyally were awestruck at the lying and skullduggery surrounding and concealing the plans for the secret bombing of Cambodia.

The war plans took shape as Nixon prepared for his first foreign tour in February. The code name for the bombing of Cambodia was Menu; its components were Breakfast, Lunch, Snack, and so on. Kissinger would concede it was a tasteless choice.

On February 19, four days before his departure for Europe, Kissinger told the president how the Menu attacks would be carried out and assured him that they could be concealed from the American people.

Nixon approved the plan in principle. He held off on launching the attacks until, as Kissinger put it, a suitable pretext could be found. On his flight from Washington in the early morning of February 23, Nixon learned that the Vietcong had started "lobbing a few shells into Saigon," as Kissinger phrased it. The president ordered Kissinger to put the plan into motion—and to keep it secret. Nixon delivered this order to Kissinger while they sat on Air Force One, parked on the tarmac at the Brussels airport—and then Nixon went off to lunch with the king and queen of Belgium.

Haldeman stayed on the plane, making sure that Nixon's orders were executed. Even Haldeman, who knew Nixon's taste for intrigue as well as anyone, was amazed. The plans Kissinger carried out that day were "so secret at the time that I was afraid to say anything," Haldeman wrote in his personal diary. He felt he was "entering an entire new world."

The flight records for the B-52 bombers carrying out the attacks would be falsified by the top American commander in Saigon, Gen. Creighton Abrams. His accomplice would be the commander of American forces in the Pacific, Adm. John McCain, whose son, later a senator, was a prisoner of war in Vietnam.

"In order to set the stage for a possible covert attack, and clear the books on this matter within the Bureaucracy, we should send a message to General Abrams authorizing him to bomb right up to the Cambodian border," Kissinger told Nixon in writing before the plans were executed. A routine request for a B-52 strike on a Communist target in South Vietnam would serve as a cover for a Menu strike in Cambodia. The B-52 pilots and navigators (not the rest of the crew) would receive secret orders from ground controllers directing them to strike targets inside Cambodia. On the bombers' return, two sets of flight reports would be filed, one true, one false.

The execution of the Menu plan was three weeks away.

* * *

Air Force One flew on from Brussels to London, Bonn, Berlin, Rome, and finally to Paris, where Nixon had meetings set with one of his heroes, President de Gaulle of France, and the far less stalwart Vice President Nguyen Cao Ky of South Vietnam.

In his role as the leader of the free world, Nixon loved the pomp of red carpet receptions and state dinners with democrats and dictators alike. He was obsessed with the tiniest aspects of these trips. He demanded "an extraordinary amount of detailed planning, making the visit seem more like a movie script than a spontaneous visit," remembered Robert Oakley, later the State Department's counterterrorism chief. Oakley was stationed at the American embassy in Paris when Nixon arrived to meet de Gaulle. One among a thousand questions from the White House: How many steps would the president have to walk from the entrance to a table at Versailles? "We would have to chart the room that the president was going to enter and then describe—step by step— exactly how he would proceed to his seat."

At the CIA station's secure conference room inside the American embassy in Paris, Nixon sat down face-to-face with Vice President Ky, a flamboyant air force officer who had led a military junta in South Vietnam and evinced no taste for democracy or the rule of law. Nixon sought to reassure Ky of America's commitment to Vietnam.

"Must convince them & American people we have an earnest desire to end the war," read Nixon's handwritten notes of the March 2 meeting. He told Ky to trust him. He would not sell out South Vietnam to the Communists. "We are not going to double-cross you," Nixon said. "We honestly are your friends."

Nixon returned to the United States and retreated to Key Biscayne to brood over the decision to bomb Cambodia. Kissinger urged him to pull the trigger. "Hit them," he told the president in a telephone call on March 8.

"Our military effort leaves a great deal to be desired, but it remains one of our few bargaining weapons," Kissinger wrote in a memo to Nixon that same day. "The guerrillas operate by terror or assassination; our side requires massive military effort. . . . De-escalation would amount to a self-imposed defusing of our most important asset and the simultaneous enhancement of this most important asset—terrorism. We would, in effect, be tying the hands of our forces in Vietnam."

Nixon agreed. He was ready to recalibrate the balance of terror.

One week later, on the afternoon of Saturday, March 15, back in Washington, Nixon took a fifty-five-minute swim in the heated White House pool. He got out of the water and called Henry Kissinger three times.

Each call evinced an escalating state of fury.

The first call lasted six minutes. "The President ordered the immediate implementation of the Breakfast Plan," Kissinger's notes read.

The second call lasted one minute. The president commanded that the secretary of state and the American ambassador in Saigon be kept in the dark until the B-52s had passed the point of no return.

The third call to Kissinger was as blunt as it could be. "Everything that will fly is to get over to North Vietnam," the president said. Kissinger's notes read, "There will be no appeal" from the Pentagon or the State Department. "He will let them know who is boss around here."

The full scope of the destruction the United States unleashed on Cambodia remained unrevealed for three decades, due to the deliberate falsification of the bombing records, authorized by Nixon and executed by Kissinger, Haig, and General Abrams. The falsification violated the military laws of the United States. The bombing of a neutral nation arguably violated the laws of war.

In November 2000, Bill Clinton became the first American president since Nixon to visit Vietnam. To help in the search for unexploded bombs, which remained a lethal threat there and in Laos and Cambodia, Clinton made public an air force database that contained a staggering statistic.

Between March 1969 and August 1973, America dropped 2,756,727 tons of bombs on Cambodia. That figure was nearly five times greater than previously known, exceeding the tonnage of all Allied bombing during World War II, including Hiroshima and Nagasaki. No one knows how many Cambodian civilians were killed, perhaps one hundred fifty thousand.

Kissinger told Defense Secretary Laird that the president had approved the bombing of Cambodia on March 16, the night after the first B-52s attacked. He said the decision was one that Nixon could never avow.

CHAPTER FIVE

"The center cannot hold"

GENERAL ABRAMS was outraged. One week after the great waves of B-52 attacks began, a wire service reporter in Saigon named Jack Walsh filed a story saying Abrams was "seeking permission" to bomb enemy sanctuaries in Cambodia. It ran on the front page of the *Washington Star* on March 25, 1969.

Abrams fired off a top-secret cable to the chairman of the Joint Chiefs of Staff, Gen. Earle Wheeler, calling the story a disaster. His fury was mild compared to Richard Nixon's.

Leaks plague every president, but none more than Nixon. His passion for secrecy equaled his hatred for reporters—a high standard. One month after the story appeared, on April 25, Nixon met with J. Edgar Hoover and Attorney General John Mitchell in the Oval Office. Mitchell sat quietly, as was his habit, puffing clouds of smoke from his pipe, listening as Hoover told the president that there was only one way to deal with leakers. And that was to wiretap them. As Nixon put it, wiretapping was "the ultimate weapon."

Nixon immediately called Henry Kissinger into the meeting and told him to take responsibility for stopping the leaks—starting by tapping members of his own NSC staff. "Henry himself was, in a sense, the target of all this suspicion," said Kissinger's aide Peter Rodman. "He was under pressure to show nobody on his staff" was leaking information. "Here he was in this room with J. Edgar Hoover, John Mitchell, Richard Nixon, and they're saying, 'Let's do some taps.'"

On the morning of May 9, Kissinger called Hoover, furious over a front-page story in the *New York Times*. The reporter, William Beecher, based at the Pentagon, had filed a careful report stating that B-52s had struck several of the enemy's camps inside Cambodia. No public outcry resulted. No congressional hearings ensued. What was really happening—a massive attack on a neutral nation, concealed by falsified Pentagon reports—did not come out until 1973.*

Kissinger told Hoover that the *Times* story was "extraordinarily damaging" and "dangerous." He hoped Hoover would help him "destroy whoever did this" by wiretapping reporters and their suspected sources at the NSC, the Pentagon, and the State Department; Kissinger would select the targets. The taps also remained secret until 1973. Their targets included thirteen American government officials and four newspaper reporters. Daily summaries of the White House wiretaps went from the FBI to the president's closest aides. This continued for twenty months—until Nixon installed his own secret taping system in the White House.

The taps revealed nothing but "gossip and bullshitting," as Nixon inelegantly put it on his own tapes. "The tapping was a very, very unproductive thing. I've always known that." But it was Nixon's first clear step over the line of the law. The president could order warrantless wiretaps against suspected foreign spies. But these were American citizens. Nixon and Kissinger later argued that the tapping was within the realm of the president's national security powers. It was not.

Some of the targets of the taps had long assumed they were spied upon by foreign intelligence services. "But I didn't think it was being done by the White House," said Ambassador William H. Sullivan, a distinguished diplomat who helped Kissinger open a secret channel of

---

* More than four years passed before Maj. Hal Knight, a former air force officer, told the Senate Armed Services Committee that he had destroyed records of the bombing of Cambodia and substituted false reports of attacks on cover targets in South Vietnam.

communication with the leaders of North Vietnam. When Sullivan later found out that his own government was tapping him, he assumed that Nixon had ordered the surveillance in a fit of drunken rage. "It probably came from Nixon personally," Sullivan said. "He was given to exploding—particularly in the course of an evening—if he had had a few drinks." Sober or not, Nixon had "an almost paranoid fear that people were not trustworthy," said Col. Richard Thomas Kennedy, the National Security Council's staff director for planning and coordination from 1969 to 1974.

Winston Lord, one of Kissinger's most devoted aides, was among those tapped. "You cannot square a personal friendship and total trust and intimacy with his authorizing of tapping your phone," Lord later reflected. "You can't run a government that way."

Nixon's spying on Americans went far beyond these taps, as a National Security Agency history declassified in 2013 disclosed. An NSA "watch list" began growing in October 1967, the result of LBJ's suspicions that antiwar activists were being financed by Moscow. It kept growing under Nixon: sixteen hundred Americans appeared on the list by 1973. The official NSA history states bluntly that the program was "disreputable if not outright illegal."

The NSA is a military intelligence service whose charter was to target foreign spies and suspected terrorists, not American citizens who questioned the president's foreign policies. The watch list was an antecedent to the far more extensive NSA surveillance program ordered by President George W. Bush; the distinct difference was the direct targeting of high-profile American citizens as opposed to high-value foreign terrorists.

The NSA history notes that the watch list grew to include the *Washington Post* humor columnist Art Buchwald and *New York Times* journalist Tom Wicker—both fired words, not weapons—"and even politicians such as Frank Church and Howard Baker." Church and Baker were U.S. senators. Church was a liberal Democrat who sponsored the first major bipartisan moves against the war. Baker was the Republican who famously asked at the 1973 Watergate hearings, "What did the president know and when did he know it?"

The FBI and NSA taps, like so much that would come to torment Nixon, were all about the war abroad and the war at home. No one ever said it better than Haldeman himself: "Without the Vietnam War there would have been no Watergate."

* * *

Nixon's greatest domestic enemy was the peace movement, which rose with every American who fell in Vietnam. By the end of March 1969, that death toll had reached 33,641, surpassing that of the Korean War.

That same week, Nixon devoted one of his first major public statements to the growing demonstrations on college campuses across the country. "This is the way civilizations begin to die," Nixon said. "The process is altogether too familiar to those who would survey the wreckage of history: assault and counterassault, one extreme leading to the opposite extreme, the voices of reason and calm discredited.

"As Yeats foresaw, 'Things fall apart. The center cannot hold,'" he warned. "None of us has the right to suppose it cannot happen here."

Many knew by heart the next lines of the Irish poet's "The Second Coming," written months after World War I ended.

> *Mere anarchy is loosed upon the world,*
> *The blood-dimmed tide is loosed, and everywhere*
> *The ceremony of innocence is drowned;*
> *The best lack all conviction, while the worst*
> *Are full of passionate intensity.*

The president and his speechwriters rarely wove poetry into their political rhetoric, but this verse was apt. Nixon really did fear anarchy in America. The American people truly were weary of the blood-dimmed tide. And the four-star generals genuinely feared Nixon would fall apart in the face of the growing opposition to the war.

"The subject of U.S. casualties is being thrown at me at every juncture: in the press, by the Secretary of Defense, at the White House and on the Hill," General Wheeler, chairman of the Joint Chiefs of Staff, wrote to General Abrams in Saigon on April 3. "I am concerned that decisions could be made in response to strong pressure inside and on the administration to seek a settlement of the war." Both men had been commanders in World War II under General Eisenhower, who had died the week before, on March 28. Like Ike, they wanted to fight and win.

But these were men who had won their stars commanding soldiers in a war of unconditional surrender; their tanks and their artillery and above all their thinking about how to fight a war were rusty. America's generals were confounded by Asian guerrillas. They did not trust Nixon to lead them to victory. The mistrust was mutual.

* * *

The president led a National Security Council meeting the week of Eisenhower's death, seeking a way to end the American role in the war before the year was over. The CIA's director, Richard Helms, gave his unvarnished analysis. Two weeks of nonstop B-52 bombing in Cambodia had had no visible impact on North Vietnam's military capabilities. The leaders of South Vietnam were not leading their own soldiers. It was pointless to send more American troops into battle without a strategy.

"We need a plan," the president said. "We are working against a time clock. We are talking six to eight months."

"We must get a sense of urgency in the training of the South Vietnamese," Nixon continued. "How do we de-Americanize this thing?" De-Americanize meant using Asians to fight Asians while pulling out Americans, changing the color of the anticommunist corpses on the battlefield.

Secretary of Defense Laird thought it was the wrong word, too negative. He said, "What we need is a term—*Vietnamizing*—to put the emphasis on the right issue." Thus began Vietnamization, a spur-of-the-moment strategy to turn a hopeless war over to our hapless allies.

"We should agree to total withdrawal of U.S. forces but include very strong conditions which we know may not be met," Nixon said. "There is no doubt that U.S. forces will be in Vietnam for some time, something like a large military assistance group, but our public posture must be another thing."

Our public posture must be another thing—that was classic Nixon, the trickster with two faces, as Martin Luther King Jr. had seen him. If sincere, a genius; if not, dangerous.

He would slowly pull American troops out of the Vietnam War—and then try to proclaim peace. As he drew down American forces, he would train and equip the army of South Vietnam. He would send Kissinger in secret to negotiate with Hanoi for a cease-fire. But if that strategy failed, the Communists could be victorious. In the end, "Vietnamization" could doom South Vietnam. And if it failed and Saigon fell, the long war would end in the death of one nation and the disgrace of another.

On April 3, the same day that General Wheeler put his worries about an American withdrawal into words, Kissinger wrote to Nixon: "We must convince the American public that we are eager to settle the war, and Hanoi that we are not so anxious that it can afford to outwait us."

"Our best course would be a bold move of trying to settle everything at once," Kissinger proposed. He would sit down in secret with the Soviet ambassador in Washington, Anatoly Dobrynin, and say that a settlement in Vietnam and a pact on limiting the superpowers' nuclear arsenals were inextricably linked. He was going to try to enlist the Soviet Union, Hanoi's most powerful ally, as a partner for peace in Vietnam. If this tactic succeeded, it could alter the course of the Cold War. Kissinger now understood the president's passion for the big play, the grand bargain.

He put this in writing to Ambassador Dobrynin.

> The President has reviewed the Vietnam situation carefully. He will not be the first American President to lose a war, and he is not prepared to give in to public pressures which would have that practical consequence. The President has therefore decided that he will make one more effort to achieve a reasonable settlement. . . .
>
> U.S.-Soviet relations are therefore at a crossroads. The President is eager to move into an era of conciliation with the Soviet Union on a broad front. As a sign of this, he is willing to send a high-level delegation to Moscow to agree with the Soviet Union on principles of strategic arms limitations. He is also willing to consider other meetings at even higher levels.
>
> The President will give this effort in Moscow six weeks to succeed.

Kissinger concluded that this was "the only way to end the war quickly and the best way to conclude it honorably." But he warned Nixon it would work only if the president were prepared "to take tough escalatory steps if Moscow rejects the overture."

He called the president in Key Biscayne on April 5 to get the go-ahead to meet with the Soviet ambassador. He got it. But Nixon already had determined to "take tough escalatory steps." Before hearing what the Soviets had to say about strategic nuclear weapons or making plans to withdraw ground troops from Vietnam, he first would increase the military pressure on the enemy. He wanted to apply the stick before dangling the carrot. As a committed cold warrior, he believed that the Communists understood the logic of force far better than the language of reason.

"Even without a reason, we ought to go ahead and crack them pretty hard in the North," Nixon said. "Crack this one, and crack another one. Plenty of places to hit. . . . The necessity for the North Vietnamese to know that there's still a lot of snap left in the old boys is very important. And I don't know any other way to do it."

* * *

As Kissinger was talking war and peace with the Soviet ambassador on April 15, Nixon learned that North Korea had shot down an American spy plane in international waters over the Sea of Japan. Thirty-one Americans were killed aboard the navy EC-121 aircraft operated by the National Security Agency. Another newly declassified NSA history and other recently released documents show that the Pentagon proposed to strike back with nuclear weapons.

Nixon first weighed seizing a North Korean ship sailing the high seas under a Dutch flag, which the State Department ruled an act of piracy. "The President said to find a way that international law can be breached," Haig's notes from an April 15 conversation with Kissinger read. "The U.S. became a great nation by breaking international law. The President said we certainly have concluded that we won't just sit here and do nothing."

But that is what he did—nothing. The next morning, he presided over a full-scale National Security Council session in the White House Cabinet Room, which included the chairman of the Joint Chiefs, who rarely attended such meetings. Haig's notes are the sole record.

General Wheeler reviewed the military options, one of which was to attack North Korea with "Honest John" missiles, artillery rockets carrying atomic warheads with a payload of thirty kilotons each, roughly equal to two and a half Hiroshimas. This act "would trigger retaliation," the general noted. The prospect of that attack, and the retaliation, gave everyone pause. The United States had fought the Korean War before.

"That is a very tough one to bite," Kissinger told the president after the meeting. "We might have to go to tactical nuclears."

Nixon stared into the abyss of nuclear war and turned away. He considered other acts of war, such as bombing North Korea's military bases. As Haig recollected in a 2007 oral history for the Nixon Presidential Library, the hawks on the NSC staff recommended "immediate military action against the North by taking out one of their airfields, and, at the same time, to tell Moscow that our toleration days were over. This included the determination to settle Vietnam immediately, with or without the Soviet Union and if the Soviet Union were to join the other side, we were prepared for that contingency as well." This, like the nuclear option, raised the possibility of a Third World War.

Kissinger, as he often did, played a double game. He said he sided with the hawks, but he warned the president that Secretary of State Rogers would openly oppose an attack, a revolt that the new administration could ill afford. That left Nixon with no option but a meager show of force: sending a flotilla of navy ships into the Sea of Japan. It was only a show. North Korea went unpunished. Nixon had frozen in the face of a Communist attack. "We do not do a thing with 31 lives missing," he sighed.

The president later regretted this decision bitterly. Haig recounted, "Nixon told me it was the worst mistake of his presidency not to respond early on in a decisive way to convince both Moscow and whoever else, Hanoi, Pyongyang, or any one of the camp that this was a different America."

One consequence of the EC-121 calamity was Nixon's near-complete loss of faith in his secretary of state, Bill Rogers. Thereafter, Kissinger became the president's diplomat in chief, opening secret negotiations with the Soviets, the North Vietnamese, and, through interlocutors, the Chinese in 1969. Rogers was to know nothing about such talks.

"Nixon did not trust the State Department," said Kissinger's Russia hand, Peter Rodman. "There were a number of issues—whether it was Vietnam or relations with the Soviets—where the first few things that Rogers did were the exact opposite of what Nixon wanted. . . . Nixon decided that he would rather do these things himself. He had Henry there to do it. Henry and he had an ideological affinity. They both looked at the world in the same way."

"The price you pay," Rodman said, "is a demoralization of the rest of the government."

* * *

Nixon had another reason for wanting complete control over the State Department. It had nothing to do with diplomacy. It was about dollars. The wealthiest Nixon campaign contributors were well aware that "ambassadorships were being sold to the highest bidders," said Samuel F. Hart, a Foreign Service officer for twenty-seven years who himself served as an ambassador under President Ronald Reagan.

This practice did not start with Nixon, but it was during his presidency that it became blatant and dangerous—another step down the road to Watergate.

Vincent de Roulet arrived as the newly appointed ambassador to Jamaica in 1969, sailing in on his ninety-foot yacht, *Patrina*, soon to be joined by seventeen of his racehorses. He was a ne'er-do-well who'd married rich; his mother-in-law, an immensely wealthy heiress, was a major Nixon fund-raiser. He had contributed $75,000 to the 1968 Nixon campaign (a sum equal to $513,000 today).

The chief political officer at the American embassy in Jamaica, Kenneth Rogers, remembered Ambassador de Roulet's tenure as a series of political disasters and racist jibes, ending only when the government expelled him and the president of Jamaica told the U.S. Department of State that "Vincent De Roulet was no longer 'persona grata.' He was not permitted to return."

Nixon appointed Turner B. Shelton, a crony and contributor of long standing, as ambassador to Nicaragua. Shelton had been the American consul general in Nassau, the Bahamas, where Nixon was a frequent visitor during the 1960s. His appointment shocked the career Foreign Service officers who served with him.

"I think he had something on them, on the White House and on Nixon," said James R. Cheek, a senior American envoy who became President Clinton's ambassador to Argentina. Strong evidence suggests that Shelton was a go-between for secret cash contributions to Nixon from donors, including the deeply eccentric billionaire Howard Hughes, who sojourned in the Bahamas and moved to the Nicaraguan capital during Shelton's tenures.

Shelton had "contributed heavily to the Richard Nixon political trajectory over many years," said Charles Anthony Gillespie Jr., later the American ambassador to Chile under Presidents Reagan and George H. W. Bush. "Turner B. Shelton was called a Hollywood producer. Now, I'm not an expert on Turner B. Shelton, but my understanding is that what Turner really produced best were what were called 'blue' movies. Whatever else he did . . . he contributed chunks of this money to Richard Nixon's campaigns over the years. He obviously merited an appointment and he got the Embassy in Nicaragua."

Shelton's shady reputation was exceeded by his devotion to the crooked dictator who ran Nicaragua, Anastasio Somoza. "Shelton didn't want any of our cables or reports to go in to Washington," said Ambassador Cheek, then Shelton's underling at the embassy. "Somoza's corruption and suppression and disappearing people . . . was supposed to be all censored out."

"He was very close to Somoza," Cheek said—so close that the dictator put the American ambassador's image on newly issued Nicaraguan currency, the twenty-córdoba bill—but "Shelton's toadying to Somoza and almost worshiping him didn't bother the White House at all."

At the start of the Nixon administration, Sam Hart was based at the American embassy in Costa Rica. "We had a career Foreign Service officer as ambassador there," he recalled. "He was told that he was not going to be kept on, and was moved out, anticipating the arrival of Mrs. Ruth Farkas. She and her husband owned Alexander's Department Store in New York and pledged a quarter of a million dollars to Richard Nixon's presidential campaign in '68"—equal to almost two million dollars today.

But "word got out that Ruth Farkas was not coming, because she and her husband had major-league problems with the IRS," Ambassador Hart said. "And even Richard Nixon couldn't fix that." Nixon's personal lawyer and political bagman, Herbert Kalmbach, fixed things for Farkas: after she pledged three hundred thousand dollars to his '72 reelection campaign, the president appointed her ambassador to Luxembourg, a far more luxurious post.*

The going price rose as the reelection neared. "Anybody who wants

---

* The Nixon Library holds evidence of the sale of ambassadorships: an undated handwritten note by Haldeman reading: "Farkas—250 for Costa Rica" and memos to Haldeman concerning Kalmbach's handling of ambassadorships for other well-heeled campaign contributors.

to be an ambassador must at least give $250,000," the president instructed Haldeman in June 1971.

This conduct had consequences. Kalmbach later pleaded guilty to selling ambassadorships for Nixon's benefit. He had several million dollars in unspent campaign cash on deposit in 1969, and some of that money wound up in a secret reelection fund Nixon began building shortly after he first took office. The cash helped finance an undercover private eye who worked for the White House, Jack Caulfield, who began spying on Nixon's political enemies in July 1969—days after Nixon commanded his aides to activate "dirty tricks" against the president's political opponents, as Haldeman's diary records. And three years later, some of the slush funds Kalmbach controlled would serve as hush money for the Watergate burglars.

* * *

Contributors who wanted something for their money often were received at the "Florida White House," in Key Biscayne, or the "Western White House," also known as LaCasa Pacifica, in San Clemente, California. Nixon escaped to these retreats frequently for long weekends and, increasingly, for weeks on end.

The Key Biscayne compound contained five well-appointed waterfront bungalows. Nixon flew there fifty-nine times as president, spending 198 days and nights. He passed almost as much time at San Clemente. Both of Nixon's hideaways were built with help from C. G. "Bebe" Rebozo, a Cuban American banker, and their mutual friend Bob Abplanalp, known as the spray valve king. Both men had been Nixon's financiers for years. Nixon liked to bend an elbow with Rebozo whenever time permitted, relaxing his mind, sometimes past the realm of reason. When Nixon really wanted to unwind, he and his drinking buddy Bebe took a helicopter from Key Biscayne to Walker's Cay, Abplanalp's private island in the Bahamas. What went on in the cay stayed in the cay.

San Clemente was far more formal, an elegant ten-room mansion built in the 1920s, on a twenty-eight-acre estate with flowering gardens and a seven-hole golf course overlooking the Pacific Ocean. It stood forty miles south of the tiny town where Nixon was raised, but light-years away from its dusty poverty.

Nixon would reside there for a month at a time. He liked to invite world leaders and Hollywood celebrities, laying charms on conservative stars such as John Wayne and Clint Eastwood and Governor Ronald Reagan of California, though he regarded the governor as an amiable dimwit with no political future. Nixon summoned his senior military and diplomatic officers to San Clemente, where they delivered the latest grim reports on Vietnam. He frequently ordered White House aides to fly in from Washington on a moment's notice to confer on the crisis of the day.

He tried to relax in his retreats, but he remained a restless man. Aides who met with Nixon in California and Florida often found him seething in self-imposed isolation. While light sparkled on the water and warm winds stirred the air, Nixon drew the blinds against the sun in Key Biscayne, and set a fireplace blazing in an air-conditioned room sealed off from the Pacific breezes in San Clemente. He sat in the shadows, communing with the only man in whom he could confide: himself.

"He had no hobbies," said Alexander Butterfield, a senior Nixon aide, one of only four men who knew about the president's secret taping system at the White House, installed in February 1971. "The Presidency was his hobby. He meditated, he thought, he pondered. He worked on his yellow pad. He thought things over. . . . He seemed to me preoccupied with the Presidency . . . preoccupied with his place in history, with his Presidency as history would see it."

* * *

Nixon believed beyond doubt that history would record his presidency as a great turning point. America would either be resurrected as the world's singular superpower or fall on the sword of Vietnam.

"This country could run itself domestically without a President," Nixon told the most prominent presidential biographer of the era, Theodore White. "You need a President for foreign policy."

His Cabinet and his White House staff soon realized that Nixon cared little about domestic affairs, least of all housing, health, education, welfare, and civil rights. Unless an issue could be leveraged for political advantage leading to Nixon's reelection, it was a waste of time. "He believed in nothing," said James Farmer, assistant secretary at the Department of Health, Education, and Welfare and one among very few black Nixon appointees. "He was neither moral nor immoral, but was amoral; he made decisions based on how they would affect him politically, not based on whether they were right or wrong."

Nixon made a halfhearted attempt to create a Domestic Council that could be a counterpart to the National Security Council. Much of the work initially fell to his White House aide Daniel Patrick Moynihan, a future Democratic senator from New York. But Nixon agreed wholeheartedly when Moynihan, in despair, told him he *"can't* have a Domestic Program."* The president had defined no domestic agenda; his Cabinet officers were in constant conflict over everything from economics to education; Congress rejected more than two-thirds of the new legislation proposed by the White House in 1969. The president concurred that it was "politically impossible" to tackle the nation's domestic problems in his first term. Far better, he concluded, "to get rid of things that don't work, and try to build up the few that do."

Getting rid of things was the heart of Nixon's domestic policy—especially erasing Lyndon Johnson's Great Society programs for the poor and politically dispossessed. When Moynihan advised that the issue of race relations could benefit from "benign neglect," the phrase fit the president's thinking perfectly. But these were ill-chosen words. "Regarding domestic policy, which Nixon dismissed as 'building outhouses in Peoria,' his disdain for the subject did not, alas, produce benign neglect," the conservative columnist George Will noted. It proved malign and malevolent. The war on poverty proved to be more of a war on the poor.

"If it's called racism, so be it," Nixon told Haldeman; he said he could not communicate with black people, "except with Uncle Toms." The blacks, the liberals, the college kids and their professors would not vote for him no matter what he did, Nixon thought, so it was pointless to appease them.

Nixon and Attorney General Mitchell pushed constantly for Congress to pass war-on-crime laws (harsher drug penalties, expanded wiretapping statutes), and they won some of those battles. But with few exceptions, new laws that changed America passed in spite of Nixon, not because he fought for them. He signed sweeping legislation such as the National Environmental Policy Act with gritted teeth; he believed "that we're catering to the left in all of this and that we shouldn't be. They're the ones that care about the environment, and that they're trying to use the environmental issue as a means of destroying the system."

The president spent far more energy trying to destroy the cornerstones of the Great Society, particularly LBJ's grandest endeavor for the poor, the Office of Economic Opportunity. He ordered two young eager-beaver staffers, Dick Cheney and Don Rumsfeld (two future secretaries of defense), to attack the OEO, which included Head Start, for schooling young children; Legal Services, providing lawyers to the poor; VISTA, or Volunteers in Service to America, created as a domestic Peace Corps; and a wide array of health and education projects.

Rumsfeld was Cheney's boss at the OEO. "He didn't know anything about the war on poverty," Cheney said, laughing, in a 2000 oral history interview, shortly before he became vice president. Neither, it must be said, did Cheney.

Nixon gave these men their first taste of executive power, and they liked it. They were proud foot soldiers in an army of young conservatives doing battle for the president.

"The Nixon administration came in disliking OEO intensely and I could never understand why Don took the job," said Frank Carlucci, another future secretary of defense recruited by Rumsfeld. "They kept calling me and telling me to kill it, to kill this or kill that."

Carlucci believed the OEO had achieved one major success: "to provide upward mobility for the people who were poverty-stricken and in the low-income brackets. An awful lot of the leadership came up through these programs," leaders who were not white men, "including people who became subsequently members of Congress." A program that helped to produce black leaders was anathema to Nixon; the informal compendium of his political opponents that came to be known as "the enemies list" contained every black member of Congress. The "OEO was the enemy," Carlucci concluded. "There's no question there was a very strong emotional feeling on the part of the president. He did not like the Great Society."

Nixon found fighting that enemy far easier than the one he faced half a world away.

* * *

"I want to end this war," President Nixon said in his first televised address to the nation about Vietnam, on May 14, 1969. He said he would not accept a peace settlement amounting to "a disguised American defeat."

Nor would he try "to impose a purely military solution on the battle-field."

So how would he end the war or win the peace? His speech was "totally unintelligible to the ordinary guy," Haldeman wrote in his secret diary. Nixon still searched for a strategy.

"Our fighting men are not going to be worn down," the president vowed. But the American people were worn out by four years of lethal combat; public support for the war was falling. As Nixon spoke, one of the more vicious clashes of the war was raging. The Battle of Hamburger Hill left 113 American soldiers dead and 627 wounded, all for control of a strategically pointless mountain.

His audience had heard empty words, and Nixon sensed that the speech was a flop. Six days later, on the Senate floor, Edward Kennedy of Massachusetts, the slain president's brother and sole political heir, spoke in language that seemed clearer to the citizenry. He called it "senseless and irresponsible to continue to send our young men to their deaths to capture hills and positions that have no relation to ending the military conflict."

The president convened a joint meeting with his Cabinet and the National Security Council the next day to make his position perfectly clear: North Vietnam was hell-bent on victory, and he would never let that happen. "We are talking to an enemy whose first objective is not peace," he said. "We need to threaten that if they don't talk they will suffer." The path to peace would have to be blazed by bombs.

"What is on the line is more than South Vietnam," Nixon warned: America's standing in the world was in peril. "If a great power fails to meet its aims, it ceases to be a great power," he said. "The greatness fades away."

CHAPTER SIX

"Madman"

THE PRESIDENT and his political opponents began preparing for a long battle on the home front as the summer of 1969 approached. Feelings on college campuses were already so fevered that President Nixon canceled his commencement speech at Ohio State University—an institution far better known as a football powerhouse than as a radical hotbed—for fear of student protests. His decision came on the strong recommendation of Attorney General John Mitchell.

In turn, Nixon ordered Mitchell to take extraordinary measures against the campus activists, the liberals, and the leftists planning to mount national protests against the war, including a march on Washington. Mitchell already had demanded and received a federal indictment against some of the most vocal leaders of the antiwar movement on charges of conspiracy to riot. During Mitchell's years as attorney general, the Justice Department brought many such political conspiracy charges, but in the end nearly every case came to nothing; the defendants were acquitted or the cases dismissed, often due to the unconstitutional conduct of the government.

Some of the steps Nixon and Mitchell took matched the harshest government crackdowns of the McCarthy era. The attorney general revived the Justice Department's Internal Security Division, which had been all but dormant for a decade. Its leader was J. Walter Yeagley, who had been an FBI agent chasing the nation's top Communists on sedition charges in 1948 when the young Richard Nixon was in hot pursuit of Alger Hiss. Twenty years after its heyday, the red hunt was renewed. Working closely with his old boss J. Edgar Hoover, Yeagley and his Internal Security force, along with a new Justice Department squad aimed solely at campus radicals, began compiling and cross-indexing files on nearly seven hundred fifty thousand potentially subversive American citizens and organizations.

Mitchell's number two man at the Justice Department, Richard Kleindienst, testified to Congress on May 22 that the government would round up radicals and revolutionaries and put them in detention camps if necessary. Few knew that Director Hoover himself began to draw up a blueprint for that drastic action back in 1948; Congress, at his urging, had passed an emergency detention law allowing suspected American subversives to be imprisoned without trials or hearings.

The first big antiwar marches were still months away. But they would come in waves, hundreds of thousands of people, the great majority among them ordinary citizens who had never before challenged the government or questioned its authority. Come the fall, there would be more protesters in the streets of America than soldiers at arms in Vietnam.

"I think there is a much deeper conspiracy than any of us realize," Nixon told Kissinger in a conversation about the coming march on Washington. "I will have to nail these people."*

* * *

On June 7, 1969, President Nixon flew from Washington for a face-to-face meeting with his partner in the war, President Nguyen Van Thieu of South Vietnam. Meanwhile, Kissinger held another secret meeting with Soviet ambassador Dobrynin in Washington. The ambassador asked what he should tell his superiors about the state of U.S.-Soviet relations.

---

* The time would come when Nixon had seen one march too many. On May Day 1971, seven thousand protesters were arrested in the vicinity of the Justice Department headquarters and detained in Washington, DC's football stadium, the largest mass arrest in the history of the United States.

"I said that everything depended on the war in Vietnam," Kissinger reported to Nixon "If the war were ended, he could say that there was no limit to what might be accomplished"—including an end to twenty years of nuclear weapons tensions.

Nixon and Thieu met at Midway Island, in the middle of the Pacific Ocean, where the United States had struck back at Japan six months after Pearl Harbor, in one of the greatest naval battles in history.

Thieu, a career military officer, had survived a series of political plots and coups; he had reasons to be suspicious of the intentions of the United States. Only three weeks before President Kennedy's assassination in 1963, the United States had tacitly backed the military revolt in which Thieu's predecessor, Ngo Dinh Diem, was murdered. Thieu suspected that Nixon would not be bearing glad tidings, and his instincts were precise.

The president said he soon would withdraw twenty-five thousand U.S. troops, less than 2 percent of the American combat force in the war. "Vietnamization" was about to begin.

"We have a difficult political problem," Nixon explained, according to the written memorandum of their private conversation. "The U.S. domestic situation is a weapon in the war." The troop withdrawal was required as a political gesture to Congress and public opinion; without popular support, America could not deploy more soldiers.

Thieu said he had the same problem, but in a mirror image. If American forces flagged, his government might fall. "What made the middle ground in Saigon so uncertain was the fear that the U.S. would withdraw support," he said. "Hence, many politicians were holding themselves available for a coalition government" with the Communists of North Vietnam. Hanoi's generals understood how political pressures and public opinion shaped war plans in Washington and Saigon.

Thieu warned of "a sagging of spirit in Saigon" and a rising belief that America would impose political concessions on his people. He recognized that Americans desired peace. He understood the difficulties for the president of a large army abroad incurring constant casualties. "We have kept saying the war is going better. We must now prove it," Thieu said. "The war in Vietnam is not a military one and neither side can win militarily." Political warfare trumped firepower; the support of the people of America and Vietnam mattered more than military might. The policy of slowly withdrawing American troops, "if not handled carefully, could be misunderstood by the North Vietnamese and their allies."

Nixon did not handle it carefully.

On June 19, at a news conference at the White House, a reporter asked the president to respond to the assertion of LBJ's last secretary of defense, Clark Clifford, that one hundred thousand American troops ought to be withdrawn by the end of 1969 and that all ground troops ought to be out by the end of 1970. "I would hope that we could beat Mr. Clifford's timetable," Nixon said.

He had no reason for raising such hopes. He had made a purely political statement; little would please the American people more than bringing the boys back home. But no such plan and no policy existed.

Nixon went on to say that, in addition to withdrawing ground troops in eighteen months, he was not politically "wedded" to the Thieu regime or opposed to a cease-fire. Kissinger despaired at the potential political consequences of these off-the-cuff comments. "He feels it will probably mean collapse of South Vietnam government in near future and will result in South Vietnamese troops fighting us," Haldeman wrote in his secret diary that night. "Thieu will consider it a betrayal, as will all South East Asia, and it will be interpreted as unilateral withdrawal."

Nixon had come to office hoping to end the war in a matter of six months. Kissinger was "discouraged because his plans for ending war aren't working fast enough and Rogers and Laird are constantly pushing for faster and faster withdrawals," Haldeman noted on July 7. "He wants to push for some escalation, enough to get us a reasonable bargain for a settlement. . . . Big meeting about this tonight on the *Sequoia*."

The *Sequoia* was the presidential yacht, built by a wealthy Philadelphia family in 1925 and then sold to the government during the Depression. Every president since Herbert Hoover had used it, usually for pleasure. The July 7 cruise was all business: four hours of Nixon thinking out loud with Kissinger, Rogers, Laird, Mitchell, and the president's top military and intelligence officials, covering every aspect of American policy and strategy in Vietnam. Though no formal record of the meeting exists, General Wheeler of the Joint Chiefs of Staff noted that the president said that public support for the war would hold "until about October," when the big antiwar protests were set to start. By then, he believed, the United States would either have to strike a peace deal or strike North Vietnam with great force.

As Nixon recalled in his memoirs and on tape, that night on the *Sequoia* was when he decided to go for broke. If bargaining would not end the war, then bombing would. He had a new deadline in mind: November 1. On that date in 1968, LBJ had stopped the bombing of North Vietnam and established the peace talks in Paris. Nixon decided that November 1, 1969, would be the right time to start bombing North Vietnam again. He seemed indifferent to the fact that the date fell two weeks before the planned climax of the peace protests, a nationwide march on Washington.

Now Nixon, the great strategist, and Kissinger, the great tactician, started making new plans. They would devise a shock-and-awe bombing campaign. They would use diplomatic subterfuges. They would play with public relations. They would undertake secret operations. And they would use psychological warfare, playing mind games with Moscow and Hanoi.

Kissinger immediately enlisted an unlikely warrior: Leonard Garment, a Nixon confidant from the New York law firm that had employed the president and John Mitchell, now a White House counselor. Garment was a genial oddball among his straitlaced colleagues: a liberal, a hipster, a musician. He was headed to Moscow to represent the United States at an international jazz festival set for July 14 when Kissinger called him in for a talk.

Kissinger told Garment that, since he was known to be close to Nixon, he would be buttonholed by Soviet intelligence officers seeking insights into the president's mind. "Convey the impression that Nixon is somewhat 'crazy,'" Kissinger said, "unpredictable and capable of the bloodiest brutality." Sure enough, shortly after arriving in Moscow, Garment was invited to meet a delegation led by a senior adviser to the Soviet leader, Leonid Brezhnev, including several men whom he assumed to be KGB spies. As directed, Garment told them that Nixon was a madman: "a dramatically disjointed personality . . . capable of barbaric cruelty . . . predictably unpredictable, a man full of complex contradictions, a strategic visionary but, when necessary, a coldhearted butcher."

And "strange to say," Garment wrote three decades later, "everything I said about Richard Nixon turned out to be more or less true."

* * *

On July 22, 1969, Nixon took off on an around-the-world tour, beginning with a flight to the South Pacific to witness the return of Apollo 11, the spacecraft that had carried the first men to walk on the moon. After seeing the landing capsule streak like a meteor across the starry night sky, and greeting the astronauts aboard a World War II aircraft carrier, the exuberant president described their journey as "the greatest week in the history of the world since Creation."

Nixon was embarking on a journey that he hoped would change the geopolitical globe. The next day, July 25, at the Top o' the Mar officers' club on the island of Guam, an American territory sixteen hundred miles south of Japan, the president delivered an informal briefing to reporters. He proclaimed a policy soon known as "the Nixon Doctrine." He said that, apart from nuclear weapons, the military defense of America's Asian allies would increasingly be the responsibility of those nations themselves, not the United States. This was Vietnamization writ large.

The doctrine was more a public relations play than a master plan. But Nixon emphasized it with foreign leaders and American ambassadors during the first three stops on his tour: the Philippines, Indonesia, and Thailand. Each nation was ruled by reliably pro-American autocrats. Each played its role in the Vietnam War, providing military bases, combat troops, and weapons.

"We are going through a critical phase for U.S. world leadership," Nixon told ten American envoys convened at the U.S. embassy in Bangkok. "The American people never wanted to be world leaders in first place and maybe that's why we have never had a world policy," he said. "What really rides on Vietnam is whether the U.S. people are going to play a big role in the world or not."

Stopping next in Saigon, Nixon met with President Thieu again. Thieu wondered if the president's pronouncement could encourage Russia and China to persuade their comrades in North Vietnam to sign a peace settlement at the Paris peace talks. "We have been using every diplomatic and other device we know to bring pressure on the Soviets," Nixon said.

China, he said, was another question.

The president's entourage aboard Air Force One included Haldeman,

Kissinger and members of his National Security Council brain trust, and a few trusted senior State Department officers. The president and Kissinger had plans so clandestine, so tightly compartmented, that seatmates had to keep secrets from one another. The Nixon Doctrine had come as "a complete and utter surprise," said John Holdridge, Kissinger's top East Asia hand at the NSC. "I was astonished"—even though his close friend and State Department counterpart Marshall Green was on the trip and had drafted the doctrine.

But then, Holdridge had a secret of his own to keep.

"Between Jakarta and Bangkok," Holdridge recalled, "Henry asked me to draft a cable to the Chinese, proposing that we get together to talk."

"I very happily sat down and worked. I said that we should not look to the past, but look to the future. There were many things that we had in common. There were many issues that were of mutual value, and we should address them, and let's get together. I gave the draft to Henry. He looked at it, gave his characteristic grunt, said nothing, turned around, and went back into the Presidential compartment."

Three days later, on August 1, Nixon met Yahya Khan, the president of Pakistan, a professional soldier who had been his army's commander in chief. Nixon asked for his help in delivering the cable to China requesting a meeting at the highest levels. Yahya said he would convey the message personally to China's prime minister, Zhou En-lai.

This was Nixon's first knock at the door to the Great Wall. As we now know, China was unlocking the door that same month. The heavens were in alignment.

In 1969, Chairman Mao had tasked four senior military marshals to study China's strategic policy. Throughout the spring and summer, Chinese and Soviet armies had been skirmishing. Moscow was debating whether to bomb China's nuclear arms facilities. That August, Beijing faced a huge new deployment of Soviet forces massing at China's border at Kazakhstan. At the very moment Nixon was seeking a secret American rapprochement with China, two of the marshals on Mao's task force, Chen Yi and Ye Jianying, proposed playing "the card of the United States." Marshal Chen specifically recommended high-level talks with Washington. Mao accepted their report.

Nixon played the next card on the penultimate stop of his world tour: a meeting with the ruler of Romania, President Nicolae Ceauşescu.

Huge crowds chanting, "Neek-zon! Neek-zon!" lined the streets of Bucharest to greet his motorcade. Nixon had a soft spot for the Communist dictator, because he believed Ceaușescu might serve as a mediator between the United States and China. "In 25 years, China will have a billion people," Nixon told Ceaușescu on August 2. "One billion Chinese fenced in is a bomb about to explode," he added, "a terribly explosive force that may destroy the peace of that time." The Romanian agreed to tell his Chinese comrades that, as Nixon put it, the Americans wanted "to open communications channels with them, to establish relations."

Nixon also asked Ceaușescu to be a diplomatic broker between the United States and the Soviet Union, in part so Moscow could help him deal with Hanoi. "There is nothing more important to me than to end this war on a fair basis," he said. "It could make possible U.S.-Chinese relations, and would help relations with the Soviet Union. All this is possible."

Nixon strongly suggested he would escalate the war if North Vietnam did not agree to a peace deal soon. The enemy's leaders "continue to fight in Vietnam, thinking that public opinion will force us to capitulate," he told Ceaușescu, speaking more frankly than he did with the American people. By November, Nixon warned, there would be hell to pay if North Vietnam did not make peace: "I never make idle threats; I do say that we can't indefinitely continue to have 200 deaths per week with no progress in Paris."

Kissinger split off from the president's traveling party and went to Paris the next day, delivering through diplomatic channels a letter from Nixon addressed to Ho Chi Minh, the leader of North Vietnam since World War II. The message proposed a new set of negotiations in Paris, to be conducted in a completely clandestine manner by Kissinger himself.

The Pentagon, the State Department, and the CIA were to know nothing about this; Nixon and Kissinger alone would negotiate an end to the war with Ho's personal emissary from North Vietnam.

* * *

After Nixon's world tour ended, he retreated to spend a month at the Western White House, La Casa Pacifica in San Clemente. The president tried to relax, but war and crisis kept him anxious and ever restless; twice during August, he awoke in the middle of the night fearing he was having a heart attack.

On August 14, 1969, Nixon convened the National Security Council in San Clemente. Those gathered at the Western White House included Nixon, Kissinger, Rogers, Laird, Helms, and Mitchell.

The main subjects were China and the Soviet Union, whose armies were clashing in a border battle and whose leaders had nuclear weapons at hand. Nixon startled his national security team by taking China's side. Moscow "may have a 'knock them off now' policy," the president said. "We must think through whether it is a safer world with China down." Nixon believed it was best to see that the largest Communist nation in the world survived.

Nixon's fear of a cataclysmic clash between China and Russia was a remarkable foresight. Four days later, William L. Stearman, the State Department's ranking intelligence expert on Hanoi, who was about to join Kissinger's staff, sat down to lunch at a Washington hotel with Boris N. Davydov—officially a diplomat, in reality a spy stationed at the Soviet embassy. Such conversations, often stranger than fiction, were part of the unwritten code of conduct between the Cold War combatants.

"Davydov asked point blank what the US would do if the Soviet Union attacked and destroyed China's nuclear installations," Stearman wrote in a top-secret memo that went straight to Kissinger. "What would the US do if Peking called for US assistance in the event Chinese nuclear installations were attacked by us?"

Kissinger called a crash meeting in San Clemente with Attorney General Mitchell, CIA covert operations chief Thomas Karamessines, and the handful of senior State and NSC experts he trusted.

If the border battle went nuclear, "the consequences for the US would be incalculable," Kissinger said. "We must make this very plain to the Soviets despite the US nuclear policy in Europe," which included an all-out attack with thousands of nuclear weapons if Soviet troops crossed into West Germany. "It would be helpful to know something about what DEFCON should be entered into," he added, if "the Soviets were to knock out the Chinese nuclear capacity."* Three weeks later, both the Soviet Union and China conducted nuclear weapons tests. The cataclysm never

---

* DEFCON stood for "defense readiness condition." There were five escalating levels. DEFCON 5 meant all was calm; 4 was an alert; 3 meant the air force was ready to mobilize in fifteen minutes; 2 was the verge of nuclear war; and 1 was the war itself. The United States had gone to DEFCON 2 only once, during the 1962 Cuban missile crisis.

came, but it was now clear to all that Moscow and Beijing were implacable enemies.

On August 30, Nixon passed an almost completely pleasant day at San Clemente, swimming and walking on the beach with Bebe Rebozo. Then came a message from Kissinger.

Ho Chi Minh had answered his letter proposing secret peace talks. The reply was defiant.

"The longer the war goes on, the more accumulates the mourning and burdens of the American people," Ho wrote to Nixon, who underlined the last sentence of this passage.

> I am extremely indignant at the losses and destruction caused by the American troops to our people and our country. I am also deeply touched at the rising toll of death of young Americans who have fallen in Vietnam by reason of the policy of American governing circles. Our Vietnamese people are deeply devoted to peace, a real peace with independence and real freedom. *They are determined to fight to the end, without fearing the sacrifices and difficulties in order to defend their country and their sacred national rights.*

Ho Chi Minh—an adopted name meaning "he who enlightens"—was born the son of Vietnamese peasant farmers in 1890, the same year as Eisenhower. He moved to Paris and joined the Communist Party after World War I. He had been an agent of the Soviet Comintern, the global Communist alliance created by Lenin. Moscow helped him establish the Indochinese Communist Party in 1930. At the time of his contact with Nixon, Ho had been fighting for independence for four decades. France had occupied Vietnam and Cambodia and called their colonial land Indochina. Ho defeated the French in May 1954, with military aid from China. That same year, the Americans took up the fight against communism in Vietnam, with small groups of military advisers and intelligence officers. By the time American combat forces invaded Vietnam in 1965, the Soviets, not the Chinese, were Ho's main military suppliers.

Ho was now seventy-nine, an international symbol of revolutionary warfare, an icon in the Communist world, and, as he wrote to Nixon, "determined to fight to the end" to defeat the United States.

He died three days after Nixon read his letter.

Would Hanoi lose its resolve without its legendary leader? Who would emerge as the enemy's chief strategist? No one in the White House, the Pentagon, or the CIA had the slightest idea whether Ho's death would change the course of the war or increase the chance for peace. American intelligence on North Vietnam's political intentions was at best informed speculation, a fact that drove Richard Nixon mad with rage.

"We tried every operational approach in the book, and committed our most experienced field operatives to the effort to get inside the government in Hanoi," CIA director Richard Helms wrote long after the war was lost. "Within the Agency, our failure to penetrate the North Vietnamese government was the single most frustrating aspect of those years. We could not determine what was going on at the highest levels of Ho's government, nor could we learn how policy was made or who was making it." At the root of this failure was "our national ignorance of Vietnamese history, society, and language," Helms admitted. Know your enemy is the oldest rule in the book of war; America broke it. Without knowing the enemy's intentions and capabilities, America's soldiers and spies were fighting a ghost army in Vietnam—Helms used the word "incubus," a demon that comes in nightmares—and it stayed shrouded in darkness during a decade of slaughter.

* * *

By the time Nixon returned to Washington on September 9, his resolve to defeat North Vietnam by any means had steeled. "I was ready to use whatever military pressure was necessary to prevent them from taking over South Vietnam by force," he wrote in his memoirs. "Kissinger and I developed an elaborate orchestration of diplomatic, military, and publicity pressures we would bring to bear on Hanoi."

The instruments in this orchestra included plans for an all-out attack in Vietnam, a worldwide nuclear alert aimed at the Soviets, and a speech to the American people scheduled for Nixon's new D-day for the war, November 1.

The president met with Kissinger, Rogers, Laird, Mitchell, and Helms at the White House on September 10 to talk about Vietnam. Kissinger had prepared a deeply pessimistic report for Nixon. "The pressure of public opinion on you to resolve the war quickly will increase—and I believe increase greatly—during the coming months," it read. "The plans for student demonstrations [beginning] in October are well known, and while many Americans will oppose the students' activities, they will also be reminded of their own opposition to the continuation of the war." Nixon underlined that sentence.

"I do not believe that with our current plans we can win the war within two years, although our success or failure in hurting the enemy remains very important," Kissinger continued. "Hanoi's adoption of a strategy designed to wait us out fits both with its doctrine of how to fight a revolutionary war and with its expectations about increasingly significant problems for the U.S." The president underlined those words, too.

Kissinger recommended bombing the enemy so hard that they would sue for peace. He and his staff had been drafting an attack plan code-named Duck Hook, with a "sharp escalation" of violence and "sharp military blows" aimed to force Hanoi to capitulate. An unsigned memo of a Duck Hook meeting Kissinger held in the White House Situation Room showed that Soviet perceptions of Nixon's rage were part of the plan: "If USSR thinks President is a madman, then they've driven him to it and they'd better help calm him down."

Duck Hook included attacks against twenty-nine major targets in North Vietnam: bombing and mining the country's main port city, Haiphong, and obliterating six central electric power stations, four airfields, the nation's major factory plants and warehouses, its principal bridges and rail yards, and the levee system in the Red River Delta, which irrigated the rice fields that fed the nation.

Nixon, Kissinger, and Haldeman flew down to the Florida White House in Key Biscayne to weigh the plan on October 3, the day after the president received it. Haldeman's handwritten diaries recorded four hours of talks, in which "P" is the president and "K" is Kissinger.

[Nixon held] one of those mystic sessions, which he had obviously thought through ahead of time. . . . Wants large free chunks of schedule time to work on Vietnam decisions. . . .

Then had session with K, and he is of course very concerned, feels we only have two alternatives, bug out or accelerate, and that we must escalate or P is lost. He is lost anyway if that fails, which it well may. K still feels main question is whether P can hold the government and the people together for the six months it will take. His contingency plans don't include the domestic factor. . . .

It's obvious from the press and dove buildup that trouble is there, whatever we do.

The dove buildup was imminent and immense. Hundreds of thousands of Americans across the country were about to join peaceful antiwar protests in October. A huge march on Washington would follow in mid-November. Nixon set his speechwriters working on his address to the nation set for November 1. He did not know if he would speak about war or peace.

* * *

Three days after the Key Biscayne meeting, on October 6, Kissinger called Secretary of Defense Mel Laird with a highly unusual request: "Could you exercise the DEFCON?" he asked. "The President will appreciate it very much." The orders went out to the Joint Chiefs on October 9: immediately prepare "an integrated plan of military actions to demonstrate convincingly to the Soviet Union that the United States is getting ready for any eventuality on or about 1 November 1969."

As often happened when Kissinger issued orders in the president's name, Laird wondered what the hell was going on. DEFCON was no exercise: it was a worldwide alert with hundreds of aircraft, thousands of military officers, and many megatons of nuclear weapons placed on high readiness. Nixon wanted to convince the Soviet Union and North Vietnam that the United States was ready to go nuclear to end the Vietnam War by November 1. The global mobilization ran from October 13 to October 30, climaxing in a squadron of B-52 bombers carrying nuclear weapons out of Alaska to the edge of the North Pacific.

Laird, born in 1922, is alive at this writing, as is Kissinger, born in 1923—the last surviving members of Nixon's inner circle. The documents on the alert were declassified in 2011, but Laird gave an interview about the DEFCON test a decade before. Nixon was playing a gigantic bluff. "This was one of several examples of what some referred to as the 'madman theory,'" Laird said. The test was intended to show that "you could never put your finger on what he might do next."

The madman theory's proofs include the DEFCON test, Haldeman's memoirs, Kissinger's instructions to Len Garment to tell the Russians that Nixon was crazy, and the Duck Hook plans, which aimed to show the president as "a madman."

Nixon believed that Eisenhower had ended the Korean War in 1953 with a secret signal sent through diplomatic channels that he might nuke Pyongyang unless the Communists sued for peace. Hard proof of that harsh threat is lacking, but brinkmanship was at the core of American foreign policy for much of the Cold War.

Nixon was probing for a reaction from Moscow that would signal a stand-down by their comrades in North Vietnam. But Hanoi's leaders, the Politburo that succeeded Ho's death, showed no sign that their will to win had changed. Nixon's idea that he could coerce peace through violence started to crumble. He rejected twelve drafts of the war speech he intended to give on November 1. A late draft announced punishing bombings against North Vietnam, promised more if the enemy would not talk peace, and pronounced the attacks the most inescapable decision of his life. Nixon ripped up all his speechwriters' drafts, canceled Duck Hook, wrote an entirely new speech, and delivered it to millions of people on television on November 3.

* * *

He read from a typed text, grim-faced, a golden curtain behind him, a television camera's eye staring at him.

"Tonight—to you, the great silent majority of my fellow Americans—I ask for your support," he said. "I pledged in my campaign for the Presidency to end the war in a way that we could win the peace. I have initiated a plan of action which will enable me to keep that pledge. The more support I can have from the American people, the sooner that pledge can be redeemed; for the more divided we are at home, the less likely the enemy is to negotiate at Paris. Let us be united for peace. Let us also be united against defeat. Because let us understand: North Vietnam cannot defeat or humiliate the United States. Only Americans can do that."

The "silent majority" was a phrase with a long provenance. For centuries, it had been used to eulogize the dead. In 1902, Supreme Court justice John Marshall Harlan spoke of the Civil War combatants who "long ago passed over to the silent majority." The peace marchers were coming to Washington in memory of the dead in Vietnam—and they forced Nixon to cancel the planned attacks at the last minute.

The three-day gathering in Washington culminated in a candlelight march on the evening of November 14, each of tens of thousands of silent protesters carrying a small flame and the name of an American soldier killed or a Vietnamese village destroyed in the war; on the following day, 325,000 people gathered around the Washington Monument, the largest political protest in the history of the United States.

On the night of the candlelight march, three of Kissinger's staff were down in the basement of the White House working late on another speech about the war. One of them, William Watts, stepped out of the Southwest Gate one flight up to light a cigarette. He looked out at the silent line of illumination in the street. He saw his wife and his three daughters, holding candles, marching against the war.

He thought, "I am on the inside, the enemy."

CHAPTER SEVEN

"Don't strike a king unless you intend to kill him"

Nixon BELIEVED that the fate of the United States depended on defeating the nation that Kissinger called "a fifth-rate agricultural power." It was a question of national survival.

"If we fail we have had it," the president told the Joint Chiefs, Kissinger, Mitchell, and Laird on October 11, as the big antiwar protests began. Adm. Thomas H. Moorer of the Joint Chiefs wrote in his diary after the meeting, "The President stated that a great power must go on this basis: 'Don't strike a king unless you intend to kill him.'" Nixon did not intend to be killed by skinny guerrillas in black pajamas.

When Nixon took the oath of office, Vietnam had been LBJ's war. It was Nixon's now. Seeing no path to peace with honor, he was looking for ways to win it and demanded new plans for victory through firepower. At the start of 1970, he contemplated sending the fearsome fleets of B-52s (each equipped to carry sixty thousand pounds of bombs) to strike North Vietnam's soldiers as they traveled south along the Ho Chi Minh Trail.

The Ho Chi Minh Trail was the Communists' essential supply line—a network of hundreds of interwoven pathways running from North Vietnam through Laos and Cambodia into South Vietnam. Soldiers moved on foot, on bicycles, oxcarts, horses, and occasionally elephants, carrying food, weapons, and military materiel. The trail kept the Communists armed and fed as they went into battle against South Vietnam. As American involvement in the war escalated, the trail system moved westward, away from the border of South Vietnam and deeper into Laos and Cambodia, where canopied jungles provided cover from air attacks and concealment for camps.

The U.S. Air Force had struck the trail since 1965, to little avail. The CIA had been fighting a secret war, alongside Laotian paramilitary fighters, using the tribesmen's knowledge of the steep terrain and dense forests. They sought to sever the trail, with little success. American war planes had been bombing the Communists' Cambodian encampments for months. Returning pilots reported that they were blowing holes in the jungle, which seemed an apt image for the air war. The U.S. embassy had no ambassador or CIA officers in Cambodia, so information on what was happening there was scant.

The Ho Chi Minh Trail might have looked like nothing more than a network of primitive footpaths, but it proved to be one of the most potent factors in the war. To sever the trail, and kill the enemy soldiers who traveled on it, American aircraft would have to drop many more bombs in disguised raids beyond the battlefronts of Vietnam, the CIA would have to step up paramilitary missions in Laos, and Communist camps in Cambodia would have to be attacked with ground troops.

* * *

Nixon's decisions balanced on a knife edge. He could make tangible military gains on the battlefront at an incalculable political cost on the home front. There would be hell to pay if Congress and the American people found out that the war was being fought far beyond the borders of Vietnam.

"We have the following problem," Kissinger told President Nixon on January 26, 1970. "The North Vietnamese are building up a large concentration in Northern Laos. There are 14,000 troops." But, Kissinger warned, "we have not used B-52s in Northern Laos before. There were no targets there."

"What if it comes out?" Nixon asked. Then he answered his own question: "Fighting the war in Laos . . . that's the problem."

Nonetheless, Nixon approved B-52 strikes on February 17. U.S. Air Force bomb-damage assessment teams reported the next day that the dead were too many to count; drinking water was scarce for many square miles as "rotting cadavers had contaminated the region's streams." Thousands of soldiers and villagers died; a biblical flood of refugees walked many miles from their homes seeking food, water, and shelter. But "the bombing was basically ineffectual," said Charles E. Rushing, then the political counselor at the American embassy in Laos. Though the Communists suffered "stunning casualties," Rushing remembered, "it didn't stop them."

The American press in Saigon quickly reported the attack, citing Pentagon sources. Nixon's wrath at this leak was immense; he tongue-lashed Admiral Moorer, the incoming chairman of the Joint Chiefs. The president was so angry that the admiral feared Nixon would never authorize another carpet bombing. He was dead wrong.

* * *

One secret stayed secret during 1970: Kissinger's private negotiations in Paris with Le Duc Tho, a senior leader of the Politburo of North Vietnam, which had accepted the American proposal for clandestine peace talks. No one in the Nixon administration outside the president, Kissinger, and a handful of aides was aware that these meetings, held at a villa outside Paris, were taking place—not the secretary of defense, not the secretary of state, not the director of central intelligence.

Le Duc Tho became, through these talks, the chief representative of North Vietnam after the death of Ho Chi Minh. He was fifty-nine years old, white-haired, black-suited, battle-hardened. He had been a revolutionary for forty years, serving as a soldier, a politician, and a diplomat. On February 21 he made the most straightforward declaration to Kissinger that would take place during their talks, which would continue for three more years.

"In this war we have had many hardships," Tho said. "But we have won the war. You have failed."

Kissinger was shocked. "What?" he sputtered.

"We have won the war," Tho repeated. "You have lost the war, the longest and most costly in your history. This is not just our own view. Americans also think that."

"If you prolong the war, we have to continue to fight," he told Kissinger. "If you intensify the war in South Vietnam, if you even resume bombing North Vietnam, we are prepared. We are determined."

"This is our iron will," he said. "We have been fighting for 25 years, the French and you. You wanted to quench our spirit with bombs and shells. But they cannot force us to submit. You have threatened us many times. . . . President Nixon also threatens us."

"You talk a great deal about peace," Tho said. "President Nixon talks about peace. . . . You talk peace, but you make war."

* * *

The president led a full-scale National Security Council conclave at the White House on February 27. The war council resembled a game of liar's poker.*

"I want to run through the Laos situation," Nixon said. "There are no present plans to put in troops." Laird corrected that misstatement: "We do insert some from time to time on the Ho Chi Minh trail," he said, referring to highly classified operations that Congress had unearthed but not disclosed.

"That is all right," Nixon said. "We bomb the Ho Chi Minh trail and we will continue to do so. I say that categorically."

But the question of combat operations in Laos remained. "Have we lost anybody there?" Nixon asked. Helms replied, "Five CIA men have died; four in helicopters shot down and one by accident." This was a major misrepresentation of the human costs of the secret war.

The president asked Laird about the level of American bombing in Laos; Nixon did not have the facts at hand. The defense secretary said the number of tactical air raids by fighter-bombers had increased fourfold from 1968 and now stood at 3,428 a month, at a cost of two billion dollars a year.

"We don't have to stop," Nixon said. "I don't care what they say. . . . There is no problem about getting into a deeper involvement in Laos."

---

* The NSC meeting included President Nixon, Vice President Agnew, Secretary of State Rogers, Secretary of Defense Laird, Attorney General Mitchell, the outgoing Joint Chiefs chairman General Wheeler, Nixon's congressional liaison Bryce Harlow, Kissinger, and the NSC aide William Watts, the man who three months before had watched from inside the White House as his wife and his three daughters marched against the war. Watts served as the silent note taker.

The president turned to Rogers: "Where do we stand?" he asked him.

"We are heading to a serious problem with Congress," said the secretary of state. "They are looking for an issue, and this is it. They see in it a repetition of Vietnam. A replay in escalation is occurring. Our sorties have been doubled. B-52 strikes have taken place."

"We have refused to make anything public," Rogers said. "How can I defend keeping this secret?"

Mitchell argued against any testimony to Congress: "That just opens Pandora's box," he said.

Laird offered a compromise: a presidential statement on the extent of the American war in Laos. "How we handle this is a major issue of credibility of this Administration," he said. "If we tell a good story here it will quiet down. Why hide everything?"

"We must lay it out," the president concurred. "There are no ground forces, and there will be none without going to Congress. . . . We must write in a simple way. There is a lot of confusion on this. I don't want any questions left."

After the NSC meeting broke up, Kissinger warned Nixon that it would be difficult to "lay it out" in "a simple way," given the long and deadly history of covert American operations in Laos. But Nixon waved him off.

"We won't mention that," he told Kissinger. "I'll have to fuzz their capacity. Non-combative and none killed." Winston Lord, newly appointed as Kissinger's special assistant, was assigned to draft the presidential white paper on Laos. Kissinger vetted it. On March 6, 1970, President Nixon released it from the Florida White House in Key Biscayne.

"There was a phrase in that paper that no American had ever been killed in combat in Laos over the previous 20 years or so," Lord remembered. This was an utter falsehood, which Lord blamed on the CIA. But responsibility for this lie ultimately lay with Nixon, who had decided to "fuzz" the issue, and with Kissinger, who knew better.

"I knew it wasn't true," Kissinger told Haldeman on March 9. "The President should have never made the statement."

The truth was that, at that time, American casualties in Laos totaled close to three hundred soldiers, airmen, covert operations officers, and civilian support staff killed, captured, or missing.

America's secret war in Laos involved a multitude of CIA officers commanding tribal warriors, a chain of CIA civilian contractors who saw combat, and special operations soldiers who planted motion-detecting sensors where they thought the North Vietnamese would be coming south. And, lost to memory, "a lot of very young and very able Air Force officers" were assigned to attack enemy convoys along the Ho Chi Minh Trail, as Kissinger's trusted aide John Holdridge later recounted. "A lot of these poor guys got shot down, and nobody seems know what happened to them. Out of all the POWs or people who were MIAs I think we only recovered a handful, 10 or 12, something like that, from Laos."

"The rest just disappeared," he said. "This is one of the great tragedies of the whole war."

* * *

Kissinger returned to Paris on March 16 to resume his secret talks with Le Duc Tho. This time he delivered a clear warning that the war might intensify to include American attacks on Communist troops and camps in Cambodia.

"We regard the presence of non–South Vietnamese forces in sanctuaries in neighboring countries as having a direct impact on the war and as being part of the problem—particularly those in camps along and near the borders of South Vietnam," Kissinger said. The American negotiating position now included a demand that "all the bases in Cambodia and Laos along the frontier and the infiltration trails should be closed."

Tho was defiant. "It is our firm conviction that so long as you prolong and intensify the war, you will meet defeat," he said. "If you failed in Laos and Vietnam, how can you succeed in Cambodia?"

President Nixon answered with brute force.

CHAPTER EIGHT

"A pitiful, helpless giant"

NIXON WAS sleepless, soul-searching. His demonic insomnia returned. "I don't think he ever slept," Haig recalled. He dealt with it at night by drinking. The president by day fell into a dark state of portents and omens. Talking with Haldeman about past presidents' auras of omnipotence, he suddenly started planning the precise details of his own funeral.

He had predicted that 1970 would be the worst year of his first term. He again proved prescient. The president's popularity plummeted eleven points in public opinion polls taken in March. The endless war was the cause. The toll Vietnam was taking was measured not only in military caskets but in wounds of the mind; an increasing number of veterans were shell-shocked or heroin-addicted. When they returned, they found the war had come home with them, a battle within the American body politic. And all the while, Americans were still dying in combat, a thousand every month.

On March 19, 1970, Kissinger told a trusted colleague about a brutal telephone conversation he had just held with the president. Kissinger told Nixon that "there wasn't much we could do militarily" to force North Vietnam to settle or surrender. The president "went through the roof." He demanded a new set of war plans—a "hard option"—and he wanted it on his desk that day.

Kissinger became frantic. He had been meeting daily with the nation's military and intelligence chiefs. LBJ's October 1968 decision to stop bombing North Vietnam had frustrated and infuriated them. But no one had any hard options. No one had any new ideas.

The written notes of a White House war council convened on March 23 convey their conundrum: "Mr. Helms said that if the enemy believed we might bomb North Vietnam, something might be achieved. Mr. Kissinger asked how this message could be conveyed to North Vietnam. General Wheeler said it would be clear if we actually did some bombing."

Then came a coup out of nowhere. That week, a right-wing military junta took power in Cambodia. Battle-hardened Communist forces started moving toward the Cambodian capital, Phnom Penh, two hundred miles northwest of American military headquarters in Saigon.

The Cambodian army was hopeless—"totally unprepared for combat" against the Communists. "It lacked experienced leaders, corruption was prevalent among its officers, and pay was low," according to a recently declassified American military history. Its principal active duty in the past decade had been draining swamps and digging ditches.

A clash between these mismatched armies was certain. Cambodians and Vietnamese had hated one another—politically, tribally, racially—for centuries. Soon the bodies of four hundred massacred Vietnamese were found floating down the Mekong River in Cambodia.

Nixon instinctively embraced the right-wing leader of the Cambodian coup, a general no one knew well, but with a name no one could forget: Lon Nol. "President Nixon asked me to draft several personal Nixon-to–Lon Nol telegrams containing rather extravagant expressions of friendship and support," recalled Marshall Green, the assistant secretary of state for East Asia. "I was concerned that Lon Nol would read into these messages a degree of U.S. military support and commitment that exceeded what our government could deliver on—given Congressional attitudes in particular. I also regarded Lon Nol as lacking the qualities needed to lead his country out of its mess."

As the mess deepened daily in Cambodia, Nixon ordered the CIA into the fight. "I want Helms to develop & implement a plan for maximum assistance to pro-U.S. elements in Cambodia," he instructed Kissinger in writing. That meant untraceable money and guns, preferably Swiss gold and an arsenal of Communist-bloc weapons such as AK-47 assault rifles, which the Cambodians could claim they had captured from the Vietcong.

The CIA director promised to support Nixon's "military effort against the Viet Cong in Cambodia . . . by the provision of covert economic and political support." This proved difficult in the short run. Cambodia, with no American ambassador, no CIA station chief, and no CIA or military intelligence officers on the ground, was terra incognita as a war zone. The American embassy was in the hands of a few Foreign Service professionals—diplomats, not warriors.

Casting around the world, Helms called upon John Stein, a veteran CIA officer with plenty of paramilitary experience in Africa but none in Indochina. Stein reported back to the CIA and the White House shortly after his arrival in Cambodia. He got straight to the point: "Here was another small Southeast Asian country where nobody knew what was going on." The new Cambodian regime "had come to the conclusion that somebody had to help them, and that this somebody was the U.S. With more fighting on their hands, their morale needed bucking up. The only way at the moment to give this bucking up was to give the AK-47 package and provide a Swiss bank account."

Nixon approved fifteen hundred assault rifles and ten million dollars in untraceable CIA cash for Lon Nol, a down payment on a far greater commitment coming soon.

* * *

That same week, America's central outpost in Laos faced a deadly siege by a gathering of North Vietnamese soldiers at the CIA's mountain redoubt in Long Tieng. If it fell, Laos itself could collapse into chaos or face the threat of Communist control. The crisis demanded immediate action but offered no easy solution. Kissinger had to plead for the president's attention.

"Poor K," Haldeman noted sardonically in his March 24 diary entry, "no one will pay attention to his wars, and it looks like Laos is falling."

On March 25, Nixon met for three hours with Kissinger, Helms, and key members of the National Security Council. The president, Kissinger noted drily, wasn't inclined to let Laos go down the drain. Helms was blunt: the United States had to ask the right-wing military junta in

Thailand to send battalions of troops into Laos, widening the covert war without telling Congress.

The CIA director wrote for the record, "Apologizing for my vulgarity, I told the president that I realized this was a 'shitty' decision to ask a President of the United States to make, but in light of all the factors it seemed a desirable thing to do. Nixon commented that it had been necessary to do a number of unpleasant things recently and that this was one more that could be taken on as well."

The next afternoon, Kissinger called Nixon in Key Biscayne, at the start of a four-day Easter weekend.

"The Thai battalion, are we going to get them in there?" Nixon asked.

"That's done," Kissinger replied.

"There's going to be no announcement," the president said. "We are just going to do it. We don't have to explain it." With that, Nixon tried to take his mind off life-and-death issues. He spent the next three days sailing, sunbathing, and drinking in Key Biscayne and the Bahamas with Bebe Rebozo.

Kissinger sent an attention-getting intelligence report to Key Biscayne on Friday morning, March 27: North Vietnam had placed its military forces on alert in Cambodia. Nixon's immediate response was to order the air force to step up the bombing of Communist targets in Cambodia. His nightmare was that Cambodia would fall, providing a permanent base for the armed forces of North Vietnam. If Laos fell, too, American soldiers would face Communist forces on three fronts. The United States, with all its military might, could lose the war, the American embassy in Saigon a garrison encircled by Asian guerrillas.

The political situation at home was no better than the military situation abroad.

Secretary of Defense Laird warned Nixon on Tuesday, March 31, that the Senate was prepared to cut off funds for American air strikes in Laos and Cambodia. Nixon responded that he would "fight such a limitation to the death."

The Senate also rejected the nomination of Judge G. Harrold Carswell, the second of two third-rate conservatives whom Attorney General Mitchell had personally selected for Nixon to elevate to the Supreme Court. A ranking Republican member of the Senate Judiciary Committee famously said in support of Carswell, "There are a lot of mediocre judges and people and lawyers. They are entitled to a little representation, aren't they?" Not on the Supreme Court, the Senate decreed. Nixon privately blamed Mitchell for the politically tone-deaf nominations—the attorney general's prior selection, Judge Clement Haynsworth, was rejected for his record of racism—but he took his wrath out on the Senate.

"Multiple unsolvable problems bearing in," Haldeman noted.

Nixon responded to the Senate's resistance with unalloyed rage. "Set up political attack," he commanded Haldeman. "Have to declare war."

The president ordered two retired New York City police officers, overseen by Ehrlichman, to conduct undercover investigations of his Senate opponents—notably, Teddy Kennedy, Edmund Muskie, Birch Bayh, and William Proxmire, four prominent Democrats who fought Nixon's military policies and his Supreme Court nominees—as part of what Nixon called "an all-out hatchet job on the Democrat leaders," including the use of the Internal Revenue Service to investigate their finances.

The ex-cops Nixon hired were Jack Caulfield, a member of the White House staff handling "special assignments" such as launching IRS audits, and Tony Ulasewicz, who was paid off the books with secret 1968 campaign cash doled out by Herb Kalmbach, Nixon's political bagman. "Tough Tony" trailed Kennedy for nearly two years. The Department of Dirty Tricks was on the case.

* * *

On April 4, 1970, Kissinger reconvened in Paris with Le Duc Tho, who grasped America's strategic problems as acutely as Kissinger and described them with greater accuracy.

"We have no intention of using Laos to put pressure on you in North Vietnam," Kissinger falsely asserted. The CIA and its Lao tribesmen were running cross-border sabotage attacks into North Vietnam at that very moment. "As for Cambodia, we have no intention of using Cambodia to bring pressure on Vietnam." That was not true.

Le Duc Tho responded: "This does not conform with reality. The Vietnamese have a saying that you can't use a basket to cover a lion or an elephant."

"I like that," Kissinger replied.

"It is quite true," said Le Duc Tho. "While you are suffering defeat in Laos and Vietnam, how can you fight in Cambodia? You have sowed the wind, and you must reap the whirlwind."

By April 19, the Communists were twenty miles from the Cambodian capital of Phnom Penh. President Nixon, in Hawaii to greet the astronauts returning from the nearly fatal Apollo 13 moon mission, was briefed by Adm. John McCain, the commander in chief for the Pacific. McCain, whose son was still a prisoner of war, captivated Nixon with a hair-raising report. The president ordered McCain to return with him to San Clemente on April 20 and meet with Kissinger.

The gist of McCain's briefing was grim: if the Communists took Cambodia, South Vietnam might be next, and the war would be lost. McCain emphasized "the need for speed in view of the precarious situation." He thought the United States should send every weapon it could find to Phnom Penh, South Vietnam's troops should attack across the Cambodian border, and squadrons of B-52s should bombard the Communists.

The Joint Chiefs of Staff claimed to have located the enemy's headquarters inside Cambodia: what the United States was calling the Central Office for South Vietnam, or COSVN. American war planners envisioned it as the Communists' nerve center, a bamboo Pentagon concealed beneath the jungle's canopy. They thought that if you could blow up COSVN, you could cripple the enemy's capacity to command and control attacks on American forces in South Vietnam. And McCain said the United States should destroy it and win the damn war.

Nixon's meeting with Admiral McCain amid the blooming springtime gardens of the Western White House was a fatal turning point. American boots were about to hit the ground in the bomb-cratered wastelands of eastern Cambodia.

Nixon, Kissinger, and McCain "discussed possible cross-border attacks into Cambodia," reads a unique account in a recently declassified Joint Chiefs history. "If such operations were mounted, the President asked, what would be the best mix of US and South Vietnamese forces? Or should only [South Vietnamese] troops be used, with the United States furnishing air and artillery support from within South Vietnam? Admiral McCain assured the President that plans were being prepared on an urgent basis and would be submitted to the Joint Chiefs of Staff as quickly as possible. The President . . . already sanctioned the provision of financial support to the Cambodian Government as well as the supply of captured weapons for the Cambodian forces."

The Joint Chiefs quickly assembled tons of weapons for the Cambodian army. Scouring the arsenals of every American ally in Asia for captured Communist weapons—Indonesia was especially helpful in supplying fifteen thousand AK-47 assault rifles—dealing in black markets to procure the proper bullets, and stripping shelves of carbine rifles from stockpiles in Saigon, American military officers in Saigon assembled ten packages, each sufficient to arm a thousand soldiers, containing eight hundred carbines, fifty pistols, thirty light machine guns, one hundred submachine guns, thirty rocket launchers, twenty light mortars, and ammunition.

That was the easy part. Now the president needed a plan for the invasion of Cambodia and the destruction of COSVN.

But Nixon never understood that COSVN was not a place. It could not be bombed. It had no address. It was a small mobile group of Communist officers. They could be located only by the radio signals they transmitted. Yet even that location was fixed only by the antennae they used for their transmissions, which could be miles away from the men who were on the air.

And the enemy always seemed to know when the B-52s were coming. North Vietnam's intelligence on America's intentions was far better than America's intelligence on its enemy's plans.

* * *

Nixon did not sleep for more than an hour or two on the night of Tuesday, April 21. Before dawn, he dictated a disturbing note to Kissinger: "I think we need a bold move in Cambodia, assuming that I feel the way today (it is five AM, April 22) at our meeting as I feel this morning to show that we stand with Lon Nol. I do not believe he is going to survive. There is, however, some chance that he might and in any event we must do something."

The aforementioned meeting was a National Security Council conclave. Nixon demanded that no staff attend and that no one take notes. But Admiral Moorer and General Wheeler left detailed accounts of the meeting in the files of the Joint Chiefs.

Nixon immediately authorized large cross-border attacks by South

Vietnam into Cambodia, with support from American artillery and fighter jets. He said that he had not yet decided the question of American ground forces attacking Cambodia.

The war council was split three ways. Laird and Rogers wanted the invasion limited in depth and restricted to the soldiers of South Vietnam. Kissinger favored an attack on the two Cambodian sanctuaries, in areas called the Parrot's Beak and the Fishhook—but without American ground troops. The military wanted an assault on the Communists in Cambodia and the spectral COSVN headquarters, with American soldiers leading the charge. So did Vice President Spiro Agnew, whose personal qualities included a lack of tact. Agnew said he objected to "all the pussyfooting." Nixon resented the implication that he was not being tough enough. The "pussyfooting" remark provoked Nixon to go for an all-out attack with American ground forces.

The Joint Chiefs of Staff never drew up a formal plan for the Cambodian operation. There wasn't enough time. But three of Kissinger's most loyal NSC staff members, Winston Lord, Tony Lake, and Roger Morris, knew of the coming invasion. They warned Kissinger that it would create "a political storm here, as it would be the most shocking spur to fears of widening involvement in U.S. ground combat in Southeast Asia."*

At 7:20 a.m. on April 24, Nixon, still sleepless, summoned Kissinger, Moorer, and Helms to the White House. In a fury, the president said that Secretary of State Rogers and Secretary of Defense Laird were sabotaging plans for the invasion. "P is moving too rashly without thinking through the consequences," Haldeman noted in his diary that evening. Kissinger called Helms to ask him what he thought of Nixon's decisions. Helms replied, "It seemed to me that if he is prepared for the fallout, then it is the thing to do. He obviously was."

"It is worth it?" Kissinger asked. Helms hoped so.

Rogers and Laird continued to object to the invasion of Cambodia until April 28. That morning, the president ordered them into the Oval Office, where the attorney general laid down the law: there would be no arguments, no dissent. In silence, they were dismissed from the room.

---

* Lake, Morris, and William Watts resigned from the NSC in protest of the Cambodian invasion. Lord stayed on and was rewarded for his loyalty. Two decades later, President Clinton made Lake his national security adviser.

Mitchell wrote: "The President stated that the purpose of the meeting was to advise those present of the decisions he had reached. . . . .There was no discussion."

* * *

On Thursday, April 30, after another night with one hour of sleep, the president made a nationally televised speech to the American people announcing the invasion of Cambodia.

"This is not an invasion of Cambodia," he said, a classic Nixon contradiction.

"I say tonight: All the offers and approaches made previously remain on the conference table whenever Hanoi is ready to negotiate seriously. But if the enemy response to our most conciliatory offers for peaceful negotiation continues to be to increase its attacks and humiliate and defeat us, we shall react accordingly.

"My fellow Americans, we live in an age of anarchy, both abroad and at home. We see mindless attacks on all the great institutions which have been created by free civilizations in the last 500 years. Even here in the United States, great universities are being systematically destroyed. Small nations all over the world find themselves under attack from within and from without.

"If, when the chips are down, the world's most powerful nation, the United States of America, acts like a pitiful, helpless giant, the forces of totalitarianism and anarchy will threaten free nations and free institutions throughout the world."

Secretary of State Rogers was in his hideaway office on the seventh floor of the State Department headquarters that night with Marshall Green, the assistant secretary of state for East Asia. Green remembered: "As Nixon concluded his maudlin remarks about the US otherwise appearing as a pitiful, helpless giant, Rogers snapped off the TV set, muttering, 'The kids are going to retch.' He clearly foresaw how the speech was going to inflame the campuses. That was several days before Kent State."

CHAPTER NINE

"An unmitigated disaster"

THE MORNING after the speech was May Day. The storm already had started on the nation's campuses. College newspapers called for a national student strike. A new march on Washington was set for the coming week.

After suffering another insomniac night, Nixon went to the Pentagon, where the Joint Chiefs showed him maps detailing where Communist forces occupied Cambodia. They depicted four major sanctuaries far beyond the targets of the invasion. "I made a very uncharacteristic on-the-spot decision," Nixon wrote in his memoirs. "I said, 'I want to take out all those sanctuaries. Make whatever plans are necessary, and then just do it. Knock them all out so that they can't be used against us. Ever.'"

To some of the officers at the Pentagon, the president seemed unhinged. Haldeman concurred. "P was really beat," he wrote in his diary a few hours later. "Really needs some good rest."

Leaving the briefing, trailed in the lobby of the Pentagon by a few reporters with tape recorders, Nixon compared American soldiers ("They're the greatest") with American students ("these bums, you know, blowing up the campuses"), a statement that he later realized only "added fuel to the fires of dissent."

On Monday, May 4, Haldeman went to Nixon's Executive Office Building hideout with some bad news. "Something just came over the wires about a demonstration at Kent State," Haldeman said. "The National Guard opened fire, and some students were shot."

"Are they dead?" Nixon asked.

"I'm afraid so," Haldeman said. Two protesters and two passersby had been killed, and nine injured, by the salvo of gunfire at the Ohio campus.

Haldeman's diary recorded the president's distress: "He's very disturbed. Afraid his decision set it off. . . . Really sad to see this added to his worries about the war. He's out on a tough limb, and he knows it. This makes it a lot worse, as he has to take the heat for having caused it. . . . Obviously realizes, but won't openly admit, his 'bums' remark very harmful."

In a telephone conversation later that day with Kissinger, Nixon stiffened his spine. "We have to stand hard as a rock," he said. "If countries begin to be run by children, God help us."

Kissinger played the tough guy: "K. wants to just let the students go for a couple of weeks, then move in and clobber them," Haldeman recorded. How they could be hit with anything harder than the bullets of the National Guard was not the question: "K. very concerned that we not appear to give in in any way. Thinks P. can really clobber them if we just wait for Cambodian success."

* * *

"The Cambodian incursion was an unmitigated disaster," begins a National Security Agency history of the battle, declassified in 2013.

"The most famous (or infamous) event of the incursion was the attempt to 'get COSVN,'" the NSA history reads. In April, the small, mobile Communist intelligence headquarters' radio antennae were located just inside the Cambodian border, about ninety miles northwest of Saigon, targeted by U.S. aircraft equipped with a multitude of electronic components. But COSVN was constantly on the move—"usually to get out of the way of B-52 strikes (which, as we know, were predicted with great accuracy by North Vietnamese intelligence), and repeated air strikes over the years had never succeeded in doing any effective damage," the NSA report records.

William Lloyd Stearman, later Kissinger's in-house expert on Hanoi and the longest-serving staffer in the history of the National Security Council, remembered vividly when he first heard that Nixon was going after COSVN, in the early hours of the invasion. "By the time I had stopped laughing, I almost felt like crying," Stearman said. "I then wondered who in the hell had briefed the President on this."

It turned out to be Kissinger.

"COSVN was a floating crap game," Stearman said. "There was simply no way you were going to be able to go in and capture COSVN. What, I wondered, did he think COSVN was all about anyway? COSVN mostly consisted of a bunch of huts and some files which could be moved quickly."

"The press got hold of the COSVN story" within two weeks, the NSA report continued, and it "became common knowledge to the American people." The pressure from the White House and the Pentagon "to locate and overrun (or at least bomb) COSVN became considerable" as the press picked up the theme of an elusive enemy. "But the military system moved too slowly. COSVN was able to evade every B-52 strike and every ground maneuver."

After five years of combat, American military commanders still did not comprehend that SIGINT (signals intelligence, the NSA's unique capability) could fix the location only of the enemy's antenna: "The transmitter, to say nothing of the headquarters itself, could be miles away. Moreover, the military targeting system seemed inflexible—SIGINT reports that COSVN had pulled up stakes from location A and was now at location B were not enough to get a strike cancelled or diverted."

The NSA report concludes, "American bombs tore up miles of jungle, and troops floundered through a trackless quagmire of Cambodia in pursuit of COSVN. They never caught up with the headquarters, which moved safely to central Cambodia ahead of the advancing allies." The invasion killed many enemy soldiers and destroyed large stocks of their weapons and rice. But it did not change the course of the war.

Protest against the invasion erupted nationwide—not only students but university presidents, not only scraggly leftists but Wall Street lawyers, not merely three NSC staffers but hundreds of State Department employees now openly opposed Nixon's conduct of the war. With a national day of protest (Saturday, May 9) looming, Nixon knew he had to mobilize public support from his political allies.

* * *

Enter Charles W. Colson. The thirty-eight-year-old lawyer had signed on as a White House counsel in November 1969, a liaison with labor unions and other special interests, and he quickly caught the president's eye.

"His instinct for the political jugular and his ability to get things done made him a lightning rod for my own frustrations," Nixon wrote. "When I complained to Colson, I felt confident that something would be done. I was rarely disappointed."

Colson's job, as he himself put it, was "attack and counterattack." And in that role, "he'll do anything," Nixon later said on tape. "I mean anything." Colson now received his first assignment as the point man for domestic political warfare. He joined a meeting of an "Action Group on Cambodia" convened by Nixon in the Roosevelt Room of the White House. Taking action in the spirit of Kissinger's encouragement to "really clobber" the president's political enemies, Colson telephoned his contacts at the New York City construction union council led by Peter J. Brennan.

On Friday, May 8, hundreds of hard hats carrying lead pipes and crowbars attacked antiwar protesters at Broad and Wall Streets, cracking heads and breaking bones. More than seventy people were injured. The hard hats got an invitation to the White House that month, and Brennan later became Nixon's labor secretary. As footage of the fracas ran on the evening news, tens of thousands of protesters were gathering in Washington from across the country, trucks were transporting soldiers to batten down in the Executive Office Building for the night, and two rings of buses barricaded the White House.

* * *

Nixon called a White House press conference at the unusually late hour of 10:00 p.m. On deadline, with minutes to write and file their stories, the White House reporters went brain-dead. Nothing about Cambodia and COSVN, nothing about the hard hats, thank you and good night. No one asked about the president's mood and motives at a moment of national crisis.

Nixon was on the verge of a nervous breakdown: he stayed up all night again, "agitated and uneasy," in his own words, frantically making more than fifty telephone calls and finally calling upon his valet, Manolo Sanchez, to accompany him to the Lincoln Memorial so he could rap with the young people protesting the war. Word spread quickly that the president was on the loose amid the hippies. The White House aide Egil "Bud" Krogh was on duty that night. Krogh vividly recalled:

> Four-thirty in the morning, I was in the Secret Service command post, and over the loudspeaker came the words, "Searchlight is on the lawn"—Searchlight being the President's Secret Service code name—and I immediately punched in Ehrlichman's home number . . . and said, "The President is out and about, and I think he's on the lawn in the Rose Garden." And he said, "Go over and render assistance right now." And so I did . . . and found out where the President was going and followed him up to the Lincoln Memorial. Couldn't have gotten there more than two or three minutes after he got there, went up the stairs to see what was going on, and found him in discussion with, at the start, 10 to 15 young people, students who had come in from all over the East Coast.

The only reliable record of the president's words on the steps of the Lincoln Memorial exists in the real-time accounts of three young women who talked with him face-to-face: Lynn Schatzkin, Ronnie Kemper, and Joan Pelletier.

"He didn't look at anyone in the eyes; he was mumbling," Schatzkin said. "As far as sentence structure, there was none."

"Somebody would ask him to speak up," Kemper said. "And that would jolt him out of wherever he was and he'd kind of look up and shake his head around, but then he'd go back to looking at his feet and he was gone again. . . . There was no train of thought."

"Nothing he was saying was coherent," Pelletier said. "At first I felt awe, and then that changed right away to respect. Then as he kept talking, it went to disappointment and disillusionment. Then I felt pity because he was so pathetic, and then just plain fear to think that he's running the country."

Nixon was "flushed, drawn, exhausted," Krogh said. "I saw him in probably the most psychologically exposed, raw period of his presidency."

Nixon went to the Capitol; he wanted to show its chambers to Sanchez, who had never been inside. Haldeman corralled him there at 6:15 a.m. The president demanded a plate of corned beef hash at the Mayflower Hotel; he got it. Haldeman urged him to get some rest, but Nixon still could not sleep, and he rattled around the White House all day without purpose as a peaceful protest of about one hundred thousand people swirled about him.

"The weirdest day so far," Haldeman wrote in his journal entry for Saturday, May 9. "Very weird. P. completely beat and just rambling on, but obviously too tired to go to sleep. . . . I am concerned about his condition. . . . He has had very little sleep for a long time." Over the next days, Haldeman added ominous notes. He demanded that the president take a five-day weekend in Key Biscayne. But that proved futile. "The unwinding process is not succeeding," he wrote during the Florida retreat. "More of the same. He just keeps grinding away." And this: "P. won't admit it, but he is . . . letting himself slip back into the old ways." That meant hitting the bottle: Nixon, desperate for respite, was drinking heavily night after night.

Kissinger, keenly aware of the precarious presidential state of mind, the recent revolt of his key staffers, and the wiretaps he and Haig maintained on government officials and newsmen, kept note takers away from every White House decision on the conduct of the war for the next month. Yet these decisions can be reconstructed from documents declassified in the past three years.

Nixon commanded new covert actions by the CIA against the Communists in Vietnam, Laos, and Cambodia. Nixon approved secret support for a regiment of Thai soldiers, unfortunately named the Black Panthers, to fight in Cambodia. Nixon ordered both B-52 and fighter-bomber attacks far deeper inside Cambodia than he ever admitted. The Communists staged a disciplined withdrawal from the bombardments.

The Senate, now increasingly well informed by the Pentagon and the State Department, voted on June 30 to cut off funds for the war in Cambodia and Laos. Though the measure was symbolic—Nixon would have vetoed it—it marked the first time that the president's power as a commander in chief at war was challenged by a vote in Congress. The invasion of Cambodia also drew the first calls for the impeachment of Richard Nixon.

In the United States, his most dangerous enemy now was not the armies of citizens marching in the streets, but a handful of senators sitting in the Capitol.

* * *

For more than a year, ever since the first press reports that the United States was bombing Cambodia, the Senate Foreign Relations Committee and its staff had been conducting a highly classified investigation of America's conduct of the war. They were asking themselves a fundamental question: what were the limits of the war powers of the president?

The president commanded that strict rules be set for the Senate's closed-door hearings, curtailing the testimony of witnesses and censoring the committee's final report on the grounds of national security. The Senate's probing so worried Kissinger that he held Situation Room strategy sessions about counteracting Senate investigators who had been "scooping up secret data all over the world," Haldeman noted in his diary. "Question now is how to avoid having our key people testify, big question of executive privilege."

It became *the* big question for Richard Nixon. Executive privilege was the dubious idea that a president could disregard any demand by Congress or the courts for evidence or testimony. It presumed he was above the law. In his escalating confrontations with Congress, Nixon's counsel ultimately asserted in court that "the President wants me to argue that he is as powerful a monarch as Louis XIV, only four years at a time."

But the president was no monarch. The Constitution made him commander in chief of the army and the navy, not the American people. It said that only Congress could declare war, only Congress had the power to make treaties, and only Congress could spend the money that the Treasury collected in taxes from American citizens.

Over the course of their yearlong investigation, the senators were discovering that the United States had spent many hundreds of millions on secret military and intelligence operations in Thailand, Laos, and the Philippines—all devoted to winning in Vietnam and all based on pacts far beyond what the Senate had approved and financed. In effect, they were secret treaties, struck without the knowledge of Congress, supporting a war Congress had never declared. Congress had abdicated power; the president had usurped it.

The few senators privy to this growing body of knowledge began to contemplate cutting back the president's use and abuse of his war powers. Slowly and cautiously, in the summer of 1970, they started to sharpen a sword against him.

These hearings were led by Stuart Symington, the secretary of the air force when Nixon first came to Washington in 1947, the man who helped get the B-52 bomber off the ground in the early years of the Cold War, and a senator from Missouri since 1953, when Nixon became vice president. Symington's sole colleague in charge of the proceedings was Senator J. William Fulbright of Arkansas, chairman of the Senate Foreign Relations Committee from 1959 to 1974.

The senators were startled and ashamed to discover how they had ceded their power to presidents—and Nixon was not the first. The story traced back through Presidents Johnson and Kennedy, as the Pentagon Papers, the secret history of the war in Vietnam, would soon reveal.

Explosive classified testimony from the CIA detailed the personal corruption of American-backed strongmen in Asia. The White House demanded the deletion of evidence on the dirty dealings of President Ferdinand Marcos of the Philippines, where the United States had major air and naval bases for the Vietnam War. Marcos had been skimming American aid since 1965. The passage read, "Marcos and his wife . . . have accumulated approximately $100 million during his term in the presidential palace." He accumulated billions before he was overthrown by a popular revolution after twenty years in power.

Some of the report's most sensitive sections dealt with the use of American power in Thailand and Laos. America's dealings with the Thai military traced back to 1954. They included hundreds of millions of dollars in military spending, the coordination of secret bombing campaigns, and the financing of combat operations by paramilitary forces, all based on secret pacts going back to 1965.

The Pentagon had paid $702 million to construct military bases in Thailand for fifty-five thousand American troops. It had laid out $80 million a year to the Thai military junta for the services of an eleven-thousand-man combat division in South Vietnam. The CIA had fixed elections and financed the junta to keep the military in power. It had armed and trained Thai paramilitary forces for combat in Laos, where an indigenous tribe called the Hmong had worked with CIA officers for many years to fight North Vietnamese forces from mountain redoubts near the Ho Chi Minh Trail.

Those payments were among many that President Nixon, and President Johnson before him, had approved to conduct covert paramilitary operations, support allied leaders, and swing elections in nations throughout the world. They had thought it especially important to provide the appearance of democracy among America's authoritarian Asian allies.

Tens of millions in political payoffs flowed annually via the CIA's cache of classified funds for this purpose. President Nixon had personally approved cash payments to the Thai generals in 1969 and 1970. They pretended to hold elections, but they soon suspended their constitution, disbanded parliament, and reimposed martial law. The generals told their friends at the American embassy that "democracy doesn't work."

The CIA had shored up President Thieu of South Vietnam with millions designed to create the illusion of a democratic government in Saigon, including supposedly independent political parties, citizens' groups, and a free press. But Thieu clearly preferred bullets to ballots. He had pocketed the CIA's cash, and when he ran for reelection he was unopposed. Although Kissinger and the NSC staff despaired over the political situation in Saigon, the White House and the CIA kept the secret subsidies flowing to Saigon. The hope that democracy could be created with dollars never died.

The Senate hearings, in their classified sessions, revealed in detail how American ambassadors in Thailand and Laos coordinated secret bombing raids around the clock. In tense proceedings, the senators closely interrogated Leonard Unger, the American ambassador in Thailand. James Marvin Montgomery, Unger's chief political and military officer, sat by his boss's side, flanked by Richard Helms, the CIA's chief.

"The dominant emotion that came across that green baize table was one of embarrassment," Montgomery recalled. "These Senators had voted for these authorizations and appropriations all of these years and never asked any questions" about where the money went or how it was spent. "They had been content, up until this point, to let the President of the United States act like a Prime Minister with a solid Parliamentary majority behind him," Montgomery said. "We are a Congressional democracy, which is something different. In many ways these Senators had sort of abdicated their responsibilities since the beginning of World War II and they never really took them back until this set of hearings. . . . This was the beginning of Congressional reassertion of its prerogatives and authority—not just in Southeast Asia but in the conduct of foreign policy as a whole."

In Thailand, for example, Ambassador Unger received a telegram every day from the Seventh Air Force headquarters in Saigon laying out the missions carried out in Laos by bombers based at U-Tapao, a huge Thai airfield built with American funds. "The Thai let us do just about whatever we wanted to do," said Montgomery. "However, this arrangement drove the Pentagon nuts, because none of it was written down." It wasn't written down because it was secret. Congress had known nothing about the bombing. The CIA's payoffs to the Thai junta had helped keep it that way.

But Senators Fulbright and Symington were now "aware of our attacks and will press for an answer," President Nixon told Prince Souvanna Phouma, the prime minister of Laos, according to a written memo of their October 1969 conversation in the White House. "President Nixon said he completely approved the bombing and would do more but the problem is a domestic political one—whether the US will become as deeply involved in Laos as in Vietnam. . . . This is a very delicate political issue and we have been trying to dance around it as much as possible."

The Senate hearings, published in heavily censored volumes during the summer and fall of 1970, compelled Congress to ban the introduction of U.S. combat troops into Laos and Thailand. The fact that the United States was bombing the Ho Chi Minh Trail in Laos was the only classified aspect of the hearings that leaked. It had become an open secret in the Senate, and Nixon admitted it after the press reported it months later. But there he drew the line on public disclosure of secret warfare.

The line would not hold for long.

*　*　*

On Friday, June 5, 1970, Nixon called all his intelligence chiefs to the White House—Richard Helms, J. Edgar Hoover, Adm. Noel Gayler of the National Security Agency, and Lt. Gen. Donald Bennett of the

Defense Intelligence Agency. "The President chewed our butts," General Bennett vividly recalled.

Nixon said that "revolutionary terrorism" was now the gravest threat to the United States. Thousands of Americans under the age of thirty were "determined to destroy our society" through their "revolutionary activism," and "good intelligence," he said, was "the best way to stop terrorism."

But he was not getting good intelligence. Nixon demanded "a plan which will enable us to curtail the illegal activities of those who are determined to destroy our society."

Nixon had been complaining about this intelligence gap for a year, obsessed with the idea that American radicals were being financed and directed by America's foreign enemies. In March 1970, Haldeman had ordered Tom Charles Huston, a twenty-nine-year-old army intelligence veteran and, in his own words, "a hard-core conservative," to act as the White House liaison to all the intelligence services, to convene them, and to write the plan Nixon demanded. Huston went to Hoover's intelligence chief, Bill Sullivan, who had the outlines of the plan already in hand. He had been working on it for two years, partly in the hope of winning Nixon's approval to succeed J. Edgar Hoover, who was seventy-five years old and starting to falter.

The program that quickly emerged was called the Huston Plan. The FBI's agents and their counterparts would be free to intensify the electronic surveillance of American citizens, read their mail, burglarize their homes and offices, step up undercover spying on college campuses—in short, keep on doing what the Bureau had been doing for decades, but in closer coordination with the CIA and the NSA, and with the secret imprimatur of the president of the United States.

Nixon knew, and Huston reminded him in writing, that many of these acts were clearly illegal. But Nixon believed that if a president did it, it was not illegal.

The president said he approved the plan. But Hoover flew into a rage when he realized that it would have to be carried out with his signature and on his authority—not Nixon's. The president had not signed it; his approval was verbal, not written. "I'm not going to accept the responsibility myself anymore, even though I've done it for many years," Hoover said. "It is becoming more and more dangerous and we are apt to get caught."

Hoover demanded a meeting with Nixon, and he stared the president down. Though Nixon believed that "in view of the crisis of terrorism," the plan was both "justified and responsible," John Mitchell convinced him that Hoover would find a way to leak the plan if ordered to sign it.

The new White House counsel, thirty-one-year-old John W. Dean, took charge of preserving the essential elements of the plan. Huston recalled, "Haldeman basically gave him the portfolio to try and work out with the Attorney General whatever they could salvage." They salvaged much of it. Undercover operations against the left expanded. Electronic surveillances and surreptitious entries increased. These operations sometimes took place at the command of Attorney General Mitchell, sometimes on orders from the president himself. And in months to come, they would come on the orders of White House aides who had arrogated these powers to themselves.

* * *

Nixon wandered in, unannounced, to one of Kissinger's crisis meetings on Cambodia in the White House Situation Room on June 15, 1970. To Kissinger's distress, the president's rambling speech there was recorded by a note taker. Kissinger sent a summary of Nixon's remarks to the participants at the meeting, warning that it was "absolutely for your own personal use and should not be distributed elsewhere."

The president used the words *psychological* and *psychological warfare* repeatedly, almost compulsively, as he stressed the political impact of the invasion. He proclaimed that, despite the edict of Congress to end American involvement in Cambodia after July 1, "we would continue our interdiction," using airpower as freely as possible.

"This interdiction, the President stated, should be interpreted broadly, and it was very important that everybody in Defense knew this. The President reiterated that he believed it necessary to take risks now regarding public opinion, so as to see that Cambodia maintained its neutrality and independence. Perhaps there were those who would disagree, but the president himself felt that we should take these risks."

He wanted to see a report every day on "what we are doing in the Cambodia area on the diplomatic, intelligence, military, and supply sides, and would watch closely the developments in these fields. It was his judgment that it was no good going way out, but it was worth taking risks."

At 7:45 that evening, the president called Kissinger. "I just hope they got it," he said. "We're going to take some gambles."

He repeated four days later: "There were a great number of people in the press and in Congress who have a vested interest in seeing us fail," he said. "This was a game for them, and we should counter-play." He would see to it that the war went on, Congress or no Congress. Though American ground forces were withdrawn by the end of June, American bombers and fighter jets flew their deadly missions in Cambodia until August 1973.

The Nixon administration drew from all its military assistance programs worldwide to find money to support the war in Cambodia; direct military aid to Lon Nol rose from $8.9 million in 1970 to $185 million in 1971. Nixon had sent Al Haig, now a one-star general, as his secret envoy to Cambodia to coordinate the delivery of weapons. One of the few Americans stationed in Phnom Penh, Andrew Antippas, the political officer at the American embassy, vividly remembered his arrival on a CIA aircraft.

"We were instructed to receive him and take him to visit Lon Nol," Antippas said. "We were all wondering who this brigadier general was. Brigadier generals in the Vietnam War were as common as doughnuts. In fact, they went out to get the coffee. We went out to the airport and met the aircraft. The brigadier general who arrived—very recently promoted to brigadier general—was named Alexander Haig. . . . This was his first big assignment under Henry Kissinger. He was told to 'go out and find out what the hell's going on in Cambodia.'"

A straightforward assessment came from Emory C. Swank, a distinguished Foreign Service officer whom Nixon named as ambassador to Cambodia in July 1970. "Phnom Penh did not need an Ambassador," he said, "but a worker of miracles."

An equally grim report by the CIA arrived on August 6, shortly after Swank's appointment. "The communists have overrun half of Cambodia, taken or threatened 16 of its 19 provincial capitals, and interdicted—for varying periods—all road and rail links to the capital, Phnom Penh," the report began. North Vietnam's soldiers and guerrillas "move at will, attacking towns and villages in the south and converting the north into an extension of the Laos corridor and a base for 'peoples' war' throughout the country and in South Vietnam as well."

But Nixon remained delusional on the subject of the Cambodian invasion. His disturbing opinions were shared by few if any American soldiers or spies. He thought the invasion a triumph of presidential power that would demoralize the enemy, destroy a potential Communist attack on Saigon, shore up morale among American troops, and turn the tide of the whole war.

He said explicitly, if inexplicably, to Kissinger on October 7 that it would prove the decisive battle, the bold decision that would lead to an imminent American victory in Vietnam.

"Listen, Henry," Nixon said, "Cambodia won the war."

CHAPTER TEN

"Only we have the power"

Richard Nixon restored a measure of calm to his troubled mind after a two-week retreat to San Clemente during August and early September 1970. He was determined to rebuild his reputation as a master of politics and his self-regard as a great statesman.

He returned to the White House on September 8 thinking as he had at the start of his presidency: he would make a move toward Moscow in his search for a way out of Vietnam. He thought the Soviets might be amenable: they had been seeking a summit meeting from the start of his administration.

Nixon decided to invite the Soviet foreign minister, Andrei Gromyko, to Washington in late October 1970—two weeks before the American midterm elections—to plan a summit conference with the Soviet leader Leonid Brezhnev. Nixon would propose a cease-fire in Vietnam in return for a negotiated political settlement of the war. The Soviets somehow would have to support Nixon's stance despite their alliance with Hanoi.

"Plan is for P to meet Gromyko the 22nd, then announce Summit for next year," Haldeman wrote. "Another good maneuver before elections." But the summit would be a long time coming. So many differences separated the Soviets and the Americans that it would take the better part of two years before they signed treaties and drank toasts.

Nixon toured Europe in late September and early October, his itinerary shaped in part by getting out the Catholic vote in the coming elections. He met with the pope. He made a pilgrimage to the graveyard of his ancestors in County Kildare, Ireland. And he conferred with the Spanish dictator Francisco Franco, the neofascist who had fought communism since 1936 and imposed Catholic values on Spaniards ever since.

He and Franco talked mainly about the Soviets. Generalissimo Franco warned that they were "seeking to trap and weaken us. We could play the game with them but we should remember this."

Nixon concurred. "We should bear in mind that—though the leadership had changed—their aims were still the same," he said to Franco. "They had the same missionary zeal to expand Communism all over the world and we should not forget this."

* * *

On October 12, as he got ready to hit the campaign trail, the president spoke his mind with unusual clarity. He delivered a speech—billed as "deep background, not attributable in any way," and thus never reported—to a small group of news executives selected from states where Republicans hoped to pick up Senate seats.

Nixon rarely spoke this forthrightly in public. A transcript of his remarks remained sealed in the Nixon archives until 2011.

"The differences between the United States and the Soviet Union are so deep and so profound that they are not going to be resolved by the two top leaders of the countries sitting down and getting to know each other better, not by smiles, not by handshakes, not by summit conferences," Nixon said. Though "we are going to continue to be competitors as long as this generation lives," the president continued, "we can have a sound basis for a meaningful settlement of major differences."

Foremost was the war in Vietnam. "They would prefer to see the Communists prevail," he said. "That does not mean, however, that the Soviet Union and the United States, because we differ as to how it should be settled, will allow that difference to drag us into a major power confrontation." For if that confrontation ever came, "whoever pushes the button may kill 70 million approximately, and the other side will also kill 70 million." No president had ever stated the human consequences of nuclear war quite so precisely.

Nixon saw three realms of common interest to negotiate with Moscow: "avoid war, reduce defense expenditures—at least don't see them go up—and third, the whole area of trade." These would be the basis for the beginning of his dialogue with the Soviets, if and when that dialogue began.

Finally he turned to the home front. "A very substantial number of Americans," he said, "are very tired of America's playing an international role. They want to get out of Vietnam. . . . Looking at the enormous problems at home—the problems of the cities, the problems of the country, the problems of the environment, the problems of the educational system, the problems of taxes, the problems of prices—a number of American people say, 'Look at all we have done since World War II. Let's concentrate on our problems at home, build a strong America, not worry about the rest of the world.'"

Nixon would have none of that. "If we are going to the sidelines," he said, "there are going to be only two major contestants left on the field. The one will be the Soviet Union and the other will be Communist China."

"Leadership in the free world is still ours. Only we can do this. Only we have the power, only we have the wealth to play this role," he concluded. "We have ended three wars in this century. We have ended World War I, we have ended World War II, we have ended Korea. We have never had a generation of peace. What we are trying to do is to end this war and to avoid other wars in a way that we can have a goal that all Americans want, a generation of peace for the balance of the century."

This theme, "a generation of peace," became Nixon's mantra in foreign affairs. The old cold warrior was wise enough to know he had to talk with his enemies to win in Vietnam. But he did not know the language of peace and reconciliation.

* * *

Ten days later, Nixon met with Soviet foreign minister Gromyko for more than three hours, first in the Oval Office with their aides, then alone with their interpreters in the president's Executive Office Building hideaway. Gromyko, who had held his post since 1957 and had served as ambassador to the United States during World War II, was perfectly diplomatic, but deeply pessimistic about Vietnam. He said there was no prospect for peace "unless the United States was willing to work out the timing for withdrawal of its troops, and agreed to the establishment of a coalition government for South Vietnam." Both men knew the government of South Vietnam would refuse a coalition with the Communists unless coerced. But the men emerged from their face-to-face encounter in a friendly mood, having secured an informal agreement for a summit meeting at an undetermined future date.

"P. obviously enjoyed the confrontation," Haldeman wrote. "Says talking with Communists is easier than others because they are hard, tough, blunt, direct—no diplomatic flummery. Coming out of EOB they started down opposite sides of the center hand rail—Gromyko moved over & said 'we should have no rail between us.'"

Kissinger advised Nixon that the meeting with the Soviet foreign minister had come at "a moment of unusual uncertainty in both capitals concerning the intentions and purposes of the other side." He saw little promise of real progress. Nixon's own handwritten notes of the day reflect that uncertainty. "Put the past behind," he scribbled—and then, in the next line: "where do we go from here?"

He put the question more directly to Kissinger: "The US—what it will be like for the next 25 years depends on whether we have the guts, the stamina, the wisdom to exert leadership. . . . People may want to put their heads in the sand; they may want to clean up the ghettos. All right, we will get out of the world. Who is left?"

He answered his own question: Russia and China. Richard Nixon would not let them run the world. "We are going to continue to be competitors as long as this generation lives," he had said. That struggle was playing out on all corners of the earth.

* * *

On October 22, at the hour Nixon and Gromyko sat down in the White House, a fusillade of gunfire rang out on the streets of Santiago, Chile, five thousand miles south of Washington. A gang of assassins murdered Gen. René Schneider, the commander of the Chilean army.

The killing was the denouement of a desperate CIA covert action in Chile, ordered by Nixon himself, to stop the democratic election of a leftist president named Salvador Allende by any means necessary. Ever since Nixon became vice president in 1953, the United States had run coups, backed right-wing dictators, and sought to subvert leftists throughout Latin America, from Bolivia to Brazil and from the Texas border down to Tierra del Fuego. In the last months of the Eisenhower administration, as Nixon knew all too well, these plots included the attempted assassination of Cuba's Fidel Castro.

Many members of Chile's political establishment and military leadership knew the CIA had been working against Allende and his allies for years. But Chile had been a democracy for decades. The election of Allende, who counted Castro among his allies, would be proof that a left-wing leader could take power with political legitimacy in Latin America. The fact that Allende had won a plurality of the popular vote in September infuriated Nixon. On September 15, 1970, after hearing that Allende had won, despite millions already spent by the CIA against him in conventional political warfare, Nixon personally ordered Richard Helms to stop him from taking office.

The CIA director told eight of his most senior officers that Nixon had ordered the Agency to stop Allende (if necessary, by backing a military coup) and to keep their plans hidden from the secretary of state, the secretary of defense, and the American ambassador to Chile.

Under law, the Chilean Congress was to ratify Allende's election on October 24. The CIA had seven weeks to reverse the results of a democratic election. The Agency divided the task into Track One and Track Two. Track One's main tactic was to buy enough votes in the Chilean Senate to block Allende's confirmation. Track Two was a coup. The CIA's covert action chief, Thomas Karamessines, kept Kissinger posted at the White House. David Atlee Phillips, a twenty-year veteran of covert operations, led the Chile task force at CIA headquarters. He thought the operation was doomed from the start.

"Anyone who had lived in Chile, as I had, and knew Chileans, knew that you might get away with bribing one Chilean Senator, but two? Never. And three? Not a chance. They would blow the whistle," Phillips said in classified testimony to the Senate five years later. "They were democrats and had been for a long time." As for Track Two, Phillips said, "the Chilean military was a very model of democratic rectitude." Their commander, General Schneider, had proclaimed that the army would obey the Constitution and refrain from politics.

An apoplectic Kissinger had commanded Karamessines to send a flash cable to the CIA station chief in Santiago on October 7: CONTACT

THE MILITARY AND LET THEM KNOW USG [U.S. government] WANTS A MILITARY SOLUTION, AND THAT WE WILL SUPPORT THEM NOW AND LATER . . . CREATE AT LEAST SOME SORT OF COUP CLIMATE. . . . SPONSOR A MILITARY MOVE.

Assassination plots against political leaders had been anathema to Helms ever since the killing of President Kennedy. He would not allow American fingerprints on a rifle aimed at Allende. But the CIA could find an ambitious Chilean general willing to carry out the military solution Nixon and Kissinger commanded. Using the time-honored tactic of bribery, the CIA suborned Gen. Camilo Valenzuela, chief of the Santiago garrison, and developed a coup plot that looked like a three-cushion pool shot.

First, soldiers would kidnap General Schneider and fly him to Argentina, removing the constitutional commander of the army. Then the military would order the Chilean Congress to dissolve before Allende's election was affirmed. Finally, they would take power in the name of the armed forces.

The CIA gave Valenzuela fifty thousand dollars, three submachine guns, and a satchel of tear gas canisters—all approved by Karamessines and the hidden hand of Henry Kissinger. But word of the plot spread within the Chilean military. By October 13, Washington's intentions were so widely known that one of the South American nation's few right-wing generals, Roberto Viaux, widely regarded by his fellow officers as a dangerous fool, was ready to commandeer a coup on his own. The CIA's station chief in Santiago, Henry Hecksher, cabled Washington: A VIAUX COUP WOULD ONLY PRODUCE A MASSIVE BLOODBATH.

That provoked the following response from the White House, via the CIA's channels: IT IS FIRM AND CONTINUING POLICY THAT ALLENDE BE OVERTHROWN BY A COUP.

On October 22, General Schneider lay mortally wounded. Shortly thereafter, Salvador Allende was confirmed by Congress as the constitutionally elected president of Chile by a vote of 153 to 35. It took days before the CIA discovered, to its collective relief, that Viaux's thugs were the assassins, not the Agency's hirelings in Valenzuela's garrison. The CIA did not have General Schneider's blood on its hands. But the Agency left the scene of the crime with Allende in political triumph and the president of the United States in a profound fury. Nixon would have his revenge. Three years later, on September 11, 1973, the coup he'd commanded would come, inaugurating seventeen years of dictatorship in Chile, a generation of political repression, and thousands of deaths.

* * *

The president returned to campaigning, crisscrossing the country on behalf of the nation's Republican candidates. He loved the details of politics, the private machinations and the cold calculations. But he often loathed the business of being a politician, pressing the flesh in public, glad-handing, backslapping. More than once he said that being president would be a great job if you didn't have to deal with people.

When he left Washington, traversing twenty-two states in seven days, he found the political climate cold and the mood of the nation grim.

Nixon had accomplished little in foreign affairs thus far. His domestic policy team had "come up with nothing," as he told Haldeman and Ehrlichman in September—no new ideas, no impelling initiatives. Unemployment was rising to 6 percent, the highest in a decade. Nixon's own popularity ratings were falling toward 50 percent. His private polls predicted that the Republicans would lose thirty seats in the House and perhaps a senator or two as well.

He had neither wanted nor planned to hit the stump in 1970, but he felt impelled to go out into the country, knowing he would confront hostile faces in the crowd. In New Jersey, a young man shook his hand, then shouted, "You're guilty of murder every day you fight this war." After a speech at the Municipal Auditorium in San Jose, California, on the evening of October 29—a grueling day that had started at a breakfast in Chicago and encompassed five cities—a crowd of two thousand demonstrators surrounded Nixon's motorcade chanting, "One, two, three, four, we don't want your fucking war!" Haldeman recorded, "We wanted some confrontation and there were no hecklers in the hall, so we stalled departure a little so they could zero in."

Nixon later wrote, "I could not resist showing them how little respect I had for their mindless ranting. I stood on the hood of the car and gave the V-sign that had become my political trademark. It had a predictable effect. . . . Suddenly rocks and eggs and vegetables were flying everywhere." The Secret Service went into emergency evacuation mode, and the motorcade moved on, behind what Haldeman described as "a terrifying flying wedge of cops." Safely back in San Clemente that night, Nixon reflected, "As far as I knew this was the first time in our history that a mob had physically attacked the President of the United States."

* * *

Nixon knew that Vietnam and its war-damaged veterans were the main source of the nation's anger and despair. Each day of the war remained dreadful; four hundred Americans were dying in Vietnam every month. The peace talks in Paris were at a stalemate. The court-martial of William L. Calley was imminent. A lieutenant at the My Lai massacre, when American soldiers slaughtered South Vietnamese civilians suspected of harboring Communists, Calley was in a military stockade awaiting trial for premeditated murder. A conviction could lead to a death sentence. The case was emblematic of a war in which the moral imperative had gone AWOL.

Reenlistment among officers was falling, along with the morale of combat troops. Insubordination was rising. So was the use of 95 percent pure heroin among American soldiers.

The dope flooded Saigon in the summer of 1970. A potent dose was available for two dollars in bars, brothels, and barracks, thanks in part to America's allies, crucial go-betweens in the drug trade. In September 1970, army medics questioned and tested more than three thousand soldiers of the Americal Division, where Lieutenant Calley had served. They found that 11.9 percent had tried heroin and 6.6 percent continued to use it. Larger government studies estimated that perhaps one-third of American soldiers tried heroin in Vietnam; among those, roughly half came home hooked. Though the statistics and the studies were arguable, tens of thousands of heroin addicts coming home was a war wound America was ill-equipped to handle.

Nixon's response was to create a White House task force to attack the heroin trade. John Ehrlichman told his young aide Egil Krogh to take the assignment. Bud Krogh was thirty-one years old; he had worked for Ehrlichman at his Seattle law firm before coming to the White House and saw his boss as a mentor and a family friend. He had been hired to handle domestic legal affairs; he knew nothing about global narcotics smugglers. But after visiting Vietnam and Thailand, he would come to understand that some of the traffickers—Golden Triangle warlords who grew the poppies, government ministers and military commanders who helped turn opium into the heroin that hit the American bloodstream—were ostensibly on our side in the war on communism. These same men helped carve the heroin trail. Our allies had become our enemies.

* * *

The November 1970 vote left President Nixon with an increasingly hostile Congress, including several senators who could be strong candidates against him in two years. Postelection punditry painted the 1970 election as "a significant political failure for me and a serious setback to my chances for being re-elected," he wrote. "The problems we confronted were so overwhelming . . . that it seemed possible that I might not even be nominated for re-election in 1972."

He felt he had reached the lowest point of his presidency. To be defeated in reelection would be akin to death for Richard Nixon. He began planning strategies that would keep him in the White House for six more years. He determined to be "absolutely ruthless" in his pursuit of an overwhelming reelection in 1972.

Nixon dictated political orders that ran to hundreds of pages, and he held strategy meetings with Haldeman, Mitchell, and Colson that rambled on for six hours. Haldeman was astounded at the "amazing array of trivia" and the "obsessive boring-in."

By November's end, Nixon made some fateful decisions. John Mitchell would leave the Justice Department and run the 1972 campaign. Covert surveillance and "dirty tricks" would intensify against Nixon's strongest potential rivals, Senators Ted Kennedy of Massachusetts and Ed Muskie of Maine. Chuck Colson had a private detective following Kennedy twenty-four hours a day. Haldeman was organizing reams of phony mailings under Muskie's name that were designed to offend conservative Democrats. Nixon intensified the "Townhouse Operation," where meetings were held in Washington to collect and distribute three million dollars in secret campaign funds. Haldeman, overseeing the operation, noted on November 19 that Nixon's lawyer Herb Kalmbach had been retained to spend half his professional time for the next two years "handling super fat cats and special assignments" to finance Nixon's reelection.*

---

* Among those who received money from the Townhouse Operation in 1970 was the forty-first president of the United States. Watergate prosecutors concluded that "George Bush received a total of approximately $112,000 from the townhouse opera-

Even Nixon staffers at a remove from the Oval Office noticed the change coming over the White House. David C. Miller Jr., later an American ambassador under President Reagan, had worked for Attorney General Mitchell at Justice for eighteen months, serving as his confidential assistant. Then he went to the White House, where he worked with John Dean, the counsel to the president. Shortly after he arrived, Dean presented him with a startling proposal.

"John Dean asked me if I would set up a safe house here in Washington for the use of the president," Miller recalled. Why? Miller asked; the CIA did that kind of thing. Dean answered, "He wants this to be a completely covert White House operation."

"I knew at that point that I was going to have to leave. I just said to myself: 'This is insane,'" Ambassador Miller recounted in 2003. "The challenge that John faced, and it was a challenge that sunk any number of youngsters at the White House, was the question of loyalty to their principal: Mr. Haldeman in John's case, Mr. Ehrlichman in Bud Krogh's case."

Bud Krogh had performed with aplomb on the drug task force. Perhaps his most spectacular achievement in December 1970 was handling Elvis Presley's unsolicited visit to Nixon at the White House, where Elvis sought an appointment as a "Federal Agent-at-Large" in the war on drugs and presented the president with a Colt .45 pistol. The reward for Krogh's dedicated service was a far more astonishing assignment. At Ehrlichman's command, Krogh was soon running a secret White House intelligence unit called the Plumbers.

"Their principals asked them to do things that were unwise and ultimately illegal," Ambassador Miller said. "It was a lack of judgment, of wisdom, more than a lack of intelligence. That was really a catastrophe." And, as a consequence, "most of my friends eventually wound up in the Watergate affair, and of course, many went to prison." The president— the ultimate principal—was at times "a very wise man." He also was "quite dangerous."

---

tion in connection with his 1970 Senatorial campaign." Under the 1970 campaign laws, this was not illegal. But the laws governing the reporting of campaign contributions were about to change, posing immense problems for Nixon and his reelection committee. After Bush's unsuccessful Senate race in 1970, Nixon named him ambassador to the United Nations and, in 1973, chairman of the Republican National Committee.

The dangerous side soon became the dominant side of the Nixon White House. In the coming months, the stoic and staunch Haldeman began to strain against the six-hour sessions of political trivia with the president. When Nixon's mind was wandering, his discourse was like a dog walking in circles before it lay down. Haldeman, to his credit, recorded every one of Nixon's ideas before the installation of the White House tapes. Both the journals and the tapes depict a president who was brusque and brutal, often witty and wise, but at times interminably indecisive. When his mind was made up, often in a state of rage, he issued irrational orders—fire all the Jews at the Internal Revenue Service, cut the CIA's budget in half immediately. Haldeman would carefully note the president's ill-considered ideas and make sure they died stillborn.

Catastrophically, Chuck Colson began to supplant Haldeman as the president's sounding board. "He started vying for favor on Nixon's dark side," said Bryce N. Harlow, a White House counselor and congressional liaison for the president. "Colson started talking about trampling his grandmother's grave for Nixon and showing he was as mean as they come."

"It was the 'in' thing to swagger and threaten" as the president's reelection campaign geared up, Harlow said. "Everybody went macho." Colson lacked judgment and wisdom. He would, as Nixon said approvingly, do anything.

CHAPTER ELEVEN

"We're not going to lose this war"

Two days before Christmas 1970, President Nixon determined once again to "break the back of the enemy," as he told Admiral Moorer, chairman of the Joint Chiefs of Staff.

His idea was to invade Laos and sever the Ho Chi Minh Trail. But Congress had barred Nixon from deploying American combat troops in Laos. So Nixon commanded the South Vietnamese Army—trained, equipped, and supported by the military might of the United States—to conduct the invasion and capture a crossroads of the trail. If the plan worked, it would vindicate Vietnamization.

Nixon sent General Haig to Saigon to sell President Thieu on the hastily conceived operation. Thieu would have to mobilize his forces rapidly in coordination with the American commanders in Saigon. Haig returned with high hopes, still seeing the light at the end of the tunnel.

The three-part plan was set by the morning of January 26, 1971. Phase one: American soldiers would set up a base near the Laotian border in South Vietnam. American helicopter gunships would bring South Vietnam's troops into battle and back them with the firepower of B-52s, fighter-bombers, and artillery. Phase two: those troops would drive into Laos and seize the town of Tchepone, described by American intelligence as a military nerve center for the Communists. Phase three: South Vietnamese soldiers and American firepower would destroy the enemy's forces and supply lines along the Ho Chi Minh Trail, slicing the enemy's lifeline like a knife cutting an artery.

But by that evening, a potentially fatal problem emerged.

The enemy had discovered the invasion plan through its intelligence agents in South Vietnam. It was well prepared for the attack. The looming disaster was laid out in a page from Haldeman's daily journals declassified in November 2014.

> Tuesday, January 26th. Henry got me into the office just as I was going home, to go over the general plan that they're really up to. They're planning a major assault in Laos which, if successful, and Henry fully believes it will be, would in effect end the war, because it would totally demolish the enemy's capability. The problem is that it will be a very major attack, with our troops massed heavily on the Laotian border. And . . . we've discovered that the enemy has our plan and is starting to mass their troops to counteract.

The president knew this. The next day, in the Oval Office, with Kissinger, Laird, Rogers, and Helms all present, Admiral Moorer said that "we had received intercepts yesterday which confirmed that Hanoi was aware of the general plan," according to Haig's written notes of the meeting. But Nixon disregarded the danger. He would depict the operation as a defensive raid on an enemy stronghold; thus "there could be no perception of defeat."

The secretary of state dissented: "He did not agree with the connotation that the Laos operation was merely a raid. The public would want to know why we were disturbing the balance in Southeast Asia and we should inform them that it was a massive attack." Rogers went on to say, "The risks appear very high. The enemy had intelligence on our plans and we were now asking the South Vietnamese to conduct an operation that we refused to do in the past because we were not strong enough. If they were set back in the operation we would be giving up everything we had achieved."

Nixon ignored him. Haig's notes conclude, "The President directed that the situation be played out."

The confrontation was among the most intense during Nixon's first two years in the White House. "The pressure back here is up to explosive proportions," Admiral Moorer cabled from the Pentagon to Gen. Frederick C. Weyand, the deputy commander of American forces in Saigon. Weyand responded that the clash would be "the real turning point of the war."

The United States and its allies had not engaged in a set-piece battle—clashing at a chosen time and place—in two years. Nor had the South Vietnamese Army ever conducted any attack of this size and scope.

The operation was prepared with excessive speed. American and South Vietnamese military commanders received operational plans on February 2. They had four days to get ready. They mistrusted the judgment of their leaders in Washington and Saigon, they were deeply skeptical of one another, and they knew it was folly to proceed with the knowledge that the enemy had the plan. Nevertheless, "prodded remorselessly by Nixon and Kissinger," as Haig put it, they bowed to the will of the White House.

"The best legacy we could leave," Nixon told Kissinger, "is to kick the hell out of Vietnam."

* * *

The South Vietnamese Army code-named the attack Lam Son 719, in tribute to a legendary warrior who had routed Chinese invaders five centuries before. It began with a bad omen: death by friendly fire. A U.S. Navy fighter-bomber struck a South Vietnamese brigade at the Laotian border on the evening of February 6, killing six soldiers and wounding fifty-one.

The plan did not survive contact with the enemy. Once inside Laos, America's allies were outclassed and outnumbered. On the battlefield, they met a superior North Vietnamese force that had been prepared for eight months. The command group that oversaw and defended the Ho Chi Minh Trail had amassed sixty thousand troops—including five main force divisions, eight artillery regiments, three tank battalions, six antiaircraft regiments, and eight sapper battalions. The heavy artillery, the antiaircraft guns, the tanks, and the troops were dug into caves and concealed in killing field formations along the only main route westward into Laos. North Vietnamese military historians called it "our army's greatest concentration of combined-arms forces . . . up to that point" of the war.

A harrowing, horrifying series of firefights and helicopter flights finally brought elements of the First Infantry Division of the South Vietnamese Army close to their strategic objective: the supposed Communist stronghold at Tchepone. What they found was described in a report by a South Vietnamese infantry commander, Maj. Gen. Nguyen Duy Hinh.

> Tchepone, a tiny town whose civilian population had fled long ago, now had only scars and ruins left. By this time, it had become more of a political and psychological symbol than an objective of strategic value. There was nothing of military importance in the ruined town; enemy supplies and war materiel were all stored in caches in the forests and mountains.

To save face, President Thieu ordered his First Infantry troops to secure Tchepone, "primarily for its propaganda and morale value," General Hinh reported. "At the price of 11 helicopters shot down," Thieu's soldiers created an operations base ten miles distant from the town. The enemy waited until the base was established, then began raining heavy artillery down upon it. President Thieu, having created the illusion of taking Tchepone, started to retreat almost immediately.

* * *

"We're not going to lose it. That's all there is to it," Richard Nixon said to Kissinger on February 18, as Lam Son 719 became a debacle. "We can't lose. We can lose an election, but we're not going to lose this war, Henry. . . . North Vietnam can never beat South Vietnam. Never."

This was one of Nixon's first conversations recorded on his Oval Office tapes, installed two days before. The Secret Service had placed five hidden microphones in the president's desk and two more near the sitting area by the fireplace. The Oval Office telephones were linked to the taping system; two more mikes were hidden in the Cabinet Room. The tapes revolved on reel-to-reel decks in the White House basement. Two months later Nixon also bugged his hideaway office in the Executive Office Building, adjacent to the White House. Four people knew: Nixon and Haldeman, along with Alexander Butterfield, deputy assistant to the president, and Al Wong, the Secret Service agent who oversaw the tapes.*

Kissinger, as was his wont, concurred with the president's resolve. "We can win in '72," he said. "Yeah, maybe," Nixon replied. "But right now, the important thing is to see this miserable thing through."

On February 26, less than a month after Nixon authorized the invasion of Laos, Admiral Moorer said, "This is the moment of truth for South Vietnam." And the truth was, as Nixon said, miserable. The battle had become a rout. THE PRESIDENT'S DECISION TO SUPPORT LAM SON 719 WAS BASED ON HIS CONFIDENCE THAT THE LAOS TRAIL NETWORK WOULD BE DISRUPTED, Kissinger cabled Ambassador Ellsworth Bunker in Saigon on March 1. FRANKLY, I AM BEGINNING TO WONDER WHAT IF ANYTHING HAS BEEN ACHIEVED IN THIS REGARD.

The answer was nothing. The U.S. Air Force already had bombed eastern Laos so hard that it looked like "the surface of the moon," said Richard C. Howland, then the State Department's political counselor in Laos, later an American ambassador under President George H. W. Bush. "Yet the Ho Chi Minh Trail was still operating."

Nixon now began bombing North Vietnam again, in violation of the bombing halt LBJ had ordered as part of his peace talks in October 1968—the same negotiations Nixon had helped to sabotage. These strikes were intended in part to destroy Communist surface-to-air missile attacks against B-52s flying in support of Lam Son 719. But they were also part of President Nixon's deepening determination to carry the war to the enemy with airpower.

Kissinger asked his covert action committee, "Why is it that Hanoi doesn't get tired?" No one knew. "They've now fought for ten years against us. They must've lost at least 700,000 men," he told Nixon on March 18. "They've had a whole young generation that are neither productive in North Vietnam or, for that matter, even breeding."

"Why, good God," Nixon replied. "There's no men."

But there were. North Vietnam concentrated forty-five thousand soldiers for a counterattack to drive their foes out of Laos in mid-March.

---

* In 1972, Nixon expanded the taping system to Camp David. The last of more than 3,700 hours of tapes was declassified in August 2014, forty years after Congress ordered them released "at the earliest reasonable date."

President Thieu unilaterally decided on a complete withdrawal, without telling the Americans, after losing three thousand soldiers going into battle. "It would be hard to exaggerate the mystification and confusion caused here by [Thieu's] rapid pull-out from Laos," Kissinger wrote in a back-channel message to Ambassador Bunker. Haig reported from Saigon that the South Vietnamese Army had "lost their stomach for Laos and the problem isn't to keep them in but rather to influence them to pull out in an orderly fashion."

The retreat was worse than the assault. The Communists turned the one road out of Laos into a highway of death, blowing up the first and last vehicle of each escaping convoy and then picking off the troops trapped between. An American airlift saved thousands of lives; its unforgettable image is a photo of South Vietnamese infantrymen desperately clinging to the skids of an American helicopter evacuating the battlefield. *New York Times* reporter Gloria Emerson interviewed survivors: "What has dramatically demoralized many of the South Vietnamese troops is the large number of their own wounded who were left behind, begging for their friends to shoot them or to leave hand grenades so they could commit suicide before the North Vietnamese or the B-52s killed them."

In all, nearly 9,000 South Vietnamese soldiers were killed, wounded, or captured during the forty-five-day Lam Son operation. The Americans sustained 102 dead, 215 wounded, and 53 missing in action, losses due largely to the fact that 92 U.S. helicopters and 5 fighter jets were destroyed by the enemy. General Hinh concluded that Lam Son 719 was no more than "a bloody field exercise" that destroyed men and morale for no military gain. Hanoi's official history of the battle bluntly called it "a concrete demonstration . . . that our army and people were strong enough to militarily defeat the 'Vietnamization' strategy of the American imperialists."

Nixon said the opposite in an address to the nation on April 7. "Tonight I can report that Vietnamization has succeeded," he said, and so he would withdraw one hundred thousand more American soldiers from combat by the end of 1971. But Lam Son 719 was a political defeat for the United States and a public relations disaster for Nixon's presidency—and he knew it. His popularity ratings fell 13 percent during the invasion.

"The war has eroded America's confidence," Nixon said to Kissinger. "The people are sick of it."

Kissinger told him that his domestic enemies "want to destroy you and they want us to lose in Vietnam." Those goals were identical, Nixon said. "If they destroy me," they would destroy the chance for victory on the battlefield. "Everything has to be played, now, in terms of how we survive."

He was speaking of his own political survival in the 1972 elections. Vietnam, he said, was the only issue that counted. When Kissinger tried to make Nixon focus on nuclear arms control talks with the Soviet Union, the president brushed him off. "All of this is a bunch of shit, as you know. It's not worth a damn," Nixon told him.

"Let's forget the Russian thing and the rest at the present time," the president said. "The game is where it is. All that matters here is Vietnam now."

His gamble in Laos forced him to realize that the ground war was a lost cause. That left him with a stark choice. Either Kissinger would have to strike a peace deal in Paris or Nixon would have to bomb North Vietnam into submission. He thought the latter a more likely way out of the war.

"We'll bomb the goddamn North like it's never been bombed," he told Kissinger on the eve of his April 7 speech, every word recorded on tape. "We'll *bomb* those bastards, and then let the American people—let this country go up in flames."

* * *

A week before, Lt. William Calley had been sentenced to life imprisonment at hard labor for premeditated murder at the My Lai massacre, where more than five hundred men, women, and children were killed. His jurors were six military officers, all but one Vietnam veterans. Within hours, over the strong objections of the secretary of defense, President Nixon ordered Calley moved from a military stockade to a more comfortable confinement: house arrest at the barracks of his home base of Fort Benning, Georgia. Three years later Nixon commuted his sentence. Calley went free.

Calley's crimes were not unique; there had been many My Lais. No one knew better than the twelve thousand members of a burgeoning group called Vietnam Veterans Against the War. On April 22, 1971, the Senate Foreign Relations Committee heard testimony from the group's spokesman, who had served as a navy lieutenant in Vietnam. In time the witness became the chairman of that same committee; at this writing, he serves as the U.S. secretary of state. John Kerry, in his well-bred Ivy League voice (Yale '66; Skull and Bones), told the senators that his group had taken statements from more than one hundred fifty honorably discharged veterans about war crimes they had committed in Southeast Asia. "They relived the absolute horror of what this country, in a sense, made them do," he said. "Raped, cut off ears, cut off heads, taped wires from portable telephones to human genitals and turned up the power, cut off limbs, blown up bodies, randomly shot at civilians, razed villages in fashion reminiscent of Genghis Khan, shot cattle and dogs for fun, poisoned food stocks, and generally ravaged the countryside of South Vietnam."

Kerry continued:

> Now we are told that the men who fought there must watch quietly while American lives are lost so that we can exercise the incredible arrogance of Vietnamizing the Vietnamese . . . the process by which the United States washes her hands of Vietnam . . . so that the United States doesn't have to admit something that the entire world already knows, so that we can't say that we have made a mistake. Someone has to die so that President Nixon won't be, and these are his words, "the first President to lose a war."
>
> We are asking Americans to think about that because how do you ask a man to be the last man to die in Vietnam? How do you ask a man to be the last man to die for a mistake?

"Where are the leaders of our country?" he concluded. "Where are McNamara, Rostow, Bundy . . . now that we, the men they sent off to war, have returned? These are the commanders who have deserted their troops. And there is no more serious crime in the laws of war. The Army says they never leave their wounded. The marines say they never even leave their dead. These men have left all the casualties and retreated behind a pious shield of public rectitude."

Haldeman himself told Nixon that the witness had been highly impressive. He predicted, "You'll find Kerry running for political office." At that very hour, Kerry was hurling the medals he had won in Vietnam (the Bronze Star, the Silver Star, and three Purple Hearts) on the ground before the Capitol, inaugurating a week of protests that drew at least two hundred thousand marchers to Washington.

* * *

Another Vietnam veteran, Daniel Ellsberg, had determined that he had a way to end the war. Ellsberg, once a hawk, had become a dove with talons, and he had gotten his grip on a copy of a highly classified seven-thousand-page study known as the Pentagon Papers. At the time of Kerry's testimony, Ellsberg was trying to convince members of Congress to put the Papers into print. He scared off committed antiwar senators such as the Foreign Relations Committee chairman, J. William Fulbright, and George McGovern of South Dakota. They thought that placing forty-seven volumes of top-secret documents in the *Congressional Record* might not be illegal but it was surely impolitic.

The Pentagon Papers, commissioned by Defense Secretary Robert Strange McNamara in 1967 and completed just before Nixon took office in 1969, detailed the history of the Vietnam War, beginning with the first American involvement in the conflict in 1954. They explicitly described the decisions of Presidents Kennedy and Johnson, along with the national security advisers whom John Kerry had called out by name, Walt Rostow and McGeorge Bundy. The gist was that America's military and civilian leaders had been lying to one another, and to the American people, about the course and the conduct of the war. The greatest lie was that there was light at the end of the tunnel. Tens of thousands of Americans had died in the darkness, searching for the illusory illumination of peace.

McNamara himself put it this way in 2003: "Any military commander who is honest with himself, or with those he's speaking to, will admit that he has made mistakes in the application of military power. He's killed people unnecessarily—his own troops or other troops—through mistakes, through errors of judgment. A hundred, or thousands, or tens of thousands, maybe even a hundred thousand. . . . The conventional wisdom is don't make the same mistake twice, learn from your mistakes. And we all do. Maybe we make the same mistake three times, but hopefully not four or five."

The lessons contained in the Pentagon Papers were that Americans might not have to suffer through three, four, or five more Vietnams. But those lessons had not been learned. Almost no one had read the Papers.

Ellsberg had taken a copy from his workplace at the RAND Corporation. The pleasantly situated Pentagon-backed institute, across the street from the Pacific Ocean in Santa Monica, California, had been formed after World War II to connect military officers with defense intellectuals to create war plans. RAND (short for "research and development") was in effect the unofficial West Coast branch of the National Security Council.

Ellsberg knew his way around Washington. He had been a marine lieutenant with a Harvard degree and had served two years in Vietnam. As a Defense Department analyst and a key contributor to Henry Kissinger's first major presentation to President Nixon on national security, he had traversed the vast pastel halls of the Pentagon and perched in the suites of the NSC. But now his trip from the corridors of power to the counterculture of the peaceniks took on the fervor of a religious conversion. He believed the Pentagon Papers had the power of a talisman. If the American people read them, the scales would fall from their eyes and they would rise up as one and demand peace in Vietnam.

After byzantine negotiations that left both men embittered, a *New York Times* reporter named Neil Sheehan obtained a set of Ellsberg's photocopies of close to six thousand pages of the Papers. Sheehan was a passionate and painstaking reporter who had covered Vietnam going back to 1962. He had only one flaw: he wrote with the speed of a stonecutter. He needed help to get the story out.

At about the same time that John Kerry was testifying before the Senate, the editors of the newspaper recruited a team of reporters sworn to secrecy, rented a suite of rooms at the Hilton hotel on Sixth Avenue in Midtown Manhattan under assumed names, and went to work trying to turn thousands of pages of documents into hundreds of column inches of newspaper stories.

Word got out. Two men deeply familiar with the Pentagon Papers learned that they had been leaked to the *Times*: Leslie Gelb, who had directed the report at the Pentagon, and Morton Halperin, who had worked with Gelb, and then under Kissinger at the National Security Council. Kissinger had wiretapped Halperin, without a judge's warrant or a court order, from May 1969 to February 1971. The taps never caught a leak of classified information but, fatefully, they recorded some of his conversations with Daniel Ellsberg. This would prove to be a signal moment in the annals of government wiretapping—and in the presidency of Richard Nixon.

Gelb and Halperin were ensconced at the Brookings Institution, a liberal think tank in Washington, in late May 1971, when Gelb got a call from a *Times* reporter asking about the origins of the Pentagon Papers. Gelb immediately went to Halperin's office down the hall. Both had no doubt who had given the Papers to the paper; nor did Kissinger and Haig. And they all knew there would be hell to pay. The biggest leak of classified information in the history of the United States was about to hit the front page of the *New York Times*.

Only one man thought he knew how to play this potential catastrophe of national security to the president's advantage, and that was Richard Nixon himself.

CHAPTER TWELVE

"It's a conspiracy"

RICHARD NIXON woke up a happy man on the morning of Sunday, June 13, 1971. The day before, he had given away his beloved daughter Tricia in marriage in the White House Rose Garden. Gray skies had threatened, but the rain never fell. A photo of a beaming president, the bride on his arm, filled the left-hand columns above the fold of the Sunday edition of the *New York Times*.

There was more good news, though it did not appear in print. After two years of secret entreaties, the Communist leaders of China had sent word that they were ready for a rapprochement. They had telegraphed through diplomatic channels that they would receive Nixon and Kissinger. The two fought privately over who would go first but settled on a secret mission by Kissinger, to take place in a few weeks, laying the groundwork for an official state visit by Nixon. The president hoped that this breakthrough would change the world—alter the architecture of the Cold War, compel the Soviets toward détente, convince Hanoi to make peace.

At 12:18 p.m., Al Haig spoiled Nixon's day of rest with a telephone call. Had the president seen the story to the right of the wedding photo?

"This goddamn *New York Times* exposé of the most highly classified documents of the war . . . is a devastating security breach of the greatest magnitude," General Haig said. Nixon had not read the story, the first in a series that was set to run for ten days, but Kissinger had. The Pentagon Papers were in part a devastating indictment of the presidents who had driven the United States into covert operations and armed combat in Vietnam. The conduct of the war since Nixon lost to Kennedy in 1960 had been a series of blind stabs and blunders.

"It just shows massive mismanagement of how we got there. And it pins it all on Kennedy and Johnson," Kissinger told the president three hours later. Nixon laughed with pleasure. Then his mood darkened. He said, "This is treasonable action on the part of the bastards that put it out."

Attorney General Mitchell wanted to go to court to stop the presses. "Hell, I wouldn't prosecute the *Times*," Nixon told Ehrlichman on June 14. "My view is to prosecute the goddamn pricks that gave it to them." Among the pricks, Nixon told Haldeman on June 15, was probably Daniel Ellsberg. But, he said, his anger building, this leak was part of a larger plot. "Goddamn it," the president roared, pounding his desk, "somebody's *got to go to jail.*"

"It's a conspiracy, Bob," the president said. "We're going to fight with everything we've got."

* * *

Mitchell's view on prosecution prevailed. The Justice Department sent a telegram to the newspaper demanding that it cease publication. It threatened a criminal indictment of the *Times* under the Espionage Act of 1917, a law used chiefly, since World War I, against political dissenters, not spies. On June 16 it won a temporary restraining order barring the *Times* from running the series on the grounds that publication would cause "immediate and irreparable harm" to American national security. The injunction moved swiftly toward the Supreme Court.

The president and his aides, having read what had been published before the injunction, now had a fuller grasp on the potential political power of the Pentagon Papers. "You can blackmail Johnson on this stuff," Haldeman told Nixon in the Oval Office on June 17. He was sure the Papers contained the inside story of the October 1968 bombing halt and the confrontation over Nixon's suspected sabotage of Johnson's peace plan. The Papers, as the Sunday *Times* story had noted, also revealed that the Kennedy administration had aided and abetted the military coup that led to the killing of President Diem of South Vietnam in November 1963, only three weeks before JFK was assassinated.

Nixon wanted a copy of the Papers, but no one in his administration seemed to know how to find one. The White House intelligence staffer Tom Charles Huston, the man behind the highly illegal Huston Plan for break-ins and bugging, was convinced that the Papers' principal author, Les Gelb, had a set locked away at the Brookings Institution, along with a study of LBJ's October 1968 bombing halt.

"Do you remember Huston's plan? Implement it," President Nixon ordered Haldeman and Ehrlichman, in Kissinger's presence. "I mean, I want it implemented on a thievery basis. Goddamn it, get in and get those files. Blow the safe and get it." Brookings never was burglarized, but other plans to commit crimes in the name of national security began taking shape within a few days.

On June 28, Ellsberg gave himself up at the federal courthouse in Boston. He faced up to 115 years in prison under the Espionage Act. He said, "As an American citizen, as a responsible citizen, I could no longer cooperate in concealing this information from the American public. I did this clearly at my own jeopardy and I am prepared to answer to all the consequences." He was the Edward Snowden of his day, with a crucial difference: he chose not to flee but to stand and fight.

On June 30 the Supreme Court ruled 6 to 3 for the *Times*. "Only a free and unrestrained press can effectively expose deception in government," Justice Hugo Black wrote in his concurring opinion. By then, Nixon had already taken the first steps to create a White House task force to carry out the purpose of the Huston Plan: the Special Investigations Unit. As the president ordered, it would implement the plan: break-ins, burglaries, bugging. Assigned to stop the leaks that exposed deception in government, the unit inevitably became known as the Plumbers.

* * *

"You need a commander" for these missions, Nixon told Haldeman on July 1. It could not be John Mitchell: "It just repels him to do these horrible things." It could not be John Ehrlichman: "He's got to decide whether we're going to pollute Lake Erie or some damn thing."

Then Nixon had an inspiration: "It could be Colson."

Nixon called Ehrlichman and Chuck Colson into the Oval Office. Colson told the president he had just the man for the job. "He's hard as nails," Colson said. "His name is Howard Hunt." Colson's friend since college, E. Howard Hunt was fifty, graying, and washed up after two decades at the CIA. His career in the world of covert operations had gone off the rails after the Bay of Pigs invasion, when 1,189 Cuban exiles trained by Hunt and his colleagues died trying to overthrow Fidel Castro in 1961. He had made a second living writing spy novels and working as a shadowy security consultant.

Colson said Hunt had admired Nixon since the investigation and prosecution of Alger Hiss. Nixon approved heartily: he said he wanted to go after Ellsberg "just like I took on the Hiss case." Hunt would become a White House consultant, effective immediately, with a desk and a safe in the Executive Office Building, under Colson's command.

"We're up against an enemy, a conspiracy," Nixon declared. "They are using any means. *We are going to use any means.* Is that clear?" That was Richard Nixon at his worst, playing politics as a game without rules.

The world was about to witness the president at his best, a political genius and grand strategist, bringing secrets to light, and to immense acclaim.

On that same day, July 1, Nixon gave Kissinger his marching orders for his secret mission to China.

"I just want to make that big play," he told Kissinger.

"Mr. President," Kissinger replied, "it's the big play."

The mission was to set a meeting in Beijing in 1972. The Soviets would then be compelled to invite Nixon to a Moscow summit, and to settle their differences on everything from nuclear weapons to the war in Vietnam. Finally—and this was the greatest hope—Moscow and Beijing together would help the United States end the war in time for Nixon's reelection in November 1972.

Nixon ordered Kissinger to emphasize "fears of what the president might do in the event of continued stalemate in the South Vietnam war." Nixon said, "We're not going to turn the country over—17 million people—over to the Communists against their will . . . with the bloodbath that would be sure to follow."

The two had agreed earlier on using the "madman" gambit in the next round of negotiations with North Vietnam. "You can say 'I cannot control him.' Put it that way," Nixon said.

"Imply that you might use nuclear weapons," Kissinger responded.

"Yes," the president said.

The China trip had been two years in the making. On August 1, 1969, on a visit to Pakistan, Nixon had asked President Yahya Khan to deliver the proposal for a meeting to China's prime minister, Zhou En-lai. On October 25, 1970, the two presidents had met again, at the White House. "I understand you are going to Beijing," Nixon said to Yahya. "It is essential that we open negotiations with China."

On May Day 1971 a message from Zhou En-lai had arrived, sent through Pakistan's ambassador to the United States: "The Chinese Government reaffirms its willingness to receive publicly in Beijing a Special Envoy of the president of the U.S. (for instance, Mr. Kissinger) or the U.S. Secretary of State or even the president of the U.S. himself for a direct meeting and discussions," it read. "It is entirely possible for proper arrangements to be made through the good offices of President Yahya Khan" of Pakistan.

Who would go first, Nixon or Kissinger? "President Nixon was ambivalent," said Kissinger's top assistant, Winston Lord. "It might take away from the drama" if his national security adviser made the first contact. "Of course, from the beginning, Kissinger wanted to go. He thought that he was the best person to handle it, and I think that he was. Not to mention Kissinger's ego, sense of history, and so on."

Hours after the message from Zhou En-Lai arrived, Kissinger sent a cryptic cable to the American ambassador in Pakistan, Joseph Farland, summoning him to a meeting in Palm Springs, California. The ambassador was familiar with foreign intrigues—a former FBI agent, he had served on sensitive diplomatic and intelligence missions for many years—but "this was about as mysterious as you can get," he recounted in a State Department oral history.

He flew across the Pacific to Los Angeles, where he was met on the tarmac by a twin-engine jet. "I was trying to figure out whose plane this was," said Farland. "I was looking in the ashtrays to see if there were any paper matches or anything else. It appeared that it was [Frank] Sinatra's plane." In Palm Springs, at the home of a wealthy Republican campaign contributor, Farland met Kissinger, relaxing on the patio in a sport shirt with a drink in his hand.

"I was anything but relaxed," the ambassador recounted. "I said, 'Henry, I've come halfway around this damn earth and I don't know why.'"

Kissinger said he had plans for an around-the-world trip, first stop Saigon, then India and Pakistan, then Paris. Once he got to Pakistan, "I want you to put me into China," he told Farland. The ambassador had two months to figure out how to smuggle Kissinger into Beijing undetected by the press.

"On the way back, I thought of nothing else but how to do it," Farland said. He devised an elaborate scheme to allow Kissinger to seem to disappear for two to three days, using a cottage controlled by his embassy in the town of Murree, a former hill station of the British Raj outside the capital. The question remained: how to fly him into China in secret, keeping the possibility of an American rapprochement under cover.

Ambassador Farland went to see President Yahya after many a sleepless night. "I have something very serious to talk to you about," he said. Yahya grinned. "I said, 'Do you know what I'm going to talk about?' He said, 'I think I do.' I said, 'Has somebody been talking to you?' He said, 'Somebody has been talking.' I said, 'I need one of your airplanes to fly to China.' He said, 'You have it.'"

Kissinger back-channeled a message to Zhou En-lai saying he would be flying in a Pakistani aircraft to Beijing at dawn on July 9. Ambassador Farland issued a statement the night before, saying Kissinger had "Delhi belly" (food poisoning) and would be recuperating in Murree. At 4:00 a.m., Kissinger and his party, including his NSC aides Winston Lord and John Holdridge, boarded their jet. To their surprise, four Chinese officials, including Chang Wenjin, a foreign ministry official and later the Chinese ambassador to Washington, already were on board. One of the two Secret Service agents accompanying the American delegation was so shocked he almost drew his gun.

The plane took off and rose over the Himalayas. Holdridge said, "We were stepping into the infinite."

Lord recalled: "As the sun came up, we were passing K-2, the second highest mountain in the world. . . . We were going to the most populous country in the world, after 22 years, and there were all of the geopolitical implications of that. There was the anticipation of meeting with Zhou En-lai, this great figure, and there was the excitement and anticipation of those talks. There were the James Bond aspects of this trip, since it was totally secret."

They landed at a military airport south of Beijing. They debarked into black limousines and, with blinds drawn and red flags flying, sped past the Great Hall of the People to the Dayoutai guesthouse for VIPs. They sent a one-word message to Washington: EUREKA.

* * *

Zhou En-lai came to greet them. The premier was seventy-three, elegant, and charming. His intelligence and cunning had made him a leader in the Chinese Communist Party for fifty years. He had lived through hardships barely known to the Americans, who saw Chairman Mao as a mysterious emperor, not a murderous monster. They knew little of his regime, which had killed tens of millions of people over two decades through deadly politics and disastrous economics.

Over the next two days, Kissinger and Zhou talked for seventeen hours, mostly haggling over the wording of the forthcoming communiqué. Kissinger wished it to appear that the Chinese wanted Nixon to come. Zhou wanted it to appear that Nixon wished to come. After a full day, they were at an impasse. Frustrated, both sides broke off.

"Kissinger and I and the others walked around outside, because we knew that we were being bugged," said Lord, the future American ambassador to China. "Probably the trees were bugged, too. Who knows? I remember that we waited for hours and hours. The Chinese were probably trying to keep us off-balance. . . . Most likely, Zhou En-lai had to check with Mao."

Finally, they worked it out: the Chinese were inviting Nixon because they had heard about his interest in visiting China. It had taken twelve hours to arrive at this formulation.

In the hours that followed, Zhou was "as forthcoming as we could have hoped" on the subject of Vietnam, Kissinger reported to Nixon. "For ideological reasons, he clearly had to support Hanoi. On the other hand . . . he did not wish to jeopardize the chances for an improvement in our relations, especially after I explained the positions we had taken in Paris and warned of the danger of escalation if negotiations failed."

Before they left, the Americans were treated to a banquet hosted by Zhou. "Here we saw just how clever Zhou En-lai was," said Lord. Zhou managed to criticize the excesses unleashed by Mao without actually criticizing Mao. Zhou himself had been imprisoned in his office by Mao's shock troops, the Red Guards, during the Cultural Revolution of the 1960s.

The Americans, exhausted but exhilarated, finished drafting the communiqué, returned to Pakistan, resumed the charade worked out by Farland, and immediately flew to Paris, where Kissinger held another round of secret talks with Hanoi's delegation on July 12. He reported to Nixon that the North Vietnamese "repeatedly stressed—in an almost plaintive tone—that they wanted to settle the war. They expressed a great desire to reach agreement quickly, and voiced what appeared to be genuine concern about the delay which might result from debate about a withdrawal date."

On July 15, Nixon announced that he had sent Kissinger to the People's Republic of China, that Zhou had invited the president to visit China, and that Nixon had accepted. "I have taken this action because of my profound conviction that all nations will gain from a reduction of tensions and a better relationship between the United States and the People's Republic of China," he said in a nationally televised address. "It is in this spirit that I will undertake what I deeply hope will become a journey for peace, peace not just for our generation but for future generations on this earth we share together."

The proclamation was wildly popular throughout the world. As Nixon had anticipated, it shocked the Russians into proposing their own 1972 summit meeting. It raised hopes in the White House that Beijing and Moscow would pressure Hanoi into a peace deal. And it made Nixon appear, in the eyes of millions of Americans, a master of global strategy—not merely the leader of the free world but *the* world leader. The big play looked as if it had gone according to plan.

"Kissinger and I thought, somewhat naively, that we had pulled off two historic encounters in one trip: the opening toward China and moving toward settling the Vietnam War," Lord recounted. "That latter idea was a wildly premature judgment."

"I remember that we debated which was the more historic and important, getting the war over with or arranging for the opening to China. We said, 'Wasn't it a great achievement to do both in one trip?'"

* * *

Five days after his proclamation that he would go to China in the name of world peace, the cold warrior within Richard Nixon went back to work.

He formally set the Plumbers in motion against the political conspiracy that threatened his power on the home front. John Ehrlichman had delegated the task of assembling a team to his trusted aide Bud Krogh, whose official title was deputy assistant to the president.

"Krogh and his guys are going to pull together the evidence," Ehrlichman assured Nixon in the Oval Office on July 20.

Krogh selected G. Gordon Liddy as a key member of the Plumbers. A former FBI agent, Liddy was forty, mustachioed, politically ambitious, and, putting it politely, hotheaded. He joined forces with Howard Hunt, the reticent retired CIA officer recruited by Colson. They made an ill-suited team. Liddy was loud, flamboyant, and reckless. Hunt was quiet, cautious, and covert.

Two weeks after Ehrlichman's assurances to the president, Krogh met with Liddy and Hunt in Room 16, in the basement of the Executive Office Building, across from the White House. Hunt proposed a burglary to steal derogatory information about Daniel Ellsberg from the office of his psychiatrist, Dr. Lewis Fielding, in Beverly Hills, California. The goal was to defame him and destroy him in the Pentagon Papers case. Liddy said such black-bag jobs were standard operating procedure in the FBI's national security investigations. He said he had pulled off a few in his day.

"I listened intently," Krogh wrote in 2007. "At no time did I or anyone else there question whether the operation was necessary, legal or moral. Convinced that we were responding legitimately to a national security crisis, we focused instead on the operational details: who would do what, when and where. . . . The premise of our action was the strongly held view within certain precincts of the White House that the president and those functioning on his behalf could carry out illegal acts with impunity if they were convinced that the nation's security demanded it."

Krogh sent a memo to Ehrlichman recommending that "a covert operation be undertaken to examine all of the medical files still held by Ellsberg's psychiatrist." Ehrlichman gave his approval in writing— "if done under your assurance that it is not traceable"—and labeled the job "Hunt/Liddy Special Project No. 1" in his notes. The team, aided by Cuban Bay of Pigs veterans, hit Dr. Fielding's suite on the night of September 3. They trashed the office but found nothing on Ellsberg.

"Where does Krogh stand now?" Nixon asked Ehrlichman in the Oval Office on September 8. He was investigating Ellsberg and other national security matters, the president's chief domestic adviser reported, and aiming to undermine antiwar Democratic senators whom Nixon saw as likely opponents in the 1972 election.

Ed Muskie of Maine already was the target of political sabotage overseen by Chuck Colson; Teddy Kennedy of Massachusetts was under full-time surveillance by Colson's operatives. Nixon himself had ordered the "permanent tails and coverage on Teddy and Muskie."

"We ought to persecute them," Nixon told Ehrlichman. "On the IRS, if you can do it, are we looking into Muskie's returns?" he asked. "Teddy?" Ehrlichman assured the president that there would be persecution aplenty.

"We had one little operation. It's been aborted out in Los Angeles," Ehrlichman told the president. "But we've got some dirty tricks under way. It may pay off."

CHAPTER THIRTEEN

"I can see the whole thing unravel"

THE COURSE of the war in Vietnam and the conduct that led to Watergate merged in a conversation between President Nixon and his ambassador to South Vietnam, Ellsworth Bunker, three days after the Pentagon Papers became public.

"Our goal is clear," Nixon said. "Our goal, now, is that, as we come to the—near the end of this long road is to succeed. We can succeed. You agree?"

Bunker did. He always saw the light at the end of the tunnel.

"But, on the other hand, we must not give our enemies—and I'm not referring to our enemies in North Vietnam, but our enemies in this country—we cannot give them the weapons to kill us with," the president warned.

Nixon's most powerful enemies in this country were the U.S. senators trying to stop the war by cutting off the billions needed to sustain combat forces. One such bill had come to a vote in the Senate in September 1970. Its main sponsor was Sen. George McGovern of South Dakota, who had flown thirty-five bombing missions against Germany during World War II. Minutes before the vote, McGovern rose to speak:

Every senator in this chamber is partly responsible for sending 50,000 young Americans to an early grave. This chamber reeks of blood. Every Senator here is partly responsible for that human wreckage . . . young men without legs, or arms, or genitals, or faces, or hopes.

There are not very many of these blasted and broken boys who think this war is a glorious adventure. Do not talk to them about bugging out, or national honor or courage. . . . We are responsible for those young men and their lives and their hopes. And if we do not end this damnable war those young men will someday curse us for our pitiful willingness to let the Executive carry the burden that the Constitution places on us.

Congress was not ready to carry that burden—not yet. McGovern's words shocked the sensibilities of some senators. His measure was defeated by a 55–39 margin. The strongest antiwar legislation enacted in 1971 was a call for an end to American military operations in Vietnam at "the earliest practicable date," subject to the return of all American prisoners of war. But a dozen more stop-the-war amendments were under consideration in the fall of 1971. One in particular demanded a free and fair vote in South Vietnam, where President Thieu was running unopposed.

"There are no fair elections in Southeast Asia," Nixon told Bunker and Kissinger. "You know that."

The primary goals of the CIA's covert action program for South Vietnam were to "re-elect Nguyen Van Thieu," to elect "twenty individuals to the Lower House . . . responsive to CIA direction," and to create pro-American political leaders "to play a vital role in the political struggle on the ground against North Vietnamese political agents," the Agency reported to Nixon and Kissinger. The CIA already had spent millions financing seemingly independent political parties, newspapers, unions, and other facades of democratic institutions—all for naught, with most of the money wasted or stolen by Thieu and his ministers. Two months before the October 1971 elections in South Vietnam, it was clear that Thieu would be the only candidate.

North Vietnam's negotiators in Paris had demanded that Thieu step down or form a coalition government with the Communists as a key to any peace deal. Their strategy was to try to get Nixon to do what they wished: to overthrow the government of South Vietnam.

But he could not "turn on Thieu," Kissinger told Nixon.

"Turn on him? Never, never," Nixon said. "We must never do that. . . . Never, never, never, never."

That would be surrender. Yet the fixed election troubled Thieu's American sponsors. "Unless there is a real contest," Ambassador Bunker reported to the White House from Saigon on August 20, "his moral and legal authority to govern will come into question. Divisiveness, not unity needed to face a determined enemy, will result." Two weeks later, on September 2, Thieu reaffirmed that he would run unopposed.

When Kissinger held another clandestine negotiating session with North Vietnam's representatives in Paris on September 13, the two sides had nothing of substance to say. "For the hundredth [*sic*] and twentieth time I tell you the question is not whether to support or give up Thieu, but what process will shape the future of Vietnam after the settlement," Kissinger told the Communists, his frustration mounting. After "the shortest meeting on record," he told Nixon, they acknowledged they were at an impasse and made no plans to meet again.

On his return from Paris, Kissinger composed a deeply pessimistic report to the president. Hanoi, he wrote, in a passage Nixon highlighted in pen, would soon demand a rapid American military withdrawal from Vietnam—and link Thieu's removal to the release of America's prisoners of war. "The heart of the problem," Nixon wrote in the left-hand margin of the paper.

"A swift collapse in South Vietnam would seriously endanger your effort to shape a new foreign policy role for this country. The impact on friends, adversaries and our own people would be likely to swing us from post–World War II predominance to post-Vietnam abdication," Kissinger warned. "An ignominious rout in Vietnam would leave deep scars on our society, calling into question the heavy sacrifices and fueling the impulses for recrimination."

Nixon had to win a war in which his enemies seemed inexhaustible, his allies undependable, his generals incompetent, and his aims scattershot. He wanted to bring the fight to the Communists, but at the same time he wanted American combat deaths to go down—irreconcilable goals. His troops kept in a defensive crouch. He raged at his top commander in Saigon, Gen. Creighton Abrams, for publicly discussing the pace of the American pullout of combat forces. "I think we have to consider withdrawing the son-of-a-bitch," Nixon told Kissinger on September 14, 1971, or "get someone second in command that will keep him from drinking too much and talking too much."

But if Nixon had trouble with his commanders in Vietnam, the trouble among the officers and conscripts who served them was deeper. As American combat soldiers pulled out of Vietnam—troop levels fell from 539,000 in June 1969 to 239,000 in June 1971—morale among those remaining plummeted, too.

"Having been in the military, I could see the signs," said Howard H. Lange, a State Department official who worked closely with American combat and intelligence officers in Hue, a base for the disastrous Lam Son 719 operation. "The kids showed no pride in appearance and they weren't disciplined. I saw written in the dust on the back of a truck in Da Nang: 'Get me out of this hell.'" Lange was dismayed by the despair among American soldiers "who saw the war in the bitterly memorable phrase as 'unwanted and unending, pursued by the unwilling, for the ungrateful.' It was a grim picture."

Nixon was equally embittered by the unending war, a battle begun by President Kennedy and intensified a hundredfold by President Johnson. He wanted out of that hell as badly as that soldier in Da Nang. He deeply desired to be done with Vietnam, to have some kind of peace deal, when he ran for reelection in 1972. John F. Kennedy and Lyndon B. Johnson and a Congress controlled by Democrats had started the war, Nixon reflected in anger, and now he had the burden of ending it. If he did not, he feared, any antiwar Democrat might defeat him—a dove like McGovern or, worst of all, Teddy Kennedy, a prospect he found personally and politically appalling, a dirty trick that history might play on him.

* * *

President Nixon addressed the war with unusual candor at a White House news conference on Thursday, September 16, 1971.

Did the one-man race for the presidency in South Vietnam affect his war strategy? "We have to keep in mind our major goal," Nixon said: ending the war "in a way that will leave South Vietnam in a position to defend itself from a Communist takeover."

What about the Senate bill to cut off aid to South Vietnam unless President Thieu held a fair election? "We presently provide military and/ or economic aid to 91 countries in the world," Nixon said. "In only 30 of those countries do they have leaders who are there as a result of a contested election by any standards that we would consider fair."

Would Thieu's reelection do anything for American hopes for a democratic Vietnam? "No," Nixon said bluntly. "That objective will not be met, perhaps for several generations."

He added an ominous note. Senators were suggesting "that the United States should use its leverage now to overthrow Thieu. I would remind all concerned that the way we got into Vietnam was through overthrowing Diem, and the complicity in the murder of Diem; and the way to get out of Vietnam, in my opinion, is not to overthrow Thieu."

A more inquisitive press corps might have wondered aloud why Nixon was digging up America's role in the November 1963 assassination of President Diem. They would have been astounded at the answer.

* * *

Over the next seventy-two hours, the president made three bold decisions. Each deepened the connection between Watergate and Vietnam.

He told Ehrlichman to have the details of the Diem assassination on his desk within a week. Nixon believed that President Kennedy was directly complicit in the murder of Diem, and that the killing was the original sin that had drawn America into Vietnam. He was convinced that proof of the crime lay somewhere in classified CIA cables, and that Howard Hunt was the man to find them, leak them to a reporter, and use the leak to destroy Teddy Kennedy's political career by smearing President John F. Kennedy as an assassin.

"He started the damn thing!" Nixon said in a taped telephone conversation with his spiritual adviser, the Reverend Billy Graham. "He killed Diem!" The story was not quite that simple.

Then the president told Haldeman to set up a meeting in which he intended to fire J. Edgar Hoover for refusing to conduct illegal bugging and break-ins against Nixon's political enemies. Nor would that prove an easy matter.

Finally, he ordered the bombing of North Vietnam, north of the demilitarized zone, to resume immediately. Not all these conversations were taped, but in those that were recorded, Nixon was at his most intense.

The president was pleased when Kissinger told him that the Pentagon was prepared to send "everything that flies in a stretch of 20 miles north of the DMZ" in an intense raid against North Vietnam.

"Good," Nixon replied. "They've been asking for it."

"You think of this miserable war—and, first of all, Henry, it isn't a miserable war," said the president, contradicting himself before coming to his point. "The goddamn war was fought for a great cause," preserving America's global power by fighting communism in Asia. "We didn't have to get into it, to begin with. But once in it, this war could have been ended in a year or two years," Nixon continued. "Using our air power we could have knocked those bastards right off the lot—"

Kissinger interjected: "The war would be history."

"And with a victory," Nixon said with a sigh.

On September 20, as the new bombing runs began, Nixon led a National Security Council meeting in the Cabinet Room. He continued to reflect on the killing of Diem. "The behavior of the U.S. in Vietnam has not really been all that bright," the president said. "After the murder of Diem, for us to say that Thieu is out because he didn't do what we wanted—I can see the whole thing unravel starting from Southeast Asia, Indonesia, and Thailand, and all the way to Japan. What we really confront is what has been a long and terrible trial for U.S. foreign policy: will it fail or succeed?"

At that moment, next door in the Executive Office Building, Howard Hunt was using an old typewriter, a copying machine, a razor blade, and Scotch tape to forge a set of diplomatic cables that could directly pin the Diem killing on President Kennedy. He had been unable to find damning classified documents that lay hidden in the files of the CIA and the State Department and the JFK Presidential Library.

JFK and some of his advisers had in fact given their tacit support to a regime change in South Vietnam. But the driving force behind the 1963 coup had been the newly appointed American ambassador in Saigon, Henry Cabot Lodge, Richard Nixon's running mate in the 1960 presidential election.

On his sixth day in Saigon, Lodge had cabled Washington: WE ARE LAUNCHED ON A COURSE FROM WHICH THERE IS NO TURNING BACK: THE OVERTHROW OF THE DIEM GOVERNMENT. At the White House, JFK approved, overruling his closest advisers. On November 4, 1963, alone in the Oval

Office, President Kennedy dictated a tape-recorded memo about the Diem assassination. "We must bear a good deal of responsibility for it," he said mournfully, eighteen days before he himself was murdered.

But Hunt had been unable to produce the evidence Nixon wanted. So he fabricated it. Colson attempted to leak the fake cables to a reputable journalist, without success. Then Hunt showed them to an old CIA colleague, Lucien Conein, who had been an eyewitness to the 1963 coup. Conein shortly thereafter appeared on a two-hour NBC television documentary about Vietnam. A review of the program in the *New York Times* by Neil Sheehan, the reporter who had obtained the Pentagon Papers, said Conein's interview in particular left little doubt that "the Kennedy Administration was deeply implicated in the coup plot" that had led to Diem's death.

Faking diplomatic cables was a dangerous business. But it was child's play compared to trying to fire J. Edgar Hoover, the FBI's director since 1924.

Nixon had Hoover to breakfast at the White House on Monday, September 20, 1971, a few hours before the NSC meeting on Vietnam. He was furious at the director's reluctance to perform break-ins for the White House, but he was afraid Hoover would wreak his revenge if Nixon demanded his resignation. Nixon quailed, not for the first time, in fear of Hoover's wrath.

For weeks thereafter, Haldeman, Ehrlichman, Mitchell, and Dean all pushed the president to force the old man out. "We have those tapes, [the transcripts of] wiretapping we did on Kissinger's staff, the newspapermen and so forth," Mitchell told the president on October 8, 1971. "Hoover is tearing the place up over there trying to get at them."

Ehrlichman explained, "Hoover feels very insecure without having his own copy of those things because of course that gives him leverage with Mitchell and with you—and because they're illegal." The possibility of Hoover's blackmailing the president hung in the air.

Mitchell continued: "Hoover won't come and talk to me about it. He's just got his Gestapo all over the place. . . . I've got to get him straightened out, which may lead to a hell of a confrontation."

Nixon once again tried to steel his resolve. "He ought to resign," the president said. "He's too old."

"He's getting senile, actually," Mitchell said.

"He should get the hell out of there," Nixon replied, but "he's got to go of his own volition. That's what we get down to. And that's why we're in a hell of a problem. . . . I think he'll stay until he's a hundred years old."

Nixon concluded, after reconsidering the question for the fourth time on October 25, that he had too much to fear from Hoover, the man he had called his closest personal friend in his political life. "We've got to avoid the situation where he could leave with a blast," Nixon said. "We may have on our hands here a man who will pull down the temple with him, including me."

* * *

With the 1972 election now a year away, Nixon finally settled on a military and political strategy of sorts. John Mitchell would resign soon as attorney general, for a last hurrah as Nixon's campaign manager. Many of Haldeman and Ehrlichman's best and brightest aides would move to campaign headquarters, one block away from the White House.

The boys in the basement at the Executive Office Building, the Plumbers, would develop a war plan against all Nixon's opponents, using all the tricks in the book, financed in part by the slush fund of campaign cash held by Nixon's lawyer, Herb Kalmbach; operating in secrecy; run in theory by the reelection committee but in reality overseen by no one.

And in Vietnam, the president would use all the force at his command to bring the enemy to sue for peace by Election Day. "We will bomb the bejeezus out of them," he told Kissinger in the Oval Office on November 20. "To hell with history. . . . Just knock the shit out of them."

"That's the best—I had not thought of that," Kissinger said. He was a master at telling Nixon what he wanted to hear.

"Do they realize that they have to deal with, here, a man who if he wins the election will kick the shit out of them, and if he loses the election will do it even more?" Nixon went on, his voice becoming more and more forceful. "Did that ever occur to you?"

"I—I have to say, honestly, it did not," Kissinger replied, in a tone more admiring than aghast.

"I'd finish off the goddamn place," Nixon said. "Knock the shit out of them—and then, everybody would say, 'Oh, horrible, horrible, horrible.'" And he laughed with pleasure at the thought.

CHAPTER FOURTEEN

"It is illegal, but . . ."

Richard Nixon believed he was at his best in a crisis—sharper, stronger, tougher. When India and Pakistan went to war at the end of 1971, he armed the outgunned Pakistanis: a very tough call, utterly illegal, in blatant violation of an international weapons embargo.

But the president hated India with a passion: "These people are savages," he said bluntly. And as Kissinger put it, Nixon had "a special feeling" for Pakistan's military dictator, Yahya Khan: the general who had created the crucial link to China.

The long and unhappy alliance between the United States and Pakistan went back to the Eisenhower administration, when Pakistan provided secret airfields for flights of the CIA's U-2 spy plane over the Soviet Union. The United States provided military assistance in return. Pakistan itself was created by the catastrophic British Partition of India in 1947, which led to hundreds of thousands of deaths as Muslims and other minorities fled to the newly created West Pakistan and East Pakistan. The two Pakistans, flanking India and separated by twelve hundred miles, never were one nation in reality; that fiction was created by partition. Their deep political differences exploded into violent conflict in the spring of 1971, after the first free elections in East Pakistan gave General Yahya's opponents a measure of power.

General Yahya, who ruled from West Pakistan, imposed martial law on the East. His soldiers indiscriminately killed his opponents; the death toll ran well upward of one million. As late as December 2014, his political allies were still being convicted of war crimes. "The Pakistani army was just murdering people," said Nicholas A. Veliotes, then a State Department official, later ambassador to Egypt under President Reagan. "There was a genocide plan there: anyone who was educated, the Paks were going to kill." American diplomats who witnessed the onslaught bluntly called it genocide in a rebellious report to Washington on April 6, 1971, signed by the American consul general in East Pakistan, Archer Blood. The "Blood Telegram" boldly condemned the Nixon administration's failure to denounce the atrocities.

Nixon deliberately did nothing. *"Don't* squeeze Yahya," he wrote in a note to Kissinger on April 28, underlining the first word three times.

India, the world's most populous democracy, had received billions in American economic assistance over the years. But in August 1971, shortly after Nixon announced the opening to China—the Chinese and the Indians had fought a vicious border war nine years before—India signed an alliance with the Soviets. This infuriated Nixon. "If they're going to choose to go with the Russians, they're choosing not to go with us," he told Kissinger. "Goddamn it, who's giving them a billion dollars a year? Shit, the Russians aren't giving them a billion dollars a year."

India's prime minister, Indira Gandhi, received a politically correct reception when she visited the president on November 4, 1971. But the next day, Nixon and Kissinger said what they really thought of her.

"She is a bitch," Nixon said.

"Well, the Indians are bastards anyway," Kissinger replied. "But, Mr. President, even though she was a bitch, we shouldn't overlook the fact that we got what we wanted, which was we kept her from going out of here saying that the United States kicked her in the teeth."

President Nixon met at the White House with the Pakistani foreign secretary, Sultan Khan, on November 15, 1971. "We will do everything we can to try to help you in your cause," Nixon pledged. But a war was coming, with India's forces supporting the separatists in East Pakistan and Yahya Khan mobilizing against India.

"Yahya is beginning to feel cornered," Ambassador Joseph Farland reported to Kissinger from Islamabad on November 19. "This thing could blow." Three days later, it did. Yahya told Farland that India had attacked and that he was declaring a national emergency. The dictator sent President Nixon the message that Pakistan was at the point of no return.

"Is Yahya saying it's war?" Nixon asked Kissinger in the Oval Office.

"Yeah, they're saying it's war."

"The Indians say it isn't?" the president said.

"That's right," Kissinger replied.

The White House "didn't have any confirmation" one way or the other, Haldeman noted in his diary that night: "Our vast intelligence network doesn't seem to be able to tell us when a couple of major nations are at war, which is a little alarming, to say the least."

Kissinger sent a back-channel cable to Ambassador Farland on November 24, saying that he was convening daily meetings of his crisis team: the Washington Special Actions Group. These meetings, he wrote, led to STRICTEST PRESIDENTIAL INSTRUCTIONS TO TILT TOWARD PAKISTAN.

Nixon made this explicit in an Oval Office conversation with Kissinger and Secretary of State Rogers that same day. "To the extent that we can tilt it toward Pakistan, I would prefer to play that," Nixon said. He cautioned them: American military aid had to be completely clandestine. "I don't want to get caught in the business where we take the heat for a miserable war that we had nothing to do with," the president said.

* * *

The miserable war went ballistic on December 3, 1971. Prime Minister Gandhi charged that Pakistan's air force had bombed six Indian airfields in Kashmir and the Punjab and that artillery shells were striking Indian positions from West Pakistan.

India, Gandhi said, was going to crush its enemy.

The president was trying to unwind in Key Biscayne. "Pakistan thing makes your heart sick," he told Kissinger. "And after we have warned the bitch."

Kissinger called the next morning. "We have had an urgent appeal from Yahya. Says his military supplies have been cut off," he told Nixon. "Would we help through Iran?" The shah of Iran was a key American ally. Placed in power by a CIA coup under President Eisenhower, he bought billions in weapons from the United States. Nixon asked, "Can we help?" Kissinger replied, "I think if we tell the Iranians we will make it up to them we can do it."

The CIA station chief in Tehran met with the shah on December 5 and encouraged him to send arms and ammunitions to Pakistan. The shah indicated that he would be glad to help, on the condition that the United States replace what he sent. On the same day in Amman, the capital of Jordan, King Hussein showed the American ambassador, Dean Brown, a telegram from Yahya asking for at least eight American F-104 fighter jets from the Jordanian air force.

On December 6, back at work in the White House, Nixon authorized the arms transfers to Pakistan, on the condition that they were conducted under the strictest cover. The shah was ready and willing to help, and apparently so were the Saudis. But Nixon double-checked on the transfer of fighter jets from Jordan.

"The way we would do that is to tell the King to move his planes and inform us that he has done it," Kissinger said. "We would have to tell him it is illegal, but if he does it we'll keep things under control."

"All right," Nixon said. "That's the way we play that."

The president and Kissinger met in the Oval Office that night, after another meeting of the Washington Special Actions Group, to discuss Indira Gandhi, General Yahya, and the war. "I was too easy on the goddamn woman when she was here," Nixon said. "She suckered us. . . . But let me tell you, she's going to pay. She is going to pay."

"This has been a great operation for the Indians," Kissinger replied. "It's going to lead to the overthrow of Yahya."

"Such a shame," said Nixon. "So sad. So sad."

* * *

Nixon, Kissinger, and Attorney General John Mitchell had a long talk about the crisis on the afternoon of December 8. All three were tense and tired, Haldeman recorded. Kissinger was threatening to resign, as he often did. Mitchell was dismayed at the prospect of running Nixon's reelection campaign. The president was once again suffering his dreadful insomnia, sinking into dark moods.

Nixon said they had to "cold-bloodedly make the decision" to act. "No more goddamn meetings."

Kissinger warned that West Pakistan could be smashed by "Soviet arms and Indian military force." This would affect "many countries threatened by the Soviet Union," especially in the Middle East. China might think that the United States was "too weak" to stop the destruction of an ally. He concluded, "We could give a note to the Chinese and say if you are ever going to move, this is the time."

Nixon agreed: "All right, that's what we'll do."

Mitchell concurred: "All they have to do is put their forces on the border."

The president told Kissinger to go to New York, convene a meeting with the American and Chinese ambassadors to the United Nations, George H. W. Bush and Huang Hua, and suggest that Chinese troops should threaten India. "I tell you, a movement of even some Chinese toward that border could scare those goddamn Indians to death," Nixon said.

Using the emergency "hot line" to the Kremlin for the first time, Nixon sent a stern message to Moscow: if India continued its attacks, it could lead to a U.S.-Soviet confrontation. Then the president ordered a ten-ship navy battle group, led by a nuclear-powered aircraft carrier, the USS *Enterprise*, into the theater of war—a show of force in the Bay of Bengal, on India's southeast coast. That would really scare them, Nixon said with satisfaction.*

But soon he became apoplectic, at times apocalyptic, as he reviewed the correlation of forces. What if the Chinese moved against India and the Soviets reacted with force? The regional conflict could become a global war.

"What do we do if the Soviets move against them?" Nixon wondered on December 12. "Start lobbing nuclear weapons in?"

"That will be the final showdown," Kissinger said. "If the Russians get away with facing down the Chinese and if the Indians get away with

---

* Nick Veliotes, President Reagan's future ambassador to Egypt, was privy to Nixon's decision to deploy the *Enterprise*; he worked for the deputy secretary of state, a member of Kissinger's Washington Special Actions Group, which met daily during the conflict. "I went into my boss and I said: 'Look, this is crazy,'" Veliotes recalled in a State Department oral history. "'All we can do here is upset the Indians.'" One show of force led to another: before Nixon left office, India tested its first nuclear weapon, leading Pakistan to develop its own bomb. "And, of course, it's all justified, in retrospect, by the fact Henry was secretly negotiating with the Chinese," Veliotes said. "We had to prove to the Chinese how tough we were."

licking the Pakistanis, what we are now having is the final—we may be looking down the gun barrel."

Nixon stared down it and said, "You've got the Soviet Union with 800 million Chinese, 600 million Indians, the balance of Southeast Asia terrorized, the Japanese immobile, the Europeans of course will suck after them, and the United States the only one."

Kissinger said, "You'll be alone."

Nixon replied, "We've been alone before."

* * *

On December 16, 1971, Yahya surrendered. He fell from power. The new nation of Bangladesh emerged from the ashes of East Pakistan. India was triumphant; Nixon was enraged. "Savages," he said. "We cannot have a stable world if we allow one member of the United Nations to cannibalize another. Cannibalize, that's the word."

By then, a new war had broken out inside Nixon's White House.

Two days before, on December 14, the muckraking syndicated newspaper columnist Jack Anderson began publishing a series of articles describing Nixon's "tilt toward Pakistan" with startling accuracy. Anderson quoted word for word from the transcribed minutes of Kissinger's war council, the Washington Special Actions Group, which met in the Situation Room, the most closely guarded office of the White House. The members included the chiefs and deputies of the CIA, the State Department, and the Pentagon. The transcripts Anderson cited were classified above top secret. They came from meetings held the week before his first column went to press and painted a particularly unflattering picture of Kissinger at his most imperious and intemperate.

John Ehrlichman, playing his role as Richard Nixon's private eye, quickly and indisputably established the source for Anderson's work. On December 21, ten minutes after the president arrived at the White House by helicopter, following a flight from Bermuda, Ehrlichman delivered his devastating news in the Oval Office. The documents Anderson had quoted from were kept in "only one place in the whole federal government," he said. "And that was here, in the Joint Chiefs of Staff liaison office of the National Security Council."

"Jesus Christ!" said Richard Nixon. He did not startle easily when it came to matters of political espionage.

"There were only two men in that office, and one's an admiral, and one's a yeoman," Ehrlichman continued. A yeoman is a navy petty officer—a clerk. The man in question was Yeoman Charles Radford. He knew Jack Anderson. They were friends and fellow Mormons.

"He had dinner with Jack Anderson the previous Sunday," Ehrlichman said. "He had been stationed in India for two years. He felt strongly about the India-Pakistan thing. So there was motive, opportunity, and access."

Radford, tearfully, had confessed to all this and more. Nixon was astonished. "How in the name of God do we have a yeoman having access to documents of that type?" he asked. Ehrlichman explained that Radford had been the eyes and ears of an admiral who reported directly to the chairman of the Joint Chiefs.

Radford was not only Anderson's source. He was the officially approved spy for the Joint Chiefs inside the White House.

The yeoman kept the nation's highest military officers informed about Nixon's secret plans and political agreements, about what went on behind the scenes between the president and foreign leaders. He had "systematically stolen documents from Henry's briefcase, Haig's briefcase, people's desks, anyplace and everyplace in the NSC apparatus that he can lay his hands on, and has duplicated them, and turned them over to the Joint Chiefs, through his boss, and this has been going on now for about 13 months," Ehrlichman said.

"Has that been a Joint Chiefs practice for a long time?" Nixon asked.

"Apparently so," Ehrlichman said.

J. Edgar Hoover himself had warned Nixon before his 1969 inauguration that he should be careful about what he said on the telephone: the Army Signal Corps monitored the presidential communications system and the White House switchboard. A corporal could eavesdrop on a president. But this was inside intelligence of a higher magnitude: the four-star generals and flag admirals of the Joint Chiefs spying on Nixon, Kissinger, and the National Security Council.

"Prosecuting is a possibility for the Joint Chiefs," the president said.

He turned to the attorney general for counsel. Mitchell was succinct. Cover it up, he said. "If you pursued it by way of prosecution, or even a public confrontation," he advised, "you would have the Joints Chiefs allied . . . directly against you." Mitchell concluded: "Paper this thing over."

The dilemma was deep. It went to the heart of the Constitution's command that elected civilians must control the uniformed military. Yeoman Radford was spying on the White House because the military chiefs of the United States did not trust their civilian leaders, up to and including Richard Nixon.

Radford had confessed to countless violations of the Espionage Act, the unauthorized disclosure of classified information, which could send him to prison for life. He had acted on orders from his superior, Adm. Robert Welander, the Joint Chiefs' liaison officer at the National Security Council. Welander reported directly to Adm. Thomas Moorer, chairman of the Joint Chiefs. Both admirals were as guilty as the yeoman. Public disclosure of these facts could make the Pentagon Papers case look like a misdemeanor.

That made going after Jack Anderson a very tricky question for the president. "If you start opening upon Anderson," Attorney General Mitchell said, "Lord knows where this is going to lead."

What about the yeoman? the president asked. "You wouldn't do anything about him?" Ehrlichman said, "You can't touch him because it would—" Nixon finished the thought: "Hurt the Joint Chiefs."

The White House tapes spun as Nixon hammered his fist down on his desk, righteously appalled. "We can't have this goddamn security problem!" The case, he said, was "a federal offense of the highest order."

* * *

Ehrlichman summoned Admiral Welander to his office in the West Wing of the White House for a taped-recorded interview on December 22. Ehrlichman said at the outset that he served as "the house detective" for the president. His aide David R. Young took notes. Young, thirty-five, intelligent, intense, a lawyer interested in everything from treaties to terrorism, was a founding member of the White House Special Investigations Unit, the crew charged with stopping leaks; he had been in on the botched black-bag job against Ellsberg's psychiatrist. The placard on his door at Room 16 of the Executive Office Building read, "Plumber."

Slowly, skillfully, with increasing severity, and with significant help from Young, who had put Yeoman Radford through an intense interrogation on a polygraph, Ehrlichman wrung a confession from the admiral.

"Your alter ego, this yeoman, was at a very critical crossroads, so to

speak, in the transmission of information in the national security apparatus," Ehrlichman said. "He has access to everything": CIA reports, NSC
records, classified State Department cables, Situation Room transcripts.

"I cover the whole waterfront," said Admiral Welander, and Radford
worked "exclusively for me."

Ehrlichman dug deeper: "This Anderson stuff. Can you account
for it in any way?" The admiral admitted, "I know it all comes from my
files."

"Does Admiral Moorer know?" Ehrlichman asked.

"The most significant things," Welander said, and "he knows that
Radford picked this up."

Ehrlichman and Young pressed him harder. The more they probed,
the worse things appeared. Yeoman Radford had stolen top-secret files
from Kissinger and Haig. Radford had rifled not only Kissinger's brief-
cases but his "burn bags," copies of top-secret material designated for
destruction in the name of national security. He backhanded everything
to Welander, who slipped it all to Moorer and the Joint Chiefs. The
Joint Chiefs and their White House spies saw decision papers drafted
for Nixon before the president read them. They had their hands on
proposals for foreign policies before Nixon saw them. They learned
about Kissinger's secret negotiations with the Chinese in Beijing and
the North Vietnamese in Paris as they happened—and not even Richard Helms, the director of central intelligence, had known about *that*.

"I've got a full account of our involvement in Cambodia from Day
One, which would make the Pentagon Papers pale by comparison,"
Welander said. "Almost anything you name."

How to shut down the spy ring without rupturing relations with the
Joint Chiefs? Nixon, Haldeman, Ehrlichman, and Mitchell wrestled with
the problem that day, and the next, sitting in the Oval Office while the
lights of the White House Christmas tree twinkled nearby in the iden-
tically shaped Blue Room.

The president truly wanted to prosecute the yeoman. But Haldeman
cautioned against a criminal case. And Mitchell sided with him.

"What we're doing here is, in effect, excusing a crime," Nixon said.
"It's a hell of a damn thing to do." But the admirals and generals had to
be kept silent and loyal.

"I think they'd be shocked to know what this guy did," the president said.

"*They know!*" Ehrlichman said. "Absolutely!"

"And they knew that he was stealing from Kissinger?"

"They had to."

The hard question confronted the president. Should there be a criminal prosecution or a court-martial? There was only one other alternative: cover-up.

"That's the question now," Ehrlichman told the president on December 23. "Admiral Welander thinks that we should put the yeoman in jail. Admiral Moorer thinks we should put Welander in jail." And Haldeman said Kissinger wanted Moorer keelhauled. "As you go up the ladder," he added, "everybody's going to crucify the guy under him." Nixon, Haldeman, and Ehrlichman laughed bitterly. "Everyone else should go to jail!" the president said.

But they absolutely had to "take care of the yeoman," Nixon said with finality on Christmas Eve. "Got any ideas?" he asked Ehrlichman.

"Yeah, but they're all illegal."

"All of them illegal?" the president said with a chuckle.

"Put him in a sack and drop him out of an airplane."

"That would do it," Nixon said.

* * *

Mitchell, the chief law enforcement officer of the United States, rested his case. He firmly decreed that the best course would be to prevent this high crime from becoming public knowledge. Keep it out of court. Close the liaison office. Consign the yeoman to oblivion—Radford went to a tiny naval base in Oregon—and send his commander to sea half a world away from Washington. Mitchell himself told Admiral Moorer that his spy ring was broken.

Above all, said Mitchell, they had to stop "the fuck-up of security" inside the White House. The president agreed. "The main thing is to keep it under as close control as we can," Nixon said to him. They ordered a warrantless wiretap on Radford.

Nixon refused Kissinger's demand for Moorer's dismissal. "I don't care if Moorer is guilty," the president said. "The military must survive." Kissinger flew into a towering rage. "They can spy on him and spy on me and betray us!" he shouted at Ehrlichman. The Radford case would have very serious consequences, he warned. And it did. "The worst thing about it is . . . you start getting paranoid," Haldeman told the president. "You start wondering about everything and everybody." Nixon replied that even paranoids had enemies. "Don't be too damn sure about anybody!" he warned. "If there's ever anything important, just don't tell anybody."

"It's a horrible way to have to work," Haldeman sighed. "But it's essential."

Already secretive by instinct and experience, Nixon immediately tightened his inner circle so closely that very few people knew his mind on any crucial matter at any given time. None was in his Cabinet. Alone, unquestioned, unchallenged, Nixon ran the military, intelligence, and national security policies of the American government through Kissinger and Haig. And Kissinger himself later reflected that the Radford affair fueled a far greater disaster. While the fear and secrecy and willful ignorance might not exonerate the crimes of Watergate, he wrote a decade later, "it might partially explain their origin."

On January 5, 1972, Richard Nixon formally began his last race. He placed Mitchell, still attorney general, in charge of his reelection. Some of the most tough-minded and least-sensible aides to Haldeman and Ehrlichman moved one block down Pennsylvania Avenue, to the headquarters of the Committee to Re-elect the President, inevitably nicknamed CREEP. The Plumbers ran rampant. Very quickly, things started happening that no one knew about.

CHAPTER FIFTEEN

"Night and Fog"

NINETEEN SEVENTY-TWO should have been the greatest year of Richard Nixon's life. His visit to China was set for the end of February, and a summit meeting in Moscow would follow in the spring. The trips would appear as adventurous as the Apollo missions to the moon; no American president had ever set foot on the Great Wall or inside the Kremlin.

But Nixon, with his uncanny political instinct, foresaw trouble ahead. He wrote in his diary on his fifty-ninth birthday, January 9, 1972, that he faced "immense opportunities and, of course, equally great dangers." He knew the summitry was in some part symbolism and showmanship, acting out diplomatic games with his enemies, playing politics with the American people. His true goal was, as ever, trying to find a way out of the war.

"It isn't about China and it isn't about Russia," he told members of his Cabinet on February 2. "It's about South Vietnam."

He had resumed the bombing of North Vietnam in the hope of ending the seven-year nightmare. "Crack 'em, crack 'em, crack 'em," he ordered Admiral Moorer that same day. He wanted the rules of engagement "interpreted very, very broadly." They were. The U.S. Air Force continually bombed North Vietnam under the guise of "protective reaction strikes"—retaliation to enemy firing. The American attacks in fact had been planned far in advance, not in retaliation but as aggression, and the records were accordingly falsified. An air force general was eventually reprimanded. But he was acting on the highest authority.

The bombing began again because Vietnamization was not working, and Nixon knew it. American intelligence predicted a major enemy offensive at Easter; the South Vietnamese Army was in no shape to withstand it. The American death toll was past fifty thousand and rising. Some twenty thousand had died on Nixon's watch, a slaughter that might have ended at the start of his first term.

"Let's not have any illusions," he told Kissinger and Haldeman. "We talk about patriotism, loyalty, principle, and the rest, and we say we hope to God there's enough of that in the country . . . enough to support the bombing of the North."

"It's the hope thing," he said. "The China thing was important from one standpoint only: hope." His fellow citizens loved the Ping-Pong diplomacy and the pandas: "Getting to know you—all that bullshit."

"The American people are suckers," Nixon said. "Gray Middle America—they're suckers."

But he needed their support to win reelection—and to end the war without a retreat or a disguised defeat. The "suckers" Nixon sneered at were his core constituency: dedicated patriots who despised the pacifists and peaceniks in the Democratic Party. Nixon's potential opponents in the presidential election already were forming a circular firing squad as their first primaries approached. His political strategists already were working to ensure that the weakest candidate would be the last man standing against the president.

But for Nixon, the worst problems lay within his administration. He was barely on speaking terms with Secretary of Defense Mel Laird and Secretary of State Bill Rogers; he was sure that Laird had had a hand in the Joint Chiefs' spy ring, and he was unsure that Rogers had a shred of diplomatic judgment. He had no faith left in Gen. Creighton Abrams, his top commander in Saigon. All this made a strategy for exiting Vietnam difficult at best.

Nixon sensed that the man who would replace John Mitchell as attorney general, Richard Kleindienst, was lacking in political wisdom. Right again: Kleindienst lied at his confirmation hearings. He did not disclose Nixon's blunt order to withdraw a Justice Department brief in an antitrust case against International Telephone and Telegraph, one of the world's biggest conglomerates and a major contributor to the Republican National Committee.

Kleindienst did not know, of course, that the order was on tape.

"That brief has to be filed tomorrow," Kleindienst had told the president. "Your order is not to file?"

"My order is to drop the Goddamned thing, you son of a bitch! Don't you understand the English language?" the president shouted. "Is that clear?"

"Yeah," Kleindienst said with a nervous laugh, "I understand that."

He eventually was confirmed as attorney general. For his testimony, he became the first Cabinet officer since 1929 to be convicted of breaking the law. He would not be the last.

* * *

The miscreants gathering under John Mitchell as he prepared to take command of CREEP should have given pause to all concerned. They were putting together plots that would lead to far greater personal and political disasters.

The prelude was "Operation Sandwedge," a twelve-page plan written at Haldeman's command and under John Dean's supervision. Its author was Jack Caulfield, the former New York City police detective who served officially as a White House liaison to law enforcement, but unofficially as undercover gumshoe for Ehrlichman and Dean.

Caulfield proposed setting up a private company based in New York City to create a "covert intelligence-gathering capability" against Democratic candidates for president that would serve as a "critical contribution to the re-election of Richard Nixon." This cover organization, to be called Corporate Security Consultants International, would be financed, to the tune of four hundred thousand dollars, entirely by "lucrative consulting contracts" with "trustworthy Republican corporate giants," disguising any connection with the Nixon administration or the campaign.

Caulfield's plan specifically called for "black-bag jobs"—though he insisted later that this meant carrying covert campaign cash, not carrying out break-ins, burglaries, and bugging, as the term was used by the FBI. His spy network would set up "surveillance of Democratic primaries, conventions and meetings," to supply the Nixon campaign with "derogatory information" on the Democrats. And it would take care of security (including electronic countermeasures against bugs and taps) at CREEP headquarters. Caulfield had just the man for the job, recommended by Al Wong, the Secret Service agent who oversaw the White House taping system. The man was James McCord, a wiretapping specialist just retired after twenty-one years at the CIA.

Sandwedge aimed above all at the "penetration of nominees' entourage and headquarters with undercover personnel." Its primary target was a skilled politico, Lawrence O'Brien, the chairman of the Democratic National Committee, a Kennedy man to the soles of his patent-leather shoes. This was catnip for Nixon. He hated O'Brien with a passion—the man had run JFK's campaign headquarters in the 1960 election—and he would be happy to destroy him by any means necessary. The Sandwedge proposal suggested exploiting O'Brien's financial ties to the billionaire Howard Hughes, the inventor, film producer, Las Vegas hotel-and-casino magnate, and increasingly notorious lunatic. An IRS investigation of the reclusive Hughes, its existence known to very few people, had revealed that he had a secret $180,000-a-year contract with O'Brien as a lobbyist.*

Sandwedge looked promising at first. Haldeman had sent his twenty-eight-year-old aide Gordon Strachan to supervise work on the program with Mitchell, who was, awkwardly, still the attorney general and starting work as the chief of CREEP. Strachan had sent Haldeman talking points for a meeting on Sandwedge with Mitchell: "From the campaign funds I need $800,000—300 for surveillance, 300 for polls and 200 for miscellaneous." Sandwedge, and the $300,000 for surveillance, were templates for Watergate.

But when Dean took Caulfield to see John Mitchell on November 24, 1971, the White House cop got a brush-off and a vague offer of something better later on. (He became assistant director of the Bureau of Alcohol, Tobacco and Firearms at the Treasury Department.) Caulfield left the attorney general's office alone, and as he walked out he saw

---

* Hughes financed Republicans and Democrats alike, currying political favor. In particular, he wanted to stop the testing of nuclear weapons in Nevada, one of his many phobias. In 1970, Hughes secretly left Las Vegas for the Bahamas, where his friends included Bebe Rebozo; that year, he sent Rebozo one hundred thousand dollars in cash for Nixon's 1972 campaign.

none other than G. Gordon Liddy waiting to go in. Caulfield did not know it, but Liddy was about to hijack Sandwedge.

Caulfield took on another politically sensitive job the following week: wiretapping the president's ne'er-do-well brother Donald Nixon and monitoring his son Don Junior. Watching over Donald the elder was one of Caulfield's long-standing assignments at the White House; Donald was a miscreant, a magnet for con artists and "wheeler-dealers," as Caulfield wrote to Dean. Fifteen years before, Howard Hughes had loaned Donald Nixon Sr. $205,000 to underwrite a restaurant in Nixon's hometown, Whittier, California. The loan was a skeleton that kept peeking out of Richard Nixon's closet.

Now Donald was dealing with a far shadier financier, a world-class swindler named Robert Vesco, who had given $200,000 to Nixon's campaign coffers. Vesco and Donald Senior were trying to buy a failed and fraudulent bank in Beirut, Lebanon, whose major creditor was the U.S. government, using Don Junior as a front man.

"Donald Nixon's son—the President's nephew—came to Beirut with an entourage which included an American wheeler-dealer," namely Vesco, in December 1971, recalled Robert Oakley, then a State Department officer in Lebanon, later U.S. ambassador to Pakistan under Presidents Reagan and George H. W. Bush. "They wanted to buy the bank," but "we didn't like the smell of it. We knew that the bank had been corrupt and that the man accompanying Nixon's nephew also did not have a savory reputation."

In short order, the American ambassador to Lebanon, William Buffum, received a message from Attorney General Mitchell requesting "favorable consideration to the Nixon offer. There was also a call from Haldeman's office in the White House, making the same request," Oakley recalled. The embassy declined, and its refusal "hit a sore spot," he said. "We heard a lot of squawking and noise; we understood that the Attorney General's office denied that Mitchell had ever been involved," he said. "We had created a huge flap in Washington"—the first among many in 1972.

* * *

The office of the attorney general of the United States is an enormous room exuding the grandeur of the rule of law. On January 27, 1972, the nation's chief law enforcement office, John Mitchell, convened with another one of Haldeman's baby-faced aides, Jeb Stuart Magruder, who had cut his teeth running Don Rumsfeld's campaign for Congress a decade before and now served as Mitchell's deputy at CREEP. The president's counsel John Dean sat alongside, representing the White House.

The meeting was run by G. Gordon Liddy. Technically, Liddy's role was CREEP's in-house lawyer, but that was a cover for his real job: the White House plumber in chief. Liddy was regarded by many of his colleagues at the time, and thereafter, as a sociopath, a man to be feared.

The former FBI agent had prepared an elaborate plan code-named Gemstone—Sandwedge on steroids—which he now formally presented to Mitchell and Dean, along with seven separate flow charts propped up on easels. Gemstone was a conspiracy to violate federal laws including kidnapping, burglary, and warrantless wiretapping, all in the name of the reelection of the president of the United States.

The first of its components was Diamond. Liddy planned to kidnap anti-Nixon demonstrators at the Republican National Convention, drug them, and take them to Mexico. Had anyone present had the requisite sense of humor, he might have suggested that the hippies who were Liddy's targets might actually enjoy being drugged and taken to Mexico, but Liddy had set a grimmer tone by entitling this chart "Nacht und Nebel" ("Night and Fog"), a term used by Nazi storm troopers for disappearing people.

Opal was a series of black-bag jobs for planting bugs at key Democratic headquarters. Emerald was electronic eavesdropping on Democrats' campaign planes. Quartz was listening in on microwave telephone traffic. Topaz was photographing documents at the candidates' headquarters in Washington and the Miami Beach convention halls and hotels. Ruby would place spies in the field organizations and headquarters of the Democratic candidates for president. Turquoise would employ Hunt's compadres from the Bay of Pigs to sabotage the air-conditioning at the convention. Then came Sapphire, in which a houseboat docked in Miami Beach would be used by prostitutes who would lure politicos; and Crystal, which would record and photograph their liaisons for blackmail. Finally came a plan to finance the long-shot campaign of Representative Shirley Chisholm, the first black woman to run for president. Its intent was to divert black Democrats from their likely nominee; its code name, Coal, indicated Liddy's political and racial sensibilities.

Hunt said he could finance the entire operation for under one million dollars.

The attorney general said this was not quite what he had in mind as a campaign intelligence operation. He told Liddy to scale the plan back, come back with a more modest proposal—say, half a million—and, by the way, burn the charts.

* * *

Richard Nixon had been contemplating a plan to destroy Lawrence O'Brien for almost two years. Haldeman wrote in his diary on March 4, 1970, that Nixon wanted "to move hard on Larry O'Brien now that he's back as DNC chairman," starting by going after his income tax returns. Haldeman was warned by Tom Charles Huston, whose playbook of dirty tricks had just been printed, that "making sensitive political inquiries at the IRS is about as safe a procedure as trusting a whore." Haldeman quickly sent an "eyes only" order to John Dean to have the IRS back off an inquiry involving none other than Howard Hughes: "As you probably remember there was a Hughes/Don Nixon loan controversy years ago, and the prosecution of this case could reopen that entire issue which could be very damaging politically." Caulfield had warned Dean from the start that digging into Hughes risked a "counter-scandal."

But the White House soon discovered, through the IRS, O'Brien's secret retainer as a lobbyist for Howard Hughes. Someone made that contract disappear. "Concerning Howard Hughes," Dwight Chapin, Nixon's deputy assistant, wrote to Chuck Colson on December 12, 1970, "his retainer with Larry O'Brien was cancelled as a result of the latest escapades."

So Nixon had inside information on O'Brien. But what did O'Brien have on Nixon? Did he know Nixon himself had received secret contributions from Howard Hughes? That Bebe Rebozo was holding one hundred thousand dollars in cash from Hughes for Nixon? Or that Hughes had made another secret campaign contribution to Nixon in February 1972?

Nixon's commerce secretary, Maurice Stans, left the Cabinet that month to become the reelection campaign's finance chairman. In his first days as CREEP's chief fund-raiser, Stans flew to Managua, Nicaragua, where he met with none other than Howard Hughes. Increasingly irrational and drug-addled, Hughes had fled from a hideaway in the Bahamas, finding refuge by renting the entire top floor of Managua's best hotel. His move to Nicaragua came with help from the notorious American ambassador and Nixon crony Turner B. Shelton—and from Maurice Stans: "The Secretary of Commerce came down and cleared the way for him to be there," said Bob White, then the number two man in the American embassy. Few plausible reasons brought Stans to Nicaragua; it is implausible that he left with an empty briefcase.

Stans was facing a crucial deadline. A newly enacted law required the public disclosure of campaign contributions to political candidates, effective April 7, 1972; the law's intent was to keep suitcases crammed with cash out of the American political system. Corporate contributions were forbidden under existing law, but if they were in hand before midnight on April 6, no one would know. So Stans had ten weeks to collect as much cash as possible. He was greatly assisted by his deputy, the president's lawyer, Herbert Kalmbach. Stans worked the corporations and the executives. Kalmbach played his field of expertise: millionaires seeking ambassadorships. One, W. Clement Stone, pledged $3 million. Unfortunately, Stone wanted London, which already was occupied by Ambassador Walter Annenberg, who gave $254,000 in order to stay on. In all, Kalmbach collected $706,000 from thirteen contributors who were given ambassadorships by Nixon after the 1972 election. Together, the finance chairmen collected about $20 million for CREEP before the deadline. Campaign headquarters, and the White House itself, were awash in cash.

Nixon still worried: Did the Democratic National Committee know who had contributed to CREEP, and how much? Did O'Brien know?

* * *

John Mitchell, his campaign deputy Jeb Magruder, John Dean, and Gordon Liddy reconvened at the attorney general's office a week after their first Gemstone conference, on February 4, 1972. All four eventually went to prison for the events that resulted from this meeting. Here is where Watergate was born. No one can prove its paternity, but its progenitor was Richard Nixon, who at that date was preparing for his momentous visit to China.

Liddy presented Mitchell, Magruder, and Dean with a scaled-down version of Gemstone. The plan still focused on the bugging and wiretapping of President Nixon's political opponents. Its targets specifically included the offices of Lawrence O'Brien and the Democratic National Committee at the Watergate Hotel.

They did not get an immediate decision from Mitchell. He was in a state of misery; his wife, Martha, whom he loved dearly, had been an alcoholic and an emotional basket case for several years. He had reason to fear that she was becoming mentally ill. He was disengaged, drinking, still running the Justice Department, dreading the campaign to come. He didn't focus on the plan before him. He did not say yes or no.

Enraged, Liddy told his colleague Howard Hunt to arrange a meeting with Nixon's hard-as-nails aide Chuck Colson. They gathered in Colson's grandly appointed suite at the Executive Office Building. Liddy wanted action and he knew how to get it. He knew that Magruder, who was running CREEP during Mitchell's mental absence, was mortally terrified of Colson. He also knew that Colson had been hammering Magruder about the need for better political intelligence on the president's enemies. So he explained the impasse to Colson, who immediately picked up the telephone, called Magruder, and told him to get a decision on Liddy's plan.

"This Watergate thing kept coming back—clearly because of the Howard Hughes issue: O'Brien," Magruder recounted in an oral history recorded years later, after he had done his time in prison and become a Presbyterian pastor. "O'Brien was a consultant to Hughes; they wanted to know if Hughes knew anything that would prove negative." He finally presented the plan for Mitchell's approval seven weeks later, during a weekend at the Rebozo retreat in Key Biscayne. "Mitchell signed off on the Watergate break-in in Key Biscayne; I think we all reluctantly signed off. None of us were interested in it at the Committee; we were pushed, first by Colson, then by Haldeman. We were continually told that the president wanted it done."

All this is confirmed on a White House tape recorded on December 10, 1972, when it still seemed impossible that these plans would ruin Richard Nixon.

"I knew we were bugging the other side," Haldeman said.

"Perfectly legitimate," the president said.

"Obviously what happened," Haldeman said on this difficult-to-discern tape, "Mitchell set this apparatus up. . . . Then we started pushing . . . Mitchell was pushing on using them. There was this—"

"—paper," Nixon said.

"Secret papers," Haldeman said. "And financial data that O'Brien had."

That was the reason for the Watergate break-in: a pure product of Nixon's obsession. "If this obsession . . . seems irrational," John Dean wrote in 2014, "there was little about Watergate that was otherwise."

But Nixon tried his best to explain it in one of his last televised interviews, not long before he died. "1972, as you know, was a very big year," he said. "We went to China. We went to Russia. . . . And here was a small thing, and we fouled it up beyond belief."

"I would advise all that follow me in the position as President: do the big things as well as you can, but when a small thing is there, deal with it, and deal with it fast; get it out of the way," Nixon said. "If you don't, it's going to become big, and then it may destroy you."

CHAPTER SIXTEEN

"From one extreme to another"

So Nixon went to China. And only Nixon, cold warrior playing peace-maker, could have gone to China in that era. The trip was seen at the time as the greatest achievement of his presidency.

Nixon made sure the world saw it. Live broadcasts, via American military channels, went to the major networks. Millions sipping coffee at breakfast watched Nixon toasting his hosts with mao-tai, the potent Chinese liquor, while the Red Army orchestra played "America the Beautiful" at a sumptuous banquet.

"It had a tremendous impact back here in the United States," said Winston Lord, Kissinger's Chinese-speaking aide, who attended and transcribed all the president's meetings with the Communist leaders. "In fact, this coverage led to almost instant romance and euphoria. That was overstated. After all, horrible things were still going on in China. We swung from one extreme to another, from picturing China as an implacable enemy to a new friend."

Kissinger warned Nixon at the outset that "the intangibles of your China visit will prove more important than the tangible results." He was right. Very few knew how close the summit came to being a diplomatic debacle. And only in retrospect did future American ambassadors to China, such as Winston Lord, see that romancing the world's biggest Communist dictatorship would create new tensions and turmoil, after the euphoria was over.

* * *

Nixon and his entourage of nearly two hundred Americans spent two days flying across America and the Pacific, stopping in Hawaii and Guam. In a sign of what was to come, Nixon and Kissinger put Secretary of State Rogers and his Asia hands in the rear of Air Force One.

They landed in Beijing on February 21, 1972. The president was driven through eerily empty streets; the Chinese had barricaded the route. He engaged in informal chitchat with Prime Minister Zhou En-lai and then went to the government's guest compound, a calm oasis within the cold, gray capital. About ninety minutes later, unannounced and unexpected, Zhou arrived and asked if Nixon would like to see Chairman Mao right now—an utter surprise. The president took off with Kissinger and Lord.

"We had no idea when they'd be back, or what would happen," Haldeman wrote.

Nixon entered the leaders' compound in the Forbidden City, the immense complex of red-and-gold palaces facing Tiananmen Square, where Chinese emperors had ruled for nearly five hundred years. He walked down a dark, long hallway and into a modestly appointed study. There, attended by two nurses, sat the last of the twentieth century's great dictators, a frail old man of seventy-eight, but still projecting power.

The United States knew less about Mao's China than Mao knew about the United States. Many years would pass before Western eyes saw reliable accounts of the horrors under Mao, the many millions of deaths by starvation caused by his mad schemes to modernize China, the murderous brutality of his political purges, the merciless repression of his rule.

Mao, like Nixon, was a farmer's son, born nearly twenty years before the president, in 1893. He became one of the founders of the Communist Party of China in 1921, inspired by Lenin's Russian Revolution. In 1927, a new Chinese leader, Chiang Kai-shek, began killing and jailing Communists. Mao led a guerrilla army of peasants into the mountains, far south of Beijing. Seven years later, Chiang tried to destroy them. Mao led a strategic retreat, the Long March, to the north. Perhaps two-thirds of the original one hundred thousand Maoists survived the grim trek over mountains and through swamps. While Mao was leading the Long March, Nixon was entering law school.

Then Japan attacked China in 1937. Chiang made a desperate strategic alliance with Mao. Together, throughout World War II, they fought the Japanese. When Japan was defeated in 1945, Mao and Chiang turned on each other again, and China fell into a brutal civil war. Four years later, in October 1949, Mao triumphed and proclaimed the birth of the People's Republic of China in Beijing's Tiananmen Square. In December 1950, seven weeks after Nixon was elected as a senator, Mao sent an enormous regiment into the Korean War, where his troops slaughtered thousands of American soldiers and altered the tide of battle.

Chiang fled to the island of Taiwan after Mao's revolution and established the anticommunist Republic of China; he remained its leader, at the age of eighty-four, when Nixon arrived in Beijing. American support for Taiwan had been absolute for two decades, a political imperative for Republicans. Nixon had been Chiang's staunch supporter, like every American president since Harry Truman—until now.

* * *

Seated in plush leather armchairs in the book-lined study, Nixon and Mao began to exchange pleasantries.

"I have read the Chairman's poems and speeches, and I knew he was a professional philosopher," Nixon said. The Chinese laughed. The two sides bantered. Nixon flattered Mao: "The Chairman's writings moved a nation and have changed the world."

"I haven't been able to change it," Mao said flatly. Switching subjects, he turned to Taiwan. "Our common old friend, Generalissimo Chiang Kai-shek . . . calls us Communist bandits," the chairman said. Nixon responded, "What does the Chairman call Chiang Kai-shek?" Zhou replied, "A bandit. . . . We abuse each other." Mao said, "Actually, the history of our friendship with him is much longer than the history of your friendship with him."

Nixon said, "Yes, I know."

Mao abruptly changed topics again. "We two must not monopolize the whole show," he told Nixon. "It won't do if we don't let Dr. Kissinger have a say. You have been famous about your trips to China."

"It was the President who set the direction and worked out the plan," Kissinger said with false modesty.

"He is a very wise assistant to say it that way," Nixon responded, drawing laughter from Mao. "He doesn't look like a secret agent. He is the only man in captivity who could go to Paris twelve times and Beijing once and no one knew it, except possibly a couple of pretty girls." Now Zhou laughed as Nixon made fun of Kissinger's reputation as a swinger: "Anyone who uses pretty girls as a cover must be the greatest diplomat of all time."

Chairman Mao, who had had many concubines as a younger man, said, "So your girls are very often made use of?"

President Nixon replied, "It would get me into great trouble if I used girls as a cover."

"Especially during elections," Zhou said, still laughing.

Nixon tried to return to the hard issues between them: the two Chinas, Vietnam, U.S.-Soviet relations—"the immediate and urgent problems." But Mao said, "All those troublesome problems, I don't want to get into very much." In the remaining half hour, Nixon did most of the talking. Mao's replies were disjointed. Nixon saw the chairman starting to fade.

The president concluded: "The chairman's life is well-known to all of us. He came from a very poor family to the top of the most populous nation in the world, a great nation. . . . I also came from a very poor family, and to the top of a very great nation. History has brought us together. The question is whether we, with different philosophies, but both with feet on the ground, and having come from the people, can make a breakthrough that will serve not just China and America, but the whole world in the years ahead. And that is why we are here."

Mao responded, "It is all right to talk well and also all right if there are no agreements"—an odd note to end on. The two leaders rose, and Mao walked the Americans to the door, moving in a slow shuffle. He told the president that he was not well. Nixon said he looked good. "Appearances are deceiving," the chairman said. Mao's last public appearance had taken place on May Day 1971. He would remain an invisible emperor until he died in September 1976.

* * *

The question persisted: how would the two sides agree on a joint statement, a communiqué set to be issued at the end of the summit, in Shanghai? Zhou had suggested in his 1971 meetings with Kissinger "a different kind of communiqué, which was unprecedented in diplomatic practice, in which each side would state its own position," Winston Lord said. "We had been separated, we had been hostile to each other, and we had these continuing differences. So when we get to agreements, people will believe us because they have seen our candor beforehand."

"Frankly, this was a brilliant idea," Lord said. But nothing else had been agreed to; each word would have to be negotiated that week.

The Shanghai communiqué had to address the issue of the two Chinas. A dramatic break in the U.S. diplomatic relationship with Taiwan would appall millions of Americans, including prominent members of the Nixon administration. Among those who had declared unswerving support for Taiwan was the American ambassador to the United Nations, George H. W. Bush.

"The conventional way," Nixon said to Zhou in a brief meeting before the night's grand banquet, was "to have discussions and discover differences, which we will do, and then put out a weasel-worded communiqué covering up the problems." Zhou responded, "If we were to act like that we would be not only deceiving the people, first of all, we would be deceiving ourselves."

Through five days of pomp and pageants, featuring a visit to the Great Wall of China—"It truly is a great wall," Nixon famously said—Kissinger and Lord labored long nights with their Chinese counterparts on the wording of the communiqué. Secretary of State Rogers remained on the sidelines, shut out by Nixon's orders, at Kissinger's demand.

Nixon and Zhou spoke at length about Vietnam. The president asked the prime minister several times to send a message to Hanoi stating that Nixon wanted a military and political settlement, but without overthrowing the Saigon government. He pounded away, hoping the Chinese would help him end the Vietnam War. But that hope was an illusion.

"Why not give this up?" Zhou told him. "You should adopt a most courageous attitude and withdraw." China and North Vietnam were not the closest allies, but if the war went on, "we will, of course, continue our aid to them."

Zhou insisted time and again that "the Taiwan question is the crucial question. . . . Once agreement is reached on that, all others can be solved easily." Nixon replied, "My goal is normalization with the People's Republic. I realize that solving the Taiwan problem is indispensable to achieving that goal." But he could not allow his opponents "a chance to seize upon the communiqué and say that the President of the United States came 16,000 miles in order to repudiate a commitment to the government on Taiwan."

The president said he would have to "sell" his own secretary of state on a solution. "That is our problem." Kissinger worked all night to resolve it. The only solution, he concluded, was to allow China to call for "the liberation of Taiwan" and the withdrawal of American military forces from the island. The document was drafted. The president read it and approved.

Nixon allowed Rogers to meet Zhou at a brief meeting at the Beijing airport on February 26. But he did not allow Rogers to see the communiqué itself until some hours later, at an overnight rest stop in Hangzhou, a resort town one hundred miles outside Shanghai. Rogers showed the text of the communiqué to Marshall Green, the assistant secretary of state for East Asia and the Pacific.

Green immediately saw a fatal flaw. The communiqué had a paragraph saying that the United States reaffirmed its commitments to all its allies in Asia—with one exception. It did not even mention America's Cold War treaties with Taiwan.

"This would almost certainly be seized upon by the world press, and especially by those in the Republican party who were opposed to the President's trip," including members of Nixon's own Cabinet, who would charge that the President had sold Taiwan down the river, Green wrote in a privately published State Department memoir. The language could be interpreted as saying Beijing "could attack Taiwan without involving the U.S." The secretary of state immediately called the president's guesthouse. He got Haldeman on the phone instead. Haldeman refused to put Nixon on the line. He said the president had already approved the statement.

Hours later, after 1:00 a.m., Green was awakened by the news that "all hell had broken loose in the Presidential suite."

The mild-mannered secretary of state finally had gotten through to the president to warn him in the strongest language: do not sell out a long-standing ally. Rogers said that "this communiqué was a disaster" and that "President Nixon was going to get killed at home and around the world," Winston Lord vividly recalled many years later, and now Nixon had to make "a terrible decision."

The Politburo of the Chinese Communist Party had already approved the communiqué—and so had the president. But now Nixon feared that the press would surely ferret out the essential fact that the United States was betraying Taiwan. That could turn his great achievement abroad into a political disaster at home.

"He said: 'Henry, you've got to go back to the Chinese,'" Lord recounted, which was "embarrassing, to say the least. It was our own fault for having cut out the State Department in the negotiations. . . . The omission of Taiwan would have been glaring."

Kissinger dreaded telling Zhou En-lai that the United States needed to reopen the Taiwan issue. The public release of the announcement in Shanghai was set for that evening, Sunday, February 27—and it was already well past midnight.

* * *

The presidential party flew to Shanghai in the morning. Zhou En-lai was there, and a farewell banquet was set to take place after the formal release of the communiqué. Zhou made the rounds at the high-rise Ching Kiang government guesthouse, where the Americans were ensconced, making a point of dropping in on Secretary of State Rogers and Marshall Green, whom he had barely seen in the course of the week.

After Zhou left, the secretary of state again demanded to see the president. Haldeman recorded the confrontation: "Rogers arrived at the suite and said he wanted to see the P. The P originally first said, tell him I'm asleep or something, then he agreed to see him, and had him come in. Rogers made the point that he wasn't trying to undercut the communiqué, that he would support it, but Rogers did want it understood that there were, in his mind, some real problems. . . . P clearly hit Bill hard, and said he expected him to tell his bureaucracy to stay behind us 100 percent."

Green recalled twenty-five years later that Nixon had the penthouse suite, Kissinger was one flight below, and Rogers was on the next one down—on the thirteenth floor: "The symbolism escaped no one." He was perplexed when Kissinger invited him to join an off-the-record briefing for American reporters that afternoon. "I was not happy about the prospect of being conspicuously identified with a communiqué I found badly flawed, and it was left unclear whether that flaw would remain," he recounted. "Kissinger never told me."

Not until the briefing was under way, and copies of the communiqué circulated, was it clear that the flawed passage had vanished.

Kissinger had been up all night, working in secret to avoid a disaster of his own making, and winning Zhou's tacit approval to rework the statement. At the last minute, "Zhou En-lai handled the matter very skillfully," Lord said. "He tried to avoid making this situation any more awkward and embarrassing than it really was." And Kissinger, answering a planted question from a reporter, verbally reaffirmed America's commitment to Taiwan.

It was weasel-worded, to quote Nixon, but it worked. The president privately acknowledged, in an Oval Office talk three weeks later, that the communiqué "had very little to do with substance." The symbolism, the pictures of Nixon and Zhou feasting together, was what would endure. As Haldeman wrote, "The network coverage of four hours, live, of the banquet . . . got all the facts the P wanted, such as his use of chopsticks, his toast, Zhou's toast, the P's glass-clinking, etc. So that came off very well."

One last banquet, and many more toasts, and Nixon sat in his Shanghai penthouse, drinking a bottle of Chinese firewater and talking for hours after midnight to the exhausted Kissinger. The tireless teetotaler Haldeman took it in with his gimlet eye: "Henry sitting on the couch just itching to go to bed, which I tried to bring about several times, but the P made the point that Zhou En-lai stays up all night, so will he. He ordered some *Mao Tai* and had several of those, which he had also done at dinner, and had at least half a dozen before and during lunch today. He did finally let us go out on his terrace and take a look at Shanghai at night. . . . Obviously, he was feeling the historic nature of the occasion."

* * *

Shanghai looks east over the Pacific, toward America, and as Nixon cast his gaze over the night sky, he could foresee good fortune. In eleven weeks, he would travel to Moscow for a summit with the Soviets, signing treaties, sealing his status as a great statesman. At home, his Democratic opponents were in disarray. Only one cloud darkened his horizon.

Zhou En-lai warned Nixon on the morning of February 28, just before he left on Air Force One, "If the war in Vietnam . . . does not stop, no matter what form it continues in, it will be impossible to relax tensions." And China would continue its military, economic, and political support for America's enemy.

Twelve hundred miles southwest of Shanghai, Hanoi's leaders were preparing their biggest military campaign against the United States in four years. They had been planning the attacks for nine months. Their official military history laid out their ultimate goal: to force the United States "to negotiate an end to the war from a position of defeat."

Nixon knew the offensive was coming—and that it would come at the time and place of the enemy's choosing. He knew only one way to strike back.

"We'll bomb the hell out of the bastards. There's not going to be anymore screwing around," Nixon told Kissinger in the Oval Office on March 14. "If they think . . . I am just going to roll over and play dead, they're crazy."

CHAPTER SEVENTEEN

"This is the supreme test"

Nixon had only a month to savor the glory of his China trip. On March 30, 1972, he and Kissinger were thinking over May's summit meeting in Moscow when a news flash hit the Oval Office.

"It looks as if they are attacking in Vietnam," Kissinger said.

"The battle has begun?" asked the president. "Should we start bombing right now?" He continued: "I'm not concerned about the attack, but I am concerned about the counterattack. By God, you've got the Air Force there. Now, get them off their ass and get them up there and hit everything that moves."

North Vietnam surged south across the demilitarized zone with troops, tanks, artillery, and a few Soviet-made fighter jets. American soldiers and their allies based in northern outposts of South Vietnam (Quang Tri, Hue, Da Nang) began facing a murderous barrage. As the enemy advanced, a U.S. Marine growled at a reporter, "I don't know any more if I'm in northern South Vietnam or southern North Vietnam."

The ground war turned grim as thousands of ARVN, the troops of the Army of the Republic of Vietnam, deserted their posts and fled. Reports of a rout at Quang Tri reached the White House in seventy-two hours.

"We lose if the ARVN collapses," Nixon told Kissinger on April 3.

"If the ARVN collapses a lot of other things will collapse around here," Nixon said. "We're playing a much bigger game. We're playing a Russian game, a Chinese game, an election game—and we're not going to have the ARVN collapse."

Nixon faced fateful, fatal decisions. Bombing North Vietnam, along with inflicting death and destruction, promised dangers on political battlefronts at home and abroad. Yet the merest chance of an American military defeat could devastate his power to negotiate with Russia and China from a position of omnipotence. He feared that this would destroy his dream of creating, as he put it, a new generation of peace. Above all, he was afraid he could lose the election if it looked like he might lose the war.

"For the President, battlefield success became paramount," said Frederick Z. Brown, the American consul general in Da Nang at the time of the 1972 attack. "If that meant relying primarily upon U.S. air power rather than upon the South Vietnamese armed forces, so be it. . . . The United States replied in massive form, in a way that nobody, nobody expected."

The diaries of Admiral Moorer and H. R. Haldeman recorded the president's commands on April 4. "There will be no consideration of restraints," he told Moorer. "Everything we do must be concentrated on breaking the back of the enemy. . . . We are not going to lose this one no matter what it costs." Haldeman wrote, "The P's massing a huge attack force, naval ships for gunning from the sea, tremendous number of additional bombers, and he's going to start using B-52s for the first time to bomb North Vietnam as soon as the weather clears."

American gunships approached the coast of Quang Tri Province, prepared to bombard North Vietnam. Nixon ordered the USS *Midway* and the USS *Saratoga* into the battle. Six great warships carrying fighter jets, the most formidable naval force assembled since World War II, gathered in the Gulf of Tonkin. The president commanded that every available B-52 bomber in the air force be readied to strike the enemy's biggest cities and military targets in saturation bombings—up to nine planes, flying wing to wing, dropping seventy-five to one hundred tons of bombs each. That was the most powerful force in the American arsenal, save nuclear weapons.

Nixon demanded the maximum number of B-52 attacks (more than eighteen hundred a month) as soon as possible. But cloud cover kept the war planes waiting for clearer skies. "God Almighty, there must be something, something, something that son-of-a-bitchin' Air Force can do in bad weather. Goddamn it!" the president yelled at Kissinger.

"Mr. President," Kissinger replied, "our major thing now is to get across to the Russians, to the Chinese, and to Hanoi that we are on the verge of going crazy."

"Goddamn it," Nixon said again, praying in his blasphemous way for the clouds to part over Hanoi and the port city of Haiphong, "get that weather cleared up." Then he laughed, a low rumble from deep in his gut. "The bastards have never been bombed," he said. "They're going to be bombed this time."

The clouds broke. On April 7, seventeen B-52s hit targets near Haiphong, the first time in seven years of warfare that American bombers struck that far north and that close to Hanoi, sixty-five miles west. Three more B-52 raids followed the next week.

Nixon asked General Haig to describe a B-52 bombing. "An enormously potent ordeal, isn't it?"

"It's a frightening weapon," Haig said. "God, you know, you just see these shockwaves . . ."

"And the ground shakes?" Nixon asked.

"And the whole ground shakes," Haig said.

* * *

"I cannot impress upon you too strongly how intensely involved the president is in this operation," Admiral Moorer cabled his top commanders in Vietnam on April 8. Two days later, a newly appointed four-star air force general personally selected by Nixon, John Vogt, arrived in Saigon to take charge of the air war.

The president had given Vogt his marching orders upon his departure, as Haldeman recorded on April 6: "The P called him and really laid it to him, saying that he was making this change because it had to be done and that he was very upset with the military. . . . He then made quite a dramatic point of the fact that this may very well be the last battle that will be fought by the United States Air Force, since this kind of war probably will never happen again, and that it would be a tragic thing if this great service would end its active battle participation in a disgraceful operation that this Vietnam offensive is turning out to be."

The United States could "break the North Vietnamese," Nixon told

Kissinger on April 10, as Haldeman took notes. "We might get something settled by summer. On the other hand, if the North Vietnamese take Saigon . . . we have to admit that we've lost the war, we pull out and as the President says, he doesn't care what the domestic reaction is, because sitting in that office next year won't be worth it anyway. American foreign policy will have been destroyed."

On April 13, Nixon ordered a more massive B-52 attack, aimed at targets in and around Hanoi and Haiphong. General Abrams, the top American commander in Saigon, postponed the strike, citing the urgent requirements of the ground war. Kissinger told Moorer, "When I showed the President Abrams' message he practically went into orbit." Moorer sent a top-secret cable to Saigon the next day: THERE ARE OTHER VERY HIGH LEVEL CONSIDERATIONS WHICH DICTATE A FIRM REQUIREMENT FOR A HEAVY AIR STRIKE IN THE HANOI/HAIPHONG AREA DURING THE COMING WEEKEND. The B-52 raids began hours later and lasted for two days.

Nixon intended to blockade the port of Haiphong with mines, to prevent more Soviet arms shipments to the enemy. He wanted the bombings and the blockading to send a blunt message to the Soviets: stop arming Hanoi and support his push for peace with honor.

Kissinger was about to go to Moscow to plan the upcoming summit with the Soviet leader Leonid Brezhnev. "Any sign of weakness on our part might encourage the Soviets to provide more arms in hopes of giving the North Vietnamese a military advantage," the president told him. "What the Russians wanted to do was to get him to Moscow to discuss the summit. What we wanted to do was to get him to Moscow to discuss Vietnam." Nixon warned that he might cancel: "It was hard to see how I could go to the summit and be clinking glasses with Brezhnev while Soviet tanks were rumbling through Hue."

Nixon and Kissinger debated the next move on the morning of April 17 in the Oval Office. Kissinger reported that Moscow was still eager to receive him, even after American bombs had hit Soviet ships and injured Soviet sailors in the port of Haiphong. Nixon was dead-set on convincing the Soviets to help him settle the war. "I have to leave this office in a position as strong as I possibly can because whoever succeeds me—because of lack of experience, or because of lack of character, guts—heading a weaker United States would surrender the whole thing," he said. This pronouncement was prophetic.

Nixon said he had to think of his legacy. He wanted to be the "Man of Peace," as he put it. He wanted to create the "Generation of Peace." Tragically, the war was his only path to peace.

* * *

Kissinger was set to fly to the Soviet Union to plan for the summit on April 20. But Nixon still balked at striking bargains with the Communists. In the Oval Office, he bluntly told Kissinger to set the terms by which he would talk with his enemies. The president was explicit: if Moscow did not help him end the war, he would obliterate North Vietnam.

"I'll destroy the goddamn country, believe me. I mean destroy it, if necessary. And let me say, even the nuclear weapon," Nixon said. "We will bomb the living bejeezus out of North Vietnam, and then if anybody interferes we will threaten the nuclear weapon. . . . We are not going to let this country be defeated by this little shit-ass country."

"It's a gamble, one of these wild things," Kissinger said. "No other man in this country would have bombed Hanoi and Haiphong having an invitation to Moscow in his pocket."

Nixon concurred. "There's no President who could go to Moscow at this time, at a time Moscow is fueling a war that has cost 50,000 Americans. No President could go at this time and come back with an arms control agreement and so forth and sell it to the American people except this President. . . . This President can deliver."

Kissinger flew to Moscow with the Soviet ambassador, Anatoly Dobrynin, leaving shortly after 1:00 a.m. on April 20 on a presidential aircraft from Andrews Air Force Base, outside Washington. The trip was clandestine: the American ambassador to Moscow, Jacob Beam, never knew Kissinger was coming. Nixon awoke at 3:00 a.m. and began dictating a message to be sent from the White House Situation Room to Kissinger's aircraft before it landed: "Brezhnev is simple, direct, blunt and brutal. The sophisticated approach we used with the Chinese is neither necessary nor wise with him," Nixon said. "Brezhnev must directly be told that as long as the invading North Vietnamese are killing South Vietnamese and Americans in the South the President will have to resort to bombing military installations in the North that are supporting that invasion."

Five hours later, Nixon and Haldeman mulled over the message to Kissinger and the mission to Moscow. "I put this brutally to him, very tough," Nixon said. He began pounding on his desk. "Goddamn it, he's got to get it simple, and he's got to be direct, and he's got to get them on the subject of Vietnam. . . . I know these bastards. These people are too smart. And Henry will get his pants taken off."

"He ends up playing their game instead of ours," Haldeman said.

"Bob, his eight meetings with the North Vietnamese are not examples of good negotiating," Nixon said. "Very early in the game you've got to hit them in the solar plexus. You've got to get their attention. Stick that knife in deep and turn it. Well, that's what I was doing last night."

As soon as Haldeman left the Oval Office, Treasury Secretary John Connally entered. He was a unique member of Nixon's Cabinet. A Democrat, elected governor of Texas in 1963, Connally had been riding in President Kennedy's limousine when JFK was assassinated in Dallas and was himself shot and grievously wounded that dreadful day. Charming, cunning, silver-haired, silver-tongued, and tough-minded, he had become Nixon's confidant—so much so that Nixon thought Connally should switch parties and succeed him as president. In June 1972, Connally would resign after only sixteen months at Treasury to raise millions under the banner of "Democrats for Nixon."

Nixon immediately revealed Kissinger's secret trip to Moscow and launched into a strategy session, including his plans for blockading Haiphong and bombing Hanoi if the Soviets did not help strike a peace deal. "If they don't give anything, then we're going to be up against a hard spot," Nixon said. "If we go to a blockade, there will be all hell to pay . . . riots and all that sort of thing. But we will put it on the basis that we're going to remain until they withdraw their forces from South Vietnam and return our POWs."

"I think it's wise," Connally said. "Tough."

"They thought that because of the political situation, that I would cave—"

"Right."

"—as Johnson did."

"That's right."

"But what they didn't realize is that I know that nobody can be President of this country, and have a viable foreign policy, if the United States suffers a defeat fighting this miserable little Communist country, fueled by Soviet arms, and that the world is going to be a very dangerous place to live in," Nixon concluded. "This is the supreme test."

* * *

Kissinger sent an encoded cable from Moscow on April 21. Haig read it to Nixon, who was at Camp David, at 9:35 that night.

> "Had 4½ hour meeting with Brezhnev. Atmosphere was extremely cordial, almost effusive. His protestations of eagerness to have the summit no matter what the circumstances was at times almost maudlin, certainly extremely strong. Brezhnev is very forceful, extremely nervous, highly unsubtle, quite intelligent but not in the class of other leaders we have met. His mood can best be summed up in the following concluding quote . . . 'I would like very much for you to convey to President Nixon that I can confirm and reconfirm our views and the desire of our government to hold the Soviet-American summit meeting.'"

"That doesn't mean a thing," Nixon said. "All that is bullshit."

On April 26, President Nixon delivered a televised address to the nation on Vietnam. "I have flatly rejected the proposal that we stop the bombing of North Vietnam as a condition for returning to the negotiating table," he said. "They sold that package to the United States once before, in 1968, and we are not going to buy it again in 1972." In his memoirs, he writes, "It was a tough speech, and afterward I wished that I had made it even tougher."

The president left Camp David, flew to Key Biscayne, then took off with Bebe Rebozo to the Bahamas for a bit of respite—swimming, rest and relaxation, drinking. On April 28, reports reached Washington that Quang Tri City was about to fall to North Vietnam. Nixon, from his idyllic retreat, sent a flash message to Kissinger. He ordered the bombing of the North increased to a thousand sorties per day—requiring around-the-clock attacks, with flares illuminating the battlefield at night. Nixon added, "There are to be no excuses and there is no appeal." He then flew to John Connally's luxurious ranch outside San Antonio, Texas, to talk about fund-raising for his reelection.

Quang Tri was the first province in South Vietnam to fall. The will of South Vietnam's military leaders shattered under fire from the

Communists. More than five hundred thousand refugees fled south toward Da Nang, the coastal city where marines first landed when the Vietnam War began in 1965. American military barracks became refugee camps. The North Vietnamese pressed south, killing civilians on the road. "People didn't want to hear about it" back home, said Frederick Brown, the American consul general in Da Nang; the suffering was "overlooked by the American side. We wanted to get the hell out."

Nixon heard about Quang Tri while at the Connally ranch, on April 30. He dictated orders to Kissinger, who was stopping in Paris for another secret meeting with Hanoi's delegation: "I intend to cancel the Summit . . . unless we get a firm commitment from the Russians to announce a joint agreement at the Summit to use our influence to end the war," Nixon wrote. "We have crossed the Rubicon and now we must win." He ordered Kissinger to tell the North Vietnamese that "the President has had enough and now you have only one message to give them—Settle or else!" But the peace talks once again went nowhere.

Nixon returned to the White House on May 1. Kissinger gave him a grim report from General Abrams in Saigon. It concluded, "As the pressure has mounted and the battle has become brutal the senior military leadership has begun to bend and in some cases to break. In adversity it is losing its will and cannot be depended on to take the measures necessary to stand and fight." Kissinger began to read it to the president. Haldeman recorded: "The P kept telling him to get to the point of the summary. Henry finally did. Then the P took the report, read it himself, and we spent quite a little time just talking over the various questions of how the Vietnamese have fallen apart."

Vietnamization had become a tragic farce. Only American airpower could turn the tide of the war now. And if the tide did not turn, Nixon said, the fate of his presidency was at stake: "We will lose the country if we lose the war."

* * *

J. Edgar Hoover died in his sleep before the next dawn. He had run the FBI with an iron hand since 1924, but he had lost his grip in the last year of his life. The president pushed him aside when he refused to carry

out the bugging and break-ins that the Plumbers then undertook in his
stead. In 1972, the White House logs record, Nixon spoke to Hoover
three times for a total of eight minutes. As the end neared, "Hoover
experienced loneliness and a fear that his life's work was being destroyed,"
wrote his number three man at the Bureau, Mark Felt.

"He died at the right time, didn't he?" Nixon said on May 2. "Goddamn, it'd have killed him to lose that office. It would have killed
him."

Hoover's closed casket lay on a black catafalque in the rotunda of
the U.S. Capitol on a rainy afternoon. Gordon Liddy and Howard Hunt
sent their Cuban henchmen to beat up antiwar demonstrators who had
gathered outside the building to mark Hoover's passing.

On the morning of May 4, a few minutes after Hoover's memorial
service, the head of the Justice Department, Richard Kleindienst, telephoned a loyal assistant, L. Patrick Gray.

"Pat, I am going to appoint you acting director of the FBI," he said.

"You have to be joking," Gray replied.

Gray, crew-cut, bullet-headed, a former naval commander, had
known Nixon since 1947. Gray had been chosen for one reason: he was
fiercely loyal to the president. He revered him. He soon learned to fear
him. He immediately went to the White House, where Nixon gave him
some wisdom. "Never, never figure that anyone's your friend," the president said. "Never, never, never. . . . You've got to be a conspirator.
You've got to be totally ruthless. . . . That, believe me, is the way to
run the Bureau." Gray would learn what Nixon meant by ruthlessness.

Nixon spent the rest of the day conferring with his innermost circle:
Kissinger, Haldeman, Haig, and Connally. He had decided that he would
again address the nation in a broadcast on the following Monday, May
8. He was going to announce a major escalation of the war in Vietnam.
The secretary of defense and the secretary of state knew nothing of his
plans.

For six long hours, Nixon thought aloud. Haldeman's diary and a
short taped conversation are the only records of this fateful day.

"We were now faced with three alternatives," Haldeman recorded.
"One was to do nothing, and in effect back down on our bluff; second
would be to bomb the North, and Hanoi and Haiphong, with the atten-
dant risks, including the great risk of the cancellation of the Summit;

and the third would be to cancel the Summit ourselves and then follow it up by bombing the North."

Then "Connally leaped in," telling Nixon that "we've got to make it clear to the Russians that we are not going to be defeated, and we are not going to surrender." Connally thought nuclear weapons were the best option in Vietnam. Nixon loved his bluster and bombast. But big talk about dropping the Bomb was no strategy.

Kissinger favored mining Haiphong harbor and placing a naval blockade across the entire coast of North Vietnam. "The more the P thought about it, the more he liked Henry's ideas, as long as it was followed up with continued bombing. So that became his conclusion," Haldeman wrote. The president would announce an escalation of the air war, along with the mining and blockading, in a nationally broadcast speech on May 8. The blockade would end when America's prisoners of war were returned and a cease-fire took hold in South Vietnam.

Now Kissinger summoned Admiral Moorer to the president's Executive Office Building hideaway, where a tape was rolling.

> NIXON: Admiral, what I am going to say to you now is in total confidence. . . . I've decided that we've got to go on a blockade. It must—I'm going to announce it Monday night on television. I want you to put a working group together. Start immediately with absolutely the best people that you've got. . . . Can it be in place Tuesday?
>
> MOORER: Oh, yes, sir.
>
> NIXON: Now, what we have in mind, in addition to blockade, is that I want as much use of our air assets as we can spare . . . take out the railroad units . . . the power plants . . . the docks . . . destroy everything that you possibly can . . . in the Haiphong area. You are to aim for military targets. You are not to be too concerned about whether it slops over. . . . If it slops over, that's too bad. . . . I've made the decision and we now have no choice. . . . We will avoid the defeat of the South. . . . And that's the way it's going to be. Now, can you do that?
>
> MOORER: Yes, sir.

Much of the tape is inaudible.* Haldeman's diary fills in the blanks. "The P very strongly put the thing to Moorer that this was his decision, that it was to be discussed with no one, especially not the Secretaries or anybody at State, or anybody over in Vietnam. . . . He hit Moorer [by saying] this is a chance to save the military's honor and to save the country."

As night fell, all departed save Nixon and Haldeman. The president concluded that his speech would be "quite a dramatic step, because it is a basic decision to go all out to win the war now."

* * *

Nixon thought, above all, about his place in history.

"We've had a damned good foreign policy," he told Kissinger after breakfast on Friday, May 5. "This whole great, big, wide world, everything rides on it."

"If there were a way we could flush Vietnam now, flush it, get out of it in any way possible, and conduct a sensible foreign policy with the Russians and with the Chinese," he said, "we ought to do it, because there's so much at stake. There's nobody else in this country at the present time, with the exception of Connally, in the next four years, that can handle the Russians and the Chinese and the big game in Europe and the big game in Southeast Asia."

"Who else could do it?" he asked. "How the hell can we save the Presidency?"

"We must draw the sword," Nixon said. "I want that place, whenever the planes are available, bombed to smithereens during the blockade. If we draw the sword out, we're going to bomb those bastards all over the place."

"No question," said Kissinger.

"Let it fly," the president said. "Let it fly."

Now Nixon changed the subject to a very sensitive question. "Would you please still study the dike situation?" he asked Kissinger.

Nixon was thinking of destroying the earthen dikes in the Red River Delta of North Vietnam. They had served for centuries to irrigate crops and sustain the food chain and to protect the people from floods.

---

* The Executive Office Building taping system was faulty, and a ticking clock near a hidden microphone in the president's desk has driven transcribers to distraction for decades.

Bombing the dikes arguably would be a war crime. He had discussed the question with Kissinger in another hard-to-hear Executive Office Building tape ten days before.

"I still think we ought to take the dikes out now," Nixon had said. "Will that drown people?"

Kissinger had replied, "That will drown about 200,000 people." His voice then lowered to an inaudible mumble.

"I'd rather use a nuclear bomb. Have you got that ready?" Nixon had said. His voice was loud and clear. "I just want you to think big, Henry, for Christ's sake!"

Returning to the question that morning, Nixon said, "I need an answer on that. I don't think it's 200,000."

"I've been up to Hanoi," Nixon continued. "Have you ever been to Hanoi?" Kissinger had not. "I have, in '52," Nixon said. The dikes, he said, served "the rice lands and the rest. The people could get the hell out of there. It isn't—it isn't a huge dam. The torrents of water will go down and starve the bastards. But it'll do it. Now if that's the case, I'll take 'em out. . . ."

"I ask this question before you go," Nixon said. "A blockade, plus surgical bombing, will inevitably have the effect of bringing North Vietnam to its knees?"

"Unless the South Vietnamese collapse," Kissinger said.

"So the South Vietnamese collapse, but they still have to give us our prisoners. We've got something. America is not defeated."

"That's right."

"That's my point," Nixon declared. "America is not defeated."

The president went to Camp David that afternoon to spend the weekend writing his address to the nation on Vietnam. His thoughts ranged over the dangers and opportunities he confronted. The war had to be settled by Election Day to guarantee his victory. Early public opinion polls showed him far ahead of the potential Democratic nominees, who were committing fratricide in their party primaries. Nixon wanted to run against the ardently antiwar senator George McGovern of South Dakota. The week before, the president had ordered Haldeman to produce fake polls showing McGovern gaining strength. "The best way to assure that we could win was to pick our opponent," Haldeman wrote. "We were much happier with McGovern than other possible foes."

The president tried to unwind Sunday night by watching a British movie, *Funeral in Berlin*, starring Michael Caine as an intelligence officer handling a defecting Soviet spymaster. But he walked out midway through the second reel, got in his helicopter, and flew back to the White House.

At 9:00 a.m. on Monday, May 8, Nixon convened an extraordinary meeting of the National Security Council. It was then and there that Secretary of State Rogers, Secretary of Defense Laird, and Director of Central Intelligence Helms learned of the president's new war plans.

"The real question is whether the Americans give a damn anymore," Nixon said. "We must play a role of leadership. A lot of people say we shouldn't be a great power. . . . 'Let's get out; let's make a deal with the Russians and pull in our horns.' The U.S. would cease to be a military and diplomatic power. If that happened, then the U.S. would look inward towards itself and would remove itself from the world. Every non-Communist nation in the world would live in terror."

Twelve hours later, the president addressed the nation.

* * *

"We now have a clear, hard choice among three courses of action: Immediate withdrawal of all American forces, continued attempts at negotiation, or decisive military action to end the war," he said on the evening of May 8. "Abandoning our commitment in Vietnam here and now would mean turning 17 million South Vietnamese over to Communist tyranny and terror. It would mean leaving hundreds of American prisoners in Communist hands with no bargaining leverage to get them released.

"An American defeat in Vietnam would encourage this kind of aggression all over the world, aggression in which smaller nations armed by their major allies, could be tempted to attack neighboring nations at will in the Mideast, in Europe, and other areas," he said. "World peace would be in grave jeopardy."

"What appears to be a choice among three courses of action for the United States is really no choice at all," Nixon continued. "There is only one way to stop the killing. That is to keep the weapons of war out of the hands of the international outlaws of North Vietnam." He laid out his next steps: seeding every port in North Vietnam with mines; sending an armada into enemy waters, including aircraft carriers ferrying fighter jets; and escalating the bombing to the utmost.

He set the terms for peace: "First, all American prisoners of war must be returned. Second, there must be an internationally supervised cease-fire throughout Indochina." Then and only then, he would "proceed with a complete withdrawal of all American forces from Vietnam within 4 months."

Nixon wrote to Kissinger the next morning: "I have determined that we should go for broke. What we have got to get across to the enemy is the impression that we are doing exactly that. . . . We must *punish* the enemy in ways that he will really hurt. He has now gone over the brink *and so have we.* We have the power to destroy his war-making capacity. The only question is whether we have the *will* to use that power. . . . I have the *will* in spades."

Nixon, finding no hope in talking to Hanoi, was delivering his message with the most punishing attacks of the war. In the next five weeks, the United States launched 14,621 air strikes and 836 naval gunfire attacks against North Vietnam. The bombing campaign, code-named Linebacker, escalated throughout the summer. The ferocious waves of B-52s grew to a peak of more than 110 sorties a day. The Pentagon estimated that the attacks killed or seriously wounded a hundred thousand people in North Vietnam.

The American political divide deepened. The bombing of North Vietnam set off protests all over the United States. They swept across almost all the nation's cities and hundreds of college campuses. All began as peaceful demonstrations (marches, sit-ins, silent vigils), but police also arrested demonstrators, sometimes in violent confrontations, in at least a dozen cities, including New York, Chicago, Boston, San Francisco, and Washington.*

May 10 saw what Admiral Moorer called "the biggest dogfight since World War Two" over the skies of Vietnam. "The enemy sent up 24 MiGs, seven of which we shot down," he reported, but the United States lost

---

* After midnight on May 19, a bomb planted by members of the Weather Underground, the most violent far-left group in America, exploded in a bathroom inside the Pentagon. No one was injured, but the attack was audacious. The group set off thirty-eight bombs during the Nixon years; the FBI made no arrests. In frustration, the FBI reinstituted its practice of black-bag jobs and burglaries in the hunt for the bombers. Eventually Gray, his second-in-command Mark Felt, and his intelligence chief Ed Miller would be indicted for illegal searches and seizures carried out against friends and relatives of the Weather Underground. Charges against Gray were dropped. Felt and Miller were convicted—and President Reagan pardoned them a few weeks after he took office.

four F-4 fighter jets. All but two of the Americans shot down died in action. President Nixon still believed that American airpower would win the war (a misplaced faith), and he became infuriated when it did not break the enemy's will to fight. "The record of World War II, the Korean War and Vietnam since 1965," Helms warned at the height of the Linebacker attacks, "strongly suggests that bombing alone is unlikely to [defeat] a determined, resourceful enemy." Nixon was incredulous when he saw intelligence reports from the Pentagon and the CIA saying that North Vietnam could keep fighting for at least two more years.

"I want you to convey directly to the Air Force that I am thoroughly disgusted with their performance in North Vietnam," he wrote to Kissinger on May 19, three days before the summit meeting in Moscow began. "I do not blame the fine Air Force pilots who do a fantastic job in so many other areas. I do blame the commanders."

He then issued a breathtaking order: "I have decided to take the command of all strikes in North Vietnam in the Hanoi–Haiphong area out from under *any Air Force jurisdiction whatever.*" Nixon said he would henceforth run the air war himself, through a naval commander of his choosing. "I want you to convey my utter disgust to Moorer which he in turn can pass on to the Chiefs," Nixon concluded. "It is time for these people either to shape up or get out."

At war with his own military leaders, the president boarded Air Force One, bound for Moscow, where he would drink toasts and sign treaties with the men who were arming his enemies.

CHAPTER EIGHTEEN

"Palace intrigue"

RICHARD NIXON and Leonid Brezhnev talked of war and peace in the Kremlin. Their meetings were the first between American and Soviet leaders since 1945, when Franklin D. Roosevelt and Joseph Stalin met with Winston Churchill at Yalta, the summer home of the last czar of Russia, Nicholas II, seeking, as Churchill had said, to "guide the course of history" after World War II.

Now the great hope was that the Moscow summit could guide the world out of the Cold War. It might slow the arms race (the mad dash for military dominance) and allow détente (the relaxation of tension) to determine relations between the United States and the USSR.

But it was not to be. "The problem with the relationship when Nixon and Kissinger were in office was that détente was oversold to the American public," said Malcolm Toon, the American ambassador to the Soviet Union from 1976 to 1979. "The idea got across to our fellow Americans that we were dealing with a basically changed Soviet Union. That was not the case at all."

Brezhnev—beetle-browed, chain-smoking, sixty-five years old, gruff and brusque but capable of charm—had been a major general in the Russian army when Nixon first ran for Congress in 1946. A political commissar, he succeeded his patron, Nikita Khrushchev, as the Soviet leader in 1964. He sought to affirm Russia's standing as a super-power—no easy matter when harvests rotted in the field for want of fuel to truck them to markets while the Politburo's military spending starved the Soviet state. Brezhnev wanted détente to bring concrete benefits (such as trade deals for grain) and significant symbols (such as a linkup between U.S. and Soviet spacecraft).

Nixon saw the summit through another lens: as one more stab at a peace deal in Vietnam. He had gone to China. He was breaking bread with Brezhnev. If only he could somehow end the war by working with his enemies, he would go down as one of the greatest presidents in history.

But the formal centerpiece of the summit was a proposed strategic arms limitation treaty (SALT, for short) intended to curb the growth of the two nations' immense nuclear arsenals. The arms race had accelerated through the 1950s and '60s. Both nations could blast the world into radioactive ruins in a matter of minutes. Nixon knew that a major arms control agreement could help enshrine him as a great statesman.

Nixon, like all presidents since Eisenhower, had seen the Pentagon's plans for nuclear war. They were terrifying. In May 1969 he had been through a dress rehearsal of the first day of World War III. He had flown from Key Biscayne to Washington on the Airborne Command Post, the "White House in the Sky," a military version of a Boeing 707 converted into a flying war center, equipped to launch thermonuclear weapons across the world. "Pretty scary," Haldeman noted. Nixon had "a lot of questions about our nuclear capability and kill results. Obviously worries about the lightly tossed-about millions of deaths."

Full-scale SALT negotiations had started in November 1969. American and Soviet delegations regularly held talks in Vienna and Helsinki on how to curb the power of nuclear weapons technology: intercontinental ballistic missiles, submarines armed with city-busting bombs, and the dream of a missile defense—a prologue to President Reagan's multibillion-dollar "Star Wars" boondoggle.

Ambassador Gerald Smith, chief of the Arms Control and Disarmament Agency, led the talks for the United States. But Nixon personally disliked Smith. So Kissinger took control of the agenda through one of his six NSC subcommittees, the Verification Panel, which met in the Situation Room; its members included CIA director Richard Helms and Attorney General John Mitchell. Kissinger set up a back channel to the Soviets with Ambassador Dobrynin; Secretary of State Rogers and Ambassador Smith were not informed of these private talks.*

On the eve of the summit, Nixon realized that many devils lurked in the details of the proposed treaty.

"I read last night the whole SALT thing and I think it's going to be a tough titty son-of- a-bitch," he told Kissinger on May 19, the day before their departure for Moscow. "There's an awful lot still left to be worked out."

"The way it stands now, unintentionally, you will have to break some deadlocks," Kissinger admitted. "We have a few snags." The thorniest might be MIRV.

MIRV was the multiple independently targetable reentry vehicle—a warhead within a missile. A "MIRVed" missile could hold as many as fourteen nuclear warheads in its nose cone, each warhead aimed at a different target, multiplying each missile's destructive power immensely. The United States had a decade's head start on MIRV; the Soviets still were striving to test the technology. This constituted a huge American advantage in the arms race. Nixon called MIRVs "indispensable." He had signed a secret National Security Decision Memorandum, drafted by Kissinger's Verification Panel, flatly stating that "there would be no limitations on MIRVs" in any arms control agreement with the Soviets.

Kissinger prepared a grandiloquent list of talking points on SALT for Nixon to read on the flight to Moscow. "Never before have nations limited the weapons on which their survival depends," one passage read. There were five words about MIRVs; Kissinger would ensure they would not be limited.

"The fact that the two great adversaries could sit down and seriously discuss something as sensitive to their security as strategic arms was something of an accomplishment," said Ray Garthoff, executive secretary of the SALT delegation and deputy director of the State Department's

---

* The central role of Kissinger's top-secret Verification Panel in setting the ill-conceived terms of the arms-control talks—and setting no limits on the warheads known as MIRVs—was uncovered when the panel's minutes were partially declassified in September 2010.

Bureau of Politico-Military Affairs. But he said it was tragic that "no serious attempt was made and no agreement reached, of course, to limit MIRVs."

* * *

Nixon arrived in Moscow at 4:00 p.m. on Monday, May 22. He was escorted to an exquisite fifteenth-century apartment in the Kremlin, a suite where czars had lived. The president's security team determined that the place was bugged; thereafter, Nixon, Kissinger, and Haldeman held meetings and dictated memos inside the president's black limousine, hoping its lead-lined doors and bulletproof windows would ward off Soviet electronic surveillance.

Shortly after Nixon was ensconced in his elegant rooms, an unexpected summons arrived: "P was whisked off to meet with Brezhnev," Haldeman recorded.

They met one on one in the Soviet leader's palatial Kremlin office. Within minutes, any hope for a deal with Hanoi seemed dashed.

"The war which the United States has for many years now been waging in Vietnam has left a deep imprint in the soul of our people and in the hearts of all Soviet people," Brezhnev said. "To take in these circumstances serious steps to develop Soviet-American relations was for us not at all an easy thing."

He quickly turned to SALT. "I think we should emphasize the agreements relating to the limitation of strategic arms," he said. "I have received a report to the effect that two or three specific points now remain unresolved."

Nixon replied, "This is something that you and I have to do, Mr. General Secretary. It is we who should settle the really difficult questions. . . . If we leave all the decisions to the bureaucrats we will never achieve any progress."

"We would simply perish," Brezhnev said.

Nixon agreed: "They would simply bury us in paper."

"Such agreements do not lessen the danger of the outbreak of nuclear war," the Soviet leader said.

Nixon conceded: "We still have enough arms to kill one another many times over."

"Exactly," said Brezhnev. "I trust you will agree, Mr. President, that only a radical solution of the problem—the destruction of nuclear weapons—can really rid the peoples of the threat of nuclear war. This would be a tremendous achievement."

Banning the Bomb was not on Nixon's agenda. The war remained uppermost. He strongly suggested "a confidential talk on the Vietnam problem." He would have it. It would be harsh.

* * *

At 3:30 a.m. on May 23, 1972, after three hours of sleep, Nixon started scrawling notes for his next talk with Brezhnev. "We are great powers— We are rivals—We have different goals—philosophies," he wrote on a yellow legal pad. "Historically this means war—We have never fought a war—Neither will win a war—. Our interests will not be served— Our people do not want war."

Nixon wrote that Moscow should put itself in the place of the United States: fifty thousand dead, two hundred fifty thousand wounded, fifteen hundred missing in Vietnam. He defined what peace with honor meant for him: a cease-fire and the return of American prisoners of war. He dangled promises of great economic and political rewards for the Soviet Union in exchange for its help in ending the war. Moscow had supplied most of the weaponry that had killed or injured three hundred thousand Americans in Vietnam. If the arms shipments stopped, the war would end, the wounds would heal, and a new era of cooperation under détente would begin—"a great victory" for Washington and Moscow. There would be lucrative trade agreements, joint space missions, somber statements signed by both leaders on the pursuit of peace. Together they could build "a new world."

Their first full day of negotiations in the glittering gold-and-ivory chambers of St. Catherine's Hall was dismal, verging on disaster. Brezhnev insisted on spending a full session on SALT. But Nixon was bored to death by the details. Kissinger, the note taker at this session, sank into despair as Nixon and Brezhnev wandered into the dense brambles of nuclear weapons technology.

Brezhnev became infuriated when Nixon would not focus on the arms control deal. "We are both civilized men," he said. "We know these weapons must never be used. Perhaps we shall not be able to achieve agreement here." In a controlled panic, Kissinger cabled Gerald Smith, the chief American SALT negotiator, still sequestered with his colleagues at their headquarters in Helsinki. As Smith wrote, it was immediately apparent that Nixon did not grasp the substance of the SALT proposals: "That the President of the United States would get into such technicalities, important though they were, struck me as peculiar, if not dangerous. These first discussions of SALT appeared based on unawareness by our boss of the Helsinki record."

"The President and Kissinger perhaps had been too busy to read these reports," Smith wrote. "This fumbling start did not bode well for the summit."

* * *

The next evening, May 24, brought "the single most emotional meeting" Kissinger had ever experienced, as he described it to Nixon.

Brezhnev and Nixon signed their accord on cooperation in space, which would lead to an Apollo spacecraft and a Soyuz command module linking up above the earth three years later. It was late afternoon; dinner at eight was set at a government dacha, a country house on the banks of the Moscow River.

Brezhnev took Nixon's arm and said, "Why don't we go see it right now?"

Haldeman, trailing behind, watched in astonishment as "all of a sudden the P and Brezhnev disappeared down a corridor, zipped into an elevator, shot downstairs, came out into the driveway, popped into Brezhnev's car and roared off." Kissinger, waiting with two aides at his Kremlin residence, was aghast. He and the aides commandeered a Soviet limousine. "Followed by Nixon's own car, full of Secret Service agents beside themselves that the president of the United States had been abducted in front of their very eyes by the Soviet Union's Number One Communist," the impromptu motorcade sped out into the countryside.

Brezhnev treated Nixon to a sixty-mile-an-hour joyride on a hydrofoil, and all hands seemed in high spirits as they sat down together in the dacha at 7:50 p.m. The Russian side: Brezhnev, Prime Minister Kosygin, and Nikolai V. Podgorny, chief of the Presidium of the Supreme Soviet. The American side: Nixon, Kissinger, Winston Lord, and the NSC aide John Negroponte, who in the twenty-first century served as President George W. Bush's intelligence chief. The Americans assumed they were about to be served caviar and vodka.

What they got was a three-hour harangue on Vietnam.

"We certainly did not choose this particular time to have the Vietnam situation flare up," Nixon said, immediately on the defensive. His bombing campaign had continued almost unabated during the Moscow summit, and he realized that "this posed a very difficult problem for the Soviet leadership." He continued: "It is our intention to end the war by negotiations." But if Hanoi would not bend, "then I will do whatever I must to bring the war to an end."

Brezhnev struck back hard. "Cruel bombing has been resumed," he said. "Very cruel military actions have been taken against North Vietnam. . . . They can only amount to a deliberate effort to destroy a country and kill off thousands, millions of innocent people. For what sake is this, by what right is this being done?"

"I don't want to hurl more epithets on you. There have been quite enough epithets heaped on you as it is. But how can the methods you use now be called a method of ending the war in Vietnam?" Brezhnev said. "No bombing can ever resolve the war."

The Soviet leader kept lambasting Nixon:

> We want to sign important documents with you in which we say we want to solve all differences through negotiation, not war, and advise others to follow that path. At the same time you will be continuing the war in Vietnam, continuing to kill innocent people, killing women and children. How could that be understood?

Then Prime Minister Kosygin took the whip hand. He reminded Nixon that he had gone to the United States to meet President Johnson in 1967. "He said he would strangle Vietnam," Kosygin recounted. "To be very frank, you are acting even more cruelly than Johnson."

Kosygin was as blunt as he could be. He asked Nixon if preserving President Thieu's power in South Vietnam was worth the blood spilled in America's name. "You want to send under the axe hundreds of thousands of Vietnamese, maybe even a million, and your own soldiers, simply to save the skin of a mercenary President, so-called," Kosygin said. "If instead of continuing to support the so-called President, you could formulate proposals which would really enable to bring the war to an end, would that not be a veritable triumph?"

> We proceed on the assumption that you have another four years ahead of you as President. We believe that you do have another four years. From the point of view of history this is a brief period, but if you could find a constructive solution you would go down in history as a man who succeeded in cutting through this knot which so many American Presidents have been unable to disentangle. . . . Isn't it worth achieving this by sacrificing the rot that is the present government in Saigon?

The clock ticked toward eleven. His hosts gave President Nixon the last word. "Our people want peace," he said. "I want it too. I want the Soviet leaders to know how seriously I view this threat of new North Vietnamese escalation. One of our great Civil War generals, General Sherman, said 'War is hell.'" All Nixon sought was a way out of hell in Vietnam.

Then at last came the vodka and a five-course supper and cognac. And when they were done, after midnight, the indefatigable Gromyko was waiting for Kissinger in Moscow to go back to work on SALT.

Kissinger was mortified. He was bone-weary "after the motorcade, the hydrofoil ride, the brutal Vietnam discussion, and the heavy meal." Still worse, he had no bargaining room. He learned in a cable from Washington that the Joint Chiefs were backpedaling on points to which they'd previously agreed on SALT. Trapped between the Politburo and the Pentagon, Kissinger stalled until sunrise rather than strike a deal.

The Americans and the Soviets wasted nearly two days haggling over an issue that their SALT experts, still sitting in Helsinki, could have solved in two hours. The major sticking point was what the nuclear-armed Soviet submarine force would look like after SALT. The Americans were far ahead on this issue: their Polaris submarine-launched nuclear missiles had fourteen MIRVs. The Soviets had nothing of the sort.

So the Americans could give a little without affecting the balance of power. But they did not want to appear to give an inch, lest they incur the wrath of the hawks back home. "The real problem," Haig astutely wrote in a back-channel message to Kissinger from the White House on May 25, "is not the strategic implication of the compromise but rather the problem of the President's public image and credibility."*

After midnight on Friday, May 26, immediately following a performance of *Swan Lake* by the Bolshoi Ballet, Kissinger and Foreign Minister Gromyko reconvened in St. Catherine's Hall in the Grand Kremlin Palace. Nixon retired to his elegant residence, to await the results of what might be a last chance to settle SALT.

The question of Soviet submarine-launched ballistic missiles remained unresolved. So did a proposal limiting the increase of the dimensions of intercontinental ballistic missile silos to 15 percent. Kissinger misunderstood the 15 percent limit. The Soviets' chief nuclear weapons expert, Leonid V. Smirnov, had subtly changed a word of this clause: the *diameter* of the silo could grow by 15 percent. This let the *volume* of the silo, and the nuclear missile launcher it held, increase by 32 percent. And that gave the Soviets a chance to build far bigger missiles. Kissinger had not grasped the nuance.

It was a short meeting.

"There is no room for additional compromise," Gromyko said.

"Then this makes it impossible to reach agreement," Kissinger replied.

Smirnov turned to Kissinger and bade him good night. "After the ballet, have nice dreams," he said. "Swans. Not evil forces."

* * *

Everything changed overnight. At 10:00 a.m., Ambassador Dobrynin knocked on the door to Kissinger's room in the Kremlin. He said the Politburo had convened at breakfast to vote on the SALT text. At 11:15 a.m., Kissinger and Dobrynin met Gromyko and Smirnov in St. Catherine's Hall.

"There are two questions left open from yesterday," Gromyko said. "First is your formula [for] submarine-launched ballistic missiles permitted for the U.S. and the U.S.S.R. That is accepted. Hooray!"

---

* Haig sent a second cable to Kissinger on May 25 saying that Defense Secretary Laird, Director of Central Intelligence Helms, and Admiral Moorer insisted on an agreement limiting the Soviets to no more than 950 submarine-launched ballistic missiles. Moscow would have to dismantle 240 older missiles to reach that limit.

"Hooray!" Dobrynin said.

"Second," Gromyko continued: "'The size of land-based ICBM silo launchers will not be *substantially* increased.' We accept your proposal"— the 15 percent solution. Gromyko said he was ready to sign that day. Kissinger was stunned by the suddenness of it all. "Today?" he said. "Let me talk to the President first." He left the great hall, hurried to Nixon's side, and returned seventeen minutes later. "The President agrees," Kissinger said. The Soviets and the Americans would dine together that night at Spaso House, the U.S. ambassador's residence, and then sign together at the Kremlin.

"This is a very important milestone in the relations between our two countries, and I am very proud to have had the opportunity to work with you gentlemen on it," Kissinger said.

"They were really difficult and delicate matters," Gromyko replied. "It is really a good end."

Then he switched to English: "We are *substantially* satisfied, even more than 15 percent!" The Soviets clearly were delighted by Smirnov's sleight of hand.

But Kissinger had snookered them all by keeping MIRVs out of the final agreement. "In his compulsive need to control events, Kissinger had deceived everybody"—including "the Secretary of State, Gerry Smith and his negotiating team in Helsinki, and even, at certain points, Nixon himself," said George Jaeger, a senior State Department intelligence official and nuclear arms expert under Nixon.

While the SALT treaty temporarily froze the number of missile *launchers* each nation could build, it stood silent on the number of *warheads*. Unleashed, unlimited, the American nuclear warhead stockpile grew sixfold over the next decade. "Not one U.S. program was stopped by SALT," Kissinger himself told the Verification Panel in 1974. "Indeed, several U.S. programs were accelerated [and] the warhead advantage of the U.S. doubled." Significant cuts in the nations' nuclear arsenals came only after the Cold War ended and the Soviet Union dissolved.

"The MIRV explosion was especially devastating and discouraging," wrote William Hyland, a CIA veteran and Kissinger's nuclear weapons expert at the NSC. "The first strategic arms agreement actually produced a sizeable buildup in strategic weaponry." In a rare confession of error, Kissinger later said, "I wish I had thought through the implications of a MIRVed world."

In short, the talks had spurred the arms race they were supposed to control.

* * *

Nixon and Kissinger, elated and expansive, spoke with Brezhnev at his Kremlin office before dinner, seeking common ground on the question of the ever-growing conflict between the Arabs and the Israelis. They had gone to war in 1967 and the threat was "an explosive one," the Soviet leader had said earlier in an aside to Nixon. "If we let events run their course war may start anew."

Now Brezhnev renewed that warning. "There are in the world today many who are eager to depict the confrontation as not between Israel and Arabs but between the Soviet Union and the U.S.," he said. "If we gloss over this . . . there will be a cold war and confrontation between our two nations."

Nixon replied that if Moscow kept arming the Arabs and America kept arming Israel without working for a settlement, "there will be a war" and "it will involve us." He said that Kissinger and Dobrynin, the masters of secret diplomacy, had to find a way to avoid that war. By September, Nixon said, "We can try to get to the nut-cutting part of the problem. I don't know if that will translate!"

The Russian interpreter did his best. Nut cutting is turning a bull into a steer.

"The question," said Kissinger, "is whose are being cut."

The banter continued at dinner. Nixon invited Brezhnev to the United States. Would June 1973 be convenient? Brezhnev said he would be delighted. Nixon said Vietnam surely would be settled by then; Washington and Moscow could be closer once the war was over. Nixon harked back to the World War II alliances of Roosevelt, Churchill, and Stalin; the president said that he and Brezhnev should always have a private channel open between them.

The grand finale at Spaso House was a flaming Baked Alaska. "The Americans really are miracle workers!" Brezhnev exclaimed. "They have found a way to set ice cream on fire!"

Richard Nixon rose at 3:00 a.m. in the Kremlin on May 29, took out a yellow legal pad, and began writing notes for a speech to a joint session of Congress that he planned to deliver in three days. What he had accomplished in his mission to Moscow was the work "not for a summit of one summer—but of many years." He had reached out across oceans and nations to America's enemies so that the world might "turn away from war to peace." He wrote that "all Americans want more than anything else a world of peace." And he asked them to trust in him to create that world.

A few hours later, Nixon and Brezhnev reviewed the communiqué that would close the summit. It was a bland statement when compared with a single minute of their conversation that morning.

"How would you see it if we sent one of our highest leaders to talk to the Vietnamese?" Brezhnev asked. "We cannot absolutely guarantee complete success. But we would like to take this step to find the best solution." He said he believed Nixon truly wanted to end the war.

The president said, "It would be very constructive to stop all the killing right now." Nixon later said it was the most startling moment of the summit. But it did not stop the killing.

* * *

Nixon took a strange detour on his way home from Moscow. Rather than heading west to Washington, he flew two thousand miles south to see the shah of Iran. His stay lasted twenty-two hours and left a long and lasting scar.

The shah, installed on the Peacock Throne by a CIA coup under President Eisenhower in 1954, saw himself as the rightful inheritor of a 2,500-year-old line of Persian kings, and his nation as the only stable sovereignty between Europe and Japan. Nixon saw the shah as an ally with billions of dollars in oil revenues and an insatiable appetite for state-of-the-art American weapons.

Nixon and Kissinger sat down with the shah at his sumptuous palace on May 30 and 31. "At the conclusion of the discussion," the State Department's official diplomatic record reads, "the President agreed to furnish Iran with laser bombs and F-14s and F-15s," America's most advanced fighter jets. The deal was more complicated than that. The president had promised to provide the shah with "all available sophisticated weapons short of the atomic bomb," as a top NSC aide wrote to Kissinger a few days later. The shah was ready to pay any sum to buy the weapons. And America's arms manufacturers were eager to sell them to him.

Nixon fed the shah phalanxes of war planes, smart bombs, helicopters, naval destroyers—anything he desired. "That was a fateful, disastrous step, because the Shah was a megalomaniac. He had been pushing us for years to let him have all this military equipment, and we'd kept him on a short leash until then," recalled Andrew Killgore, a State Department political consul in Tehran. The military hardware "piled up in gigantic amounts, covering mile after mile after mile, up hills and mountains, down valleys, with huge fences around it, gathering dust in the sun."

The arms transactions became sordid; Iran's vice minister of war, General Hassan Toufanian, would demand and receive a two-hour meeting at the Pentagon with Secretary of Defense Donald Rumsfeld in 1976. The general named the American military contractors who had paid tens of millions of dollars in bribes for multibillion-dollar contracts with the shah. He pointed out that Pentagon procurement officers had greased the wheels for the weapons manufacturers. Rumsfeld expressed mild dismay and sent the general away.

The shah would spend twenty-five billion dollars on American weapons after Nixon's visit. The kickbacks and crooked contracts degraded a generation of Iranian military and government officials. And not even Iran could pump enough oil to both pay for the weapons and provide for its people. Throughout the seventies, the rich grew richer, the poor poorer, the regime more repressive, the resistance stronger. Few Americans saw it coming, but the shah's corruption led to a world-shaking revolution in 1979. We live with its consequences today.

Shortly after Nixon left Tehran, John Connally arrived for his share of caviar. Connally had resigned as treasury secretary, effective June 12, to raise money for Nixon's reelection. He was on a thirty-five-day world tour, mixing the business of politics with the pleasure of serving as the president's confidant with chiefs of state. He dined privately with Nixon at San Clemente upon his return.

The American ambassador in Tehran was Joseph Farland, who had received the post as a reward for smuggling Kissinger from Pakistan into China. Farland, in a State Department oral history recorded in 2000, said that Connally made an extraordinary approach to the shah in the Saadabad Palace.

"He wanted a conversation with His Imperial Majesty," the ambassador said. "He wanted to go by himself. That smelled of something, palace intrigue of some magnitude. I just was not going to have it and I told him so, that if he wanted a conversation with His Imperial Majesty, I was going.

"We got in the car and started down the hill and he said, 'Would you mind closing that window between us and the chauffeur? I want to speak to you in confidence. I want you to do the following,' which I thought was very inappropriate."

Ambassador Farland, according to the official transcript of the oral history, then rubbed his thumb and forefingers together: the universal hand signal for bribery.

"You're making the money motion," Farland's interlocutor noted.

"It was either for himself, for the political campaign, or to be divided up," Ambassador Farland said. "It was inappropriate and, as far as I'm concerned, illegal."

Back home, Richard Nixon was riding high. It was now clear that George McGovern would be the Democratic nominee for president, a prospect that delighted Nixon. The president decided to spend a long weekend in Key Biscayne and the Bahamas with his buddies Bebe Rebozo and Bob Abplanalp, enjoying their camaraderie and cocktails.

Before he left the White House on Friday, June 16—the eve of the break-in at the Watergate Hotel—he tossed a book into his briefcase along with a sheaf of memoranda for the coming campaign. He had been meaning to read the book since the Moscow summit. It was the final volume of Winston Churchill's history of World War II, *Triumph and Tragedy*.

CHAPTER NINETEEN

"We have produced a horrible tragedy"

AT 12:45 A.M. on Saturday, June 17, CREEP's security chief, James McCord, and his crew of four Cuban Americans tiptoed into the offices of the Democratic National Committee's headquarters at the Watergate Hotel.

The air hung thick and heavy in Washington. The skies started trembling from the faraway force of Hurricane Agnes, which passed by Florida and began sweeping up the Eastern Seaboard of the United States that weekend, killing 119 people and inflicting billions of dollars in damage—at the time, the most devastating storm in American history.

The president and his men were far-flung: Nixon was in the Bahamas, and Haldeman in Key Biscayne, where both felt the hurricane's lashing wind; Mitchell and his CREEP chieftains were in California, gathering millions at a campaign fund-raiser; John Dean was somewhere over the Pacific, flying back from a junket in the Philippines. Only Ehrlichman stood watch at the White House.

All these men told so many lies in the weeks and months ahead that it took two years of federal investigations, congressional hearings, and criminal trials to establish the essential elements of the Watergate story. But Nixon knew in a matter of days that the break-in would afflict him and his closest aides. He began trying to stop the wheels of justice from turning.

The four Cuban Americans accompanying McCord had been anti-communist activists for years: Bernard "Macho" Barker, a longtime Miami real estate agent; Eugenio Martinez, a legendary sea captain still on a CIA stipend; Virgilio Gonzales, a locksmith who ran the Missing Key Company in Miami; and Frank Sturgis, a soldier of fortune. All four were recruited by the CIA veteran Howard Hunt, all had played bit parts alongside Hunt in the Agency's attempts to overthrow Fidel Castro, and all believed the Watergate job was part of the effort by the United States to stop the spread of communism in the Western Hemisphere.

The burglars, under the command of CREEP counsel Gordon Liddy, had rented rooms at the Watergate hotel and office complex and at the Howard Johnson Motor Lodge across the street. Liddy and Hunt had a clear line of sight out their windows at the Howard Johnson to the Democratic National Committee's Watergate office. They had bugged the DNC's telephones three weeks earlier; one of the bugs malfunctioned, and the information gathered from the other was all but worthless.

Their objective on June 17 was to enhance the electronic surveillance and to photograph or steal as many files as possible at the DNC. Had all gone smoothly, their second target that night would have been George McGovern's campaign headquarters.

Shortly after 2:00 a.m., a squad of plainclothes police officers, alerted by a Watergate security guard, entered the DNC with guns drawn and arrested McCord and the Cubans, all neatly dressed in business suits and wearing thin rubber gloves. Hunt and Liddy, hearing urgent walkie-talkie warnings from McCord that the jig was up, fled as fast as they could.

McCord was carrying electronic eavesdropping gear. Wiretapping was a federal crime; the police called in the FBI. Special Agent Angelo J. Lano was on the case at 8:00 a.m. Together, armed with search warrants, the police and the FBI started collecting evidence. They found $5,900 in $100 bills and, in Macho Barker's pocket, the keys to the Howard Johnson hotel rooms. Barker's and Martinez's address books were at the Howard Johnson, and inside both books were Howard Hunt's telephone number at his White House office.

McCord and the break-in crew were arraigned that afternoon. The five men had given false names—all belied by FBI fingerprint files. The risk that they would flee if released was high; so, thus, was their bail. The judge asked their occupations. Anticommunist, said one of the Cubans. Retired, said McCord. From where? asked the judge. CIA, McCord mumbled.

* * *

On Monday, June 19, John Dean had a very unpleasant talk with Gordon Liddy. They met by prearrangement as Liddy skulked past the western edge of the White House grounds, across the street from CREEP headquarters, where he had spent the weekend shredding files.

Liddy confessed that he had recruited McCord for the Watergate burglary, linking the crime to CREEP. Worse yet, he and Hunt had used two of the Miami Cubans now jailed for the Watergate break-in to ransack Daniel Ellsberg's psychiatrist's office—which connected the Ellsberg job to Watergate *and* the White House. Liddy had violated an essential element of espionage by entwining two separate covert operations. Any close investigation of one could uncover the other.

Dean reported all this to Ehrlichman—who relayed the bad news to Haldeman in Key Biscayne—and he strongly suggested, not for the last time, that the White House hire an experienced criminal lawyer.

Nixon delayed his return to the White House until after Hurricane Agnes was well past Florida. Late on Monday evening, June 19, flying north on Air Force One, Haldeman told Nixon the disturbing news about McCord's arrest—and McCord's connection to Liddy and CREEP. The next day, Nixon and Haldeman had an eighty-minute talk—the tape with the infamous "eighteen-and-a-half-minute gap," deliberately erased, a destruction of evidence only the president or a close aide could have committed. Haldeman's diary for Tuesday, June 20, fills in part of the gap: "We got back into the Democratic break-in again. I told the P about it on the plane last night. . . . The more he thought about it, it obviously bothered him more, because he raised it in considerable detail today. I had a long meeting with Ehrlichman and Mitchell. We added Kleindienst for a little while and John Dean for quite a while. The conclusion was that we've got to hope the FBI doesn't go beyond what's necessary in developing evidence and that we can keep a lid on that, as well as keeping all the characters involved from getting carried away with any unnecessary testimony."

Haldeman walked into the Oval Office at 9:30 a.m. on Wednesday, June 21. The president did not say good morning. "What's the dope on the Watergate incident?" Nixon asked. Haldeman had learned a great deal of inside dope in the past hour: Liddy had talked to Mitchell's lieutenant Fred LaRue, at LaRue's apartment at the Watergate Hotel, and added alarming details to what he had told Dean. The gist was that if anyone ever looked inside the campaign's ledgers, they would see that the Watergate money trail went to the top of CREEP. And Liddy had hinted at blackmail. He said CREEP had an obligation to pay for the bail, the legal expenses, and (by implication) the burglars' silence.

Trying to protect Nixon from the worst of it, Haldeman simply explained that Liddy and Hunt had masterminded the Watergate break-in. "Does it involve Mitchell?" the president asked. He answered his own question. "Probably did. But don't tell me about it. . . . If Liddy'll take the rap on this, that's fine." Haldeman thought Liddy would take the fall but that scapegoating him might not suffice.

If Mitchell, as campaign manager, was implicated in the crime, the consequences could be incalculable. Mitchell wanted the FBI's acting director, Pat Gray, to force the Bureau to back off the case. Nixon concurred.

That afternoon, Gray convened his first Watergate meeting at FBI headquarters. Mark Felt, his number-two man, was at the table, along with the special agent in charge of the Washington field office and the chief of the FBI's Criminal Investigative Division. Gray instructed his men to go slow on interrogating White House personnel. He also said he had agreed to John Dean's demand that Dean sit in on the FBI's interviews.

Gray did not inform his top officers that he would secretly feed Dean dozens of daily summaries of the FBI's Watergate investigations and interrogations.

On Thursday, June 22, FBI agents questioned Charles W. Colson, special counsel to the president, with Dean sitting by his side. Colson mentioned that Howard Hunt had an office safe in the White House. Dean denied knowledge of it. Safe? What safe? He had lied to the FBI, a felony punishable by five years in prison. In fact, Dean had already ordered a team of government locksmiths to open the safe. He knew what was inside: a bagful of McCord's wiretapping equipment, psychological profiles of Ellsberg prepared by the CIA at Hunt's request, phony cables Hunt fabricated on the 1963 killing of President Diem, and a loaded .25-caliber revolver.

That evening, Gray told Dean that some FBI agents, looking at the CIA connections of five of the six burglars, suspected they had stumbled on a covert Agency operation. Dean shared this information with Mitchell, who had a flash of inspiration: suppose the White House could convince Gray that Watergate was indeed the CIA's work? Then the Bureau, under protocols designed to keep it from tripping over the Agency, would have to back off.

Since this supposition was false, using the CIA to block an investigation by the FBI constituted a criminal obstruction of justice.

Dean relayed Mitchell's brainstorm to Haldeman, who passed it on to the president shortly after 10:00 a.m. on Friday, June 23. Nixon thought it sounded like a great idea. The newly appointed deputy director of central intelligence, Lt. Gen. Vernon Walters, a Nixon crony of long standing, would tell Gray to stand down the FBI investigation in the name of national security.

"Good deal!" Nixon said.

Walters was in Gray's office by 2:30 p.m. brandishing the shield of secrecy. Gray agonized for days, a roiling battle raging in him between his loyalties and his respect for the law. Then, on June 28, he answered a call from the White House.

John Dean handed Gray two white manila envelopes: documents taken from Hunt's safe. "These should never see the light of day," he told Gray. "They are such political dynamite their existence can't even be acknowledged. I need to be able to say that I gave all Hunt's files to the FBI. That's what I'm doing." Gray chose his course: he eventually destroyed the evidence.

That same day, June 28, Nixon arrived at his desk exhausted; he had been unable to fall asleep until dawn. He had resolved overnight that John Mitchell would have to resign. He hated to do it, but he had to keep the taint of a third-rate burglary from touching his campaign. Mitchell officially stepped down three days later, pleading the pressures of caring for his increasingly deranged wife. The story was that he did it for love.

Under the delusion that he had contained the political consequences of Watergate, Nixon returned to his great passion: destroying his enemies at home and abroad.

* * *

The tone and tenor of Richard Nixon's reelection campaign was reflected in a written report that Al Haig submitted to the president on June 28. The day before, at Nixon's direction, Haig had visited former president Lyndon B. Johnson at his Texas ranch.

"President Johnson told me that he considered a McGovern Presidency a disaster," Haig recorded. "He noted that McGovern supporters had totally devastated the Democratic party machine in Texas by employing the most irresponsible and revolutionary campaign tactics." Expanding on what LBJ had said during their seven-hour conversation, Haig wrote to the president:

> I think we must be very, very wary of the strong possibility that Hanoi has been in close touch with McGovern or McGovern elements. . . . I have never for a moment doubted the total and complete collaboration between Hanoi and the McGovern camp and especially those individuals around McGovern. If we proceed under any other assumptions, we are totally naive.

Haig's accusation of treason resounded throughout the Nixon White House. "This arrogant son of a bitch is a traitor," Colson wrote of McGovern. "Instead of running for President, he should be running from the gallows." Pat Buchanan, one of Nixon's favorite speechwriters, put together what he called an "Assault Book," containing "enough McGovern statements, positions, votes, not only to defeat the South Dakota Radical—but to have him indicted by a Grand Jury."

Senator McGovern was no radical, though he had been steadfast against the war. He pledged to withdraw all American forces from Vietnam within ninety days of his inauguration. But the chance of his being inaugurated evaporated shortly after he won his party's Democratic nomination on July 12, 1972.

The Democratic convention in Miami was the most disorganized event of its kind in modern times. McGovern gave his acceptance speech at 2:48 a.m.—prime time on Guam, as Nixon noted—after a political circus in which thirty-nine people were nominated for vice president, including Chairman Mao. "It was a nightmare for me," McGovern said years later; "it was one of the most costly mistakes of the campaign that we frittered away that prime time when the country, for the first time, could have seen me on my turf, in control."

McGovern, without much forethought, chose Sen. Thomas Eagleton of Missouri as his running mate. It was soon revealed that Eagleton's medical history included twenty years of manic depression and extensive bouts of electroshock therapy. First McGovern said he stood behind Eagleton "one thousand percent." Then he forced him off the ticket.

Even without these fiascoes, McGovern's campaign was doomed before it began. On May 15, a lunatic with a handgun had shot and nearly killed George C. Wallace, the right-wing racist who, running as a Democrat, had won the Maryland and Michigan primaries that same day. Now Wallace was in a wheelchair; he could not run for president. Nixon had won 43.4 percent of the vote in 1968, Wallace had won 13.5 percent, and every Wallace voter then was a likely Nixon voter now. Presidential polls in August reflected those numbers almost exactly. Nixon was heading for a landslide in November—unless the Watergate story came out.

* * *

"We're sitting on a powder keg," Haldeman told the president in the Oval Office on August 1, and "it's worth a lot of work to keep it from blowing." But the damage was being controlled. Liddy had sworn a blood oath of silence. The Cubans were out on bail. Hush money had started flowing.

"Hunt's happy," Haldeman said.

"At considerable cost, I guess?" said the president.

"Yes," said Haldeman.

"It's worth it," Richard Nixon replied.

Kissinger told Nixon on August 2 that Hanoi might settle the Vietnam War before the election—"if you stay ten points ahead." Both men wanted to believe that North Vietnam would rather sign a peace deal than face the wrath of a reelected president.

"Frankly, I'd like to trick them," Nixon said. "I'd like to do it in a way that we make a settlement, and then screw them in the implementation, to be quite candid."

"Well, that we can do, too," Kissinger said.

"We could promise something, and then, right after the election, say Thieu wouldn't do it," Nixon said. "Just keep the pressure on."

The president was unsure South Vietnam could survive until November. If the war was still on, he would destroy Hanoi and Haiphong after the election, he vowed. But "the advantage, Henry, of trying to settle now, even if you're ten points ahead, is that then you assure a hell of a landslide," he said. "You'd have a mandate."

"And you have the goddamned nightmare off your back," Kissinger replied.

"It *is* a nightmare. It's a nightmare being there," Nixon said. "This war is over by the end of this year," no matter what it took. "Vietnam poisons our relations with the Soviets, and it poisons our relations with the Chinese. We have suffered long and hard—and God knows how do we get out of it?"

"They are bastards," Kissinger said. "They would love it best if you got defeated."

"Sure," Nixon said. "Or shot."

"They hate you, and they hate me," Kissinger said. "But the question is now: how can we maneuver it . . . so that it can look like a settlement by Election Day?"

For the next three months, under Nixon's direction, Kissinger worked nonstop to find something that would "look like a settlement" before the election. That, Kissinger promised, would "finish the destruction of McGovern" and give Nixon the mandate he desired. The destruction of McGovern was uppermost in Nixon's mind the next morning, August 3. "What in the name of God are we doing on this score?" he yelled at Haldeman and Ehrlichman in the Oval Office. "What are we doing about their financial contributors?" he asked. "Are we running their tax returns?"

"Not as far as I know," Ehrlichman said.

"We'd better forget the goddamn campaign right now," Nixon raged. "We have all this power, and we're not using it." The president recorded in his diary that night: "All of our people are gun-shy as a result of the Watergate incident and don't want to look into files that involve Democrats." Nixon was chagrined that he had not used his "enormous powers" to dig into the Internal Revenue Service records of his political enemies. He promised himself that would change after the election.

Nixon flew to the Republican National Convention in Miami Beach on August 22, 1972. He had been renominated by a vote of 1,347 to 1. He wrote in his memoirs, "My eyes burned from the lingering sting of

tear gas"—police had confronted thousands of antiwar protesters outside the convention center—"as I entered the hall to accept my fifth and
last nomination." The delegates shouted, "Four more years! Four more
years!"

Eight days later, Haldeman walked into Nixon's office at the Western
White House in San Clemente. "Bad news," he said glumly. "I really
mean it—it's really bad." He handed the president the latest Gallup poll.
Nixon: 64 percent. McGovern: 30 percent. Undecided: 6 percent. The
two men smiled with pleasure.

* * *

The future of Richard Nixon's second term pivoted on two fateful conversations on September 15, 1972: first with Dean, then with Kissinger.

That day, a federal grand jury had indicted Liddy, Hunt, McCord,
and the Cubans for the break-in and bugging at the DNC headquarters.
But the charges stopped there. The Watergate prosecutors had hit a stone
wall.

John Dean joined the president and Haldeman in the Oval Office
at 5:27 p.m. Richard Nixon later denied he had ever met Dean until 1973.

"Well, you had quite a day today, didn't you?" Nixon said.

"Quite a three months," Dean replied.

"How did it all end up?" Haldeman asked.

"Three months ago I would have had trouble predicting where we'd
be today," Dean said. "I think that I can say that fifty-four days from
now that not a thing will come crashing down to our surprise." He was
referring to the time left until Election Day.

The president was well pleased with Dean. "The way you've handled
it, it seems to me, has been very skillful, because you—putting your fingers in the dikes every time that leaks have sprung here and sprung
there. . . ." With Watergate seemingly stanched, Nixon warmed to the
prospect of revenge in days to come. "All of those that have tried to
do us in . . . are asking for it and they are going to get it," he said. "We
haven't used the Bureau and we haven't used the Justice Department,
but things are going to change."

But at "the Bureau," the FBI, the number-two man, Mark Felt, and
his colleagues were convinced they had to do something regarding the
government of Richard Nixon.

They suspected a conspiracy to obstruct justice was going on at the

White House. They thought the president had placed Pat Gray in charge of the FBI as part of that conspiracy. Gray's appointment "hurt all of us deeply," said Charles Bolz, the chief of the FBI's accounting and fraud division. Felt was Hoover's rightful heir. "Felt should have moved up right there and then," Bolz said. "And that's what got him into the act. He was going to find out what was going on. . . . And, boy, he really did." Felt was "Deep Throat," the *Washington Post's* best source on Watergate. "I knew somebody would break," Nixon would say bitterly after the first piercing newspaper articles started appearing in late September.*

Six hours later, Kissinger sat down with the president. Kissinger had spent much of the past month traveling the world—to Saigon, to Moscow, and to Paris, where he held another clandestine meeting with the top representative of North Vietnam, Le Duc Tho, a member of the enemy's Politburo.

At long last, Le Duc Tho wanted to talk peace.

"He said: 'You have to tell us if you want to settle it,'" Kissinger reported to the president. "I said: 'Yes, we want to settle it.' He said: 'Give me a day.' I said: 'Well, October 15th.' He took my hand and said: 'Our first agreement. We'll settle it October 15th.'"

Nixon was stunned and skeptical. October 15 was one month away.

"What do you think his reason is?" the president asked.

"I think they are terrified of you getting re-elected," Kissinger replied. "I said: 'You and your friends have turned this election into a plebiscite on Vietnam. . . . The President is going to have a majority for continuing the war.'"

---

* "We know what's leaked and we know who leaked it," Haldeman told the president on October 19 (Nixon White House Tapes, Oval Office). "Is it somebody in the FBI?" Nixon asked. "Yes, sir," said Haldeman. "Very high up."

NIXON: Somebody next to Gray?

HALDEMAN: Mark Felt.

NIXON: Now why the hell would he do that?

HALDEMAN: It's hard to figure. . . . If we move on him, then he'll go out and unload everything. He knows everything that's to be known in the FBI. . . . Gray's scared to death. . . .

NIXON: What would you do with Felt? . . . Christ! You know what I'd do with him? Bastard!

Attorney General Kleindienst, following orders from the White House, told Gray five times to fire Felt. The acting director could not find the will to do it.

But Kissinger also reported that what "Thieu is really afraid of is a cease-fire." Somehow the president would have to negotiate an end to the war with his allies as well as his enemies.

* * *

"We set up dinner on the *Sequoia* tonight, Kissinger, Haig and I with the President," Haldeman recorded on the night of September 28. Kissinger was convinced that "the North Vietnamese do want to settle. The hang-up still is dumping Thieu. . . . What he wants to do is send Haig to Saigon tomorrow, have him meet with Thieu, and get an agreement from Thieu to secretly agree to step down, sometime around January."

For days on end they wrestled with the Vietnam dilemma. "I know we have to end the war," Nixon said on September 29. "But if we end it in the wrong way, we've got a hell of a problem—not in the election. Forget the election. We'll win the election. We could surrender in Vietnam and win the election."

"What do we require Thieu to do?" he asked. "If he does get out, does it unravel in South Vietnam?"

Kissinger predicted, presciently, that even if there were an official cease-fire and American troops withdrew, the fighting between North and South Vietnam might have no end in sight. "Thieu doesn't want a cease-fire," Kissinger said. "He doesn't want us out. I mean, let's face it: the real point is that our interests and his are now divergent. We want out. We want our prisoners. We want a cease-fire. He wants us in. He thinks he's winning. And he wants us to continue bombing—"

"For another two or three years," Nixon said. "Jesus Christ, it's a hell of a choice."

Haig was about to go to Saigon as a special envoy to President Thieu. "Make it very clear to him," Nixon told Haig later that day. "He can't just assume that because I win the election that we're going to stick with him through hell and high water. This war is not going to go on. God-damn it, we can't do it. . . . We've got to get the war the hell off our backs in this country. That's all there is to it."

Haig pointed out, "Of course, if it looks like it could cause a public break . . ."

The president finished the thought: "That would be bad," he said. "A public break would hurt us. That'd hurt us in the election."

Kissinger then said, in so many words, what Nixon knew all too well.

After twenty thousand American combat deaths on his watch, the president could be accused of imposing a deal on Thieu that could have been struck back in October 1968.

Nixon weighed this possibility. Then he continued to instruct Haig on how to talk to Thieu: Nixon had stood by South Vietnam in the face of overwhelming opposition. Nixon had "no support. The House was against him. The Senate was against him. The media was against him. The students had rioted. All sorts of hell-raising. He's made these tough decisions." Now Thieu had to give him something in return.

He gave Nixon the back of his hand.

"We have a major crisis with Thieu," Kissinger told Nixon at Camp David on October 4. "He rejects every proposal we've made, every last one of them."

"We can't have a huge bust-up with Saigon before the election," Kissinger said. "Afraid not," Nixon replied. "Of course Thieu knows that. . . . What is his line?"

"His line is that he's the government of South Vietnam, that the North Vietnamese are the aggressors and they've got to leave," Kissinger said. "He is playing '68 all over again. . . . He figures if he can survive now 'til the 7th and just dig in then we'll have to yield."

"He's got to trust the President. He's never let him down," Nixon said, referring to himself, as he did more and more often, in the third person.

Kissinger was set to talk to North Vietnam's Paris delegation in four days. "Supposing we don't get to an agreement," he suggested. "We are in good shape as far as Thieu is concerned. If we do get to an agreement I will just have to go out and . . ."

"And cram it down his throat," said the president. "After the election we'll do what we goddamn well please."

* * *

But Hanoi was thinking one step ahead of the next election.

"We must concentrate our efforts on doing whatever it takes to resolve our first objective, which is *to fight to force the Americans to withdraw*," Le Duan, North Vietnam's Politburo chief and the nation's top decision maker since Ho Chi Minh's death, wrote in a formal decision in September. Le Duc Tho received his orders in Paris shortly before Kissinger arrived. The Politburo told its chief negotiator to give the Americans the concessions they sought. Thieu could stay in office. The

South Vietnamese government could remain as well. A cease-fire in place, with Communist forces controlling some of South Vietnam, would take hold. An election commission, with Communist representation, would reach a political settlement.

These were simply tactics to Hanoi, all aimed at achieving their strategic goal: an American military withdrawal. The North Vietnamese calculated that without American support Saigon would fall.

At 7:00 p.m. on Thursday, October 12, after a sixteen-hour session in Paris, Kissinger, accompanied by Haig, returned to the White House. They walked into the president's Executive Office Building study, outfitted with leather armchairs, a wet bar, and hidden microphones. Nixon and Haldeman were waiting. The president made Kissinger a scotch and soda, Haig a martini. Whatever Nixon made for himself, he was soon high.

"Well, you got three out of three, Mr. President," Kissinger said— China, Russia, Vietnam.

"You got an agreement?" said Nixon. "Are you kidding?"

"No, I'm not kidding," Kissinger said.

Nixon laughed with pleasure and turned to General Haig.

"I'm going to ask Al, because you're too prejudiced, Henry. You're so prejudiced to the peace camp that I can't trust you. Don't you think so, Al?"

"Yes, sir," Haig said. He was not laughing.

NIXON: What about Thieu?

HAIG: It isn't done.

KISSINGER: Well, that's the problem. . . . Here is what we have to do: I have to go to Paris on Tuesday to go over the agreed things word-for-word. . . . Then I go to Saigon to get Thieu aboard. . . .

NIXON: Won't it totally wipe out Thieu, Henry?

HALDEMAN: Yeah.

KISSINGER: Oh, no. It's so far better than anything we discussed. He won't like it because he thinks he's winning, but here is the deal, just to give you the main points. . . .

NIXON: We can do that after.

KISSINGER: All right, afterwards. . . . We are getting out of this with honor.

NIXON: Henry, let me tell you this: it has to be with honor. But also it has to be in terms of getting out. We cannot continue to have this cancer eating at us at home, eating at us abroad. . . . You use that term . . . "with honor"?

KISSINGER: "With honor."

NIXON: Do you use it? Apprise me, Al. "Honor"?

HAIG: Sure. . . . Thieu's got his rights. . . .

KISSINGER: Thieu can stay. No side deals.

NIXON: Why can he? How? Under what conditions?

KISSINGER: There are no conditions. Thieu can stay. The only thing we agreed was that Thieu will talk to the other side—

NIXON: Um-hmm.

KISSINGER: —about setting up something that will be called the National Council for National Reconciliation and Concord. . . .

NIXON: They're leaving Thieu in. They're in. And they're supposed to negotiate a National Council? Thieu will never agree, they'll never agree, so they screw up, and we support Thieu, and the Communists support them, and they can continue fighting, which is fine. . . . Let me come down to the nut-cutting, looking at Thieu. What Henry has read to me, Thieu cannot turn down. If he does, our problem will be that we have to flush him, and that will have flushed South Vietnam. Now, how the hell are we going to come up on that?

Over dinner, the three men drank the president's best wine, a '57 Château Lafite Rothschild. (A rare event, noted the abstemious but ever observant Haldeman. The president almost always saved the finest vintages for himself, the bottles discreetly wrapped in a white linen napkin by his valet, while others were served California *vin ordinaire*.)

Haldeman soberly recorded in his diary that night, "The P kept interrupting Henry all through the discussion. He obviously was all cranked up and wasn't listening to the details. . . . The real basic problem boils down to the question of whether Thieu can be sold on it and if he doesn't buy it, there's no option but to flush him, because we can't turn down the offer: we're trapped now." Haldeman's entry for the next day reads, "Both the P and Henry are realizing in the cold gray light of dawn today that they still have a plan that can fall apart . . . although Henry's convinced that he's got it settled and that it will work out and that we can talk Thieu into it."

On October 18, Nixon sent Kissinger to Saigon carrying a handwritten note in which the president pledged his devotion to Thieu and the survival of South Vietnam as a free country. Over the next seventy-two hours, Kissinger tried to convince Thieu to sign the Paris Peace Accords. It was futile. Communication between the two men broke down. So did the secure communications system in the embassy, forcing Kissinger to use a bulky scrambling machine in Ambassador Bunker's bedroom to send increasingly frantic bulletins to Haig. Coding and decoding their conversations took hours; their messages overlapped; their signals were crossed; anger and frustration between Kissinger and his military aide mounted.

* * *

On October 22, Haldeman recorded: "The Vietnam deal blew up this morning. Thieu stonewalled Henry. We're back in the soup."

Kissinger wrote in a cable from Saigon that day: "Thieu has just rejected the entire plan or any modification of it and refuses to discuss any further negotiations"; he demanded instead "total withdrawal of North Vietnamese forces, and total self-determination of South Vietnam."

"It is hard to exaggerate the toughness of Thieu's position. His demands verge on insanity," Kissinger wrote in a second message. "He stated that we have been colluding with Moscow and Peking for months against him."

The ambassador sent a third report. Thieu had said, "The South

Vietnamese people will assume that we have been sold out by the U.S. and that North Vietnam has won the war. . . . If we accept the document as it stands, we will commit suicide—and I will be committing suicide."

On October 26, 1972, Kissinger returned to Washington, where he convened an unusual public press conference. In one of the most striking statements in the history of American warfare and diplomacy, he said, "We believe that peace is at hand."

Nixon, Kissinger, and Haig wrote of this moment in their memoirs.

Nixon: "I knew immediately that our bargaining position with the North Vietnamese would be seriously eroded and our problem of bringing Thieu and the South Vietnamese along would be made even more difficult."

Kissinger: "'Peace is at hand' would provide a handy symbol of governmental duplicity in the continued bitter atmosphere of the Vietnam debate."

Haig: "The President regarded Kissinger's gaffe as a disaster."

* * *

Richard Nixon was reelected president of the United States on Tuesday, November 7, 1972. Though it was the first election in which eighteen-year-olds could vote, the turnout was a mere 55 percent, one of the lowest recorded in the twentieth century. Nearly thirty-four million eligible voters did not bother to cast a ballot for president. But neither the spreading stain of Watergate nor the bloodshed in Vietnam stopped the second-greatest landslide in the history of the presidency. Nixon took forty-nine of the fifty states and won 60.7 percent of the popular vote to McGovern's 37.5 percent.

At 2:30 a.m. on Wednesday, Nixon ordered up some bacon and eggs from the White House mess for himself, Haldeman, and Colson. They had a quiet celebration. Later that day, he sent Haig to Saigon to hand-deliver a letter for Nguyen Van Thieu.

> Dear Mr. President:
>   On this day after my reelection I wish to reopen our dialogue about the draft agreement to end the war. . . . For you to pursue what appears to be your present course . . . would play into the hands of the enemy and would have extremely grave consequences for both our peoples and it would be disaster for yours.

Not long thereafter, Thieu's ambassador to the United States, Tran Kim Phuong, came to see Henry Kissinger in the White House. "Your Government has managed to enrage the President almost beyond belief," Kissinger told him. "Saigon has attacked me as betraying you, and I am attacked here as being a murderer. . . . Saigon thinks, that clever Kissinger, he wants the Nobel Prize. We will wear him out and get to President Nixon."

"It is a tragedy," Kissinger said. "We have produced a horrible tragedy."

CHAPTER TWENTY

"A hell of a way to end the goddamn war"

THE DAY after his overwhelming reelection, Richard Nixon summoned every member of his Cabinet to the White House. The president was in a dark mood for a man in a moment of triumph. "I am at a loss to explain the melancholy," he wrote five years later, but on reflection, he thought the incubus of Vietnam and the impending trial of the Watergate burglars were haunting him.

Quoting Benjamin Disraeli, Britain's prime minister a century before, Nixon told his Cabinet that he wanted no "exhausted volcanoes" in his government. He left abruptly. Haldeman rose and told everyone to turn in their resignations, effective by the end of Nixon's first term in January 1973.

The president had been planning this for a long time. "We've got to really do something regarding a new government," Nixon had told Haldeman seven weeks before. "Tear the State Department to pieces. . . . The Treasury bureaucracy is bad and so is Justice. . . . Helms has got to go and we should get rid of the clowns [at the CIA] by cutting personnel forty percent. The information they develop is worthless. . . . The real problem is, of course, Defense. . . . He wants to tell all hands that everybody should resign" the day after the election.

"It was done in an appallingly brutal way. It just left people stunned," said George P. Shultz, who served Nixon as secretary of labor and secretary of the treasury. "It was cruel." Nixon realized in retrospect that "it was a mistake. I did not take into account the chilling effect this action would have. . . . The situation was compounded by my own isolation at Camp David, where I spent eighteen days in the four weeks after the election."

In the solitude of his mountain retreat, Nixon planned to tear down the pillars of the political establishment, rebrand the Republican Party in coalition with conservative Democrats, create what he called a New Majority to last until the end of the twentieth century, and destroy the remnants of LBJ's Great Society once and for all.

He began by dismantling his national security team. He fired CIA director Richard Helms. He started to "tear the State Department to pieces" by replacing the career diplomats of the Foreign Service with politically loyal appointees. Nixon vowed to "ruin the Foreign Service. I mean ruin it." He intended to remove Secretary of Defense Laird and Secretary of State Rogers as soon as possible. Laird was ready to leave—but Rogers was unwilling to resign. "Wants me to talk to Rogers, make the point that . . . anyone who's been in for four years should go," Haldeman noted in his November 14, 1972, diary entry. "Finish in a blaze of glory with the Vietnam peace signing."

Nixon even reconsidered the wisdom of retaining Kissinger—whose psychological stability he questioned in solitary conversations with Haldeman and Haig—for the peace he had promised was nowhere at hand.

"That goddamn Thieu," Kissinger said in a telephone call to the president at Camp David on November 15. "I don't see how he can continue to stall," the president replied. "What in the hell is he going to do?" Thieu's intransigence had put Hanoi's leaders in "a very tough frame of mind," Kissinger said—but "I think at this moment they are less of a problem than Thieu."

If Nixon recalled his own conspiracy with Thieu to scuttle the peace talks in 1968, such thoughts went unrecorded.

* * *

With grim resolve, Kissinger returned to Paris and presented North Vietnam with a list of sixty-nine proposed changes in the Peace Accords, all intended to mollify America's ally in Saigon. "The list was

so preposterous, it went so far beyond what we had indicated both publicly and privately, that it must have strengthened Hanoi's already
strong temptation to dig in its heels," Kissinger later admitted.

Hanoi did so. In response, Nixon dictated a back-channel cable to
Kissinger on November 24 with a dramatic threat: I WOULD BE PREPARED
TO AUTHORIZE A MASSIVE STRIKE ON THE NORTH if the talks broke off, the presi-
dent said. The war would go on.

Nixon knew this was a great risk. WE ALL MUST REALIZE THAT THERE IS NO
WAY WHATEVER THAT WE CAN MOBILIZE PUBLIC OPINION BEHIND US. THE COST IN
OUR PUBLIC SUPPORT WILL BE MASSIVE, he predicted in the cable. Congress
might cut off all funds for combat, Nixon feared; the American people
would likely be appalled.

"It's just a hell of a way to end the goddamn war," the president told
Haig in the Oval Office on November 30. "I didn't want the goddamn
thing," the president raged, referring to Kissinger's "peace is at hand"
proclamation. "But you know why he did that? He wanted to make peace
before the damned election."

That day, the president called the Joint Chiefs, led by Admiral
Moorer, to the White House. He told them to develop a plan to bomb
North Vietnam as never before if the peace deal did not take hold.

"Above all," he said, "B-52s are to be targeted on Hanoi."

Nixon saw only one way out: an unprecedented attack by squadrons
of B-52 bombers aimed directly at the capital of North Vietnam, civilian casualties be damned.

"Start bombing the bejeezus out of them," the president said. "We
can go 'til the Congress comes back" from adjournment—after the New
Year. "I don't see any other way we can survive this whole goddamn
thing."

* * *

On December 5, Nixon gathered his innermost circle at Camp David—
Haldeman, Ehrlichman, and his favorite hard-charging counselor,
Chuck Colson—for five days of deliberation over Vietnam. Haldeman
wrote that their long talks were "really agony." The question was "who
is to blame for the breakdown? K wants the P to blame North Vietnam"
in a televised address to the American people. "The P's concern is that
this just ties him in with a failure."

The consensus at Camp David was that Kissinger was on the edge of sanity. Nixon said that "the real problem is we have a weak link as a negotiator," Haldeman wrote. "He wanted to be sure I read Hutschnecker's book *The Will to Live*." (Arnold Hutschnecker was a psychotherapist whom Nixon had consulted off and on for twenty years.) "He thinks the thesis . . . is clearly related to K's suicidal complex."

They decided to reject Kissinger's advice on the Paris talks and tell him "it would be a mistake to break it off and the P to go on TV with chapter and verse as to why the negotiations have failed," Haldeman recorded. "We're in the Christmas season now, people feel good, and so on, they don't want to hear all this." Nixon still had a shred of hope: "The President feels we just can't spend any more; any more money, lives, time, effort, agony on the war. That we can get out now. . . . We should keep the hopes alive."

* * *

Hopes were dashed. On December 12, in Saigon, Thieu gave a speech to his legislature flatly rejecting any peace agreement. In Paris, the talks broke off. In Washington, Nixon faced a seismic split within his government.

That day, Secretary of Defense Laird sent a long and impassioned message to the president arguing for an immediate cease-fire. Laird said he and Admiral Moorer had agreed that Nixon had "only one viable realistic choice. That choice is to sign the agreement now." Nixon could end the war before Christmas, bring American prisoners of war home, receive an accounting of soldiers missing in action—and let Thieu fend for himself. Otherwise, Laird warned, the president would lose more than support from Congress and the American people: "I am concerned that you are putting in jeopardy your reputation as a world leader and your future effectiveness on the world scene."

Nixon did not reply to Laird. At 10:45 a.m. on Thursday, December 14, Admiral Moorer sent word to the air force high command that major attacks against North Vietnam were "definitely on the front burner."

At that same hour, Kissinger returned to the White House from Paris, cursing the Vietnamese. "They're shits," he said. "Tawdry, miserable, filthy people. They make the Russians look good."

"And the Russians make the Chinese look good, I know," Nixon reasoned with his enraged aide. "You've got to remember who the enemy are. The enemy has never changed. The election didn't change it. The only friends we've got, Henry, are a few people of rather moderate education out in this country, and thank God, they're about 61 percent of the people, who support us," the president said. "Looking back, we probably should have let it wait 'til the election, and the day after the election: *Whack!*"

So began the countdown to the Christmas Bombing of 1972. There would be only one respite once it began. "I don't want anybody flying over Christmas Day," Nixon said. "People would not understand that. There's always been a truce: World War I, World War II, and so forth."

The commander in chief said to Kissinger, "Get rested and get ready for all this and go out there and just remember that when it's toughest, that's when we're the best. And remember, we're going to be around and outlive our enemies. And also, never forget, the press is the enemy."

"On that, there's no question," said Kissinger.

"The press is the enemy. The establishment is the enemy. The professors are the enemy," Nixon said. "Write that on the blackboard 100 times and never forget it."

* * *

On Saturday night, December 16, Nixon held a Christmas dinner at the White House for his Cabinet heads, for whom he had sharpened the guillotine blades to fall in a few weeks. Anne Armstrong, a Republican National Committee chairwoman newly appointed as a counselor to the president, rose to give a toast. In one breath, she praised Jesus Christ, the Prince of Peace, and "the P . . . the man who has done the most for peace in our history," Haldeman recorded. "A potential awkwardness didn't seem to develop."

The president spoke to Kissinger on December 17. "The whole thing that counts is how we look four years from now and not how we look four weeks from now," he said. "You see, one of the beauties of doing it now is we don't have the problem of having to consult with the Congress. Nobody expects me to consult with the Congress before doing what we are going to do tomorrow."

"The '52s will shake them," Nixon predicted.

"They are double-loaded," said Kissinger. "That's like a 4,000-plane raid in World War Two. . . . It's going to break every window in Hanoi."

"Just the reverberations? Well, that should tend to shake them up,"

Nixon said. "They are going to scream. They always do. They would have screamed otherwise but for the fact that the talks were broken. Now we'll give them something else to scream about."

Nixon went to Camp David at 4:46 p.m. Forty minutes later he telephoned Admiral Moorer at home to give the green light. Moorer wrote in his diary, "He emphasized that 'the strikes must come off' and that he did not expect any excuses. I carefully explained to the President . . . we were constrained in the selection of targets and tactics because of the weather. . . . He told me he wanted to be 'damn certain everybody understood this is for keeps.'"

Nixon called Moorer again "to stiffen his back." He warned the admiral, "I don't want any more of this crap about we couldn't hit this target or that one. This is your chance to use military power effectively to win this war, and if you don't I'll consider you responsible."

On December 18, at 7:15 p.m., Moorer sent a message to every senior American military commander in the theater of war: "You will be watched on a real-time basis at the highest levels here in Washington. We are counting on all hands to put forth a maximum, repeat maximum, effort in the conduct of this crucial operation. Good luck to all."

* * *

That night, the B-52 bombers struck the capital of Hanoi and the port of Haiphong in three great waves. Over twelve days at Christmas, 714 B-52 sorties dropped fifteen thousand tons of bombs in and around the capital and the port—a force greater than each of the atomic bombs dropped on Hiroshima and Nagasaki. The war planes inflicted immense damage, killing and wounding thousands, damaging or destroying North Vietnam's biggest railways and power plants, and terrorizing the two cities.

Nixon micromanaged the bombing, demanding more and more strikes on specific targets; Kissinger enforced his orders. "Now that we have crossed the bridge let's brutalize them," Kissinger told Moorer on the night of December 19. "You'll have massive problems with the President" if the attacks subsided.

North Vietnam struck back with surface-to-air missiles. They brought down a total of fifteen B-52s. Forty-two pilots and crewmen were killed and twenty-four captured. "The P kept coming back to the B-52 loss problem," Haldeman recorded. "It's going to be very tough to take."

On December 20, Nixon, Kissinger, and Haldeman met in the Oval Office. The president had sent Al Haig back to Saigon, just before the Christmas Bombing started, to try to strong-arm Thieu. "He got kicked in the teeth," Kissinger reported, referring to Haig. Thieu kept Haig waiting for five hours and then rejected any talk of peace. "What that son-of-a-bitch Thieu has done to us is criminal," Kissinger said. "There's almost no way we can get Thieu to go along without doing a Diem on him"— that is, overthrowing him, which was precisely what Hanoi wanted. "Thieu is an unmitigated, selfish, psychopathic son-of-a-bitch," Nixon said. Nevertheless, "we've got to continue the bombing of the North."

That same afternoon, ever restless, Nixon flew to Key Biscayne with Kissinger. Nine B-52s were downed over the next forty-eight hours. On December 22 the air force cut its sortie rate to sixty a day, trying to regroup its planes and rest its crews. Nixon was furious.

"I just came from the President and I have not seen him so outraged since I got in this job," Kissinger said in a telephone call to Admiral Moorer. "We have got to get the maximum shock effect now!" The admiral wrote in his diary, "This is a helluva way to run a war."

Nixon remained in the warm sun of his Florida retreat while Kissinger immediately returned to Washington to watch over the war. Seventy-five B-52s hit Hanoi on December 23; all returned safely. A larger attack was set for Christmas Eve. Kissinger called Nixon that afternoon. "Moorer is preparing a big strike," the president said.

"All-out," Kissinger replied. "We just got a report that they are totally evacuating Hanoi." Nixon hoped the enemy's will to fight and "the morale of their people" would be crushed.

Sleepless, Nixon opened his diary on Christmas Eve and wrote, "This is December 24, 1972—Key Biscayne—4 a.m."

"On this day before Christmas it is God's great gift to me to have the opportunity to exert leadership, not only for America but on the world," Nixon wrote. "This, on the one hand, imposes a great responsibility but, of course, at the same time the greatest opportunity an individual could have . . . the glorious burden of the presidency."

On December 26 the bombing resumed. Hanoi buckled under the immense force of the B-52s. Its leaders sent word through Paris that peace talks could resume as soon as the bombing ended. But Nixon wanted to inflict more punishment on the enemy. He did not relent. The B-52 attacks intensified to 115 sorties that day. The president took satisfaction in a readout sent by the French Foreign Ministry from its consul general in Hanoi: "I've just lived through the most terrifying hour of my life. An unbelievable raid has just taken place."

Nixon returned to the White House. On December 27 he spoke in the Oval Office with Col. Richard T. Kennedy, a senior officer on the National Security Council staff. Colonel Kennedy said he thought North Vietnam might settle, but it would not fall to its knees begging to surrender.

"Never!" Nixon said.

"To give the devil his due, the North has come down there, time after time, under the most incredibly difficult circumstances and done well. Now, that's all a matter of just plain will," Kennedy said.

"Sure," Nixon said. "They've got a greater will to win."

"We've done our best," the colonel said. "At considerable cost."

"God, yes," said the president. "God, yes. At great cost."

That night, Kissinger called to say North Vietnam had said again that it would talk peace if the bombs stopped falling. Nixon and Kissinger agreed that if Hanoi sent a third plea, they would ground the B-52s in thirty-six hours.

"We gave them a hell of a good bang," Nixon said with satisfaction. "We're punishing the hell out of them, aren't we?"

On the night of December 28, Colonel Kennedy called Admiral Moorer to report that Hanoi had "swallowed the hook." On December 29, sixty B-52s struck Hanoi and Haiphong for the last time. Twenty-four hours later, the Nixon administration proclaimed that the Paris peace talks would begin again as early as January 3, 1973—the day Congress reconvened in Washington.

And on that day, Richard Nixon learned, to his lifelong sorrow, that he had another war to fight.

* * *

The trial of the Watergate burglars would begin the next week. The White House counsel John Dean had been keeping a very close eye on the case.

Nearly a year had passed since Dean heard G. Gordon Liddy present his plans for espionage and sabotage to John Mitchell and Jeb Stuart Magruder, Haldeman's protégé and Mitchell's deputy at CREEP, in the attorney general's office at the Justice Department. Almost six months had gone by since the raid at the Watergate. The federal grand jury that indicted the seven burglars had heard testimony from Magruder, who had committed perjury, as Nixon knew, to protect himself and his superiors from prosecution.

Magruder was the director of the president's impending inaugural. He would have to decide whether to keep lying when called to testify at the trial. He was terrified. And he knew he was not the only false witness.

On the morning of January 3, Haldeman had a gut-wrenching conversation with Magruder. At 11:00 a.m., Haldeman walked into the Oval Office. "Colson could be in some real soup," he told Nixon. "Colson and Mitchell have both perjured themselves under oath," as had Magruder, before the grand jury.

"You mean Colson was aware of Watergate?" Nixon said.

"Not only was he aware of it, he was pushing very hard for results," Haldeman said bluntly.

"Who was he pushing?" the president asked.

"Magruder and Liddy," Haldeman answered. Liddy would rather die than testify. But Magruder now was caught in a perjury trap. If he kept lying under oath at the trial, he might stay out of jail—or he might ensnare himself. And if he told the truth, he could bring down Mitchell, Colson, and others very close to Nixon.

Nixon tried to absorb what he had just heard. "Does Mitchell know that Colson was involved?" he asked. "Does Colson know Mitchell was involved?"

"I think the answer is yes to both of those," Haldeman replied.

At that hour, Howard Hunt's criminal lawyer called John Dean and said that Hunt was about to crack at the prospect of prison. The federal judge in the case was John Sirica, a stalwart law-and-order conservative widely known in Washington as "Maximum John," for the severity of his sentences. The Watergate defendants were looking at decades behind bars. As Nixon learned two days later, Hunt craved a promise of presidential clemency. Hunt's wife had been killed in an airplane crash four weeks earlier; she was carrying ten thousand dollars in cash, a small part of the money that had been paid to Hunt and his coconspirators by some very senior members of the White House staff.

Many tens of thousands of dollars, much of it campaign cash held in White House safes, already had gone to keep the Watergate defendants silent and their lawyers solvent.

Winding up his conversation with the president, Haldeman said the key figures in the case would require care and feeding. "Liddy we're taking care of in one way" (stacks of hundred-dollar bills) and "we're taking care of Magruder the right way" (with a promise of a new job after the inauguration). But there would be problems galore in the days to come, during and after the trial.

"It gets down to undeniable specifics," Haldeman said. These specifics were, as the president knew within a matter of days, not merely perjury but also hush money, a multitude of felonies, and a chain of evidence reaching into the Oval Office. The strongest links in that chain were the reels of tape spinning beneath his feet.

* * *

White House staffers distant from the Oval Office saw strange things happening in the days between the election and the inauguration.

Michael B. Smith, a staunch Republican and, later, President Reagan's global ambassador for trade, was chief of presidential correspondence, in charge of 230 people who answered every letter addressed to Nixon, making each word seem convincing. "Gordon Strachan, who was one of Haldeman's young assistants, came over to me" before the inauguration, Smith remembered; Strachan had been Haldeman's liaison to CREEP. "He was carrying a black bag. He said, 'The President wants to thank everybody for what they did in the election campaign.' Strachan opened up the black bag and there was $300,000 in cash. Now, you tell me what a 28-year-old kid is carrying around $300,000 in cash for."*

"Watergate," Smith concluded, "involved arrogance, rather than malevolence. These were ruthless people. They were not corrupt in the slightest. I believe that the Nixon White House staff was probably the most pristine or puritanical staff you could ever imagine. But some of them were zealots to an extreme."

The zealot in chief was Chuck Colson. On Friday, January 5, Colson had a deep talk with Nixon about Howard Hunt, his friend of twenty years' standing.

The president wrote in his diary the next day, "Colson told me on

---

* Strachan actually was twenty-nine at the time. He was carrying the cash under Haldeman's orders. Indicted in 1974, he testified truthfully through his ordeal. All charges against him were dropped.

Friday that he had tried to do everything he could to keep Hunt from turning state's evidence. After what happened to Hunt's wife, etc., I think we have a very good case for showing some clemency." Colson continued, as Nixon wrote, that Haldeman and Ehrlichman were more deeply involved in Watergate than the president realized.

On January 8, Nixon and Colson talked again in the president's Executive Office Building hideaway. "I know it's tough for all of you," Nixon said, "for you, John, Bob, and all the rest. We're just not going to let it get us down. This is a battle. It's a fight."

Richard Nixon turned sixty the next day. How great a burden did he feel? He wrote in his diary that, ten years before, he'd felt that his life was "at an end." Now it had "turned completely around." But he knew a time bomb was already ticking for his second term, before the first one ended.

Nixon was sworn in for four more years as the thirty-seventh president of the United States on January 20, 1973. He concluded his last inaugural by saying, "We shall answer to God, to history, and to our conscience for the way in which we use these years."

CHAPTER TWENTY-ONE

"You could get a million dollars"

THE PRESIDENTIAL chalice was poisoned, drop by drop, days after the inaugural ball was over.

The Vietnam Peace Accords were signed in Paris. "After the cease-fire there will be inevitable violations," Nixon said on January 23, 1973, the day Kissinger initialed the pact. All sides broke the agreement. The war went on.* The armies of Hanoi and Saigon clashed. B-52 bombers pounded North Vietnamese troops in Cambodia and Laos. "Whack the hell out of them," Nixon commanded.

"We have a stick and a carrot to restrain Hanoi," the president told South Vietnam's foreign minister on January 30. The B-52s were a big stick.

That same day, the Watergate jury returned verdicts after deliberating for ninety minutes. Liddy and McCord were convicted on all counts. Hunt and the Cubans had pleaded guilty. All were facing decades behind

---

* "Who's causing the most violations of the agreement, the South Vietnamese?" Kissinger asked Admiral Moorer a month later. "Yes, the South Vietnamese," the Joint Chiefs chairman replied. (Minutes of Washington Special Actions Group Meeting, Washington, DC, February 23, 1973, *FRUS* X: Vietnam, January 1973–July 1975.)

bars. Judge Sirica held a post-trial hearing February 3. He bluntly stated that justice had yet to be served. He strongly doubted the government's witnesses, and he openly called on Congress to look into the case.

Nixon was outraged. "Here's the judge saying I did this," he railed to Colson in the Oval Office. "His goddamn conduct is shocking. . . . He's trying to prod the Senate into conducting a big investigation."

The Senate heard Sirica loud and clear. On February 7, it voted unanimously to create a select committee to investigate Watergate. Its chairman would be Senator Sam Ervin, a conservative Democrat from North Carolina given to country-boy maxims and constitutional admonitions. Ervin had a Harvard law degree to go with his down-home humor. His mandate was to investigate the Watergate break-in, any cover-ups, and "all other illegal, improper, or unethical conduct occurring during the Presidential campaign of 1972, including political espionage and campaign finance practices." He would receive half a million dollars to hire investigators—and the power to subpoena anyone save Richard Nixon.

The president flew to San Clemente the next day to spend a long weekend plotting to counter the Senate Watergate Committee. Haldeman, Ehrlichman, and Dean joined his strategy sessions. "We should play a hard game," Nixon said. He had two goals. He would maintain "the outward appearance of cooperation." But, in the meantime, "our objective internally should be maximum obstruction and containment, so as not to let this thing run away with us."

Back in Washington, Nixon spent much of the next week giving marching orders to his revamped national security team. The president's new director of central intelligence, James Schlesinger, was a Nixon man to the core—"I mean one that really had R.N. tattooed on him," his predecessor, Richard Helms, said—who had been an ax wielder at the Bureau of the Budget. Nixon told him to chop out the dead wood at the CIA, to purge as many people as possible, especially senior officers suspected of liberal sympathies.

Over the course of nineteen weeks, Schlesinger fired five hundred CIA analysts and more than a thousand clandestine service officers. After he received death threats over the dismissals, he hired armed bodyguards. He lasted five months as director of central intelligence.

Nixon, having rid himself of Secretary of Defense Laird, introduced the Joint Chiefs to their new boss at a formal luncheon at the Pentagon. Elliot Richardson was a genial Boston Brahmin with no military exper- tise beyond leading a platoon at the Normandy invasion under General Eisenhower in June 1944. He had been secretary of health, education, and welfare in the first Nixon administration, in charge of issues that were his cup of tea, not Nixon's.

Nixon alluded to his preference at a February 15 luncheon with Rich- ardson and the Joint Chiefs, weighing the value of the Department of Defense versus the costs of welfare. "We would like to be able to put the DOD budget into welfare," the president said, "but if we did, the world would eventually fall under the Communist system."

Richardson lasted four months as secretary of defense.

At 9:09 a.m. on February 16, L. Patrick Gray, the acting FBI director, entered the Oval Office for the second time in his life. After a nine- month delay, Nixon was submitting Gray for Senate hearings to confirm him as J. Edgar Hoover's successor, as required by law. The president was taking a huge risk.

Gray was a dutiful dullard deeply entangled in the web of Water- gate. He had destroyed evidence on orders from John Dean. He was back- handing his agents' reporting to Dean—which an FBI internal report later described as "the most serious blunder from an investigative stand- point."

Gray had made few friends at FBI headquarters, where he became known as "Three-day Gray" for the time he spent at his desk each week. He had let the FBI's number-two man, Mark Felt, control the Watergate investigation. And Felt was the key source of the front-page Watergate stories in the *Washington Post*. Nixon was one of the few people in America who knew that.* The *Post* had been the first news- paper to report that Howard Hunt and Gordon Liddy oversaw the Watergate break-in, that John Mitchell controlled a slush fund for political espionage, and that "political spying and sabotage" were at the heart of CREEP's campaign.

---

* Felt was not the only source reporters had at the FBI; at least four top agents fed the press. But Felt indisputably leaked to Bob Woodward at the *Washington Post* and to Sandy Smith at *Time* magazine. A corporate lawyer for *Time* ordered Smith to reveal his source; the attorney then called his good friend John Mitchell, which was how Nixon knew what Felt did off-duty.

Nixon quickly asked Gray how he would handle the Senate's questions about Watergate. "Would it hurt or help for you to go up there and be mashed about that?" Nixon asked.

"Mr. President, I'm the man that's in the best position to handle that," Gray said. "I've consistently handled it from the outset. . . . I think the Administration has done a hell of a fine job in going after this thing." This was bluster and bombast. "You haven't been able to do anything—or have you?—up to this point, about the leaks," Nixon asked. "The whole story, we've found, is coming out of the Bureau. . . . This stuff didn't leak when Hoover was there. I've never known of a leak when Hoover was there. I could talk to him in this office about everything. And the reason is that—it wasn't because they loved him, but they *feared* him. And they've got to *fear* the man at the top. . . . You've got to be brutal, tough and respected. . . . I understand leaking out of the CIA, those goddamned cookie-pushers. But if it leaks out of the Bureau, then the whole damn place ought to be fired."

Nixon's fury rose. "You've got to do it like they did in the war," the president said. "In World War Two, the Germans, if they went through these towns and then one of their soldiers, a sniper hit one of them, they'd line up the whole goddamned town and say until you talk you're all getting shot. I really think that's what has to be done. I mean, I don't think you can be Mr. Nice Guy over there."

"I haven't been," Gray protested. "These guys know they can't lie to me like they used to lie to Hoover."

Nixon was relentless. "I've got to have a relationship here where you go out and do something and deny on a stack of Bibles."

"Right," said Gray. "I understand."

"I don't have anybody else," Nixon said. "I can't hire some asshole from the outside." He went on, his rage simmering. "There were times when I felt that the only person in this goddamned government who was standing with me was Edgar Hoover. . . . He would break his ass if he saw something that was wrong being done, if somebody was pissing on us. . . . What you've got to do is to *do like Hoover.*"

"It's going to be a bloody confirmation," Nixon warned Gray. "You've got to be prepared to take the heat and get bloodied up. But if you do go through a bloody one, let's remember that you're probably going to be in for just four years. And then they're gonna throw you out. So let's get in there and do some good for the country. . . . This country, this bureaucracy—Pat, you know this—it's crawling with, Pat, at best, at best, unloyal people and at worst treasonable people."

"Treasonable people," Gray repeated.

"We have got to get them, break them," Nixon said. "The way to get them is through you. See?"

* * *

On February 22, Nixon smuggled Sen. Howard Baker into the presidential hideaway at the Executive Office Building. It was extremely rare for any aspect of the president's day to go unrecorded in the official White House logs. This was an exception. Senator Baker, a photogenic and politically ambitious Tennessee Republican, would be the ranking minority member of the Watergate Committee. He was eager to please the president. He laid out the committee's plans, and the next day in the Oval Office Nixon gave Ehrlichman a full account of their conversation.

"I must have scared him to death," Nixon said. "I put it very hard to Baker."

Nixon said the senators planned first to take testimony from "a lot of pipsqueak witnesses, little shit-asses, over periods of weeks to build it up, the pressure." But then, "you got to call Haldeman, you got to call Ehrlichman." The president laid down the law—or his version of it. He said he would assert "executive privilege" to keep his White House staff from being dragged before the committee.

The Constitution is silent on the question of executive privilege, and the Supreme Court had never confronted it. But two prior presidents had invoked it. One was Dwight Eisenhower; the other, Harry Truman. Twenty-five years before, Truman asserted the privilege to protect government personnel records from congressmen—most notably, Richard Nixon—chasing Communists such as Alger Hiss. This confrontation was at the center of chapter one in Nixon's 1962 memoir *Six Crises*. Back then, Nixon had fought against executive privilege. Now he had to fight for it.

But he could not invoke the privilege in order to keep the silence of people outside presidential command—such as John Mitchell, hunkered down at his New York law firm, trying to raise hush money for the Watergate defendants; Chuck Colson, who had left the White House days before; and Herb Kalmbach, the president's private attorney, fund-raiser, and financier. Each was in legal peril.

"What are they going to say?" Nixon asked, dreading the answer, though he already knew it in part. "They raised the money?"

"There's a hell of a lot of money, and it floated around, and there weren't receipts, and there was funny bookkeeping, and money went to Mexico and back, and there were just a hell of a lot of odds and ends," Ehrlichman replied.

"What'll Mitchell say?" the president wondered.

"I don't know," Ehrlichman admitted. "He's been puffing his pipe and looking at the ceiling and saying, 'You guys got a problem.'"

After discussing four more present and former White House aides who might have problems testifying truthfully, they turned to Colson.

"He'll perjure himself," said the president.

If the president's aides defied the Senate Watergate Committee when it subpoenaed witnesses, "in effect we take the Fifth Amendment," Ehrlichman said. "Is that worse?"

"Yeah, it's a cover-up," Nixon said. "The cover-up is worse than whatever comes out. It really is—unless somebody is going to jail." The president had a prescient vision of what lay ahead: a ceaseless procession of investigations, interrogations, and indictments.

"I'm not going to let anybody go to jail," he vowed. "That I promise you."

* * *

One week later, on February 27, the president summoned his thirty-three-year-old White House counsel, John Dean, for the first of thirty tape-recorded conversations they would have about Watergate over the next forty-nine days. Though Nixon droned on about the Hiss case and dreamed of a counterattack against Congress, these conversations centered on two conundrums: the cover-up and covering up the cover-up.

Nixon first asked about the sentencing of the seven Watergate defendants. Dean told him that Judge Sirica, "Maximum John," was delaying judgment day until March, using presentencing interrogations by probation officers to conduct his own inquisition into the case—and trying to coerce confessions. "This judge may go off the deep end in his sentencing," Dean warned.

Then there would be the Senate Watergate Committee to face in May. The president said he had told Senator Baker to run things just as Nixon had run the Hiss case. "But the committee is after someone in the White House," Nixon said. "They'd like to get Haldeman, Colson, or Ehrlichman."

"Or possibly Dean," said Dean.

March 1 brought a tremor of fear at the White House. On the first day of his confirmation hearings, Pat Gray testified and, trying to ingratiate himself with the senators on the Judiciary Committee, volunteered to let them see the FBI's raw and unedited investigative reports on Watergate. Handing over the Watergate files would be giving an enemy a sword. The files showed that key figures in the case had lied to the FBI. And they showed that Dean had sat in on FBI agents' interviews with every key figure in the case—to the agents' deep displeasure. If the senators saw that fact, then Dean could be called to testify under oath. Gray had put the White House one subpoena away from a potentially calamitous confrontation.

"For Christ's sake," the president said with a groan, "he must be out of his mind."

The next day, at a White House press conference, a reporter asked if the president would object to Dean's testifying about Watergate, the FBI, and the White House. "Of course," said the president. "It is executive privilege. . . . No President could ever agree to allow the Counsel to the President to go down and testify before a committee."

On March 7, Gray's increasingly contentious confirmation hearings landed John Dean on page one of the *Washington Post*. The president called Dean into the Oval Office at 8:53 a.m. They commiserated. The hearings had "morphed into a mini-Watergate hearing, with the Democrats using selected items plucked from the raw FBI material . . . to discredit him as a potential FBI director," Dean later wrote. "Remarkably, Gray just kept digging himself a deeper hole, and by thrusting me into his hearings, he provided the Democrats with sufficient leverage to kill his nomination: They asserted that if I did not appear as a witness, they would not confirm him." The president had become "totally disenchanted" with Gray. He charged Dean with subtly scuttling the nomination.

* * *

Two hours later, Nixon spoke privately in the Oval Office with Thomas Pappas, the oil company executive who had channeled more than half a million dollars to Nixon's 1968 campaign from the colonels who ran the military junta in Greece. Pappas had been instrumental in the selection of Spiro Agnew as Nixon's running mate in 1968, and he had personally contributed at least one hundred thousand dollars to Nixon's 1972 reelection. The week before his meeting with the president, he had met with the campaign's manager, John Mitchell, in New York and pledged six-figure sums to the Watergate defendants' hush-money fund.

Haldeman already had told the president that Pappas was contributing heavily to "the continuing financial activity in order to keep those people on base . . . and he's able to deal in cash." In exchange, all Pappas wanted was an assurance that his close friend Henry Tasca would be reappointed as the American ambassador to Greece. "Good. I understand. No problem," Nixon had replied.

Pappas entered the Oval Office at 10:54 a.m. Nixon gave his word on the ambassadorship and thanked Pappas profusely. "I am aware of what you're doing to help out," he said. "I won't say anything further, but it's very seldom that you find a friend like that."*

* * *

One week before, Pat Gray had turned over the FBI's Watergate files—twenty-six thick books, along with summaries and analyses—to the Senate Judiciary Committee. On March 14 the president ordered Dean to call the FBI to see if this procedure had any precedent. He said he wanted an answer in three minutes, and if he did not get it, "I'll fire the whole goddamn Bureau."

As Nixon knew perfectly well, J. Edgar Hoover had fed the House Un-American Activities Committee, where Nixon served, reams of raw FBI reports on suspected Communists and Communist sympathizers from 1948 onward. But that was different, Nixon said. Hoover had done it under the table; it was a secret transaction; it never leaked.

Dean reminded Nixon of this history after conferring with the Bureau. (It took longer than three minutes; no one was fired. That was simply the way Nixon barked commands.)

---

* Questioned under oath in 1975, Nixon denied ever selling an ambassadorship to anyone. Pappas never was charged in the Watergate scandal. Ambassador Tasca helped keep America the only developed nation friendly to the Greek junta; the United States provided arms and intelligence to dictators who jailed and tortured political foes. Congress later tried to investigate Nixon's dealings with the Greek junta. The hearings were quashed on national security grounds.

"Well," Nixon told Dean, "keep 'em scared over there."

On March 14 the Senate Judiciary Committee voted unanimously to summon John Dean. The president had precluded that; at his March 2 press conference, he'd proclaimed that the White House counsel could not be compelled to testify before Congress. Nixon, Dean, and the president's press secretary, Ron Ziegler—whose prior job before joining the Nixon team in 1962 was as a Jungle Cruise skipper at Disneyland—huddled to prepare for a news conference Nixon had set for the next day, March 15. They knew that any answers they provided on Watergate would only provoke more questions.

The president, providing guidance, said, "Give them a lot of gobble-de-gook, that's all. Then let them squeal."

Ziegler, checking his notes, said: "We've made it very clear that no one in the White House directed espionage and sabotage."

Nixon made his position perfectly clear. "Espionage and sabotage is not illegal, do you understand? That's the point I'm making. Espionage and sabotage is illegal only if it's against the government."

The president acquitted himself masterfully at the March 15 press conference, where seven of the thirteen questions dealt with Gray, Dean, the forthcoming Watergate Committee hearings. He parried every one. Why had he banned Dean from testifying at Gray's confirmation? Nixon stood upon the Constitution to justify the obstruction of justice.

> Mr. Dean is Counsel to the White House. He is also one who was counsel to a number of people on the White House Staff. He has, in effect, what I would call a double privilege, the lawyer-client relationship, as well as the Presidential privilege. . . . I consider it my constitutional responsibility to defend the principle of separation of powers.
>
> I am very proud of the fact that in this Administration we have been more forthcoming in terms of the relationship between the executive, the White House, and the Congress, than any administration in my memory. We have not drawn a curtain down. . . . All we have said is that it must be under certain circumstances, certain guidelines, that do not infringe upon or impair the separation of powers that are so essential to the survival of our system.

In that connection, I might say that I had mentioned previously
that I was once on the other side of the fence, but what I am
doing here in this case is cooperating with the Congress in a
way that I asked the then President, Mr. Truman, to cooperate
with a committee of the Congress 25 years ago and in which
he refused. I don't say that critically of him now. He had his
reasons. I have mine.

And he flatly proclaimed, "Members of the White House staff will
not appear before a committee of Congress in any formal session" at any
time. That assertion of executive privilege seemed to slam the door on
the Senate Watergate Committee once and for all.

But after the barrage of questions, Nixon asked Haldeman and
Ehrlichman if Dean should write a Watergate report to feed the hunger
of the press corps and Congress. They concluded that it would be
impossible—and potentially suicidal. Dean himself told the president on
the morning of March 16: "There are some questions you can't answer."

Minutes later, Nixon and Haldeman spoke alone in the Oval Office.
Any report Dean could write would have to reveal criminal conduct.
"Then you get into a real mess," Haldeman said. "I just wonder if it isn't
a losing game."

That afternoon, Ehrlichman laid out his own Watergate report for
the president. His synopsis was startlingly detailed. Liddy and Hunt,
spurred by Colson, demanded and received from CREEP at least one
hundred thousand dollars for the Watergate break-in. "Liddy, being kind
of a nut, sat down with Hunt and said, 'Okay, how are we going to pull
this off?' And Hunt said, 'Listen, I know five Cubans who will come up
here for that kind of dough and they'll crack the United States Treasury.'
So they had to call McCord for equipment," because the CREEP security director had eavesdropping expertise from his career at the CIA.
"McCord says, 'What the hell are you guys up to?' And they told him."

How could Dean put this on paper? It would unravel threads that
ran right to the White House. "We can't do it," Ehrlichman said suc-
cinctly. In the evening, Nixon telephoned Dean. The president still
wanted a report—even if it only added another layer to the cover-up. "I
realize the problems of being too specific," Nixon said. "Just put it in
general terms, you see? I don't know. Do you think that's possible?"

"It's going to be tough but I think . . . it's a good exercise, and a drill that is absolutely essential," Dean said. The White House counsel also had a news flash for the president: "Maximum John" Sirica would impose sentences on the Watergate defendants in one week.

In an Oval Office conversation with Dean on March 17, Nixon elaborated on what the report should say. "I think what you've got to do, John, is to cut it off at the pass," the president said. "Liddy and his bunch just did this as part of their job."

On Monday, March 19, Howard Hunt's lawyer delivered a blackmail message to Dean, face-to-face in the White House. If Hunt didn't get $122,000 in cash within forty-eight hours, he would have some startlingly seamy things to say at his sentencing. Dean called John Mitchell in New York and asked, referring to Tom Pappas, "Is the Greek bearing gifts?"

On that same day, James McCord signed, sealed, and delivered a letter to Judge Sirica. McCord had not demanded hush money. His silence had not been bought. And he had heard scuttlebutt from his fellow defendants and some of their lawyers that infuriated him. The word was that the White House wanted to lay Watergate at the feet of the CIA, where he and five of his codefendants had served. McCord was intensely loyal to the CIA and Richard Helms. The idea that the Agency could take the fall for the crime and the cover-up compelled him to compose his letter. It would be read by the judge from the bench at the sentencing, four days later.

McCord wrote, "[I]n the interests of restoring faith in the criminal justice system, which faith has been severely damaged in this case, I will state the following:"

1. There was political pressure applied to the defendants to plead guilty and remain silent.
2. Perjury occurred during the trial in matters highly material to the very structure, orientation, and impact of the government's case, and to the motivation and intent of the defendants.
3. Others involved in the Watergate operation were not identified during the trial, when they could have been by those testifying. . . .

Following sentence, I would appreciate the opportunity to talk with you privately in chambers.

The facade of the cover-up was about to crack. Judge Sirica, upon reading the letter in his chambers, turned to his law clerk and triumphantly said, "This is going to break this case wide open." Nixon's attorney general, Richard Kleindienst, wrote in his memoirs: "Future historians, in a more detached environment, might well conclude that the McCord letter was not only the turning point in Watergate but perhaps a turning point in modern civilization."

Tuesday, March 20, 1973, was the last day of Richard Nixon's presidency unscathed by Watergate. The president was still the most powerful man on earth and the leader of the free world. He hammered home that message in a speech he made that morning in the Cabinet Room of the White House to two dozen Republican leaders in Congress and the chairman of the Republican National Committee, George H. W. Bush. Fortunately for future historians, the Cabinet Room was wired.

"The only threat to the world's freedom and the world's peace is the Soviet Union today and the People's Republic of China twenty years from now," the president proclaimed. "The United States, therefore, has to use this last ultimate moment. It is the last moment because whenever we fall behind we'll have no chips at all."

"There is a chance for peace," he said. "It's never going to be because . . . Zhou En-Lai and Nixon shook hands and got to know each other; Brezhnev and Nixon hit it off because they both came from poor families; all that gobble-de-gook you read in the columns. That's all crap. It happens only because the President of the United States . . . is strong enough and respected enough to be paid attention to. We are the force for peace in the world."

* * *

On the morning of March 21, John Dean reported to the Oval Office to present a full picture of the legal problems confronting the president. Their conversation remains the most remarkable tape Richard Nixon ever recorded.

"I have the impression that you don't know everything I know—and it makes it very difficult for you to make judgments that only you can make," Dean began. "I think that there's no doubt about the seriousness of the problem we've got."

"We have a cancer within, close to the presidency," Dean said. "It's growing daily. It's compounding. It grows geometrically now."

"One, we're being blackmailed; two, people are going to start per-juring themselves very quickly that have not had to perjure themselves to protect other people. . . . And there is no assurance—"

"That it won't bust," Nixon said.

Dean began to lay out facts, many of which Nixon knew very well: "Where did it start? It started with an instruction to me from Bob Haldeman to see if we couldn't set up a perfectly legitimate campaign intelligence operation over at the Re-Election Committee." Dean con-tinued: "I came up with Gordon Liddy. . . . I was aware of the fact that he had done some extremely sensitive things for the White House . . . going out into Ellsberg's doctor's office."

"Oh, yeah," said Nixon, who had learned about that break-in from Ehrlichman.

"Took Liddy over to meet Mitchell," Dean said. "Liddy laid out a million-dollar plan that was the most incredible thing I have ever laid my eyes on: all in codes, and involved black bag operations, kidnapping, providing prostitutes to weaken the opposition, bugging, mugging teams." The review of the break-in, arrests, trial, and imminent sentenc-ing of the Watergate burglars was Dean's throat-clearing cough before the cancer diagnosis.

The burglars had demanded hundreds of thousands of dollars in blackmail to keep silent. Mitchell had raised hush money as recently as the week before from the gift-bearing Greek. Haldeman had handed over $328,000 in CREEP funds for payoffs. Ehrlichman and Dean were entirely enmeshed in the crimes and the cover-up. It all consti-tuted a conspiracy to obstruct justice, Dean told the president. "Bob is involved in that. John is involved in that. I am involved in that. Mitchell is involved in that."

Dean turned to "the continued blackmail" by the Watergate defen-dants. "It'll go on when these people are in prison, and it will compound the obstruction of justice situation. It'll cost money. It's dangerous," he said. "People around here are not pros at this sort of thing. This is the sort of thing Mafia people can do: washing money, getting clean money, things like that. . . . We are not criminals and not used to dealing in that business."

"That's right," said the president. Then he asked, "How much money do you need?"

Dean took a guess.

"These people are going to cost a million dollars over the next two years." Silence filled the Oval Office for a few seconds.

"We could get that," Nixon said. "You could get a million dollars. And you could get it in cash. I know where it could be gotten. . . . You don't need a million right away, but you need a million. Is that right?"*

"That's right," Dean said. They agreed that the immediate problem was Howard Hunt, who could sink Ehrlichman, Colson, and Dean with a single deposition. "Don't you have to handle Hunt's financial situation . . . damn soon?" Nixon said. "Either that or let it all blow right now."

"If this thing ever blows and we're in a cover-up situation, I think it'd be extremely damaging to you," Dean said. "What happens if it starts breaking, and they do find a criminal case against a Haldeman, a Dean, a Mitchell, an Ehrlichman?"

Nixon returned the conversation to the blackmail. "Let me put it frankly: I wonder if that doesn't have to be continued?" Dean kept silent, overawed at engaging in a criminal conspiracy with the president.

"Let us suppose that you get the million bucks and you get the proper way to handle it," Nixon said. "That would be worthwhile." Otherwise, "the thing blows and they indict Bob and the rest."

The president continued: "Jesus, you'd never recover from that, John."

"That's right," Dean said.

"It's better to fight it out instead," Nixon concluded.

The fight resumed the next morning. The Watergate files Pat Gray had handed to the Senate held a deadly accusation. FBI agent Angelo Lano had concluded that Dean had lied to him by concealing the existence of Howard Hunt's White House safe. Sen. Robert Byrd, a West Virginia Democrat, asked Gray on March 22 if Dean had deceived the FBI.

Gray replied, "I would have to conclude that that probably is correct, yes, sir." Lying to the FBI meant slammer time.

---

* Nixon buzzed in his secretary, Rose Mary Woods, that afternoon, and asked how much money was in a certain White House safe. "I know we still have that four hundred," she said, on tape. The four-hundred-thousand-dollar slush fund was a secret cache only she and Nixon knew about.

The president's men convened in the Oval Office. "Gray is dead on the floor," Ehrlichman told the president. "He accused your counsel of being a liar," Haldeman said sardonically. "He may be dead," Dean said with false bravado, "'cause I may shoot him." The last laughs on the White House tapes echoed and faded.

Later that day, Nixon had a heart-to-heart with John Mitchell, who had flown down from New York to consult and comfort the president. But Nixon could not be consoled. He had concluded that obstruction of justice was the only recourse. "I don't give a shit what happens," he said. "I want you all to stonewall it, let them plead the Fifth Amendment, cover up or anything else. . . . We're going to protect our people, if we can."

* * *

The president and Haldeman fled Washington for the Florida White House on the day of the Watergate sentencing, Friday, March 23. They spent more than five hours that afternoon mulling over the case while they awaited word from Judge Sirica's courtroom.

The judge read McCord's letter from the bench. "The courtroom exploded," recalled Sam Dash, a law professor preparing to serve as chief counsel to the Senate Watergate Committee. "It was a stunning development. . . . It looked as if Watergate was about to break wide open."

Sirica gaveled the court into silence. Then he brought down the hammer on the other defendants: up to twenty years for Liddy, thirty-five for Hunt, and forty for the Cubans. He said the sentences would be reduced if the men cooperated by coming clean with the Senate committee.*

Nixon and Haldeman spent four days in Key Biscayne consumed by the case. Dean holed up in Camp David laboring on a written Watergate report for the president. Haldeman called him there on March 24. Dean said, "The problem is we've been bailing out everybody else and it's gotten out of hand and compounded the problem. Now we have to protect ourselves." They spoke again the next day. "He's back to his

---

* All did except for Liddy. McCord was released on bond pending the Senate hearings. The sentences Sirica imposed were arguably a form of coercion to force the defendants to incriminate themselves. He wasn't called "Maximum John" for nothing. The prison time actually served by the "Watergate Seven" ranged from two months for McCord to fifty-two months for Liddy.

cancer theory, that we've got to cut the thing out," Haldeman recorded
in his diary. But where to make the first cut? He and Dean talked a
third time on Monday, March 26.

"He feels that Mitchell has a problem and Mitchell may not realize
it," Haldeman wrote. "Then he went into a great deal of detail on what
he sees as the really serious problems now. The main one is the blackmail situation. He says he was aware that Mitchell and others were being
blackmailed by those involved in the Watergate thing."

The two tried to tally how much already had been paid to the Watergate defendants and their lawyers through funds controlled by Mitchell, Haldeman, Kalmbach, and CREEP. It came to more than five hundred
thousand dollars. "Dean feels he's not in a position to fully evaluate the
blackmail situation," Haldeman wrote, "but it's clear that all concerned
felt there were dire threats to the White House, and when you're being
blackmailed you imagine the worst."

Haldeman spent six hours with the president that day, going in circles on the Watergate case, shrouded in misery as the sun shone on the
Florida seashore: "It's a beautiful day at Key Biscayne, which I spent
inside, locked in the P's villa. We'll leave late tonight to go back to Washington."

The president faced the prospect of the Senate Watergate Committee hearings in seven weeks. On March 27 he mused, "A committee of
Congress is a double weapon. It destroys a man's reputation in public.
And if it turns its files over to the Department of Justice for prosecution,
they will prosecute the poor bastards. . . . I did it to Hiss."

Haldeman, Ehrlichman, and Dean now began to contemplate hir-
ing criminal lawyers. All realized that "it isn't going to get any better
on Watergate," as Nixon told Haldeman in the Oval Office on March 30.
"It's going to get worse. . . . It's going to go on and on and on and on."

Nixon decided to retreat to San Clemente for a week. Before he
returned to Washington, on Sunday, April 8, John Dean held an
informal off-the-record meeting with federal prosecutors. He had told
Haldeman of his plans. Haldeman responded with a memorable admo-
nition: "Just remember that once the toothpaste is out of the tube it's
going to be very tough to get back in." By now, Dean wrote, he was
halfway out: "One foot in the White House and one foot outside it."

On April 9, Nixon and Haldeman had a hushed and haunting conversation about "recording what is going on in this room," as the presi-

dent put it. "I feel uneasy about that." The tapes could be of great value to Nixon. He could keep them for a presidential memoir that could make millions. They would protect him against the inevitability that Kissinger would write his own version of history.

But if anyone else ever heard the tapes they could pose a great danger.

"I think we should destroy them," Nixon said.

CHAPTER TWENTY-TWO

"Vietnam had found its successor"

THAT SPRING was a dark season for Richard Nixon. Each week brought deluges of bad news. The downpours turned to floods, and the rising torrents slowly eroded the stone wall surrounding the White House. The wars of Watergate consumed every waking moment.

"Vietnam had found its successor," Nixon wrote, underscoring every word.

Friday, April 13: John Dean relayed inside information from federal prosecutors to the White House, and his news was dismal, befitting the day. Dean had served as a kind of human switchboard in the cover-up, conferring with every central participant. Now he was using his lawyers to winkle information out of federal investigators, even as he dangled a promise of becoming a witness for the prosecutors.

Howard Hunt was set to appear Monday afternoon before the Watergate grand jury; he had blackmailed the White House by threatening to reveal "seamy stories," and he knew several. Up next was Jeb Stuart Magruder, whose will to continue committing perjury was weakening. If Magruder testified truthfully, he could incriminate John Mitchell—the "Big Enchilada," as Ehrlichman called him, the nation's chief law enforcement officer from 1969 to 1972, and of late the president's raiser of hush money. And if Mitchell were indicted, "that's the ball game," Nixon said.*

Saturday, April 14: Nixon spent seven hours strategizing with Haldeman and Ehrlichman, talking until midnight. They started by speculating about what Hunt might say to the prosecutors. "Question: Is Hunt prepared to talk on other activities he engaged in?" Nixon asked. These included breaking into Daniel Ellsberg's psychiatrist's office, forging diplomatic cables implicating JFK in the assassination of South Vietnam's president, and being paid for his silence at trial. The demands for money in exchange for silence had not ceased; Nixon, Haldeman, and Ehrlichman discussed how to smuggle more than $300,000 in cash out of the White House and into the hands of the convicted burglars. "Hunt's testimony on hush money," Nixon said, could lead prosecutors to the president's doorstep. They wrestled with the implications of Magruder's testimony. Ehrlichman composed an imaginary magazine story: "The White House's main effort to cover up finally collapsed last week when the grand jury indicted John Mitchell and Jeb Magruder. . . . The White House press secretary, Ron Ziegler, said the White House would have no comment." The president moaned like a wounded man.

Magruder had just pointed a dagger close to the heart of the White House. "I'm going to plead guilty" and testify for the prosecution, he told Haldeman, who taped their telephone conversation. Magruder had implicated John Mitchell that day in an informal conversation with federal investigators. "I am in a terrible position because I committed perjury so many times" in the Watergate case and the cover-up. He couldn't take it anymore, he said, and he had to seek absolution. Nixon, Haldeman, and Ehrlichman had arrived at a moment of truth— or falsehood. The Watergate break-in was one problem. The greater danger was the cover-up and the peril it posed to the president if it began coming apart.

"There were eight or ten people around here who knew about this," Ehrlichman said. "Bob knew. I knew."

Then Nixon said—as if unconscious of his rolling tapes—"Well, I

---

* The president pointed out that Mitchell had collected hush money for Hunt from Thomas Pappas five weeks before and that Nixon had personally thanked Pappas in the Oval Office.

knew." He was acutely aware that he was doomed if Dean testified about the cancer on his presidency and the million-dollar cure.

Haldeman: "If Dean testifies, it's going to unscramble the whole omelet."

Ehrlichman: "Dean seems to think that everybody in the place is going to get indicted," said—referring to himself as well as Mitchell, Haldeman, Colson, and ten more prominent presidential appointees—on charges including "paying the defendants for the purposes of keeping them, quote, on the reservation, unquote."

Nixon: "They could try to tie you and Bob into a conspiracy to obstruct justice."

As night fell, Dean returned from the Justice Department to deliver more startling news to the White House: that afternoon, Haldeman and Ehrlichman had become targets of the federal grand jury. Now no one could predict how far up the chain of command the criminal case could climb.

Ehrlichman, who recently had started taping his own telephone conversations, called Mitchell's successor, Attorney General Richard Kleindienst. He began by saying he had spent the day with the president and had made some phone calls on his behalf.

> EHRLICHMAN: The first one I talked to was your predecessor. Then I talked to Magruder. . . . He has decided to come clean.
>
> KLEINDIENST: No kidding? . . . Inconsistent with his testimony before the grand jury?
>
> EHRLICHMAN: Dramatically inconsistent.
>
> KLEINDIENST: Holy shit!
>
> EHRLICHMAN: And he implicates everybody in all directions up and down the Committee to Re-Elect.
>
> KLEINDIENST: Mitchell?
>
> EHRLICHMAN: Yep, cold turkey.

"John," the attorney general said, giving truly gratuitous legal advice, "it seems to me that you are going to have to be very careful."

* * *

The fates, so often cruel to Richard Nixon, now forced the president, Haldeman, Ehrlichman, and Kleindienst to don formal evening wear and attend the annual cavalcade of self-congratulation called the White House Correspondents' Dinner. The most prominent awards went to Bob Woodward and Carl Bernstein of the *Washington Post* for their coverage of Watergate, a slap in the president's face.

Nixon, to his credit, turned the other cheek, making mildly amusing remarks from the dais at the Washington Hilton Hotel. "It is a privilege to be here at the White House Correspondents Dinner. I suppose I should say it is an executive privilege," he began. The president praised a man with "the most difficult job in this country," his press secretary, Ron Ziegler. "I must say you have really worked him over," Nixon said. "This morning he came into the office a little early, and I said, 'What time is it, Ron?' He said, 'Could I put that on background?'"

The after-dinner receptions were still going strong, the liquor still flowing, when, shortly after midnight, Henry Petersen, chief of the criminal division of the Justice Department, telephoned Kleindienst at the hotel in a state of high agitation. He said they had to meet at once.

They gathered at Kleindienst's home, along with the four top federal prosecutors in the Watergate case, as Petersen laid out a riveting summary of the case before them. John Dean and his lawyer had been talking to the prosecutors about a proffer, a provisional statement offered in hope of immunity from prosecution. Though the government had promised him nothing, Dean had delivered a devastating account of cover-ups and conspiracies conducted by Mitchell, Haldeman, Ehrlichman, and others. Dean had never showed his hole card—what he knew about Nixon's conduct as coconspirator in chief—but the prosecutors were convinced Dean wasn't bluffing.

The meeting broke up at 5:00 a.m. "I didn't sleep but I did weep," Kleindienst remembered.

* * *

Sunday, April 15: Kleindienst called Nixon unbidden at 8:41 a.m. The president neither liked nor respected his attorney general. He saw Kleindienst as a weakling, incapable of controlling the criminal investigation threatening the White House. Kleindienst was on the verge of resigning, but Nixon was one step ahead; the president had resolved to replace him as soon as possible.

Red-eyed, tear-stained, Kleindienst talked to Nixon for seventy minutes later that morning. The recording of their conversation was cut short at a crucial moment: an entire reel of tape went missing forever from the White House. But Kleindienst vividly remembered one crucial point. He asked Nixon if a special prosecutor should take over the Watergate case. Clearly Kleindienst could not preside in a case against his close friend Mitchell. But few legal precedents guided the special prosecutor question. The Constitution commands the president to "take care that the laws be faithfully executed." But in a criminal case where evidence might be locked away within the White House, the powers of a special prosecutor might have to be settled by Congress or the Supreme Court.

Kleindienst returned at 4:00 p.m. with Petersen, who had been cleaning his boat and, as he entered the president's elegant hideaway at the Executive Office Building, wore sneakers, dirty jeans, and a T-shirt smelling faintly of turpentine. Petersen was a strong-willed man who, like Richard Nixon, had gone to work in Washington in 1947, though Petersen had been an FBI clerk and Nixon a freshman member of Congress. Petersen tried to impress upon Nixon the seriousness of the fact that Haldeman and Ehrlichman faced criminal indictments. He was struck by the calm with which Nixon took the news. If was as if Nixon already knew—and he did.

Petersen argued that Haldeman and Ehrlichman should resign forthwith. Nixon said he would defend them until they were proven guilty.

"What you have said, Mr. President, speaks very well of you as a man," Petersen replied. "It does not speak well of you as a president."

The president quickly left the White House. He spent two hours aboard the *Sequoia*, accompanied by Bebe Rebozo, who said he could raise two or three hundred thousand dollars to help Haldeman and Ehrlichman. Alcohol was involved in their colloquy. When John Dean came to the White House later that evening, at the president's request, Nixon was still under the influence.

"Clearly he had been drinking, and while not drunk, he seemed exhausted, slurring his words," Dean wrote, and the way in which Nixon spoke to him—asking leading questions, giving misleading answers—

"made me wonder (as I later testified) if he was recording me." Upon taking his leave, Dean said, "I had to muster considerable fortitude to advise the president of the United States that if he did not handle this problem correctly it could result in his impeachment."

Ehrlichman, who seems to have taken perverse pleasure in bearing bad news by phone, called Pat Gray at around 11:00 p.m. He said Dean had told federal prosecutors that Gray had taken the bogus cables from Hunt's safe—and Gray confessed that he had burned them. Gray already had perjured himself before the Judiciary Committee on this very question. Horrified at the disgrace he faced, Gray said, "What the hell am I going to do?" Ten days later, he confessed to lying and resigned as acting FBI director. In time, he considered suicide.

* * *

Monday, April 16: Dean had decided to bear witness against his White House colleagues. He went to see the president at 10:00 a.m. with a draft of a letter of resignation in his pocket. Dean said he would not lie to protect John Mitchell or anyone else conspiring in the cover-up.

Henry Petersen returned that afternoon to confront the president with fresh news from inside the Watergate investigation—all devastating for Haldeman and Ehrlichman. Haldeman had known about the plans to bug the DNC's headquarters; then he'd kept copies of transcripts from the wiretaps. Ehrlichman had demanded that Dean "deep-six" the documents from Hunt's safe (the papers Pat Gray had burned) and had then commanded Hunt to leave the country.

Finally, that evening, Nixon and Dean reconstructed from memory Liddy's original proposal to Mitchell—the buggings, the muggings, the kidnappers, the hookers—and considered whether any hard evidence, not hearsay, could hang the break-in on Mitchell.*

"Everyone's in the middle of this, John," Nixon said.

Dean handed the president a revised letter requesting a leave of absence. On that grim note, the two men parted for the last time.

---

* Did Mitchell green-light the Watergate burglary? Magruder said so; the charge is uncorroborated. If he did, said Ray Price, Nixon's favorite speechwriter, it would have been on March 30, 1972, in a late-night telephone call to Magruder from Key Biscayne, when Mitchell was likely intoxicated.

* * *

Tuesday, April 17: Watergate investigators commanded by Mark Felt knocked at the doors of 1600 Pennsylvania Avenue. "The FBI has just served a subpoena on our White House police," Ehrlichman told the president. It sought the names of the people who had been cleared to enter the White House on June 18, 1972.

> NIXON: Jesus Christ.
>
> EHRLICHMAN: Now what in the hell?
>
> NIXON: Where were we then?
>
> HALDEMAN: What date?
>
> NIXON: Ah, June 18.
>
> HALDEMAN: June 18.
>
> EHRLICHMAN: The day of the bugging. . . . I bet it's the Hunt safe thing.
>
> NIXON: I need somebody around here as counsel.
>
> HALDEMAN: And Attorney General.
>
> NIXON: I need a Director of the FBI.

Shortly before 5:00 p.m., Nixon gave a formal statement on Watergate to the White House press corps. He said that on March 21—immediately after John Dean's dire warning of a cancer on the presidency, a diagnosis that Nixon did not disclose—he had initiated "intensive new inquiries" into Watergate. "Last Sunday afternoon, the Attorney General, Assistant Attorney General Petersen, and I met at length in the EOB to review the facts which had come to me in my investigation."

"Real progress has been made in finding the truth," Nixon declared—a bit of truth, perhaps, but not the whole truth.

At 11:45 p.m., after a state dinner for the prime minister of Italy and a scintillating concert by Frank Sinatra, the president called Henry Kissinger from the White House. Their conversation went on past midnight and into the wee hours of April 18.

Nixon was slightly inebriated and deeply despondent. He spoke of "throwing myself on the sword." The idea appalled Kissinger. "You have saved this country, Mr. President. The history books will show that, when no one will know what Watergate means." But Nixon would not be consoled. "It's a human tragedy," Kissinger conceded.

Thursday, April 19: Nixon went up to the mountaintop at Camp David. After a brief White House Cabinet meeting the next morning, in which Watergate went unmentioned, he flew down to Key Biscayne, where he remained until April 24. He spent much of his four-day Easter weekend boating with Rebozo. Nixon deleted the names of his visitors from that weekend's White House logs. But one of them was Horace Chapman Rose, known as Chappie, Ike's treasury undersecretary and Nixon's occasional confidant for two decades. Toward the close of a bleak three-hour talk, Chappie Rose quoted William Gladstone, whose first term as British prime minister began in 1868, a century before Nixon was elected president. The aphorism—which may have been apocryphal—was that the first essential for a prime minister was to be a good butcher.

The president prepared his knives.

Wednesday, April 25: Nixon, Haldeman, and Ehrlichman had a harsh three-hour talk in the Executive Office Building. Ehrlichman had just learned about the White House tapes. "If matters are not handled adroitly, you could get a resolution of impeachment," Ehrlichman said, "on the ground that you committed a crime." He argued that the president should listen to the tapes and assess the threat they represented. Nixon handed this immense task to Haldeman.

Thursday, April 26: Mark Felt was certain he would be chosen to lead the FBI after Gray's fall: a grave miscalculation. He served as acting director for three hours. Instead, Nixon named William D. Ruckelshaus, the administrator of the new Environmental Protection Agency, as the acting director of the Bureau.* The mild-mannered Ruckelshaus was thunderstruck at Nixon's ferocity that day. "I had never seen the President

---

* Ruckelshaus arrived at the FBI to find a letter on his desk—Hoover's desk—signed by Mark Felt and every one of his top aides, protesting his appointment. It wasn't personal, Ruckelshaus said: "They just felt it was inappropriate to have a bird-watcher as Hoover's successor." (William D. Ruckelshaus, "Remembering Watergate," speech before the National Association of Former U.S. Attorneys, Seattle, Washington, October 3, 2009.)

so agitated," he remembered. "I was worried about his stability. . . . He was extremely bitter."

Nixon feared the legal perils he faced. "I don't think it should ever get out that we taped this office," he told Haldeman, who spent five hours that day trying to transcribe the "cancer on the presidency" conversation at Nixon's request, looking for exculpatory evidence. The president worried that "this blackmail stuff" could surface. They recalled raising the matter of hush money—"the Pappas thing"—on that March 21 tape. But Haldeman told the president that the snippet with the strongest shock was when Dean warned Nixon that "people may go to jail. . . . And that really jarred you."

* * *

Friday, April 27: Nixon fled Washington for Camp David, where he stayed for the final days of his cruel April.

Camp David is a lovely compound of wood-and-stone lodges on the Catoctin Mountain of Maryland, sixty-two miles north by northwest of the White House, deep in a forest divided by a narrow road. President Franklin D. Roosevelt had it built by government-paid laborers for the Works Progress Administration, an exemplar of the New Deal programs Nixon hated. FDR called it Shangri-La. President Eisenhower renovated it and renamed it after his grandson, David, who married Richard Nixon's daughter Julie in December 1968. Its buildings, transport links, armed security, and encrypted communications were maintained by the navy and the CIA.

In late April, the fields below Camp David fill with apple and cherry blossoms, the rising road glistens with burgeoning aspens and birches, the campgrounds bloom with daffodils and tulips. Nixon hadn't come to smell the flowers. He had come to fire Haldeman and Ehrlichman. For good measure, he decided to dismiss his attorney general, accept John Dean's resignation, and create a new palace guard.

Saturday, April 28: The president called his press secretary, Ron Ziegler, at 8:21 a.m. "That's quite a collection of headlines this morning, isn't it?" Nixon said.

The front page of the *New York Times* was covered with four big stories above the fold. One said Pat Gray had resigned as acting FBI director. "Haldeman and Ehrlichman Reported Fighting Ouster," read another. A third said: "Dean Is Reported Asking Immunity" from federal prosecution. But the double-decker headline atop page one was the shocker: "A JUSTICE DEPT. MEMO SAYS LIDDY AND HUNT RAIDED OFFICE OF ELLSBERG'S PSYCHIATRIST."

Watergate prosecutors had uncovered the raid. As Nixon now knew, Ehrlichman had signed off on the break-in. The law required the prosecutors to disclose the crime to the trial judge in the Pentagon Papers case. A dismissal of the charges on grounds of government misconduct looked inevitable.

"What the hell. We've just begun to fight, haven't we?" Nixon said to Ziegler. "After all, a hell of a lot of other crap is going to hit."

"That's right," Ziegler said.

"This is a time for strong men, Ron," the president reassured his spokesman. "Our day is going to come."

Nixon called Haldeman twenty minutes later. The president wanted Bill Rogers as his consigliere in his hour of calamity. What did Haldeman think of that? "There is a crisis here of enormous proportions," the ever loyal Haldeman told the president. "The way for him to finish his service to the nation is by moving and cleaning this up." Twenty minutes after that, Nixon called Rogers.

Nixon said to Rogers that "John and Bob are going to make their move . . . and then I'm going to move on Dean" and dismiss Kleindienst. On Monday he would address the nation on Watergate—"not for the purpose of saying everything that happened, but because I just want the country to know that I'm in charge, that we're getting to the bottom of it." He wanted Rogers to guide his hand and steel his nerves.

"What time would you like me up there, Mr. President?" Rogers asked.

"Frankly, the sooner the better," Nixon said. "I want to get it done, get it done, done."

Rogers was remarkable for making the trip at all. Nixon, after scorning and humiliating his secretary of state for four years, now craved his counsel—exactly as he had in 1952, when Rogers saved Nixon's reputation. That episode formed chapter two of *Six Crises*.

Rogers, later Eisenhower's attorney general, had taken charge when Nixon's vice presidential nomination was threatened by allegations of a political slush fund. Rogers audited the fund and found it clean, and he helped Nixon fight serious-minded newspaper editorials calling for him to withdraw his nomination. When General Eisenhower himself considered dumping Nixon, Rogers stood steadfast in support. Nixon gave Rogers a draft of a speech he had written in his defense, and Rogers gave him the courage to go on national television and read it.

Vowing that he had never made personal use of political funds, listing his meager assets, including his wife Pat's "respectable Republican cloth coat," Nixon then admitted in all candor to accepting one campaign gift—just one. A man had heard on the radio that little Julie and Tricia Nixon would love to have a puppy. A black-and-white spotted cocker spaniel arrived in a crate from Texas. The girls loved the dog and named it Checkers. "And I just want to say this right now," Nixon declared, "regardless of what they say about it, we're going to keep it." The Checkers speech was among the greatest moments in the early days of television.

Rogers had helped to salvage Nixon's reputation; the president returned the debt of gratitude by treating him like a pariah for four years. And yet Rogers returned to do one last favor for Richard Nixon before accepting, after a decent interval, his dismissal as secretary of state.

Now, on that Saturday afternoon in April, after the morning fog had burned off, Nixon and Rogers spent five hours walking the grounds of Camp David and talking about the president's political future. Nixon thought out loud about another reshuffling of his Cabinet and his staff; this quickly became a grim game of musical chairs, for he would need a new secretary of state, a new secretary of defense, a new attorney general, new FBI and CIA directors, and a new White House chief of staff—all in a matter of weeks.

Rogers returned the president's attention to the immediate crisis. He strongly agreed that Haldeman and Ehrlichman had to resign, but he balked when Nixon asked him to deliver the blow. The president pleaded for one more favor: to help him draft the speech he planned to deliver on Monday. The secretary of state felt he could not refuse this last request. The words would be far more painful to write than the Checkers speech. But both talks had the same purpose: saving Richard Nixon from himself.

* * *

Sunday, April 29, was execution day. A few weeks before, for reasons only he knew, Nixon had removed the tape recording system from his study at Camp David's Aspen Lodge, the room where he carried out his sentences against Haldeman and Ehrlichman. But their memories of that afternoon are all of a piece.

Ehrlichman wrote: "He looked small and drawn. It was impossible for me to remain composed as he told me he hoped and prayed he might die during the night. 'It is like cutting off my arm,' he began, and he could not continue. He began crying uncontrollably. . . . The Camp was in full spring bloom out there, I noticed. All the bulbs were up and out."

Haldeman recorded: "The P was in terrible shape. Shook hands with me, which is the first time he's ever done that. . . . We were looking at the tulips from the Aspen porch, talking about the beauty and all, and as we started back in, he said, well, I have to enjoy it, because I may not be alive much longer. . . . Then he went through his whole pitch about how he's really the guilty one. He said he's thought it all through, and that he was the one who started Colson on his projects, he was the one who told Dean to cover up, he was the one who made Mitchell Attorney General, and later his campaign manager, and so on. And . . . that he too probably will have to resign."

Nixon—as he would do again on a far more fateful day—invoked the sainted memory of his pious mother. "I followed my mother's custom of getting down on my knees every night and praying silently," he said to Haldeman. "When I went to bed last night I had hoped, and almost prayed, that I wouldn't wake up this morning."

Monday, April 30: Nixon awoke alone, ate breakfast alone, and apart from a brief talk with his tireless secretary, Rose Mary Woods, and a long session with his talented speechwriter Ray Price, he spent the day alone, working on his address to the nation on Watergate. The speech, as Nixon wrote years later, was the start of "an increasingly desperate search for ways to limit the damage to my friends, to my administration, and to myself."

He took his helicopter back to the White House, went to his barber, and walked into the Oval Office at 8:58 p.m., two minutes before he went on the air.

Richard Nixon, one of the most talented and tenacious presidents of the twentieth century, had the rare gift of blarney, a cajoling tongue capable of telling falsehoods with unblushing effrontery. He got off some good lines in his speech that night, such as "There can be no whitewash at the White House." But he also told seventeen palpable lies about Watergate—concerning his role in the case, his fictitious in-house investigation of the crimes, and his commitment to uncovering the full story. He wrapped up his speech and then got rip-roaring drunk, as evidenced by his increasingly incoherent telephone calls, between 10:00 p.m. and midnight, to Haldeman, Rogers, Colson, the Reverend Billy Graham, and his new nominee for attorney general, Elliot Richardson. "Goddamn it," he told Haldeman, "I'm never going to discuss the son-of-a-bitching Watergate thing again—*never, never, never, never.*" He had the gall to say to Rogers, whose forced resignation as secretary of state was imminent, "*You're* the Cabinet now, boy," and then laughed. "No bullshit."

Rogers advised him: "Get some sleep now."

* * *

While Nixon was anguishing in the White House, the peace accords Kissinger had struck were failing in Vietnam. "Still no cease-fire and no visible movement toward a political settlement" after ninety days, Ambassador Bunker reported from Saigon.

An especially harsh series of B-52 attacks struck Cambodia that spring. These bombings, like so many before, were covert and counterproductive. They killed civilians and they drove the surviving Communist troops eastward, closer to Saigon.

These secret bombings were uncovered by an intrepid twenty-eight-year-old freelance reporter named Sylvana Foa and two Senate staff investigators, Dick Moose and Jim Lowenstein. Moose and Lowenstein were in the Cambodian capital, Phnom Penh, checking out a tip that the American embassy was coordinating the B-52 raids with the Pentagon. They had no proof until Foa struck up a conversation with Lowenstein.

"Listen," she said. "Do you want to hear something interesting?" She turned on her five-dollar pocket radio and tuned it to an open frequency. "There were American pilots talking to an American air controller," Lowenstein recalled. The embassy was vectoring the bombers to their targets, a blatant violation of the peace accords. On April 27 the staffers reported their findings to Sen. Stuart Symington, a senior member of the Senate Foreign Relations Committee.

"Symington went to the Secretary of Defense and didn't get any place; went to the Secretary of State and didn't get any place," Lowenstein said. "And, as I recall, he finally went to the President and said, 'This is what these guys say. This is what the law says. This is what this Committee is considering in terms of legislation.'"

Congress started drafting legislation to cut off funding for the war—regardless of the president's powers as commander in chief—by requiring congressional approval for any combat-related spending in Indochina. In the words of William Stearman, the NSC's senior Hanoi analyst, "The Presidency had been so weakened by Watergate that the American public, and certainly the Congress, would not continue our support for the Vietnamese forces much longer."

* * *

The mercurial Al Haig, promoted from colonel to four-star general by Nixon, was the new Haldeman and Ehrlichman—the president's chief of staff and palace guard. He was the only man Nixon could depend upon in his time of crisis. The Senate Watergate Hearings were set to begin in seventeen days—and the president had no counsel, no one in official command at the FBI or the Justice Department, and only Haig to trust.

Then another general—Vernon Walters, the president's handpicked deputy director of central intelligence, a man of impeccable discretion who had worked with Nixon since 1958—delivered a set of documents to Haig. Copies would soon be in the hands of senators and Watergate investigators.

These scrupulously maintained memoranda of conversations, memcons for short, detailed the meetings among Walters, Haldeman, and Ehrlichman during the days immediately after the Watergate break-in. They described the orders from the White House to use the CIA to turn off the FBI's investigation with a spurious assertion of national security.

May 11 became judgment day at the White House. First Haig read the memcons. They were devastating. One passage said: "It was the President's wish that Walters call on Acting FBI Director Gray and . . . suggest that the investigation not be pushed further."

Haig immediately called Nixon at Camp David. "It will be very embarrassing," Nixon said. "It'll indicate that we tried to cover up with the CIA." In a second telephone call, the president put it more bluntly: "If you read the cold print it looks terrible. . . . I just don't want him to go in and say look, they called us in and tried to fix the case and we wouldn't do it." Nixon wrote in his memoirs: "One of the things that made the memcons so troublesome was that Walters was one of my old friends; he would not have contrived them to hurt me. In addition, his photographic memory was renowned, and he was universally respected as a scrupulous and honest man."

That same morning, page-one stories described the White House wiretaps Nixon and Kissinger had placed on presidential aides and prominent reporters starting in 1969. Kissinger, who was expecting to be appointed secretary of state, brazenly denied that he had chosen the wiretap targets among his NSC staff and national security reporters; he implied he was only following orders. Nixon shouted: "Henry ordered the whole goddamn thing. . . . He read every one of those taps . . . *he reveled in it, he groveled it, he wallowed in it.*"

That same day's newspapers reported that the federal judge presiding over the espionage trial of Daniel Ellsberg in the Pentagon Papers case had dismissed the charges on grounds of government misconduct. Belatedly, the Justice Department, as required under law, had disclosed the misconduct—a warrantless White House wiretap recording Ellsberg, and the Plumbers' break-in at Ellsberg's psychiatrist's office.

The Pentagon Papers case was a total loss for the president: Ellsberg went free and the *New York Times* won a Pulitzer Prize. Nixon was embittered.

"Doesn't the President of the United States have the responsibility to conduct an investigation with regard to leaks in the goddamn place?" Nixon argued to Haig on May 11, regarding the wiretaps. "I got to go to the court to ask them? Screw the court." The court begged to differ.*

---

* The Supreme Court banned the warrantless wiretapping of Americans on the Monday after the Watergate break-in. The president had claimed he had an unassailable right to wiretap at will. In a unanimous decision, the Court wrote that the government had to obtain a judge's warrant for a wiretap: "This inconvenience is justified in a free society to protect constitutional values [and to ensure] that indiscriminate wiretapping and bugging of law-abiding citizens cannot occur" (*United States v. U.S.* District Court, 407 U.S. 297 [1972], also known as the *Keith* case). The White

John Mitchell publicly denied signing the wiretap authorizations. Nixon had a one-word response to that: "Bullshit." He was right about that. But that same afternoon, FBI agents had wrung a modicum of truth from Mitchell.

He confessed that the taps were part of "a dangerous game we were playing." He also told them where transcripts of the wiretaps might be found: in the White House safe of John Ehrlichman. The acting FBI director William Ruckelshaus recalled: "An FBI agent, sent by me to the White House to guard those records and others in Ehrlichman's office, was badly shaken when the President of the United States seized his lapels and asked him what he was doing there." He was upholding the law of the land—and helping to make a case against the president of the United States.

Nixon saw no alternative but to fight to keep these documents secret. "Good god, if we were going to stonewall executive privilege and a lot of other things we can sure as hell stonewall this," he told Haig on May 12.

How they were going to stonewall the Huston Plan was another question. Nixon had endorsed every kind of government spying on Americans—opening their mail, bugging their phones, breaking into their homes and offices—until J. Edgar Hoover himself killed the program. John Dean had placed a copy of the incendiary plan in a safe-deposit box and given the key to Judge Sirica. He intended to turn the copy over to the Senate Watergate Committee.

Nixon's constant refrain had been contempt for court rulings on wiretapping, break-ins, any aspect of "the national security thing." Nixon insisted: "I'm going to defend the bugging. I'm going to defend the Plumbers [and] fight right through to the finish on the son of a bitch." But when he thought about people actually reading the patently illegal Huston Plan, he changed his tune. "The bad thing is that the president approved burglaries," Nixon said on May 17; he could be perceived as "a repressive fascist."

House wiretaps also kept Kissinger in court for two decades. Morton Halperin, his aide at the NSC, sued Kissinger over the taps, seeking a formal written apology, not a financial windfall. It took until 1991, and a ruling from the Supreme Court, before Kissinger wrote that letter.

The tension at the White House was unbearable. With the Watergate hearings days away, Nixon screamed at his underlings as he schemed to save his presidency. Ziegler cautioned him to stay calm: "If we allow ourselves to be consumed by this—"

"—We'll destroy ourselves," the president said.

Rose Mary Woods tried to console him. She said that Dr. Hutschnecker, Nixon's psychoanalyst, had just called her: "He's thinking of you all the time and if there's anything on God's earth that he can do. . . ."

"They may kill me in the press, but they will never kill me in my mind," Nixon said. "I'm going to fight these bastards to the end."

CHAPTER TWENTY-THREE

"The President of the United States can *never* admit that"

Watergate was now more than a botched burglary. Warrantless burglaries and bugs, bald-faced lies obstructing justice, black bags crammed with hush money, B-52 bombings erased by falsified records—whether in the name of national security or the reelection of Richard Nixon—were abuses of presidential power.

Under the rule of law, the Senate Watergate Hearings were not a trial. But the rule of law had been taking a beating of late. The Justice Department and the FBI had been discredited. Few trusted Nixon to clean house rather than cover up the dirt. Piercing the shield of executive privilege that the president claimed would require a sharp force.

So the Senate unanimously commanded the new attorney general, Elliot Richardson,* a Republican stalwart who had run the Pentagon

---

* Richardson's appointment as attorney general began the second reshuffling of Nixon's Cabinet and inner circle in 1973 (a third was soon to come). James Schlesinger took Richardson's place as secretary of defense. William Colby succeeded Schlesinger at the CIA. Former defense secretary Mel Laird and former treasury secretary John Connally returned to the White House to offer Nixon advice and counsel alongside the new chief of staff, Al Haig. But no one could replace Haldeman and Ehrlichman. "I had cut off one arm and then the other" by dismissing them, Nixon wrote. "The

loyally since Nixon's second inaugural, to appoint a special prosecutor with the independent authority to investigate the president. He chose a man tailor-made to enrage Nixon: Archibald Cox, President Kennedy's solicitor general. Richardson vouched for Cox's capacity to handle "the grave, difficult and delicate issues" he would confront. Nixon described the genteel Cox as "the partisan viper . . . planted in our bosom."

The prevailing political atmosphere—in particular, the fact that Cox was investigating the president himself—compelled Nixon to make an unusual concession. He agreed that only the attorney general had the power to dismiss Cox. The special prosecutor was an independent force; the president could not slay the viper with the stroke of a pen. Cox requested and received the files of the prosecutors who had put the Watergate burglars in prison—and who were continuing to call witnesses before the federal grand jury overseen by Judge Sirica. They meticulously prepared an eighty-seven-page précis of their findings, listing twenty-seven people who were potential targets for indictment.

Number twenty-seven was the president of the United States. They cited Vernon Walters's memoranda as essential evidence. The Walters memcons, now circulating among senators and senior Justice Department prosecutors, included the meeting where Walters was told that the president wanted the CIA to shut down the Watergate investigation. The White House tape of that meeting would one day be known as the smoking gun.

The special prosecutor's power was one among many weapons aimed at the White House that spring.

* * *

Two events took place in Congress that would change history. One was without fanfare, the other without precedent.

First, the War Powers Resolution of 1973 was introduced by congressman Clement Zablocki, an unheralded Wisconsin Democrat. Its intent was to resolve the Constitution's division of military authority between the president and Congress.

The Constitution makes the president commander in chief of the

---

amputation may have been necessary for even a chance at survival, but what I had had to do left me so anguished and saddened that from that day on the presidency lost all joy for me" (*RN*, p. 849).

armed forces; it gives Congress the authority to declare war and the responsibility to support the armed forces by appropriating money. The War Powers Resolution said that the president had to consult with Congress about making war; it required a formal declaration of war, absent a national emergency caused by a surprise attack; and it gave the president sixty days to win congressional approval for financing a war. This bill would be passed into law, over President Nixon's veto, six months later. It would prove a revolutionary act.

Then, on May 11, that tumultuous day at the White House, the House of Representatives voted 219–188 to cut off funds for the bombing of Cambodia.

The transmissions picked up by Sylvana Foa's five-dollar pocket radio had reverberated around the world. This vote marked the first time the House had passed an end-the-war bill, an act within its power: under the Constitution, all spending bills must originate in the House. Between early February and the end of April 1973, the United States had dropped 83,837 tons of bombs on Cambodia, roughly seven Hiroshimas, at a cost of $159.5 million (about $840 million in today's dollars). The Pentagon had been caught trying to transfer $150 million from other operating accounts into another three months' worth of bombs for Cambodia.

Now the House had said no. If the Senate followed suit, that vote would go straight to the heart of the issues raised by the War Powers Resolution. Can the president conduct a war any way he wants? Or can Congress, since it buys the bombs and the war planes with tax dollars, control the president? Nixon could continue the bombing—and he did. But he risked laying his power on the line and provoking a constitutional crisis—and he would.

Nixon had undertaken many of the major military offensives of the Vietnam War without consulting Congress; he had created a three-billion-dollar slush fund, stashed throughout the federal government, for classified military and intelligence operations; he had established scores of secret statutes without consulting the courts—all by invoking a declaration of national emergency first proclaimed by J. Edgar Hoover at the start of the Cold War. A Senate select committee created in June 1972 was slowly and painstakingly uncovering these facts, showing how Nixon had usurped power, unconstitutionally placing the presidency above Congress and the courts.

"The balance between the three branches was under attack by Nixon," said William Green Miller, staff director of the Special Select Committee on Emergency Powers and War Powers, and later the U.S. ambassador to Ukraine. The war in Vietnam and "the misuse of power and intelligence in Watergate all are part of the constitutional debate" at the time. "The constitutional balance had to be restored."

The issues of presidential powers and presidential secrecy had been festering for years. After the War Powers Resolution was introduced, Sen. J. William Fulbright, chairman of the Foreign Relations Committee since 1959, said flatly, "Watergate is the bursting of the boil."

* * *

On May 17, 1973, Sen. Sam Ervin Jr. brought the Senate Watergate Committee to order, banging a colorful wooden gavel handcrafted by North Carolina Cherokees. "The Founding Fathers," he intoned, "knew that those who are entrusted with power are susceptible to the disease of tyrants, which George Washington rightly described as 'love of power and the proneness to abuse it.'"

The committee's first witness was Robert C. Odle Jr., the straight-arrow administrator of the Committee to Re-Elect the President. His conduct had been flawless, save for one fact: he had hired James McCord as CREEP's security director.

Odle remembered hearing about the Watergate break-in a few hours after it took place, while he was working on a Saturday morning at CREEP headquarters. "That could never happen here," Odle told a colleague. "I have this guy working for me named Jim McCord, and he has got this place really tight, and all I can say is I am glad McCord works for me." At that moment, McCord was under arrest. When Odle learned that, "I was extremely concerned," he testified. "I mean, here was our security director in jail."

"How long did you keep Mr. McCord on the payroll after the Watergate bugging?"

"About one minute," Odle answered.

The next thing he remembered was G. Gordon Liddy standing in the hallway at CREEP and asking where the paper shredder was. "I saw him with a pile of papers, perhaps a foot high," Odle told Sen. Howard Baker. The stack went into the shredder.

Despite the gravity of the moment, Odle brought levity to the pro-

ceedings. "We tried from the beginning to save documents," he testified, to show that CREEP was a "well-run, fairly thrifty campaign."
Senators, staff, and some reporters started to giggle. "That seems funny
now, I know," Odle said. "We wanted to save the documents because
we thought it might be interesting for a scholar to go back in 100 years
and . . ." At this point, the transcript shows, the hearings dissolved into
laughter. Senator Baker complimented Odle by noting that when the
committee broke for lunch, the television network covering the hearing had returned to its regular program, the popular game show *To Tell
the Truth*.

After hearing detailed testimony from the police officers who had
arrested James McCord and his Cuban American cohorts inside the
Democratic National Committee, Ervin recessed the proceedings at 5:15
p.m. The next major witness on the following day, Friday, May 18, would
be McCord himself.

* * *

Shortly before McCord arrived at the witness table, President Nixon convened a Cabinet meeting at the White House. Among those present was
the new chairman of the Republican National Committee, George H. W.
Bush.

After hearing reports on how the rest of the government was faring,
Nixon turned to the continued American bombing in Cambodia, the
upcoming summit visit of the Soviet leader Leonid Brezhnev in June,
and Watergate's effect on the American body politic.

"The problem in Southeast Asia is blown out of proportion because
of Cambodia," Nixon told his Cabinet. "The purpose of bombing is
not to get into a war in Cambodia, but to enforce the peace in Vietnam." There was no peace. At that moment, Kissinger was opening six
days of talks in Paris with President Thieu of South Vietnam and his
adversary Le Duc Tho of the Hanoi Politburo, trying to salvage the
failed cease-fire. The negotiations were fruitless; even Kissinger called
them a charade. The war went on.

The June summit with the Soviets would be "a watershed in world
history," Nixon predicted. "Either we move forward on a constructive
basis as we began last year, or we stop. If it is the latter, the world will be
a dangerous place. . . . A lot is riding on the visit." Kissinger had spent
May 4–9 with Brezhnev, trying to work out an agenda for the summit.

But he found the Soviet leader agreeable to little beyond a grand pronouncement against nuclear war.

As for Watergate, "It is rough and will get rougher," Nixon said. "The crap will fly, but don't think we have to deny every charge."

"Be proud," Nixon urged them. "Just say you don't believe the President is involved."

* * *

James McCord, not yet fifty, had spent five years at the FBI and nineteen years as a security officer specializing in surveillance and counter-surveillance at the CIA. A trusted friend in law enforcement, Jack Caulfield, John Ehrlichman's gumshoe, had recruited him as CREEP's security director.

In his explosive letter to Judge Sirica, McCord had said, "There was political pressure applied to the defendants to plead guilty and remain silent" at the Watergate burglars' trial. McCord had not pleaded guilty or taken hush money. So what was that pressure? Watergate counsel Sam Dash asked.

McCord described three clandestine meetings with Caulfield held during the burglars' trial, while he was free on bond, in January 1973. The two men talked twice at a parking area overlooking the Potomac River, and once during a two-hour car ride through the Virginia countryside. McCord said Caulfield told him he was delivering messages from "the very highest levels of the White House": Plead guilty. Stay silent. You'll go to jail for a year or less. There would be executive clemency to cut his sentence short, financial support for his family while he was behind bars, and a good job when he went free. McCord testified that Caulfield said that "the President's ability to govern is at stake"; the government might fall if the cover-up failed.

McCord had told Caulfield that he knew the president had his problems, but "I had a problem with the massive injustice of the whole trial being a sham, and that I would fight it every way I know how." In response to questions from Sam Ervin, McCord said that promises of executive clemency and clandestine caretaking also came from his codefendant Howard Hunt and Hunt's lawyer; as the evidence would show, these assurances had been extracted from Hunt's comrade and Nixon's counselor Chuck Colson.

On Tuesday, May 22, Caulfield followed McCord to the witness table, taking his oath to tell the truth. He confirmed every aspect of McCord's testimony about their secret meetings, and then he added startling details. In early January 1973, at the start of the Watergate burglars' trial, Caulfield, the acting assistant director for enforcement at the Bureau of Alcohol, Tobacco and Firearms, was attending a drug conference in San Clemente when he received a telephone call in his hotel room from John Dean.

Dean asked him to leave the hotel and call him back from a public telephone. He told Caulfield that "he had a very important message which he wanted me to deliver to James McCord." The message was: "1) A year is a long time; 2) Your wife and family will be taken care of; 3) You will be rehabilitated with employment when this is all over." Point one was an implicit promise of executive clemency; the minimum sentence that "Maximum John" could impose under federal law would be at least one year. Points two and three were explicit offers of cash in exchange for silence.

"I immediately realized that I was being asked to do a very dangerous thing," Caulfield testified. "I said to Mr. Dean that I did not think it was wise to send me on such a mission since Mr. McCord knew, as many others did, that I had worked closely with Mr. Dean and Mr. Ehrlichman at the White House."

Despite his misgivings, he met again and again with McCord. "I specifically renewed the offer of executive clemency," he testified. McCord said no. Dean instructed Caulfield before their third meeting to "impress upon him as fully as you can that this offer of executive clemency is a sincere offer which comes from the very highest levels of the White House."

Chief counsel Sam Dash had questions on this point: "You do know, do you not, that the President is the only person in this country who can grant executive clemency in a federal criminal matter?"

"Yes, sir, I do."

"Did you understand when you were speaking with Mr. Dean that Mr. Dean wanted you to transmit the message to Mr. McCord that the offer of executive clemency was made with the proper authority?"

"Yes, sir."

Millions of Americans were now glued to their television sets.

* * *

At about 4:00 p.m. on May 22, as Caulfield testified, the White House started handing out a four-thousand-word white paper, President Nixon's longest and most detailed statement about Watergate to date. Nixon had painstakingly rewritten every word of the draft and issued it in the first person—and almost every word of the preamble was false.

> I can and do state categorically:
>
> 1. I had no prior knowledge of the Watergate operation.
> 2. I took no part in, nor was I aware of, any subsequent efforts that may have been made to cover up Watergate.
> 3. At no time did I authorize any offer of executive clemency for the Watergate defendants, nor did I know of any such offer.
> 4. I did not know, until the time of my own investigation, of any effort to provide the Watergate defendants with funds.
> 5. At no time did I attempt, or did I authorize others to attempt, to implicate the CIA in the Watergate matter.
> 6. It was not until the time of my own investigation that I learned of the break-in at the office of Mr. Ellsberg's psychiatrist, and I specifically authorized the furnishing of this information to Judge Byrne.
> 7. I neither authorized nor encouraged subordinates to engage in illegal or improper campaign tactics.

Point one was true. Points two through seven were lies.

Point two: Nixon began trying to cover up Watergate six days after the break-in. He lied to White House aides, high officials of the Justice Department, the FBI, the CIA, Congress, and federal prosecutors. Four times, on tape, he suborned perjury by CREEP's second-in-command, Jeb Magruder. He withheld evidence by reflex.

Point three: Nixon twice authorized Colson to promise clemency to Howard Hunt and, as sworn testimony that very day suggested, promised clemency through John Dean to James McCord, the first man to blow the whistle on the Watergate cover-up.

Point four: Nixon, on tape, discussed hush money for Watergate defendants with Dean, Haldeman, Tom Pappas, and Rose Mary Woods.

Point five: Nixon tried to find a way to use the CIA connections of six of the seven Watergate burglars to pin blame for the break-in on the Agency. He authorized Haldeman and Ehrlichman to pressure the CIA into obstructing the FBI's investigation.

Point six: Dean told Nixon, on tape, about the Plumbers' burglary of Ellsberg's psychiatrist's office. Nixon did not look into the facts. Arguably it was a felony for Nixon to conceal his knowledge of the crime.

Point seven: Nixon, using Chuck Colson as his point man, spied on the campaigns and campaign contributors of his 1972 opponents, including George McGovern and Ed Muskie. He misused the IRS and the Secret Service in acts of political espionage.

The white paper could have been a chance for absolution. Nixon admitted that he'd authorized the White House wiretaps—but he omitted the fact that the taps never identified a leak. He promised that "executive privilege will not be invoked as to any testimony" at the Watergate hearings—but he reserved the privilege to withhold documents. He admitted the existence of the Huston Plan—but he never said, "I approved it." In that passage, he had edited out the first person singular.

The first draft had said: "'I ordered that they use any means necessary, including illegal means,'" Nixon told Haig. "The President of the United States can *never* admit that."

The cover-up of the cover-up was the penultimate act in his downfall, an approaching darkness at the end of the tunnel. The white paper would become a template for the first article of the impeachment of the president.

* * *

Yet the flickering genius of Richard Nixon flared two days later, when he gave a fiery speech to the American prisoners of war returned from Vietnam.

Nixon always spoke triumphantly of ending the war. Soldiers with boots on the ground knew better. "There's going to be a full-blown war starting up after we leave," said Col. Einar Himma, one of the last American combat officers to take off from the Tan Son Nhut Air Base in Saigon. "The fighting has never stopped anyway."

After years of secret negotiating to end the war, and the gradual replacement of American divisions by Saigon's forces under Vietnamization, what Nixon had accomplished in the end was a straight swap: the complete withdrawal of American combat forces in exchange for the release of 591 American prisoners of war. And on May 24, 1973, he invited every one of those POWs and their wives for a briefing and a reception at the State Department and supper on the White House Lawn. With 1,300 guests, it was said to be the biggest formal dinner ever held at the Executive Mansion.

When delivering his speech for the POWs, with members of the press present, Nixon was steely as a drill sergeant. "There was no plan to end the war" when he first came to office, he said. "Many of you were already prisoners of war. You had no hope."

Nixon said he had won their release through his strength—and through his secrecy. "I want to be quite blunt," he said. "Had we not had secrecy, had we not had secret negotiations with the North Vietnamese . . . you men would still be in Hanoi rather than Washington today. And let me say, I think it is time in this country to quit making national heroes out of those who steal secrets and publish them in the newspapers."

"I am going to meet my responsibility to protect the national security of the United States of America insofar as our secrets are concerned . . . so we can continue these enormously important initiatives for peace" with the Soviets and the Chinese, Nixon said. "The strength to be the peacemaker in the world—it is all right here. It is in America. It is in that Oval Office. . . ."

"Those first four years in that office were not easy ones for me," he said. "But looking toward the balance of the second four years, let me say I feel better, because out in this room, I think I have got some allies, and I will appreciate your help."

That day marked the last time that Nixon talked at length about the war during his presidency. It was striking that he spoke to such an extent about the secrecy and the solitude of his office to hundreds of men who had suffered in silence and isolation for so long.

* * *

After midnight, in the wee hours of May 25, Nixon unburdened himself to Haig on the telephone. He sounded exhausted, drunk, or both. The steel was gone. He talked bluntly about resigning: "Wouldn't it be better for the country, you know, to just check out?" Haig laughed. "No, no, seriously," Nixon said. "You see, I'm not at my best. I've got to be at my best, and that means fighting this damn battle, fighting it all-out. And I can't fight the damn battle," not with bad news hammering him hour after hour. "The goddamn thing has gotten to me. . . . And you get to the point that, well, if you can't do the goddamn job you better put somebody in there that can."

But no one could at that moment—and no one saw that fact more clearly than Nixon.

He knew (as very few did) that Vice President Agnew might soon face a federal indictment.* Next in the legal line of succession were two Democrats: the Speaker of the House, Carl Albert of Oklahoma, an alcoholic who spent two months in rehab later that year; and the president pro tempore of the Senate, James Eastland of Mississippi, a doddering plantation master and notorious racist. Neither was fit to serve. Fifth in line was the secretary of state. Nixon was about to nominate Kissinger—born in Germany and thus disqualified under the Constitution.

So Nixon had to fight the damn battle. The summer was going to be swallowed up by the Watergate hearings, though the committee was in a temporary recess and no major witnesses were scheduled for the next three weeks. During this lull, John Dean kept the press well fed, each story cutting away the president's credibility. Dean was to testify in June; Mitchell, Haldeman, and Ehrlichman throughout July. The Senate's inquisition would run into September.

The number of people privy to the deeper secrets of Watergate grew as Al Haig brought new lawyers and staffers into the Oval Office. Among them were two who learned that Nixon had had the White House wired. Nixon knew what would happen if *that* secret got out—and if Cox or Congress got their hands on his tapes.

On June 4, Nixon began listening to his taped conversations with John Dean, taking notes in preparation for Dean's public testimony, "so that we can strategize whipping this son of a bitch," as Haig put it. Steve Bull, who had succeeded Alexander Butterfield as the deputy

---

* A federal grand jury was working on a case captioned *United States of America v. Spiro T. Agnew.* Nixon had learned that Agnew was suspected of taking kickbacks from contractors while governor of Maryland—and while the vice president of the United States. Still, Nixon was pleased to have him. He saw Agnew's sleaze as insurance against his own impeachment.

assistant to the president overseeing the taping system, struggled to find the right reels; the tapes never had been catalogued. Nixon spent nine hours that day listening to his talks with Dean from March, telling Haig it was the hardest work he'd ever done in his life. He avoided the "cancer on the presidency conversation," remembering well that he had said he could raise a million dollars in hush money, recoiling at the prospect of hearing himself say it again.

Then came a shock. On June 6, one of Nixon's new in-house counsels, J. Fred Buzhardt, a highly intense lawyer imported from the Pentagon by Haig, had a meeting with Special Prosecutor Cox. Buzhardt returned to report to Nixon that Cox wanted evidence from the White House—specifically, "a tape of a conversation that you had with Dean on the evening of Sunday, April 15."

Nixon was flabbergasted.

How could Cox suspect that this tape existed? As it turned out, he had three sources: one was Henry Petersen, chief of the Criminal Division of the Justice Department; the second was John Dean; and the third was Richard Nixon himself.*

When Buzhardt raised the subject the next week, Nixon said flatly: "I have no tapes." It wasn't the first time he'd lied to Buzhardt, and it wouldn't be the last.

In a talk with Rose Mary Woods on the morning of June 12, the president became unglued. Brezhnev was arriving in four days for a weeklong summit meeting. Dean was supposed to take the stand two days after that.†

Watergate had been a tightening noose for a year. "It's almost a miracle that I've survived this," Nixon said, "this brutal assault, brutal,

---

* It will be recalled that Nixon spoke on Sunday, April 15, with both men. Petersen, clad in a filthy T-shirt, had rebuked Nixon for defending Haldeman and Ehrlichman, saying it "does not speak well of you as a president." Dean, in turn, intuited that Nixon's contrived conversation and skulking conduct that night "made me wonder (as I later testified) if he was recording me." Peterson had told Cox that Nixon had offered to let him, Petersen, listen to "a tape of a conversation" with Dean recorded that night—as Buzhardt informed Nixon on June 6. Amazingly, this tape did not exist: either a negligent Secret Service agent had forgotten to set a new reel spinning or the tape was discovered and destroyed.

† John Dean had hired a criminal lawyer, Charles N. Shaffer Jr., to help him prepare for his testimony. Dean recalled in his book *Blind Ambition* that he told Shaffer what he knew and asked the attorney what he thought. Shaffer said: "The president is a goddamn criminal, that's what I think."

brutal, brutal assault, day after day after day. . . . That impeachment crap. That's the saddest of all." Rose Mary Woods, who loved Richard Nixon, said, "You're killing yourself with the job."

"I don't mind killing myself . . . ," the president said. "I would expect to kill myself, and I would do it."

* * *

He won a brief respite—very brief—when the leaders of the Senate announced that John Dean's testimony would be postponed in deference to diplomacy. General Secretary Leonid I. Brezhnev arrived in the United States on June 16 for his weeklong summit meeting with President Nixon. They held six talks, in Washington, at Camp David, and in San Clemente. In a one-on-one conversation with Brezhnev, taped in the Oval Office on June 18, Nixon said, "We must recognize, the two of us, that I for 3½ more years in this office and the General Secretary, I hope, for that long or longer, we head the two most powerful nations. . . . And the key really is in the relationship between Mr. Brezhnev and myself. If we decide to work together, we can change the world."

But they could not work together that week. Compared with its predecessors in Moscow and Beijing, the summit was a bust. Though the two leaders signed agreements on trade and other issues, the proclamation of the prevention of nuclear war was pabulum, and they made no progress on the strategic arms limitation treaty. The reality of arms control under Nixon was best expressed years later by James Schlesinger, who served as both defense secretary and chairman of the Atomic Energy Commission, in charge of building America's nuclear arsenal: "I think that I still have the record for producing the most nuclear weapons in one year, that would have been 1972, of anyone in history."

Nixon and Brezhnev found no common ground on the pursuit of peace in the Middle East, which the Soviets thought was the most urgent issue of the time. At 10:30 p.m. on June 23 in San Clemente, Brezhnev woke Nixon out of bed with an urgent demand for an unscheduled talk—an argument about the imminence of an Arab-Israeli war. For two hours, well past midnight, Brezhnev tried to bully Nixon into signing a joint statement for peace negotiations. The United States and the Soviet Union were as contentious over the basic issues as the Israelis and the Arabs; such a pact seemed a pipe dream. Nixon thought Moscow was angling for the advantage of its allies in Egypt and Syria. The president was unmoved.

There was no talk of "the spirit of San Clemente" at the summit's end. Nixon stayed secluded at the Western White House while John Dean took the stand for a week in Washington.

* * *

Dean looked very young—he was thirty-four—and very respectable as he took the stand. He spent a full day reading a 245-page prepared statement and spent four days answering questions. All three major networks covered every minute of his testimony, and public television rebroadcast it every night. As many as eighty million Americans watched at least part of Dean's command performance.

He methodically shredded Nixon's white paper, point by point. He meticulously reconstructed their March 21, 1973, conversation about the metastasizing cancer in the Oval Office. He described in detail a corrupt administration committing crimes under the cover of national security. This portrait was composed by a man who confessed to coordinating the cover-up for the president.

Nixon realized, too late, that "we would never recover" from this portrayal. "It no longer made any difference that not all of Dean's testimony was accurate," the president wrote in his memoirs. "It only mattered if *any* of his testimony was accurate. And Dean's account of the crucial March 21 meeting was more accurate than my own."

Senator Baker, as the ranking Republican on the Watergate Committee, said that the outcome of the investigation rested on one question: "What did the president know and when did he know it?" Dean pointed to his talk with the president on September 15, 1972—the day of the Watergate burglars' indictments—as the moment the cover-up began. Since Nixon had denied meeting Dean before 1973, this seemed a definitive point. And Dean hammered it in by disclosing that the president himself had offered prosecutors "a tape of a conversation" with Dean recorded on that April night before Dean became a government witness. If there were tapes, Baker's question could be answered in full.

At 5:30 a.m. on July 12, two days after he returned to the White House from San Clemente, Nixon awoke in excruciating pain, every breath a stabbing knife in his chest. The diagnosis was viral pneumonia. The president spent the next week at the Bethesda Naval Hospital, outside Washington.

The following afternoon, Friday the thirteenth, two Watergate staff investigators, Scott Armstrong, who worked for the Democrats, and Don Sanders, who worked for the Republicans, conducted a preliminary interview with a potential witness: Alexander Butterfield, the deputy assistant to the president during Nixon's first term, the gatekeeper to the Oval Office. Butterfield, recently appointed as head of the Federal Aviation Administration, was one of seven people who knew about the tapes at the time, outside of the Secret Service technicians who handled the recording system. Butterfield had resolved that if he were asked a direct question about the tapes, he would answer truthfully.

They sat in a cluttered basement room of the Senate's offices. Sanders had a document that Nixon's counsel Fred Buzhardt had given to the Republican staff as a means of cross-examining John Dean. It was a single sheet of paper, a verbatim transcript, with a *P* for "president" and a *D* for "Dean." The investigators slid the document across the table and asked Butterfield what he made of it. That wasn't a direct question.

"I thought to myself that this had to come from the tapes—the very thing I'm worrying so much about," Butterfield remembered. "So I just hemmed and hawed."

Then Sanders, a former FBI agent, took over. "You had mentioned the Dictabelt," he said. Nixon dictated letters and memoranda on the device, and Rose Mary Woods typed them up. "Apart from the Dictabelt, was there ever any other listening device in the Oval Office?" That *was* a direct question.

During a 2012 symposium with Dean and Armstrong, Butterfield recalled:

> I knew it would be the end of my career, certainly in Washington. I just knew that. Nixon was so set on this thing being an absolute secret—and it was an absolute secret for all that time. We know that from what's on the tapes. So, I said, "I'm sorry you asked that question. Yes, there was, and that's where this document had to have come from." And then we spent forty-five minutes describing the system. I felt reasonably sure that they had not heard that from any previous witness. That secret of Nixon's was too closely held.

Armstrong ran to see the chief counsel, Sam Dash: "I blurted out, 'Sam, Nixon taped all of his conversations.'" Butterfield testified to that on Monday. It was the biggest bulletin of the year. "NIXON BUGGED HIMSELF" was the tabloid headline in the *New York Post*.

Sleepless in his hospital room before dawn on July 19, Nixon scrawled a note on his bedside pad: "Should have destroyed the tapes." But he had not. Instead, he decided, in a state of self-delusion, that "the tapes were my best insurance against an unforeseeable future."

In retrospect, Nixon wrote, "from the time of the disclosure of the tapes and my decision not to destroy them, my presidency had little chance of surviving to the end of its term."

* * *

On July 23, Senator Ervin and Special Prosecutor Cox subpoenaed a handful of tapes. Ervin wanted five for the Senate committee; Cox demanded nine for the Watergate grand jury. The president refused, citing executive privilege.

The battle was joined in Judge Sirica's court. Looking to the Constitution for guidance on executive privilege, and finding none—the Framers had rejected the idea that one branch of the government had dominion over another—the judge began to draft an order. Sirica said he would rule by the end of August on whether the president had to obey the subpoenas.

Awaiting a decision, Nixon addressed the nation on August 15. Though defiantly defending himself, he appeared to promise to regard the rule of law. "The time has come to turn Watergate over to the courts," he said. That did not mean he would turn over his tapes.

While sticking by every word of his white paper, Nixon conceded that Watergate was "not just a burglary and bugging of party headquarters but a whole series of acts that either represent or appear to represent an abuse of trust."

But, he continued, Watergate also involved "a number of national security matters," including "my efforts to stop massive leaks of vital diplomatic and military secrets."

"Many have urged that in order to help prove the truth of what I have said, I should turn over to the Special Prosecutor and the Senate committee recordings of conversations that I held in my office or on my telephone. However, a much more important principle is involved," the president insisted. "This principle of confidentiality of Presidential conversations is at stake in the question of these tapes. I must and I shall oppose any efforts to destroy this principle, which is so vital to the conduct of this great office."

That same day, after years of struggle, by order of Congress, and over Nixon's veto, the United States ceased the bombing of Cambodia. By law, the legislature was cutting off funds for the war in Vietnam. The passage of the War Powers Act was imminent. For the first time in history, the elected representatives of the people of the United States were forcing the president to sheath his terrible swift sword.

Richard Nixon, having failed to end the Vietnam War on his terms, now faced his final crisis.

CHAPTER TWENTY-FOUR

"The same enemies"

"LET OTHERS wallow in Watergate," said Richard Nixon. He fled the miasma of midsummer Washington and spent almost all the rest of August in Key Biscayne and San Clemente.

Before the White House taping system was revealed—and immediately removed on orders from General Haig—Nixon had talked a brave game. Some of the last tapes caught his fighting words.

He vowed to eviscerate Sam Ervin and the Senate Watergate Committee. "I'm going to hit them and destroy them and they'll be destroyed . . . absolutely destroyed," he told Haig in a late-night telephone call. "They don't realize what they're up against—this stupid Ervin, drinking too much, and pointing his finger. Ha!"

Calling Kissinger from Camp David, he said, "We've been at this for four years, four-and-a-half- years. . . . [I]t's virtually the same enemies, isn't it?"

"The same enemies and now trying to do legally what they tried with riots earlier," Kissinger replied.

"And in an election too," Nixon said. "They failed at their riots, they failed in the election, now they're trying to do it" with the Watergate investigation.

And he told Haldeman before his fired aide appeared before the Senate committee, "As you are well aware Bob, they're really not after you."

"Oh, hell, no," Haldeman responded with bravura.

"They're after the President," Nixon said.

But Haldeman, Ehrlichman, and Mitchell had done themselves and the president no favors in their testimony before the Senate committee. Haldeman, having heard the "you could get a million dollars" tape of March 21, swore that the president had immediately followed that statement by saying, "But it would be wrong." That was perjury. What was wrong, Nixon had said many minutes later, was granting executive clemency under extortion.

Ehrlichman, who had presided over the Plumbers, was snarling and imperious. He defended the president's national security powers, even when it came to burglary, to protect state secrets. He confronted the courtly country lawyer Herman Talmadge, a Georgia Democrat, who reminded him of the Magna Carta, the thirteenth-century foundation of Anglo-American law, and its ideal that a man's home was his castle, and that his castle could be defended against a king.

> Q: Do you remember when we were in law school, we studied a famous principle of law that came from England, and also is well-known in this country, that no matter how humble a man's cottage is, that even the King of England cannot enter without his consent?
>
> A: I am afraid that has been considerably eroded over the years, has it not?
>
> Q: Down in my country we still think it is a pretty legitimate principle of law.

The Senate gallery applauded. Ehrlichman's jutting jaw dropped. At that moment, a federal grand jury in Los Angeles was preparing a sealed indictment against him for the break-in at Ellsberg's psychiatrist's office, a Plumbers operation he had approved in writing.

John Mitchell was the worst witness of all. He was by then a broken man, destroyed by his devotion to Richard Nixon; the public breakdown of his mad wife, Martha; and his thirst for Scotch whisky. Mitchell lied under oath, attesting that he had undertaken no reelection campaign responsibilities while he was still attorney general. And he said that, in order to protect the president's reputation before the 1972 ballot, he had concealed his knowledge of what he called "the White House horrors," in particular the crimes of the Plumbers.

In a moment of truth, Talmadge again stuck in the dagger.

> Q: You placed the expediency of the next election above your responsibilities as an intimate to advise the President of the peril that surrounded him? . . .
>
> A: In my mind, the re-election of Richard Nixon, compared to what was available on the other side, was so important that I just put it in that context.

Mitchell, Haldeman, and Ehrlichman would face federal indictments in a matter of months, the grand jury handing up the case to the Watergate special prosecutor. But by then the lawyer who held that title was no longer Archibald Cox.

* * *

In the fall of 1973, Richard Nixon faced a legal confrontation that had no precedent in the history of the United States.

On August 29, Judge Sirica ordered a subpoena *duces tecum*—Latin for "bring it with you"—to be served upon the president. It demanded that he deliver to the court nine White House tapes requested by Cox so that the judge could hear them in chambers; then he would decide if they should be turned over to the prosecutor. No criminal subpoena ever had been enforced upon a president; no court ever had compelled a chief executive to turn over documents against his will.

In a statement issued from San Clemente, Nixon said he would appeal. By September, the Watergate Committee had reconvened hearings in the Senate; Sam Ervin and his investigators wanted the secret recordings, too. Nixon's counselors considered tossing the tapes into a bonfire; the threat of spending ten years in prison was a stumbling block. They asked themselves: Who would strike the match? King Timahoe?*

By the time a federal appeals court upheld Sirica's order, the presi-

---

* King Timahoe was the president's unaffectionate Irish setter.

dent already had proclaimed that he would not tear down the walls of the White House to comply with Cox or the Congress. He would abide only by a "definitive" decision by the Supreme Court. The president, when asked, would not define what he meant by definitive. He had appointed four of the nine justices; would he heed a divided court? What if the Court said to turn over the tapes and the president said no?

The nation was in uncharted territory. The only recourse under the Constitution if Nixon defied the High Court was impeachment—an indictment by the House of Representatives and a conviction by a two-thirds vote in the Senate—and no president ever had suffered that fate. The battle for the tapes continued in the courts and expanded rapidly into the political arena. A constitutional confrontation seemed imminent by October.

And October was when the Nixon administration, and the president himself, began to disintegrate.

* * *

Nixon had an ever-shifting set of schemes to avoid turning over the subpoenaed tapes. One was to fire Archibald Cox. Another was to create highly edited summaries of transcripts that might convey the gist of the tapes to the satisfaction of the courts and Congress. Or they might not.

On October 1, Rose Mary Woods took one of the nine tapes—a conversation among Nixon, Haldeman, and Ehrlichman from June 20, 1972, three days after the Watergate break-in—and began transcribing it using a new apparatus called a Uher 5000, with a foot pedal that would let her stop, start, and rewind the tape without taking her fingers off the typewriter keys. Later that day, by the president's account, she reported to Nixon that something had gone wrong: after answering the phone with the rewind pedal on, she'd returned to the tape to find a five-minute buzz in the recording where voices had once been.

Nixon checked with Haig and Buzhardt and they reported (wrongly) that the tape in question was *not* among the nine under subpoena. Nixon put the problem out of his mind and went on a long drive in a White House limousine to talk to Haig about what was really worrying him: Spiro T. Agnew, the vice president of the United States.

Nixon knew all about Agnew's crooked conduct, having been informed of the facts by Elliot Richardson, the attorney general since

May 29, and by William D. Ruckelshaus, the deputy attorney general, recently sworn in after serving seventy-nine days as the acting director of the FBI—a man Nixon called, with apparent sincerity, Mister Clean.

The evidence against Agnew was ironclad, a casebook in corruption. Five construction executives and engineers in Maryland had sworn under oath that, for eight years, beginning in 1964, they had been paying off Agnew (a county executive and the state's governor before becoming vice president) in exchange for receiving state contracts. These kickbacks, regular monthly payments of up to ten thousand dollars apiece, had continued through December 1972. Agnew at least once pocketed an envelope of cash in the basement of the White House.

For months Agnew had fought a furious battle to dodge the charges. He said flatly that he would not go to prison and he would not face an indictment. He had argued with Nixon and Richardson that the case had to be quashed. If they did not meet his demands, he threatened, he would take his case to the American people—which he did. His rabble-rousing public rants were exactly the kind of embarrassment Nixon did not need at the moment.

At 6:00 p.m. on October 9, the Oval Office gatekeeper Steve Bull announced, "Mr. President, the Vice President." Nixon and Agnew shook hands and sat down in front of the fireplace. Agnew had given in but, greedy to the last, in return for his resignation he asked the president to help him find lucrative corporate contracts abroad. As they parted, Nixon assured Agnew that he could always count on his friendship. The next day, the vice president of the United States became the former vice president. He stood in a federal courthouse in his hometown, Baltimore, Maryland, and pleaded no contest to a single charge of failing to report $29,500 in income during 1967, when he was the governor. This plea bargain, the judge said, was an unusually generous deal; he generally jailed tax evaders. The resolution was a suspended three-year sentence, a $10,000 fine, and Agnew's resignation.

On the afternoon of October 10, Nixon said to Richardson, "Now that we have disposed of that matter, we can go ahead and get rid of Cox." Only Richardson, not the president, had the legal power to do that. Nixon had struck that deal himself; at the time, the arrangement had seemed to him the line of least resistance.

* * *

Nixon had weighed four choices to replace Agnew as vice president: Ronald Reagan, the governor of California, whom he considered a lightweight; Nelson Rockefeller, the governor of New York, whom he disliked; John Connally, his former treasury secretary and trusted confidant, whom he wanted to succeed him as president; and Gerald Ford of Michigan, the Republican minority leader of the House, respected as a decent human being if not regarded as the brightest light in the legislature.

A rapid consultation with the Republican chiefs in Congress made Nixon realize that only Ford could be confirmed, as required under the Constitution, without a struggle.

A peculiarity of the American political system requires presidential appointees to undergo background checks by the FBI. A civic panic began in the quiet city of Grand Rapids, Michigan, as seventy-five FBI agents arrived and began to question anyone who had ever heard of Gerald Ford. On October 15, Bill Ruckelshaus, as the Bureau's former acting director, booked a flight to Grand Rapids, intending to quell the citizenry. He stuck his head into the attorney general's office to inform him.

Richardson looked up, his elegant visage a mask of misery.

"We've got an even worse problem than Agnew," he said.

That's not possible, Ruckelshaus said.

"Yes, it is," Richardson replied. "The President wants to fire Cox."

"He'll never do it," Ruckelshaus said confidently. "The American people won't tolerate it." He was half right. The president's problem was political, not legal. If he fired Cox, Nixon would wound himself.

Cox wanted to enforce the appeals court's order for Nixon to produce the nine subpoenaed tapes forthwith. Nixon's new gambit was to produce edited summaries of the tapes, and the tapes themselves, to the seventy-two-year-old Mississippi senator John Stennis, a highly conservative Democrat and a reliable political ally to the Nixon administration. Stennis would then verify the summaries and turn them, not the tapes, over to Cox.

But this compromise, as Nixon called it, was a calamity in the making.

Senator Stennis was known to be half deaf and in poor health, recovering from gunshot wounds suffered in a mugging months before; moreover, the senator had never agreed to a plan to review summaries, only to read complete transcripts. Three of the subpoenaed tapes could not be transcribed in any fashion: the Dean conversation of April 15 did not exist; a Nixon-Mitchell telephone call immediately after the Watergate break-in could not be found; and worse yet (if there could be worse), the tape Rose Mary Woods had been working on had an inexplicable gap—not just five minutes, but eighteen and a half minutes—made by at least five erasures, an incendiary fact that hinted at foul play.

In a letter that Haig dictated to Richardson on Friday, October 19, Nixon ordered Cox to cease and desist from seeking any more tapes, notes, or memos from the White House. He had a new incentive for this improper demand: John Dean had just agreed to plead guilty to obstruction of justice. Under the plea agreement, struck with Cox, Dean would go to prison but would first serve as a sworn government witness in any trial against the president's men or, conceivably, the president himself.

"The President all along intended either to force Cox's resignation or induce Richardson to fire him," Ruckelshaus said in 2009. "The reason was simple. Cox was getting too close. In the nine tapes in question, or those subsequently acquired by the Special Prosecutor, were several smoking guns. This was why my earlier assumption about the willingness of the President to fire Cox was wrong. The act of firing Cox was that of a desperate man. Adverse public reaction must have seemed preferable to handing your accuser the still-hot weapon with your fingerprints all over it. Richardson was attempting to work out a compromise that would accommodate all legitimate and honorable interests. The President's intentions were neither."

There matters stood on Friday evening. A showdown was certain.

On Saturday morning, October 20, Cox called a press conference. "I am certainly not out to get the President of the United States," he said, but Nixon had overstepped his powers by obstructing the work of the special prosecutor's office. The president was not complying with the law or the legal agreement that gave Cox the right to follow the evidence wherever it led. Cox would go back to court to pursue the case. And he reminded his listeners, a nationwide television audience, that the president could not fire him. Only the attorney general had that right.

Richardson, after receiving an angry telephone call from Al Haig ordering him to fire Cox forthwith, requested a face-to-face meeting with the president. The meeting took place at 4:30 p.m. It was short and ugly; Richardson was back in his office before 5:00. He was beginning to describe their confrontation to Ruckelshaus and the third-ranking man in the Justice Department—the solicitor general, Robert Bork, whose job was to represent the president before the Supreme Court—when the phone rang again. Al Haig calling: this time for Ruckelshaus. Their conversation was brief—and brutal, too. Fire Cox now, Haig said; this is an order from your commander in chief. The deputy attorney general declined. Haig then asked to talk to Bob Bork.

"Both Elliot and I had urged Bork to comply if his conscience would permit," Ruckelshaus remembered. "We were frankly worried about the stability of the government. Bork indicated to us that he believed the President had the power to fire Cox and he was simply the instrument of the exercise of that power. He thus issued the order discharging Cox."* At 8:00 p.m. on October 20, the White House announced that Richardson had resigned and Ruckelshaus and Cox had been fired. The special prosecutor's office was abolished by presidential order and sealed by FBI agents.

Cox had the last word: "Whether we shall continue to be a government of laws and not men is for Congress and ultimately the American people" to decide. That statement made the deadlines for Sunday's papers. When asked what he would do next, Cox's spokesman James Doyle said, "I'm going home to read about the Reichstag fire." That ended the constitutional cataclysm of the Saturday Night Massacre and began a political conflagration.

* * *

The battles of Watergate reached a crescendo at the moment a war in the Middle East almost went global.

On October 20, the Yom Kippur War—so called because it had started on the Day of Atonement, which observant Jews devote to

---

* In a memoir published posthumously in 2013, Bork said he went to see the president that evening, and that Nixon offered him the next available Supreme Court seat. President Reagan nominated Bork to the Supreme Court in 1987, but the Senate rejected the nomination—in part due to Bork's role in the Saturday Night Massacre.

religious reflection—had been going on for nearly two weeks. The Arabs attacked the Israelis first. American intelligence on the Middle East, which relied heavily on Israeli intelligence, was caught unaware. Syria and Egypt gained the upper hand in the first days of the war, thanks to the element of surprise and Israeli military hubris.

"All our intelligence said there would be no attack," the new secretary of state, Henry Kissinger, said at an emergency Cabinet meeting. "Why did Israel not figure there would be an attack?" He answered his own question, as was his style. The Israelis thought "there was no threat. The Arabs are too weak. So they interpreted the intelligence this way. We did the same."

Kissinger, whose Senate confirmation hearings had been marred by questions over the White House wiretaps, had taken office on September 22. He remained in charge of the National Security Council, working in uneasy alliance with Al Haig, once his underling.

As Nixon sank deeper into the swamp of Watergate, Kissinger gained an imperial power over foreign policy, and Haig behaved like the acting president of the United States.* Nixon was increasingly incapable of playing his role as the leader of the free world. This telephone conversation between Kissinger and his NSC deputy Brent Scowcroft indicated Nixon's incapacity:

> SCOWCROFT: The switchboard just got a call from 10 Downing Street to inquire whether the President would be available for a call within 30 minutes from the Prime Minister. The subject would be the Middle East.
>
> KISSINGER: Can we tell them no? When I talked to the President he was loaded.

That exchange was recorded at 7:55 p.m. on October 11, the fifth night of the war and the day after Agnew resigned.

---

* "Actually Al Haig *was* the President of the United States," said William Lloyd Stearman, at the time the chief of the NSC's Indochina staff. And "it became unpatriotic to attack Kissinger," said E. Wayne Merry, then a State Department aide for congressional relations, "even when members of Congress were very dubious about some of the things he was doing." These quotations are from the Foreign Affairs Oral History collection.

* * *

The Israelis pleaded for American arms to help repel the invaders. Kissinger, Haig, Defense Secretary James Schlesinger, and Joint Chiefs chairman Tom Moorer tried to mobilize a covert airlift of American weapons. Owing to a series of snafus, secrecy was lost, and giant U.S. Air Force cargo planes, their insignias highly visible, landed in Tel Aviv, their arrival caught on television cameras as Israelis cheered.

Both the Soviets and the Saudis had warned the Americans that this war in the Middle East was coming. The Saudis had explicitly told William Casey, the undersecretary of state for economic affairs and future CIA director, that they would use oil as a weapon unless America used its influence to pacify the Israeli army in its continuous conflicts with the Arabs. A few months earlier, Casey's assistant Willis C. Armstrong had attended a lunch with Casey, the Saudi foreign minister, and the Saudi oil minister. He vividly recalled that the Saudis had said, "If you don't do something to restrain the Israelis, there's going to be a war in the Middle East. When the war breaks out, we're going to have to put an embargo on oil to the United States." Armstrong remembered: "Casey and I looked at each other after the lunch, and I said, 'Shall we write that up?' He said, 'Nobody would believe us.' But we were warned."

The embargo began to take shape during the Yom Kippur War, shortly after the American arms shipments started arriving. The world price of oil quintupled. Soon millions of Americans began spending hours sitting in their cars, waiting in line to fill their gas tanks. Rage at the pump was nationwide.

The Soviets became deeply involved in the Yom Kippur War, resupplying their allies in Syria and Egypt. Brezhnev sent Nixon an increasingly tense series of messages, one proposing they work together diplomatically to stop the war, the second strongly suggesting that a joint U.S.-Soviet military task force serve as peacekeepers. A brief cease-fire had stopped the war, but then the Israelis broke it. The third message from Moscow was a threat: the Soviets might act unilaterally, militarily, in the Middle East to end the war.

The threat was real. American intelligence sensors in the Dardanelles, the narrow strait connecting the Black Sea to the Mediterranean, detected Soviet ships carrying nuclear arms. This startling fact was confirmed thirty years later by David Michael Ransom and Helmut

Sonnenfeldt, NSC staffers under Kissinger, though Ransom was at that moment serving as an intelligence watch officer at the State Department.

"The Soviets were shipping warheads to Egypt," said Ransom, later an American ambassador in the Middle East. "That sent Kissinger into an extraordinary series of moves to bring the fighting to an end."

The extraordinary moves began, one hundred hours after the Saturday Night Massacre, in the White House Situation Room. The principals at the meeting were Kissinger, Schlesinger, Moorer, Haig, and CIA director Bill Colby. The president was not present.

"Nixon was in his family quarters," Sonnenfeldt said. "There were rumors that he was drunk." They were not rumors.

This midnight conclave was recorded only in the diary of Admiral Moorer, declassified in 2007. Until then, the meeting remained one of the more mysterious events in modern American history.

Moorer's diary of the night of October 24 had—to use a phrase Kissinger favored—the unpleasant odor of truth. Its record begins at 10:30 p.m., when Kissinger's high-ranking aide Larry Eagleburger called Moorer for an urgent meeting in the Situation Room.

The diary begins: "We had just received a real piss-swisher from Brezhnev regarding the Arab/Israeli Conflict." (*Piss-swisher* is navy slang; its polite equivalent is pot stirrer.)

"The Brezhnev letter proposed that the USSR/US urgently dispatch to Egypt, Soviet and American military contingents to ensure implementation of the Ceasefire and, further, containing the threatening sentence: '. . . it is necessary to adhere without delay. I'll say it straight. If you find it impossible to act jointly with us in this matter we should be faced with the necessity urgently to consider the question of taking appropriate steps unilaterally.' "

All agreed that what the Soviets proposed in the Middle East was a potential disaster. If U.S. and Soviet soldiers started landing in the middle of the battle, each side standing with its allies, it could look like the opening day of World War III.

"This would not be a NATO war," Moorer wrote (his italics are verbatim). "Any direct confrontation on the ground with the Soviets would be very difficult. In short, *the Middle East is the worst place in the world for the US to get engaged in a war with the Soviets.*" No one disagreed.

"The big question then became *Why did the Soviets suddenly reverse themselves and without any warning all day then 'bang' we receive the*

Brezhnev threat?" Nobody had any clear answers. But they all surmised that the Soviets were responding to Israel's breaking the brief cease-fire. The Israeli violation of the agreement broke the camel's back, Kissinger agreed.

Kissinger had bigger thoughts, recorded word for word by Moorer: *"the Soviets were influenced by the current situation the President finds himself in . . . if the Democrats and the US public do not stop laying siege to their government, sooner or later, someone will take a run at us. . . .* Friday the Pres US was in good shape domestically. Now the Soviets see that he is, in their mind, non-functional. . . . *The overall strategy of the Soviets now appears to be one of throwing détente on the table since we have no functional President,* in their eyes, and, consequently, *we must prevent them from getting away with this."*

In the absence of a functioning president, these five men, led by Kissinger, decided to send strong signals to the Soviets to back off. They raised America's global nuclear alert level to DEFCON III, one step short of imminent nuclear war. They dispatched three warships to the Mediterranean, alerted the Eighty-Second Airborne Division, and recalled seventy-five B-52 nuclear bombers from Guam. Since that entailed the immediate movement of many thousands of American soldiers, sailors, and airmen, Moorer said the decisions would immediately be leaked— which was not a bad thing, since the Americans wanted to signal to the Soviets how seriously they took the threat.

"At 0400 we went to bed to await the Soviet response," Moorer's record ended, save for one last thought: *"If the Soviets put in 10,000 troops into Egypt what do we do?"*

The United States might have gone to war—or it might have done nothing. As Larry Eagleburger, who served as secretary of state under President George H. W. Bush, later noted, "One of the things that I recall now with a great deal more equanimity than I did at the time is what was never really understood: the degree to which the Watergate crisis, particularly in its final months, meant that if we had been put to the test somewhere in the foreign policy arena, we would not have been able to respond. We were a ship dead in the water."

Through good luck and, perhaps, blind fortune, Moscow and Washington backed away from the specter of a Third World War. Kissinger, to his great credit, began a three-year attempt to try to negotiate peace in the Middle East. To his discredit, when word of the nuclear alert leaked, as it did almost instantly, he deceived the press, saying the president had saved the day, when Nixon had spent the night in a stupor.

The other question raised by reporters was how a handful of unelected officials could raise a global military alert, mobilize the Eighty-Second Airborne, and send nuclear bombers aloft in a secret midnight meeting without consulting Congress or, as it became evident, the president. In the charged atmosphere created by the Saturday Night Massacre, it looked like the Nixon administration might indeed become a government of men, not laws.

It seemed worse to Elliot Richardson, the sacked attorney general: "A government of laws was on the verge of becoming a government of one man."

* * *

That one man had reasons to drink himself to sleep on the night of October 24. The president had said that day his enemies would assassinate him; Nixon told Kissinger that they wanted "to kill the President. I may physically die."

Real threats faced the president along with his roiling fears.

Hours before the Situation Room meeting, the House of Representatives, for the first time since 1868, began formal proceedings to impeach the president of the United States. Then Nixon's constitutional lawyer, Charles Alan Wright, announced that the White House would at last turn over the subpoenaed tapes to Judge Sirica. And Nixon caved in to demands from Republican leaders in Congress, responding to the overwhelming outrage of their constituents, to reestablish the special prosecutor's office.

The new sheriff in town was Leon Jaworski, a prosecutor of Dachau concentration camp commanders and a past president of the American Bar Association. He also was the 1972 chairman of Texas Democrats for Nixon. That fact did not immediately endear him to Cox's army of investigators, but Jaworski told them he would follow the evidence wherever it led, even into the Oval Office. Congress wanted to hear him say that explicitly.

Q: You are absolutely free to prosecute anyone; is that correct?

A: That is correct. And that is my intention.

Q: And that includes the President of the United States?

A: It includes the President of the United States.

Archibald Cox's files had been preserved, most of his staff stayed on, and the restoration of a government of laws began.

* * *

The Internal Revenue Service had discovered that Nixon had paid $792 in income tax in 1970 and $878 in 1971.* With a salary of $200,000 per year, he should have been paying considerably more. In 1969, Nixon had donated his pre-presidential papers to the National Archives and received a huge deduction, but his lawyers had backdated the deed of gift to dodge a change in the tax laws. The disclosures about his taxes were damaging; the response from the president on November 18 was disastrous.

"I am not a crook," said Richard Nixon, a retort that did not resonate among the American people.

After the Saturday Night Massacre, Nixon needed a new attorney general, his fourth in five years. He chose one of the Senate's own, William B. Saxbe, an Ohio Republican and former state attorney general, calculating he would be quickly confirmed. Saxbe was, by his own description, "a wild hare," an unorthodox Republican, but he was more than willing to take the job; he found the Senate stultifying. He went to the White House; he found the atmosphere like a hospital ward. His interview was short; Saxbe had one question. He wanted to know if the president was in any way implicated in Watergate.

"Nixon lied to me," Saxbe said.

On November 21 came the revelation in Judge Sirica's courtroom that two of the subpoenaed tapes could not be found and that the third had essentially been obliterated by the eighteen-and-a-half-minute gap. Moreover, the gap had two distinct tones: five minutes of white noise,

---

* The IRS also had discovered that Bebe Rebozo had been holding $100,000 in cash from Howard Hughes for Richard Nixon, a purported campaign contribution never delivered to Nixon's campaign. Nixon had suggested that Rebozo hang on to it for the future. But when the tax men came calling, Rebozo returned the cash to the Hughes organization. This, too, appeared unseemly to the American public when revealed in October 1973.

which could be explained by Rose Mary Woods's human error involving the foot pedal. But that noise was followed by an entirely distinct sound, like a distant whirlwind.

Called to the stand by the judge, Haig testified that only three people had had access to that tape, which recorded Nixon and Haldeman roughly seventy-two hours after the Watergate burglars had been arraigned. Those three were Rose Mary Woods, Steve Bull, and Richard Nixon. Electronics experts, including National Security Agency technicians, established that the foot pedal was not at fault. Haig suggested to Sirica that an unseen sinister force had erased the tape. The judge suspected that Nixon was the force in question. But there the mystery ended, unsolved.

And in truth what was not on the tapes was immaterial. What mattered was what was on the tapes.

By December, under orders from Judge Sirica, the special prosecutor, his investigators, and the grand jury had custody of three tapes. And the first they heard, dated March 21, 1973, was the conversation about the cancer on the presidency, highlighted by Nixon's assertion that he could get a million dollars in hush money.

"I for the first time realized that President Nixon was involved and culpably involved," Jaworski recalled in an oral history. What he could never grasp was why anyone—in particular, the president of the United States—would preserve such vividly self-incriminating evidence on tape.

Nixon now reversed his earlier private pledge to congressional leaders that he would transcribe selected tapes and make the texts public. He consulted his White House lawyers, some of whom had started to suspect that they had a crook for a client. He saw how deeply they doubted he could weather the rough passages the transcripts would reveal. But he also knew that, one way or another, through the courts or through Congress, his words on tape might soon be inscribed in counts of an indictment or articles of impeachment.

Alone in his study at San Clemente at 1:15 a.m. on January 1, 1974, the president took out a yellow legal pad and began to put his thoughts on paper. "Do I fight all out or do I now begin the long process to prepare for a change, meaning, in effect, resignation?"

He paused to reflect. He picked up his pen.

"The answer—*fight*."

CHAPTER TWENTY-FIVE

United States v. Richard Milhous Nixon

Rᴄʜᴀʀᴅ Nɪxᴏɴ's seventh crisis lasted seven months. The president's final battle to save himself began on January 3, 1974, hours after Congress reconvened. That day, White House lawyers rejected the Senate Watergate Committee's request for more than five hundred tapes and documents.

Still sleepless in San Clemente, the president made another note in his diary at 5:00 a.m. on Saturday, January 5: "Above all else: Dignity, command, head high, no fear, build a new spirit, drive, act like a President, act like a winner," Nixon wrote. "Opponents are savage destroyers, haters. Time to use full power of the President to fight overwhelming forces arrayed against us."

When he delivered his State of the Union speech on January 30, he addressed "the so-called Watergate affair." He said, "I have provided to the Special Prosecutor . . . all the material that he needs to conclude his investigations and to proceed to prosecute the guilty and to clear the innocent. I believe the time has come to bring that investigation and the other investigations of this matter to an end. One year of Watergate is enough."

The special prosecutor quickly issued a stern correction: the president had not delivered a long list of requested tapes, documents, and memos. The White House lawyers immediately responded that they would not comply with the demands.

On February 6, the House of Representatives voted overwhelmingly to begin impeachment proceedings against the president. The grueling process began in the House Judiciary Committee, which had substantial subpoena powers. The committee received a copy of Jaworski's list of crucial evidence on February 22.

Nixon wrote, "The biggest danger I saw in the year ahead was that both the Special Prosecutor and the House Judiciary committee would begin requesting more and more tapes—always with the disclaimer that each request would be the last. But there would never be an end," he feared, "until all 5,000 hours of tapes had been requested and surrendered."

He vowed not to surrender. He believed that if he were driven from office America would be undermined. But he lacked the strength to fight and lose. His beloved daughter Tricia later showed him a note from her own diary, written that winter.

> Something Daddy said makes me feel absolutely hopeless. . . .
> He has cautioned us that there is nothing damaging on the
> tapes; he has cautioned us that he might be impeached because
> of their content. Because he has said the latter, knowing Daddy,
> the latter is the way he really feels.

Her poignant note is the most powerful evidence of what Nixon knew and when he knew it.

* * *

On March 1, the Watergate grand jury handed Judge Sirica a staggering indictment.* Seven men stood charged with conspiracy to obstruct justice, including the former attorney general John Mitchell, the former

---

* Ten months later, to the day, Mitchell, Haldeman, and Ehrlichman were convicted of conspiracy and perjury. Each served a substantial sentence. Colson became a bornagain Christian, pleaded guilty to conspiracy, went to prison, and spent most of his life as an evangelical devoted to prison reform. Additional defendants were former assistant attorney general for internal security Robert Mardian (convicted at trial but acquitted on appeal); CREEP lawyer Kenneth Parkinson (acquitted on all charges);

White House chieftains Haldeman and Ehrlichman, and Nixon's amoral adviser Chuck Colson. The charges included lying to the Senate, the FBI, and the grand jury itself.

Richard Nixon was named as an unindicted coconspirator by a unanimous vote of the nineteen-member grand jury. (It was actually a 38–0 decision; each grand juror had raised both hands in unison when polled.) This astonishing fact was kept secret, under judicial seal, at the special prosecutor's request. Jaworski had political consider-ations to weigh, no less than Congress's politicians had legal burdens to bear. He thought it best for the country that a president's guilt or innocence be established by impeachment and conviction by Congress under the Constitution, not by indictment inside a courthouse.

On March 6, Nixon held a press conference and took a very pointed question. One of the perjury counts against Haldeman claimed he had lied to the Senate by averring that Nixon had said "it would be wrong" to raise a million dollars in hush money. The grand jury had heard the tape. What was the truth?

"I meant that the whole transaction was wrong, the transaction for the purpose of keeping this whole matter covered up," the president replied. "I directed that Mr. Haldeman, Mr. Ehrlichman, Mr. Dean, and Mr. Mitchell [meet] so that we could find what would be the best way to get the whole story out." These were two sentences with two bold lies. Fortunately for Nixon, he was not under oath.

Then Jaworski sought sixty-four additional tapes as evidence in the trial of *United States v. Mitchell et al.* On April 18, Judge Sirica subpoe-naed them. That set up a confrontation potentially fatal to Richard Nixon's presidency.

Among these tapes was the hottest smoking gun of all: the conver-sation about using the CIA to block the Watergate investigation.

Nixon sought a political solution to his legal crisis. He chose the edited-tape gambit—the same strategy that had created the Saturday Night Massacre. Of all Nixon's many self-inflicted wounds, this was

---

and Haldeman aide Gordon Strachan (who won a separate trial and was found not guilty). The special prosecutor struck again on March 7: Ehrlichman, Colson, and Liddy were indicted for the Plumbers' break-in at Ellsberg's psychiatrist's office. All were convicted. Ehrlichman, in a memoir, called that break-in the seminal Water-gate episode, the one that set the stage for all that followed.

among the worst, confirming an observation Haldeman had made to
the president a year before: "It is almost like we have a death wish."*

* * *

On April 29, Richard Nixon spoke for thirty-five minutes on national
television, seated next to a table stacked with binders full of expurgated
tape transcripts. He said the binders contained "all the additional
evidence needed to get Watergate behind us and get it behind us
now." They would leave "no questions remaining about the fact that
the President has nothing to hide."

The 1,308-page "Blue Book" was published by the Government
Printing Office the next day. Long excerpts immediately appeared in
newspapers and magazines. The transcripts left the American citizenry
amazed and amused and appalled.

The transcripts had been carefully edited to conceal both foul play
and foul language. Some of the censored parts were still as compelling
as the content. For instance, Dean discussing Howard Hunt's demands
for money with the president on March 21, 1973.

> D: You have no choice but to come up with the $120,000 . . .
>
> P: Would you agree that that's the prime thing that you damn
> well better get done . . . ?
>
> D: Obviously. . . .
>
> P: [Expletive deleted].

"Expletive deleted" entered the American lexicon. By May 1, publishers were printing three million paperback copies of the "Blue Book."
The transcripts read like FBI wiretaps of gangsters plotting a heist, except
that these men were sitting in the White House, not a warehouse.
Here was the president of the United States talking, in that same conversation.

---

* Haldeman's mordant comment concerned Nixon's nomination of Pat Gray as FBI
  director. Gray hung himself, and John Dean, with his testimony. In turn, that set
  Dean toward bearing witness against Nixon.

P: How much money do you need?

D: I would say these people are going to cost a million dollars over the next two years.

P: You could get a million dollars. You could get it in cash. I know where it could be gotten. . . . Who would handle it? Any ideas on that?

He did *not* say it would be wrong. The revulsion of some Republicans in Congress—the people who could protect Nixon from impeachment and conviction—was intense. "Deplorable, disgusting, shabby, immoral," said the Senate minority leader, Hugh Scott of Pennsylvania.

The White House now drew the line. Nixon would provide nothing more to the special prosecutor than the Blue Book. His lawyers moved to quash Sirica's subpoena for the sixty-four tapes Jaworski sought. The judge struck back, ordering the White House to produce the tapes forthwith. Nixon defied him. The U.S. Supreme Court, responding to Jaworski's direct appeal, agreed to take the case on an emergency basis. The High Court agreed that in July it would hear oral arguments in *United States v. Richard Milhous Nixon, President of the United States.*

The House committee's members knew the Blue Book transcripts had been falsified. The committee's chief counsel, John Doar, had six of the relevant tapes in hand. The White House had supplied them to the federal grand jury under Judge Sirica's orders; they had served as essential evidence against Mitchell, Haldeman, and Ehrlichman. Sirica took the tapes and conveyed them to the impeachment committee, a perfectly legal if completely secret procedure.

John Doar, who called himself a "Lincoln Republican," had fought bravely for civil rights as a Justice Department official in the 1960s. As chief counsel, he had been studying the constitutional standards and the legislative history of impeachment since December.* His committee's

---

* Before taking the job, Doar chatted with David Miller, a future American ambassador; they were friends from Doar's days at the Justice Department. Miller ran the White House Fellows program under Nixon; he knew many key players in Watergate. Miller left in 1971, sensing disaster approaching. "Mr. Doar knew that I had worked for President Nixon," Miller recalled in a Foreign Affairs Oral History interview. Doar asked Miller: "Is there any chance that the President did not know about what these

able and aggressive staff included a recent Yale Law School graduate named Hillary Rodham.

On May 9, Doar convened the first of eighteen executive sessions of the impeachment committee, presenting a lengthy "statement of information" that could form a template for a bill of impeachment. The committee heard witnesses ranging from John Dean to Leon Jaworski to White House lawyer James D. St. Clair. Considerable political conflict flared within the closed chambers.

The committee's thirty-eight members ranged from the most conservative to the most liberal representatives in Congress. At the center of this spectrum stood four relatively moderate Republicans and three staunchly right-wing southern Democrats; these seven men were of no one mind. Each article of impeachment might stand or fall on the way they swayed.

The Constitution says a president may be impeached for "Treason, Bribery, or other high Crimes and Misdemeanors." Treason was not at issue. Bribery was a touchy subject; many members of Congress performed unseemly favors for campaign contributors. But high crimes and misdemeanors—now, that was rich terrain. The phrase originated in fourteenth-century proceedings of the British Parliament. The history of Anglo-American jurisprudence showed that acts worthy of impeachment included the abuse of the powers of high office. "Abuse of power" was thus a high crime—and another phrase about to enter American discourse, alongside "expletive deleted."

"Obstruction of justice" was by now common parlance, owing to the criminal proceedings against the president's men. Nixon had been obstructing justice for two years, since the Watergate burglary, and his continuing defiance of the subpoenas was part of that pattern. Obstruction of justice was a felony designed to disguise a felony. And as Nixon had said more than once on tape: It wasn't the crime. It was the cover-up.

After six weeks of deliberation, the committee began drafting formal articles of impeachment against the president of the United States at the end of June. In July—after the Supreme Court heard *United States v. Nixon*—the debate would begin.

---

people were doing?" I said, "Absolutely none." President Nixon was a detail-oriented control freak and the odds that the president was not personally involved were nil. Doar said, "That's interesting."

* * *

During a seven-week stretch, from June 10 to July 29, Richard Nixon spent only seven days in the White House.

Nixon fled Washington and began an epic voyage, through the Middle East and Europe, then on to Moscow. He was determined to reappear on the global stage as the leader of the free world, the most powerful man on earth.

The sheer will Nixon showed by undertaking this trip was formidable. He began dictating his diary on tape again, a practice he had dropped for many months. Just before his departure on June 10, he recorded, "The great tragedy is that it seems to be a year and a half almost that is lost."

On top of the sadness and the stress, he was not a well man. Nixon suffered from phlebitis, a blood clot in a vein of his left leg that caused swelling and suffering. The danger of the disease is that the clot can break loose, flow into the bloodstream, enter the lungs, and create a potentially fatal embolism. The phlebitis flared up just before he took off, and it pained him.

The first stop was Salzburg, Austria, a way station intended to let the president reset his body clock before a grueling week in the Middle East. Nixon was housed at Schloss Klessheim, an imperial building inside a gated park, with a soaring salon, cream-and-gold walls, and glittering crystal chandeliers. One among the president's huge contingent was a State Department official, Alfred Joseph White, who assisted Nixon's brief chat with the chancellor of Austria, Bruno Kreisky. "He came out to greet Chancellor Kreisky," White recalled. "The limp was very noticeable. He had a haggard, grey, drawn, exhausted look and seemed in pain. The agony of his situation was plainly evident. He seemed a bent and broken man in those ghastly few minutes. His Presidency was crashing down around him, and it showed."

The next stop was Egypt, and the trip was a smashing success for all, owing greatly to dialogues between Kissinger and the Egyptian leader Anwar Sadat, which had started in November, after the Yom Kippur War, as part of Kissinger's ceaseless shuttle diplomacy among the Arabs and Israelis.

Sadat was the son of peasants but behaved as if born to the presidency. He was amenable to reestablishing diplomatic relations with the

United States, breaking Egypt's military reliance on the Soviets, and consolidating the cease-fire with Israel. In January, Sadat had formally invited Nixon for a state visit.

On June 12, in Cairo, President Sadat awarded Richard Nixon Egypt's highest civilian decoration, the Collar of the Nile. The route of their motorcade from the airport to the presidential palace was lined with as many as one million cheering Egyptians chanting Nixon's name at the top of their lungs. The president of the United States was elated. Nixon and Sadat later traveled by train for three hours to the grand palace of Alexandria. They waved from an open coach to millions more who stood along the tracks, and they were greeted at their destination by mounted lancers in splendid regalia.

By the end of his two-day visit, after viewing the Great Pyramid of Giza and signing an accord with Sadat reestablishing relations, Nixon's ecstasy at the welcome reception he'd received soothed his throbbing leg and eased his troubled mind.

"The Egyptians, as I saw, went all out," said Arthur A. Houghton III, a senior officer at the American embassy in Cairo, who witnessed it all. "The President of the United States really was an earthquake to them, the most important thing that had happened for years. They went out of their way to make it clear [that] they wanted us to be a partner in the future. Nixon was—I don't know what Nixon was. . . . But nevertheless he served the role that he needed to serve. It was a great ceremonial occasion."

Nixon's next stop was far less satisfying. On the evening of June 14 he landed in Jidda, Saudi Arabia, and remained for twenty-two hours. King Faisal, then seventy-two years old, had been a principal architect of the recent oil embargo that had crippled the American economy and sent the stock market to a four-year low. The Saudi leader now pledged to be a friend to America—and American oil companies—in days to come. Nixon welcomed the promise of amity and oil. Unfortunately, he made a serious mistake in his toast to the king.

U.S. ambassador Jim Akins "had asked the President if he wanted any texts or talking points for his speech," recalled Hume Horan, the deputy chief of mission at the American embassy in Saudi Arabia. "Nixon replied, 'No, I write my own.' So he got up there and began talking about King Faiṣal, and how wonderful it was that his father had cooperated with Lawrence of Arabia, the great role he had played in the Arab revolt, and how in his early days Faisal had been to France for the Paris Peace Conference with Woodrow Wilson. Excellent. But Nixon was speaking of the wrong Faisal! He was praising the late King of Iraq—not the Saudi Faisal, whose father had driven the Hashemites from Arabia! Jim's blood ran cold."

From there it was on to Syria, where the Hashemites once ruled. But in 1974, Syria was under the iron hand of President Hafiz Assad, the father of the present-day dictator, Bashar Assad, who was then eight years old. Nixon recounted that the young Bashar had seen the June 15 arrival ceremonies in Damascus for the president of the United States on television and had asked his father that night, "Wasn't that Nixon the same one you have been telling us for years is an evil man who is in complete control of the Zionists and our enemies? How could you welcome him at the airport and shake his hand?"

Nevertheless, Nixon recorded that he "was very impressed with President Assad," who had "a lot of charm." Nixon reestablished American diplomatic relations with the autocratic regime. He was all too often more amenable to dictators than democrats.

On June 16, Air Force One flew from Damascus to Tel Aviv, where the president and First Lady were met by Yitzhak Rabin, prime minister of Israel, and ensconced in the luxurious Suite 429 of the King David Hotel in Jerusalem. The hotel was a unique landmark in the history of Israel: the headquarters for British military officers and diplomats who governed the land known as Palestine after World War II. In 1946 a terrorist gang called the Irgun blew up a section of the hotel, killing ninety-one people, most of them British overlords.* The British Mandate crumbled before Israel's foundation in 1948; the King David's splendor was restored.

Prime Minister Golda Meir had lost her seat after the military humiliations of the Yom Kippur War, but she still had clout; she was among the toughest of a tough people. Nixon graciously toasted her. But Nixon, the first American president to visit the Jewish state, spent a tense time with the new Israeli leadership during a long June 17 meeting at the Knesset, the Israeli parliament. The Israelis were not happy that Nixon and Kissinger were negotiating with Syria and Egypt and Saudi Arabia.

---

* The Irgun was commanded by Menachem Begin, who became Israel's prime minister in 1977.

Nixon was irritated at the Israelis' attitude. To be blunt: Nixon didn't like Jews, as he said time and again on the White House tapes.

Hal Saunders, Kissinger's chief aide during the shuttle diplomacy, explained how the secretary of state skillfully smooth-talked and soothed the Israelis—diplomatic duplicity at its finest. "He stopped being the Secretary of State of the United States, who was trying to mediate an agreement," Saunders said. "He became Doctor Kissinger, an American professor, serving as a consultant to the State of Israel, who, incidentally, had shared the Jewish experience. This metamorphosis was done in a very impressive, subtle and admirable fashion." Kissinger—whom Nixon had barred from Middle East negotiations before making him secretary of state precisely because he was Jewish—salved the tensions and salvaged Nixon's visit to Israel.

They flew the short hop from Tel Aviv to Amman on the afternoon of June 17. King Hussein of the Hashemite Kingdom of Jordan had for years been a rare friend to the United States in the Middle East. Suave and politically astute, King Hussein survived through the turmoil of his time by making alliances with anyone amenable, especially the United States. America trained and equipped his air force and shared intelligence on how best to survive in a rough neighborhood rife with the fathers and grandfathers of today's terrorists.

Nixon's arrival in the wake of the Yom Kippur War was a serious security issue for the king. "This being the first visit of an American president in the Middle East with an extremely unpopular U.S.–Middle East policy in the Arab world, the Jordanians were afraid he was going to get killed," said Roscoe S. Suddarth, U.S. ambassador to Jordan under Presidents Reagan and George H. W. Bush and a senior political counsel at the American embassy when Nixon came to Amman. "Who was going to be in the flatbed truck following the Nixon car and motorcade? The Nixon advance team wanted to put all photographers and the Jordanians wanted to put all soldiers with submachine guns."

This part of the trip was dispiriting. Nixon was exhausted: he turned down a palace lunch with King Hussein. He was anxious: the news that he had been named as an unindicted coconspirator in *United States v. Mitchell* had leaked, and the Senate Watergate Committee was about to release its final report. Nixon looked "like a waxen Madame Tussaud effigy," Ambassador Suddarth said. "He just wanted to be alone and worry about Watergate."

What Nixon really wanted right then was a long rest at Camp David, away from it all in the peace and quiet of his mountaintop retreat. He flew back to America over a two-day trip, stopping in the Azores, an Atlantic Ocean archipelago about 850 miles west of Portugal, where the United States had a well-equipped air force base. The dictatorial leader of Portugal, António de Spínola, flew out to greet him after his eight-hour flight, and following some diplomatic niceties Nixon was abed by nine. Flying home across the ocean, greeted on the White House Lawn by Vice President Ford in the late afternoon of June 19, he then made brief televised remarks to the American people. Borrowing a phrase from Eisenhower, he said that waging peace was harder than waging war.

The next day, he took his helicopter to Camp David for a three-day vacation. A hard week lay ahead, including a summit with the Soviets that held few hopes for ushering in a more peaceful world.

* * *

First, Nixon flew to Brussels to attend the twenty-fifth anniversary of the founding of NATO, the North Atlantic Treaty Organization, formed after World War II, at the dawn of the Cold War, as a military and diplomatic alliance of the United States and Western Europe against the Soviet Union and its satellite states. The great leaders of that era (Eisenhower, Churchill, de Gaulle) all had died in the past decade. Their successors were by comparison second-rate.

Donald Rumsfeld had risen to become the American ambassador to NATO. Rumsfeld's counselor for political affairs, James E. Goodby, received the president at the Brussels airport. Nixon had "a face carved out of wood—no expression," Goodby said. "It was quite a shocking experience to see a president of the United States looking like that."

Nixon, in his formal address to the North Atlantic Council, NATO's decision-making body, said that he and Brezhnev had put an end to the Cold War—the struggle that was the sole rationale of NATO's existence. This bald assertion shocked leaders such as Helmut Schmidt, chancellor of West Germany, who had Communist troops garrisoned on his nation's eastern border and tens of thousands of American soldiers stationed in his country.

And then Nixon returned to Moscow, where Brezhnev jovially escorted him to a lively welcoming festival and a state dinner at the

Kremlin. A year before, in a telephone call to his daughter Julie Nixon Eisenhower, Nixon had described an animated conversation with the Soviet leader while riding on the *Sequoia* in Washington. "My god, he really thinks I'm the greatest friend he's ever had," Nixon said. "The thing is with all this wallowing in Watergate, my god, Brezhnev and I are deciding the future of the world. These bastards have got to understand that."

The fortunes of the world were unaffected by the summit. Nixon and Brezhnev still spoke of their friendship, but their nations were now at odds on nuclear arms. SALT had stalled, and they could go nowhere on arms control until the treaty was resolved. "SALT—this is the most difficult of all," Nixon said to Brezhnev on July 28. "In terms of an overriding runaway nuclear arms race, agreement on offensive arms is crucial."*

Nixon continued: "If we are unable to reach agreement or to make progress in reaching agreement in the future, inevitably the reaction will be, on our side, to go forward with our offensive nuclear weapons program; and, of course, the Soviet Union will do likewise; it is inevitable. So the question we have is whether to control the nuclear arms race before it controls us. I wish I had the solution."

On June 29, Brezhnev took Nixon and Kissinger to his dacha on the Crimean Sea, still hoping to solve the problem of MIRVs undermining arms control. "We suggest that the U.S. be limited to 1100 MIRVs and 1000 for the Soviet side," Brezhnev said the next day. "This means 100 MIRV missiles more for the American side."

Kissinger responded that "this was impossible." He continued: "We will have to stop our MIRV programs next year, but the Soviets will continue for four more years at their maximum capacity. This will be represented in the U.S. as our freezing while permitting the Soviets to catch up."

Nixon saw they were getting nowhere. He proposed a ride on Brezhnev's boat. "I agree," Brezhnev said. "It is time to go out on the water." The voyage was less joyous than the sail on the *Sequoia*. Nixon returned to Moscow downcast.

---

* The United States had a 3.5-to-1 advantage in warheads over the Soviets due to its decade-long development of MIRVs. American missiles also were more sophisticated and accurate. If the Soviet Union agreed to a freeze on nuclear weapons, it would be frozen into inferiority. The Soviets had more missiles, but in a nuclear war, targets are destroyed by warheads, not missiles.

"Sophisticates in the press and political world [will] zero in on the fact we were unable to get an agreement on further limitation of strategic arms," he told Brezhnev on July 2 at their last formal talk. "Some of the critics, we have to recognize, will jump on this and say this summit was a flop." Nixon in fact thought that the summit, the fanfare notwithstanding, had been in large part a failure.

Air Force One took him to Loring Air Force Base in Caribou, Maine, the easternmost military outpost in the United States, and then directly to Key Biscayne for the July 4 holiday. As much as he loved his role as world leader, he longed for another respite. When he returned to the Oval Office on Monday, July 8, he knew his judgment was at hand.

* * *

That was the day the Supreme Court heard *United States v. Richard Milhous Nixon*. Leon Jaworski and James St. Clair were granted three hours for oral argument, thrice the Court's standard—but this was no ordinary case. Eight of the nine justices were present. William Rehnquist, having served in the Nixon administration, recused himself.

The sole issue before the Court was Nixon's claim of executive privilege to shield his tapes from the special prosecutor. The president did not argue that he was protecting secrets of state (a stance that could have carried considerable strength), but rather that the sanctuary of the Oval Office kept presidential conversations confidential.* Congress and the courts had no right to hear them.

Jaworski's argument to the justices went directly to the High Court's earliest ruling on the separation of powers under the Constitution, the 1803 case *Marbury v. Madison*, which stated that the duty of American judges was "to say what the law is." The president had placed himself above the law by defying the subpoena for the tapes. St. Clair, by contrast, said that the Constitution commanded that only by impeachment could a president submit to the power of another branch of government; the secrecy of the tapes was a political controversy beyond the reach of the Supreme Court.

---

* The "state secrets" doctrine derived from a 1952 case where the government withheld information about an air force jet that had crashed and killed four fliers. Their widows sought compensation. The courts ruled that the jet's defective design was a state secret shielded under a principle of executive privilege.

Justice Lewis Powell, appointed by President Nixon in 1972, cut to the heart of that argument. "Mr. St. Clair," he asked, "what public interest is there in preserving secrecy with respect to a criminal conspiracy?"

St. Clair's reply was straight out of *Alice in Wonderland*: "The answer, sir, is that a criminal conspiracy is criminal only after it's proven to be criminal."

But the subpoenaed tapes were at the center of the criminal case against Mitchell and his codefendants—in which the president was an unindicted coconspirator. On one of the tapes, Henry Petersen, head of the Justice Department's Criminal Division, discussing the legal problems that might face Haldeman and Ehrlichman, had presciently and precisely explained where the president now stood: "For example, I am indicted. You're an unindicted co-conspirator. You are just as guilty as I am."

St. Clair stood by his guns. Impeachment by the House and conviction in the Senate was the only recourse—and even then, executive privilege could protect discussions of presidential conduct on the tapes. Justice Thurgood Marshall, appointed by President Johnson in 1967, thought this ludicrous.* "How are you going to impeach him if you don't know" what was on the tapes? Marshall asked. "You lose me someplace."

St. Clair had lost more than one member of the Court. After Justice Powell's death, his private papers on the Court's deliberations in *United States v. Nixon* were placed in the archives of the Washington and Lee University School of Law in Virginia. They show how the Court achieved consensus in the case.

Chief Justice Warren Burger was Nixon's confidant and the Court's most conservative member (along with the recused Rehnquist). He sometimes met in private with the president, which was injudicious. The chief justice wanted an acknowledgment that executive privilege existed. He also wanted to write the opinion of the Court in his name.

The Court's liberal justices crafted a compromise in two weeks. They convinced the chief and his conservative colleagues such as Powell that the president could not use executive privilege to usurp the Court's duty

---

* Nixon discussed Justice Marshall on a tape recorded on February 28, 1973: "Marshall, of course, is a black," Nixon said. "He is so goddamn dumb." That section of tape was redacted from public view until after Marshall died.

to say what the law was. They invoked the words of James Madison from the Federalist Papers, a foundation for the Constitution: "The accumulation of all powers, legislative, executive, and judiciary, in the same hands . . . may justly be pronounced the very definition of tyranny." The decision satisfied the chief's desire to establish a legal principle of executive privilege—and the Court unanimously ordered Nixon to hand over the tapes.

* * *

Since July 12, Nixon had been isolated at La Casa Pacifica, the "House of Peace," his home in San Clemente, huddled with a few close aides waiting for word from the Supreme Court and the impeachment committee. "I suppose it could be said this is our Seventh Crisis in spades," he wrote in his diary on July19. "We can only hope for the best and plan for the worst." On July 23, he learned that one of the conservative Republicans on the House Judiciary Committee was going to vote for impeachment.

"Well, Al," he said to Haig, "there goes the presidency."

He tried to draft a speech that night, but he was overtaken with hopelessness. In the margin of his legal pad, he wrote, "12:01 a.m. Lowest point in the presidency, and Supreme Court still to come." He could not sleep until 2:30 on the morning of July 24. The Court handed down its ruling four hours later.

Haig awakened him. "It's pretty rough, Mr. President."

"Unanimous?"

"Unanimous. There's no air in it at all."

"None at all?"

The House began its hearings against the president that evening. The drafting of three articles of impeachment went up to the last minute. The debates over the charges against the president lasted through three long nights before the first vote was taken. Nixon would not return to Washington until it was tallied.

The hearings, televised in prime time, had moments of rambling diatribes but also some reasoned discourse. Forty million Americans received an education on the principles of the Constitution, along with a bill of particulars on the high crimes and misdemeanors of a president.

The tapes were transcribed, as commanded by the Supreme Court, and prepared for publication. These words could not be deleted; they were indelible.

* * *

On July 27, by a vote of 27–11, with six Republicans joining all twenty-one Democrats, the committee passed the first article of impeachment against the president. In a preamble, it said that Richard Nixon, by obstructing justice, had violated his oath of office to defend the Constitution and to take care that the laws be faithfully executed.

The bill of particulars listed his high crimes. The president had lied. He had withheld evidence. He had counseled his aides to present false testimony. He had stonewalled the Justice Department, the FBI, the special prosecutor, and Congress. He had approved paying hush money to criminal defendants, thus "rewarding individuals for their silence or false testimony." He had tried to misuse the CIA to obstruct the FBI, a fact derived from the meticulous files of Gen. Vernon Walters. And he had "made false or misleading public statements for the purpose of deceiving the people of the United States into believing that a thorough and complete investigation had been conducted" into Watergate.

"Wherefore," the article concluded, "Richard M. Nixon, by such conduct, warrants impeachment and trial, and removal from office."

Nixon had been swimming in the Pacific while the yeas and nays were tallied. He was changing at the beach house when Ron Ziegler called. And there, looking out into the ocean, barefoot and wearing a blue windbreaker emblazoned with the presidential seal, Nixon began to realize that he might have to resign. The full House would surely pass that article—and, as Nixon was learning from his dwindling band of allies on Capitol Hill, a vote of conviction by two-thirds of the Senate was increasingly likely.

Monday, July 29, was his first full day back in Washington after more than two weeks in San Clemente. The second article of impeachment came down with an even stronger vote, 28–10. It read like a criminal indictment: the president had abused his power by interfering with the lawful conduct of the FBI, the CIA, the IRS, the Justice Department, and the special prosecutor. It made special note of the White House Plumbers, whose work was "financed in part with money derived from campaign contributions." And it cited the 1969 White House wiretaps as unwarranted "electronic surveillance . . . for purposes unrelated to national security." The second article concluded, "Richard M. Nixon has acted in a manner contrary to his trust as President and subversive of constitutional government, to the great prejudice of the cause of law and justice and to the manifest injury of the people of the United States."

The third and final article passed the next day—like the first, by a 27–11 vote. Following the patterns of fact laid down in *United States v. Nixon*, the committee accused Nixon of defying lawful subpoenas, and thus usurping unto himself "judgments necessary to the exercise of the sole power of impeachment vested by the Constitution in the House of Representatives."

Nixon could not sleep at all that night. Noting the time and date atop his legal pad—3:50 a.m. on July 31—he weighed three choices: resign, fight until impeached by the full House, or struggle through the trial before the Senate. Dawn had broken before he concluded, *"End career as a fighter."*

And then he showed Al Haig the "smoking gun" tape transcript. The words of the president recorded on June 23, 1972, were evidence of his obstruction of justice in the Watergate break-in. There they stood in black ink: his order that the CIA must tell the FBI, "Don't go further into this case—period." By command of the Supreme Court, those words would be a matter of public record in a few days. Nixon himself had said that obstruction of justice was an impeachable offense. Haig thought the smoking gun was fatal; Nixon feared the same. If he fought his impeachment, he could be convicted by the Senate. He would no longer be his own judge and jury. He would stand alone.

On August 1 the president told Haig he would resign within a week. Every preparation for the transition of power was to be conducted in complete secrecy, with one exception. Nixon instructed Haig to tell Gerald Ford: it was time for him to steel himself to be sworn into office. Ford, on the day before the vote on the first article of impeachment, had made a rousing speech in Indiana proclaiming the president's innocence. He was about to be disabused.

Then, on Tuesday, August 6, Nixon, incredibly, held a full-dress Cabinet meeting and, with a straight face, said that in the best interests of the nation he would *not* resign. He then launched into an exposition of the economic policies that the White House would propound for the next six months. Attorney General William Saxbe was appalled. "Mr. President," Saxbe said, "don't you think we should be talking about next week, not next year?" In dead silence, Nixon arose from the table and left the room.

* * *

At 9:00 p.m. on August 8, 1974, the thirty-seventh president of the United States made his thirty-seventh formal televised address to the American people. He came quickly to the point.

> I have concluded that because of the Watergate matter, I might not have the support of the Congress that I would consider necessary to back the very difficult decisions and carry out the duties of this office in the way the interests of the Nation will require.
>
> I have never been a quitter. To leave office before my term is completed is abhorrent to every instinct in my body. But as President, I must put the interests of America first. America needs a full-time President and a full-time Congress, particularly at this time with problems we face at home and abroad. . . .
>
> Therefore, I shall resign the Presidency effective at noon tomorrow.

The following morning, everyone working at the White House, from the uniformed women who vacuumed the carpets to the military officer who carried the briefcase with the launch codes for nuclear war, gathered in the elegant East Room of the White House to await the president's last words.

Nixon came out of an elevator and started walking down the corridor slowly, as if in a trance. His military aide put his hands on Nixon's chest, bracing him, telling him where he was, who was in the room, and what was about to happen. The atmosphere was overwhelmingly emotional. Many people were in tears.

Among the hundreds who saw Nixon's farewell was NSC officer David Michael Ransom, the marine veteran who had detected Soviet warheads heading toward Egypt during the Yom Kippur War.*

---

* Ransom went on to a notable diplomatic career, serving in Iran, Lebanon, Saudi Arabia, Syria, and Yemen. He was the American ambassador to Bahrain from 1994 to

"There was a hush as he went up to the podium," Ransom remembered. "People cheered and tried to cheer and applaud. He gave a speech that I could only describe as pathetic."

> I remember my old man. I think that they would have called him sort of a little man, common man. He didn't consider himself that way. You know what he was? He was a streetcar motorman first, and then he was a farmer, and then he had a lemon ranch. . . . And then he was a grocer. But he was a great man, because he did his job, and every job counts up to the hilt, regardless of what happens.
>
> Nobody will ever write a book, probably, about my mother. Well, I guess all of you would say this about your mother—my mother was a saint. And I think of her, two boys dying of tuberculosis, nursing four others in order that she could take care of my older brother for three years in Arizona, and seeing each of them die. . . . Yes, she will have no books written about her. But she was a saint.

The president concluded, "We think that when we suffer a defeat that all is ended. . . . Not true. It is only a beginning, always. . . . Never get discouraged. Never be petty. Always remember, others may hate you, but those who hate you don't win unless you hate them. And then you destroy yourself."

Ransom remembered: "I felt relief about his resignation, but I also felt a deep running admiration for a man who faced adversity so courageously. Sometimes, when you are a soldier, the enemy might overrun you; you then have a choice between surrender and fighting. My heart has always gone out to the men who keep on fighting."

The morning was cloaked with clouds. A helicopter awaited on the lawn. Nixon left the White House, said farewell to Gerald Ford, and walked to the chopper. Ransom stepped out onto a balcony to watch Nixon fly away. Two other people stood beside him. One was the White

---

1997. He received the Defense Distinguished Service Medal, the Pentagon's highest civilian award, retired from the Foreign Service, and recorded his recollections in an oral history two years before he died at the age of sixty-five in 2005.

House chef, wearing his white uniform. The other was Secretary of Defense James Schlesinger, smoking his pipe.

"Nixon flashed his double-armed signal of departure with two fingers raised in a 'V' sign and then he turned and entered the helicopter," Ransom said. "It began cranking up very slowly. Finally, there was a deafening sound. The chopper lifted off, pivoted, and disappeared into the gloom of the morning. It was almost a haunted scene."

As the helicopter faded into the fog, the three men looked at one another. Schlesinger took his pipe out of his mouth, banged it on the railing, emptying the bowl, and said, "It's an interesting constitutional question, but I think I am still the secretary of defense. So I am going back to my office." He looked at the cook and said, "What are you going to do?"

The cook said, "I'm going to prepare lunch for the president."

"I thought, 'Of course. The king is dead. Long live the king!'" Ransom said. "The cook had it right. This wasn't a matter of abstruse argument over constitutional privileges. Our state was going to carry on and the president would want lunch in about an hour and a half. So, the cook went off and prepared it.

"I've always thought of that as something very important about our country. We may stumble but we don't fall."

Epilogue

Richard Nixon fought wars he could not win, feared his enemies at home would defeat him, and felt unconstrained by law when he sought to destroy them first. That belief led him to break his oath of office and violate the Constitution. He permanently damaged people's respect for the presidency, a danger in a democracy.

And now his legacy is all around us.

Some presidents who succeeded Nixon never seemed to learn. Ronald Reagan ran covert wars overseas with clandestine funds. His top national security aides were indicted, then pardoned, by George H. W. Bush. Bill Clinton was impeached for perjury. George W. Bush's abuses of power dwarfed Nixon's—secret prisons, sanctioned torture, limitless eavesdropping, all supported by presidential fiat and secret statutes, aided and abetted by Vice President Dick Cheney. Barack Obama's administration tormented more reporters and their sources under threat of subpoena or prison than Nixon's ever did. In America, now more than ever, campaign cash from corporate magnates controls elections.

South Vietnam fell nine months after Nixon left office, as did Cambodia, which went on to suffer the torments of a tyrannical regime, and Laos, where many thousands of tribesmen who had fought alongside

Americans for twenty years fled into exile. The last Americans to leave Saigon took neither peace nor honor with them. And still we go to war without knowing our enemies, or the contour of the battlefield, or the way out.

* * *

Richard Nixon was unconditionally pardoned for the crimes of Watergate—an unpopular proclamation by President Ford—a month after he left the White House. Within six weeks, Nixon came close to dying.

His chronic phlebitis, doubtless compounded by depression, flared dangerously. He entered Long Beach Memorial Hospital near San Clemente on October 23, 1974. His physicians saw the danger. Nixon's left leg was obstructed by blood clots; if one broke loose and invaded his lungs, he would almost surely suffer a potentially fatal embolism. Without surgery, his prognosis was grim. He was sixty-one years old.

Nixon collapsed after the operation. A vein ruptured. Bleeding internally, he fell unconscious, white as a sheet, in deep vascular shock. His heart stopped. "He just flat-lined," said his White House aide Steve Bull, who was with him in the hospital. "Clinically . . . he was dead." His nurse slapped his face, repeating: "Richard! Wake up, Richard!" When he came to consciousness the next day, his doctor told him: "We almost lost you last night."

For the next two decades, Richard Nixon tried to turn his life into a parable of a man who suffered, died, and rose again.

Having taken every tape and every file he could find before he left the White House, he signed a $2 million contract for his memoirs, a 1,094-page book that he drafted with the help of the future television news anchor Diane Sawyer and his favorite speechwriter, Raymond Price. He signed a $600,000 deal with the British broadcaster David Frost for a series of interviews.

Nixon made a cunning remark near the end of his encounters with Frost. "What history says about this administration will depend on who writes history," he said. "Winston Churchill once told one of his critics that history . . . would treat him well, and his critic said: 'How do you know?' And he said, 'Because I intend to write it.' "

And Nixon did, first in his memoirs, then in eight volumes on statecraft and power. "As people look back on the Nixon administration," he said in 1988, "they're probably most likely to remember fifty years from now, one hundred years from now, that we made a difference on a very major issue. We changed the world." He and he alone had transformed the global balance of power with "the China initiative, which only I could do."

"History will treat me fairly," he concluded. "Historians probably won't."

The tales of the tapes remained untold: Nixon and his wealthy supporters fought a twenty-year battle until his death in 1994 to keep them out of the hands of historians and citizens alike. It took twenty more years, up through 2014, before the last of the tapes were released and made available for the arduous task of transcription.

The tens of thousands of recently declassified documents from his years in office, on top of the tapes, are the real history of the Nixon administration. This book's task is to tell it as it happened, in the words of the man himself—the man who said in his second inaugural address that we must answer to history, and to our conscience, for our work.

* * *

Ray Price, who was with Nixon throughout his presidency and in his exile, gave an oral history interview in 2007 to Timothy Naftali, who transformed the Richard Nixon Presidential Library from a mausoleum into a living museum.

Talking about Nixon's burdens in the Oval Office, Price said: "You have to, in some cases, sacrifice a lot of virtue. You may not have to sacrifice virgins, but you may have to sacrifice virtue sometimes. And that's the only way you get things done in the real world. It is a real world, and a lot of the critics tend to forget that the world is real. . . . And people forget he actually was human. A lot of people may not believe this, but he was."

"We don't expect our presidents to be human," Naftali said.

The two men laughed together.

"But almost all of them have been," Price said.

Judgments

President Richard M. Nixon: Named as an unindicted coconspirator by the Watergate grand jury; unconditionally pardoned by President Ford.

Vice President Spiro T. Agnew: Pleaded no contest to evaded taxes on bribes he took while in office; three-year sentence suspended.

Attorney General John N. Mitchell: Convicted of conspiracy to obstruct justice and perjury; served nineteen months in prison.

White House chief of staff H. R. Haldeman: Convicted of perjury and conspiracy to obstruct justice; served eighteen months in prison.

White House assistant to the president for domestic affairs John D. Ehrlichman: Convicted of conspiracy to obstruct justice, conspiracy to violate civil rights, and perjury; served eighteen months in prison.

White House counsel John W. Dean III: Pleaded guilty to conspiracy to obstruct justice in the Watergate cover-up; served four months.

White House special counsel Charles W. Colson: Pleaded guilty to obstruction of justice; served seven months.

White House deputy assistant to the president Dwight L. Chapin: Pleaded guilty to lying to the Watergate grand jury; served eight months.

White House aide to Ehrlichman and liaison to federal law enforcement Egil Krogh Jr.: Pleaded guilty to conspiracy to violate civil rights in his role overseeing the Plumbers; served four and a half months; license to practice law restored by the state of Washington.

Nixon attorney and financier Herbert W. Kalmbach: Pleaded guilty in connection with the sale of ambassadorships to wealthy campaign contributors; served six months; license to practice law restored by the state of California.

CREEP deputy director Jeb Stuart Magruder: Pleaded guilty to conspiracy to obstruct justice, fraud, and wiretapping; served seven months.

CREEP finance director and former commerce secretary Maurice Stans: Pleaded guilty to five misdemeanor violations of campaign finance laws; fined $5,000.

CREEP adviser and presidential aide Frederick C. LaRue: Pleaded guilty to conspiracy to obstruct justice; served five and a half months.

Watergate burglary overseer E. Howard Hunt: Convicted of conspiracy, burglary, and wiretapping; served thirty-three months.

Watergate burglars Bernard Barker, Virgilio Gonzales, Eugenio Martinez, and Frank Sturgis: Pleaded guilty to conspiracy, burglary, and wiretapping; their sentences ranged from twelve to fifteen months.

Watergate wiretapper James W. McCord Jr.: Convicted of conspiracy, burglary, and wiretapping; broke the case with his letter to Judge Sirica; served four months.

Watergate mastermind G. Gordon Liddy: Convicted of conspiracy, burglary, and wiretapping; served fifty-two months, the longest sentence of all.

Acknowledgments

One Man Against the World exists thanks in great part to three people: Stephen Rubin, the courageous president and publisher of Henry Holt and Company; Gillian Blake, Holt's extraordinary editor in chief, who gave every word meaning; and my brilliant literary agent, Kathy Robbins, who has stood by me for twenty years.

At the Robbins Office, David Halpern contributed mightily. At Holt, thanks to Chris O'Connell, Meryl Sussman Levavi, Jenna Dolan, Eleanor Embry, and Caroline Zancan.

The collected works of Richard Nixon include 2,636 hours of taped White House conversations open to the public. The struggle to wrestle them from Nixon—and the continuing effort to transcribe them—has been an epic battle. The last 340 hours of tapes were released on August 21, 2013, nearly forty years to the day after their existence was revealed at the Senate Watergate Hearings. The talented Cynthia Colonna helped me immeasurably in transcribing hundreds of crucial Nixon tapes.

All Nixon historians stand on the shoulders of Stanley Kutler, professor emeritus at the University of Wisconsin–Madison. In 1994, Kutler sued the National Archives and the Nixon estate to force the release of the White House tapes. He won. He worked tirelessly for more than twenty years to bring the truth of the Nixon administration out of the past and into the light of day. Stanley died in April 2015. I wish he could have read this book.

Harry Robbins Haldeman produced handwritten and dictated diaries that describe in minute detail the mind of Richard Milhous Nixon. Haldeman's candor can be checked meticulously against contemporaneous documents and records. Haldeman almost always got it right—and his reflections have a mordant sense of humor. Without his diaries (online and in the public domain at the Nixon Library's website), replete with passages declassified as recently as November 2014, no accurate account of Richard Nixon's presidency would be possible.

The memoirs of members of the Nixon administration are often self-serving, and sometimes demonstrably false. An exception is John W. Dean III's *The Nixon Defense*, published in August 2014. Dean—who, like Iago in Shakespeare's *Othello*, plotted to destroy his master—may not be the most reliable narrator of the Nixon tragedy, but his book is essential. With the help of forty-two Nixon Presidential Library archivists and six personal assistants, Dean transcribed a multitude of previously unpublished tapes. His book is a straightforward script of the conversations and confrontations that preceded Nixon's downfall.

Timothy Naftali led the Nixon Presidential Library for four crucial years until November 2011. He is an unsung hero of American history. I am grateful to him, his successors, and every staff member of the Nixon Library, who will serve generations of Americans throughout the twenty-first century.

The editors, historians, and archivists of *The Foreign Relations of the United States* series produce the official diplomatic history of America, published continuously since the Civil War. Their work is unique and invaluable. Laboring tirelessly—often against strong opposition from the CIA—they have printed fifty-six thick volumes of declassified documents on the foreign policies of the Nixon administration, all available online. Since 2007, these have incorporated the transcripts of hundreds of hours of conversations among Nixon, Kissinger, and their top military, diplomatic, and intelligence officials.

My mother, Professor Dora B. Weiner, is a distinguished historian. She taught me how to read and write. I am forever grateful to her.

I love my wife, Kate Doyle, who works with all her heart and soul in the name of human rights, and our daughters, Emma Doyle and Ruby Doyle, who know that American democracy is a work in progress—and that work may take a long time. We are all in it for the long haul. I dedicate this book, and my life, to them.

Notes

Abbreviations

Abrams Papers   Abrams Papers, U.S. Army Center of Military
History, Washington, DC

CIA   Central Intelligence Agency, declassified
documents

Cong. Rec.   *Congressional Record*

FAOH   Foreign Affairs Oral History Collections, online at
http://adst.org.oral-history/.

FBI   Federal Bureau of Investigation, declassified
documents

FRUS   *Foreign Relations of the United States*, 1969–1976

JFKL   John F. Kennedy Presidential Library, Boston, MA

Kissinger Papers   Kissinger Papers, Manuscript Division, Library of
Congress, Washington, DC

Kissinger Telephone
Conversations   Kissinger Telephone Conversations, Nixon
Presidential Materials, National Archives Washington, DC. Many key Kissinger conversations
quoted in this book are available online at the
Nixon Presidential Library, http://www
.nixonlibrary.gov/forresearchers/find/textual
/telcons.php. The National Security Archive, a
nonprofit research group, also holds a substantial
collection, http://nsarchive.gwu.edu/

LBJ Library   LBJ Presidential Library, Austin, TX

Moorer Diary   Admiral Thomas H. Moorer diary, declassified
sections in *FRUS* and in "The Joint Chiefs of Staff

	and the War in Vietnam," online at www.dtic.mil /doctrine/jcs-vietnam.htm
Nixon Library	Richard M. Nixon Presidential Library and Museum
NWHT	Nixon White House Tapes. A selection of the tapes is online at the Nixon Library's website at http://www.nixonlibrary.gov/virtuallibrary/tapeexcerpts/index.php
President's Daily Diary	Nixon Library online, http://www.nixonlibrary.gov/virtuallibrary/documents/dailydiary.php
Public Papers of Richard Nixon	Available online at http://www.presidency.ucsb.edu/richard_nixon.php

Author's Note

1   "I gave them a sword": Nixon interview with David Frost, broadcast May 19, 1977, broadcast on American public television stations, online at http://www.wgbh.org/programs/FrostNixon-The-Original-Watergate-Interviews-489/episodes/FrostNixon-The-Original-Watergate-Interviews-7381.

2   "a cancer within": John W. Dean to Nixon, March 21, 1973, NWHT, White House.

1: "A great, bad man"

5   *the* world leader": Jan. 2, 1971, entry in H. R. Haldeman, *Haldeman Diaries*, online at http://www.nixonlibrary.gov/virtuallibrary/documents/haldeman-diaries/haldeman-diaries.php.

5   "an indefinable spirit": Richard M. Nixon, State of the Union address, Jan. 22, 1970, Public Papers of Richard Nixon.

6   "Nixon has a genius": Martin Luther King Jr. letter to Earl Mazo, cited in Clayburn Carson et al., eds., *The Papers of Martin Luther King, Jr: Symbol of the Movement, January 1957–December 1958* (Berkeley: University of California Press, 2000), p. 481.

6   "We are still dealing with governments" and "Those Chinese are out to whip me": May 27, 1971, NWHT, Oval Office.

6   "They particularly won't believe me": April 17, 1971, NWHT, Oval Office.

7   "the environment is not an issue that's worth a damn to us": Feb. 9, 1971, entry in *Haldeman Diaries*.

7   "in the long run . . . a catastrophe": Shultz interview in Gerald S. Strober and Deborah Hart Strober, *Nixon: An Oral History of His Presidency* (New York: HarperCollins, 1994), p. 51.

7   "Nixon never trusted anybody": Helms interview with Stanley I. Kutler, July 14, 1988, Box 15, Folder 16, Wisconsin Historical Archives, Madison, WI, cited by permission of Professor Kutler.

9   "When the president does it": Nixon interview with Frost.

10   "it was 'me against the world'": Robert Finch interview, in Strober and Strober, *Nixon*, p. 49.

10   "He hears the train go by at night": Nixon address accepting the presidential nomination at the Republican National Convention in Miami Beach, Florida, Aug. 8, 1968, Public Papers of Richard Nixon.

10   "He had a lemon ranch": Richard Nixon, farewell address, White House, Aug. 9, 1974, Public Papers of Richard Nixon.

11   "The last thing my mother, a devout Quaker": Richard Nixon, *Six Crises* (New York: Simon and Schuster, 1962), p. 295.

12   "the zeal": Hoover testimony, March 26, 1947, House Un-American Activities Committee, online at http://www.digitalhistory.uh.edu/.

13 "my closest friend": May 3, 1972, NWHT, White House.

13 "the security of the whole nation and the cause of free men": Nixon, *Six Crises*, p. 37.

14 "The Hiss case brought me national fame": Ibid., p. 69.

14 "even suggesting that the presidency itself could be stolen": Ibid., p. 416.

15 "For sixteen years, ever since the Hiss case": Live footage of Nixon's "last press conference" is at https://www.youtube.com/watch?v=_RMSb-tS_OM.

2: "This is treason"

17 "In those years in limbo": Watts oral history, FAOH.

17 "When Mr. Nixon and I called on President Suharto": Green oral history, FAOH.

18 "was bound to be crucified": Doris Kearns Goodwin, *Lyndon Johnson and the American Dream* (New York: New American Library, 1977), p. 263.

19 "increasingly attracted": Bui Diem with David Chanoff, *In the Jaws of History* (Bloomington: Indiana University Press, 1999), pp. 237–44.

20 "He was in Washington when Castro took over": Woods to Haldeman, Oct. 13, 1968, Nixon Library, Nixon Presidential Returned Materials Collection: White House Special Files.

21 "between three and five million dollars": Woods to Nixon, "RE: Telephone call from Bob Hill—re Mexico," Sept. 29, 1968, Nixon Library, Nixon Presidential Returned Materials Collection: White House Special Files.

21 "someone in Johnson's innermost circle": Richard Nixon, *RN: The Memoirs of Richard Nixon* (New York: Simon and Schuster, 1978), p. 326.

22 "I immediately decided" . . . "a cynical last-minute": Ibid., p. 327.

22 "It appears Mr. Nixon will be elected": Director, NSA, to [classified], "Thieu's Views on Peace Talks and Bombing Halt," partially declassified Dec. 17, 2010, LBJ Library.

22 "Nixon was playing the problem": Rostow to Johnson, 6:00 a.m., Oct. 29, 1968, LBJ Library.

22 "He better keep Mrs. Chennault": Oct. 31, 1968, LBJ Tapes, LBJ Library.

23 "South Vietnam is not a truck": Thieu quoted in conversation between President Johnson and Robert McNamara, Nov. 1, 1968, Washington, DC, *FRUS* VII: Vietnam, July 1970–January 1972.

23 "The Republican nominee": Oct. 31, 1968, LBJ Tapes, LBJ Library.

23 "It's clear as day!": Notes of meeting, Nov. 2, 1968, Washington, DC, *FRUS* VII: Vietnam.

23 "a message from her boss": Rostow teletype to President Johnson, Nov. 2, 1968, LBJ Library.

23 "This is treason": Nov. 2, 1968, LBJ Tapes, LBJ Library.

24 "The deal was cooked": Habib oral history, FAOH.

24 "I do not believe": Telephone conversation among President Johnson, Secretary of Defense Clifford, Secretary of State Rusk, and the president's special assistant (Rostow), Nov. 4, 1968, 12:27 p.m., *FRUS* VII: Vietnam.

25 "These messages started" . . . "And it is a sordid story": Nov. 8, 1969, LBJ Tapes, LBJ Library. The bitterness lingered through Inauguration Day, January 20, 1969. LBJ's administrative aide James R. Jones, later the American ambassador to Mexico, watched it firsthand. LBJ said that Nixon was "a son of a bitch, but he's the only son of a bitch we have as President, so we have to support him. He never trusted Nixon but he wanted him to succeed. Johnson had an enormous sense of the history of the presidency and the night before the inauguration I remember he admonished all of us. . . He said: 'This plane, the United States, has only one pilot. When we go through rough weather, if everybody on the plane starts trying to take the controls and beating the pilot over the head, that plane is going to crash.'" On inauguration morning, the presidential limousine waited at the White

House for the drive to the swearing-in at the Capitol Building. "Johnson and Nixon in the back seat," Jones remembers. "All the way up there, Nixon, all he wanted to talk about was losing Texas and how he didn't intend to lose Texas in '72."

25 "We were tapped": Nixon to Haldeman, June 28, 1972, NWHT, Old Executive Office Building.

25 "he had sent two secret emissaries": CIA Saigon station, "President Thieu's Comments on Peace Talks," Nov. 18, 1968, LBJ Library.

25 "The 'X' Files": Memorandum for the record, W. W. Rostow, May 14, 1973, LBJ Library.

3: "He was surrounded by enemies"

27 Inauguration Day: Huston oral history, Nixon Library.

27 "I really need": July 1, 1971, NWHT, Oval Office.

29 "This country is going so far right you won't even recognize it": This remarkable statement by Attorney General Mitchell was reported by Kandy Stroud of *Women's Wear Daily* as "overheard" during a 1970 cocktail party at the Women's National Press Club. It was part of a long and evidently tape-recorded rant against students, professors, and the New Left shortly after the May 1970 killings of four students by National Guardsmen at Kent State University.

29 "Attorneys General seldom directed Mr. Hoover": Nixon testimony, *U.S. v. Felt*, Oct. 29, 1980, United States District Court for the Southern District, New York.

30 "I had a strong intuition about Henry Kissinger": Nixon, *RN*, p. 341.

32 "It was a bizarre way": Rodman oral history, FAOH.

32 "There was an absolute conviction": Haldeman oral history, Strober and Strober, *Nixon*, p. 183.

33 "the greatest military man I had ever met": Alexander M. Haig Jr. Oral History Interview, Nov. 30, 2007, Nixon Library.

34 "I had clearly crossed the line for the first time": John W. Dean, keynote address, "Presidential Powers: An American Debate," April 25, 2006, Center on Law and Security, New York University School of Law.

34 "convinced that Nixon's drinking could cost him any chance of a return to public life": John Ehrlichman, *Witness to Power: The Nixon Years* (New York: Simon and Schuster, 1988), pp. 37–38.

34 "house detective": Ehrlichman, "Transcription of Tape-Recorded Interview," White House, Dec. 17, 1971, Nixon Library.

35 "From the first time he ran for office": Ehrlichman interview recorded by CNN in 1988, transcript at www2.gwu.edu/~nsarchiv/coldwar/interviews/episode-16/ehrlichman4.html.

4: "He will let them know who is boss around here"

36 "to understand . . . these were horrible decisions": Haldeman oral history; Strober and Strober, *Nixon*, p. 181.

37 "Sedov said": Kissinger, memorandum of conversation, Washington, Jan. 2, 1969, *FRUS* XII: Soviet Union, January 1969–October 1970. NSC Files: Contacts with the Soviets Prior to Jan. 20, 1969. Kissinger and Sedov met at the Pierre Hotel, headquarters for the Nixon transition team.

37 "Our lines of communication": Nixon inaugural address, Jan. 20, 1969, Public Papers of President Richard M. Nixon. Nixon's handwritten notes from meetings held January 20 and 21 include the following. Of domestic and international issues, including China, he wrote in part, "Chinese Communists: Short range—no change. Long range—we do not want 800,000,000 living in angry isolation. We want contact"

(Box 1, President's Handwriting File, January 1969, Administrative Files, White House Special Files, President's Office Files, Nixon Presidential Library and Museum).

37   "In the second week of the administration": Haig oral history, Nixon Library, Nov. 30, 2007.

37   "This will be a great symbol": Vietnam, Minutes of National Security Council Meeting, Jan. 25, 1969, Nixon Presidential Materials, NSC Files, National Archives and Records Administration, Washington, DC.

38   "To preclude . . . military actions": Haig to Kissinger, Washington, March 2, 1969, "Memorandum from Secretary Laird Enclosing Preliminary Draft of Potential Military Actions re Vietnam," *FRUS* XXXIV: National Security Policy, 1969–1972. The memo describes the war plans developed by the Joint Chiefs in response to Kissinger's request on January 27, including the nuclear option.

38   "What is the most effective way to bring the war to a conclusion?": Minutes of National Security Council Meeting, Jan. 25, 1969, Washington, *FRUS* VI: Vietnam, January 1969–July 1970.

38   "Mr. Kissinger questioned": Minutes of the 303/40 Committee Meeting, Feb. 12, 1969, *FRUS* VI: Vietnam. The 303 meetings, later known as the 40 meetings, were where Kissinger and high-ranking intelligence, military, diplomatic, and national security officials made decision on CIA covert operations.

39   "I believe it is absolutely urgent": Memorandum from President Nixon to Kissinger, Washington, Feb. 1, 1969, Washington, DC, in Box 64, Vietnam Subject Files, Reappraisal of Vietnam Commitment, vol. 1, Nixon Presidential Materials, NSC Files, National Archives, Washington, DC.

39   "The question that arises": Laird to Nixon, March 13, 1969, "SUBJECT: Trip to Vietnam and CINCPAC," March 5–12, 1969, *FRUS* VI: Vietnam.

40   "lobbing a few shells into Saigon": Kissinger to Nixon, March 10, 1969, "SUBJECT: Dobrynin–Rogers Conversation on the Paris Negotiations," *FRUS* VI: Vietnam.

40   "so secret . . . entire new world": Feb. 24, 1969 (Brussels), entry in *Haldeman Diaries*.

40   "In order to set the stage": Kissinger to Nixon, "Consideration of B-52 Options Against COSVN Headquarters," Feb. 19, 1969, Top Secret, declassified 2006, *FRUS* VI: Vietnam.

40   "an extraordinary amount of detailed planning": Oakley oral history, FAOH. Nixon's obsession with detail was everyday life at the White House. The scripting of the presidency was a daily burden, part of the immense pressure Nixon imposed on himself and his inner circle. He would stop in the midst of deliberations over the war to demand that soup and salads be banned from White House dinners. His highest-ranking staffers took orders in the Oval Office about "whether or not the curtains were closed or open, the arrangement of state gifts, whether they should be on that side of the room or this side of the room," his aide Alexander Butterfield said; before every ceremonial occasion at the White House, the president needed to know "whether the military would be to the right or the left, which uniforms would be worn by the White House police, whether the Secret Service would salute during 'The Star-Spangled Banner' and sing"—and this level of preoccupation applied to "all Presidential activities."

41   "Must convince them": Notes by President Nixon of a meeting, Paris, March 2, 1969, *FRUS* VI: Vietnam.

41   "We are not going to double-cross you": Telegram from the embassy in France to the Department of State, Paris, March 2, 1969, memorandum of conversation among the president, Vice President Ky, Ambassador Lam, the secretary of state, Ambassador Lodge, Ambassador Walsh, and Dr. Kissinger, *FRUS* VI: Vietnam.

41   "Hit them": March 8, 1969, Kissinger Telephone Conversations.

41   "Our military effort": Kissinger to Nixon, March 8, 1969, "SUBJECT: Reflections on De-escalation," *FRUS* VI: Vietnam.

41   "The President ordered": Memorandum for the record, March 15, 1969, "SUBJECT: March 16 Rocket Attack on Saigon," Nixon Presidential Materials, NSC Files, National Archives, Washington, DC.

5: "The center cannot hold"

43   Abrams was "seeking permission": Surprisingly, this important story languished for six weeks until the *New York Times* followed up on it. "Although President Nixon became concerned over these two stories and the threat they posed to secrecy . . . Nixon need not have worried," a declassified U.S. Air Force history of the Vietnam War reflected. "Possibly put off the track by the lack of reaction from military leaders and civilian authorities, the press failed to pursue the matter. As it turned out, more than four years elapsed from the first Menu bombing in 1969 until Maj. Hal Knight, a former Air Force officer, told the Senate Armed Services Committee in 1973 that, while serving at a Combat Skyspot radar site, he had destroyed records of strikes in Cambodia and substituted reports of attacks on cover targets in South Vietnam." Bernard C. Nalty, *Air War over South Vietnam 1968–1975*, Air Force History and Museums Program (Washington, DC: U.S. Air Force, 2000), pp. 127–32.

43   "the ultimate weapon": Nixon deposition, recorded in San Clemente, CA, Jan. 15, 1976, *Halperin v. Kissinger*, U.S. District Court, Washington, DC. Nixon gave this deposition in connection with the White House wiretaps. Kissinger finally settled the case in 1991, when he wrote an apology to his former aide Halperin, whom he had selected as a wiretap target in 1969.

44   "Here he was in this room with J. Edgar Hoover": Rodman oral history, FAOH.

44   "destroy whoever did this": Hoover memorandum of conversation with Kissinger, May 9, 1969, FBI.

44   "gossip and bullshitting": Feb. 28, 1973, NWHT.

44   tapping was within the realm: The taps were clearly illegal. The prevailing law, the 1968 Omnibus Crime Control and Safe Streets Act, dealt specifically with the issue. While prohibiting all wiretapping and electronic surveillance by persons other than law enforcement authorities (and even then, under strict rules), it stated that "nothing . . . shall limit the constitutional power of the President . . . to protect the nation against *actual or potential attack or other hostile acts of a foreign power*, to obtain *foreign intelligence information* deemed essential to the security of the United States or to protect national security information against *foreign intelligence activities*." I have emphasized the passages with the word *foreign*. Nothing in that law allowed the wiretapping of Americans who were not foreign spies.

44   "But I didn't think it was being done by the White House": Sullivan oral history, Strober and Strober, *Nixon*, p. 99.

45   "an almost paranoid fear": Kennedy oral history, FAOH.

45   "You cannot square a personal friendship": Lord oral history, FAOH.

45   "disreputable if not outright illegal": Thomas R. Johnson, *American Cryptology During the Cold War, 1945–1989: Book III: Retrenchment and Reform, 1972–1980*, Center for Cryptological History, National Security Agency, p. 85. This unique National Security Agency history was written in 1998 and declassified, with significant deletions, in 2013, available online at https://www.nsa.gov/public_info /_files/cryptologic_histories/cold_war_iii.pdf.

46   "Without the Vietnam War": H. R. Haldeman, *The Ends of Power* (New York: Times Books, 1978), p. 117.

46   "This is the way civilizations begin to die": Nixon statement on campus disorders, March 22, 1969, Public Papers of Richard Nixon.

46   "The subject of U.S. casualties": Wheeler cable to Abrams, April 3, 1969, Abrams

Papers, U.S. Army Center of Military History. Cited in *History of the Joint Chiefs of Staff: The Joint Chiefs of Staff and the War in Vietnam, 1969–70*, Historical Division, Joint Secretariat, JCS, p. 51, available online at http://www.dtic.mil/doctrine/doctrine/history/jcsvietnam_69_70.pdf.

47   "We need a plan": National Security Council meeting, March 28, 1969, Box TS 82, NSC Meetings, Jan.–March 1969, Top Secret; Sensitive, in Kissinger Papers. These minutes were based on notes taken by Haig that were typed by a White House secretary; Haig made corrections by hand to the typed transcript. CIA director Richard Helms gave Nixon the Agency's collective opinion that the United States had no strategic concept or coherent policy in Vietnam, the outlook there was for five or six more years of continuing war, it would be pointless for Washington to send more U.S. troops to Vietnam, and if South Vietnam's leaders could not make it on their own the United States "ought to get out." Helms notes, Job No. 80B01285A, DCI, Box 11, Folder 5, CIA.

48   "We must convince the American public": Kissinger to President Nixon, April 3, 1969, "SUBJECT: Vietnam Problem." This document contains the message delivered to the Soviet ambassador, *FRUS* VI: Vietnam.

48   "the only way to end the war quickly and the best way to conclude it honorably": Ibid.

49   "Even without a reason": Telephone conversation between President Nixon and Kissinger, April 5, 1969, 9:45 a.m., Kissinger Telephone Conversations, Library of Congress, Washington, DC.

49   Another newly declassified NSA history: *United States Cryptologic History*, Crisis Collection, Vol. 3: *The National Security Agency and the EC-121 Shootdown*, NSA, 1989, declassified May 13, 2013. Online at https://www.nsa.gov/public_info/_files/cryptologic_histories/EC-121.pdf.

49   "The President said to find a way": Telephone conversation between President Nixon and Kissinger (notes by Haig), April 15, 1969, *FRUS* XIX: Korea, 1969–1972.

49   "Honest John": Minutes of NSC meeting, April 16, 1969, ibid.

50   "That is a very tough one": Telephone conversation between President Nixon and Kissinger, April 17, 1969, ibid.

50   "immediate military action against the North": Haig Oral History Interview, Nov. 30, 2007, Nixon Library.

50   "We do not do a thing": Telephone conversation between President Nixon and Kissinger, April 17, 1969, *FRUS* XIX: Korea.

50   "Nixon told me": Haig Oral History Interview, Nov. 30, 2007, Nixon Library.

50   "Nixon did not trust": Rodman oral history, FAOH.

51   "ambassadorships were being sold to the highest bidders": Hart oral history, FAOH.

51   "Vincent De Roulet was no longer 'persona grata'": Rogers oral history, FAOH.

51   "I think he had something": Cheek oral history, FAOH.

52   "contributed chunks of this money": Gillespie oral history, FAOH.

52   "We had a career Foreign Service officer": Hart oral history, FAOH.

52   "Anybody who wants to be an ambassador must at least give $250,000": June 23, 1971, NWHT, Oval Office.

54   "He had no hobbies": Butterfield testimony, House Judiciary Committee impeachment hearings, July 2, 1974. Transcript on line at http://watergate.info/judiciary/BKITOW.PDF.

54   "This country could run itself domestically": Nixon interview cited in Margaret MacMillan, *Nixon and Mao: The Week That Changed the World* (New York: Random House, 2008), p. 8.

54   "He believed in nothing": Farmer oral history, Strober and Strober, *Nixon*, p. 110.

55　he *"can't* have a Domestic Program": Moynihan quoted in March 11, 1969, entry in *Haldeman Diaries*.

55　"Regarding domestic policy, which Nixon dismissed as 'building outhouses in Peoria'": Will quoted in "Up Front," *New York Times Book Review*, May 11, 2008, http://www.nytimes.com/2008/05/11/books/review/Upfront-t.html.

55　"If it's called racism, so be it" and "Uncle Toms": Feb. 27 and April 2, 1970, entries in *Haldeman Diaries*.

55　"that we're catering to the left": Feb. 9, 1971, entry in ibid.

56　"He didn't know anything about the war on poverty": Cheney oral history, Miller Center, University of Virginia, Charlottesville, VA, recorded March 16–17, 2000.

56　"The Nixon administration came in": Carlucci oral history, FAOH.

56　"to provide upward mobility" . . . "OEO was the enemy": Ibid.

56　"I want to end this war": Nixon address on Vietnam, May 14, 1969, Public Papers of Richard Nixon, full text online at http://www.presidency.ucsb.edu/ws/index .php?pid=2047.

57　"totally unintelligible to the ordinary guy": May 14, 1969, entry in *Haldeman Diaries*.

57　"Our fighting men": Nixon address on Vietnam, May 14, 1969.

57　"senseless and irresponsible": Sen. Edward M. Kennedy, Cong. Rec., May 20, 1969.

57　"We are talking to an enemy": Nixon meeting with Cabinet and NSC, May 15, 1969, Nixon Presidential Materials, White House Special Files, National Archives, Washington, DC.

6: "Madman"

59　Hoover himself began to draw up a blueprint: Hoover's plans are detailed in an FBI document, "CIA Requests for Information Concerning Aliens," dated November 19, 1948, and declassified under the Freedom of Information Act (FOIA) nearly sixty years later. Despite the document's title, 97 percent of the people listed as potential candidates for preventive detention by the FBI were Americans.

59　Congress . . . had passed: The long-forgotten Emergency Detention Act of 1950 became the subject of congressional hearings in 1971 after the mass arrest of six thousand protesters in Washington. While six detention camps were established and funded by the Congress, none of them was ever used.

59　"I think there is a much deeper conspiracy": Nov. 14, 1969, Kissinger Telephone Conversations.

60　"everything depended on the war in Vietnam": Memorandum from Kissinger to President Nixon, June 13, 1969, Washington, DC, *FRUS* XII: Soviet Union.

60　"We have a difficult political problem": Memorandum of conversation, June 8, 1969, Midway Island, *FRUS* VI: Vietnam.

60　"a sagging of spirit": Ibid.

61　"if not handled carefully": Ibid.

61　"He feels it will probably mean collapse of South Vietnam": June 19, 1969, entry in *Haldeman Diaries*.

61　"discouraged because his plans" and "He wants to push for some escalation": July 7, 1969, entry in *Haldeman Diaries*.

61　"until about October": *History of the Joint Chiefs of Staff: The Joint Chiefs of Staff and the War in Vietnam, 1969–70*, Historical Division, Joint Secretariat, JCS, pp. 56–57: "On the evening of 7 July the President met with his key advisers to review Vietnam policy. . . . Political climate was considered at some length, and General Wheeler later told CINCPAC [Adm. John S. McCain] and COMUSMACV [Gen. Creighton Abrams] that 'the political situation here is not good.' The President considered that public opinion would hold 'until about October,' when some further action on his part would be required." The complete text of this history is online at http://www.dtic.mil/doctrine/doctrine/history/jcsvietnam_69_70 .pdf.

62 "Convey the impression that Nixon is somewhat 'crazy'": Leonard Garment, *Crazy Rhythm* (Boston: Perseus Books, 1999), pp. 174–77.

63 "We are going through a critical phase": Nixon remarks, July 29, 1969, U.S. embassy, Bangkok, *FRUS* XX: Southeast Asia, 1969–1972.

63 "We have been using every diplomatic and other device": Memorandum of conversation, Nixon and Thieu, July 30, 1969, Saigon, *FRUS* VI: Vietnam.

64 "a complete and utter surprise": Holdridge oral history, FAOH.

64 "Between Jakarta and Bangkok": Ibid.

64 Yahya said he would convey the message: Pakistan's ambassador to the United States, Agha Hilaly, met with Kissinger's NSC aide Harold H. Saunders after Nixon returned to Washington in August 1969. Ambassador Hilaly had a ten-page memo from his president on the meeting with Nixon in Pakistan—a unique record. It said that "President Nixon stated it as his personal view—not completely shared by the rest of his government or by many Americans—that Asia can not move forward if a nation as large as China remains isolated. He further said that the US should not be party to any arrangements designed to isolate China." He asked President Yahya to convey his feeling to the Chinese at the highest level: "When President Yahya said it might take a little time to pass this message, President Nixon replied that President Yahya should take his own time and decide for himself the manner in which he would communicate with the Chinese.

"Hilaly said that Zhou En-lai had been invited to Pakistan and had accepted, but that it was not clear when he would come. He said President Yahya might, in a conversation with the Chinese Ambassador, simply say that the United States had no hostile intent toward Communist China but he would wait until he saw Chou En-lai to convey President Nixon's specific views."

Saunders told the ambassador: "We would like to establish a single channel for any further discussion of this subject should President Yahya have any questions about what President Nixon intended or any impressions of Chinese views which he might wish to relay to President Nixon. We would like to see Ambassador Hilaly and Dr. Kissinger as the two points of contact." Memorandum of conversation, Aug. 28, 1969, Washington, DC, *FRUS* XVII: China, 1969–1972.

64 "the card of the United States": Xiong Xianghui published the first documented records of Mao's task force. Xiong Xianghui, "The Prelude to the Opening of Sino-American Relations," Chinese Communist Party History Materials, no. 42 (June 1992), excerpts online at http://www2.gwu.edu/~nsarchiv/NSAEBB/NSAEBB145/.

65 "In 25 years": Private meeting between President Nixon and Ceaușescu, Aug. 2, 1969, Bucharest, *FRUS* XXIX: Eastern Europe, Eastern Mediterranean, 1969–1972.

65 "All this is possible": Memorandum of conversation between the president and President Ceaușescu, Aug. 2–3, 1969, Bucharest, *FRUS* XXIX: Eastern Europe.

65 "continue to fight in Vietnam": Ibid.

66 Nixon convened the National Security Council: President Nixon's notes on a National Security Council meeting, Aug. 14, 1969, San Clemente, CA, *FRUS* XVII: China.

66 "may have a 'knock them off now' policy": Minutes of meeting of the National Security Council, Aug. 14, 1969, San Clemente, CA, *FRUS* XII: Soviet Union. Kissinger, in his memoirs, called Nixon's tilt toward China in its clash with the Soviets a "revolutionary thesis": the president had declared that "we had a strategic

interest in the survival of a major Communist country, long an enemy, and with which we had no contact."

66 "Davydov asked point blank": William L. Stearman, memorandum of conversation, Aug. 18, 1969, Washington, DC, "SUBJECT: China: US Reaction to Soviet Destruction of CPR Nuclear Capability," *FRUS* XII: Soviet Union.

66 "the consequences for the US would be incalculable": Memorandum for the record of the Washington Special Actions Group meeting, Sept. 4, 1969, San Clemente, CA, *FRUS* XII: Soviet Union.

67 "The longer the war goes on": Kissinger to President Nixon, Aug. 30, 1969, "SUBJECT: Response from Ho Chi Minh," *FRUS* VI: Vietnam.

68 "We tried every operational approach in the book": Richard Helms, *A Look over My Shoulder* (New York: Random House, 2003), pp. 310–11.

68 "I was ready to use whatever military pressure was necessary . . . to bear on Hanoi": Nixon, *RN*, pp. 393, 398.

68 "The pressure of public opinion": Kissinger to President Nixon, Sept. 10, 1969, Washington, DC, "SUBJECT: Our Present Course on Vietnam," *FRUS* VI: Vietnam.

69 "sharp military blows": Kissinger to President Nixon, Oct. 2, 1969, Washington, DC, "SUBJECT: Contingency Military Operations Against North Vietnam," *FRUS* VI: Vietnam.

69 "If USSR thinks President is a madman": Vietnam, Contingency Planning, Sept. 12, 1969, Kissinger Papers.

69 "[Nixon held] one of those mystic sessions": Oct. 3, 1969, entry in *Haldeman Diaries*.

70 "Could you exercise the DEFCON?": Transcript of telephone conversation between Kissinger and Secretary of Defense Laird, Oct. 6, 1969 (declassified Oct. 14, 2011), Washington, DC, "The Joint Chiefs of Staff Readiness Test," in *FRUS* XXXIV: National Security Policy.

70 "an integrated plan": Memo to General Wheeler, Oct. 9, 1969, Records of the Chairman of the JCS, Earle Wheeler Papers. The document originally was obtained by William Burr of the National Security Archive under the FOIA, and first cited by Burr and Jeffrey Kimball in "Nixon's Secret Nuclear Alert: Vietnam War Diplomacy and the Joint Chiefs of Staff Readiness Text, October 1969," *Cold War History* 3, no. 2 (January 2003).

70 "the 'madman theory'": Laird interview with William Burr, June 18 and Sept. 6, 2001, National Security Archive, George Washington University.

71 "Tonight—to you, the great silent majority": Nixon address to the nation on the war in Vietnam, Nov. 3, 1969. Public Papers of President Nixon, full text online at http://www.presidency.ucsb.edu/ws/index.php?pid=2303.

72 "I am on the inside, the enemy": Watts oral history, FAOH.

7: "Don't strike a king unless you intend to kill him"

73 "a fifth-rate agricultural power": Kissinger, memorandum of conversation, "SUBJECT: Vietnam," Aug. 4, 1969, Ministry of Foreign Affairs, Paris. Full text online at http://nsarchive.gwu.edu/NSAEBB/NSAEBB193/HAK-8-4-69.pdf

73 "If we fail we have had it" and "'Don't strike a king'": Adm. T. H. Moorer, memorandum for the record, Oct. 11, 1969, Washington, DC, "SUBJECT: JCS Meeting with the President," *FRUS* VI: Vietnam.

74 "We have the following problem" . . . "What if it comes out?": Transcript of telephone conversation between President Nixon and Kissinger, Jan. 26, 1970, 3:30 p.m., Washington, DC, Kissinger Papers.

75 "rotting cadavers": Admiral Thomas Moorer, JCS 2610 message to Admiral John McCain, Feb. 18, 1970, Abrams Papers, cited in William M. Hammond, *Public Affairs: The Military and the Media, 1968–1973*, Center for Military History, Washington, DC, 1996.

75 "the bombing was basically ineffectual": Rushing oral history, FAOH.

75 "We have won the war" . . . "You talk peace, but you make war": Memorandum of conversation, Feb. 21, 1970, 4:10 p.m., Paris, *FRUS* VI: Vietnam.

76 "I want to run through the Laos situation" . . . "I don't want any questions left": Minutes of the National Security Council Meeting, Feb. 27, 1970, Washington, DC, *FRUS* VI: Vietnam.

77 "I'll have to fuzz their capacity": Transcript of telephone conversation between President Nixon and Kissinger, Feb. 27, 1970, Washington, DC, Kissinger Telephone Conversations, cited in *FRUS* VI: Vietnam, document 190, editorial note.

77 "There was a phrase in that paper": Lord oral history, FAOH.

77 "I knew it wasn't true": Transcript of telephone conversation between Kissinger and Haldeman, March 9, 1970, Washington, DC, Kissinger Telephone Conversation, cited in *FRUS* VI: Vietnam, document 190, editorial note.

78 "a lot of very young and very able Air Force officers": Holdridge oral history, FAOH.

8: "A pitiful, helpless giant"

79 "I don't think he ever slept": Haig Oral History Interview, Nov. 30, 2007, Nixon Library.

79 "there wasn't much we could do militarily," "went through the roof," and a "hard option": From minutes of Washington Special Actions Group meeting, March 19, 1970, Washington, DC, footnote 12: U. Alexis Johnson Files, Telcons, March–April 1970, *FRUS* VI: Vietnam.

80 "Mr. Helms said": Minutes of Washington Special Actions Group meeting, March 23, 1970, Washington, DC, *FRUS* VI: Vietnam.

80 "totally unprepared for combat": *History of the Joint Chiefs of Staff: The Joint Chiefs of Staff and the War in Vietnam, 1969–1970*, p. 149.

80 "President Nixon asked me to draft" . . . "to lead his country out of its mess": Marshall Green oral history, FAOH.

80 "I want Helms to develop": Kissinger to President Nixon, March 19, 1970, Washington, DC, *FRUS* VI: Vietnam.

81 "military effort against the Viet Cong in Cambodia": Helms to Kissinger, March 23, 1970, "SUBJECT: Proposals to Sustain the Present Regime in Cambodia," *FRUS* VI: Vietnam.

81 "Here was another": Memorandum of conversation, April 18, 1970, Washington, DC, "SUBJECT: Dr. Kissinger's Conversation with CIA Officer Recently in Phnom Penh." *FRUS* VI: Vietnam.

81 "Poor K": March 24, 1970, entry in *Haldeman Diaries*.

82 "Apologizing for my vulgarity": Helms memorandum for the record, March 25, 1970, Job 80–B01285A, Jan 1–June 30, 1970, DCI Helms Files, CIA.

82 "The Thai battalion": Telephone conversation between Nixon and Kissinger, March 26, 1970, Nixon Presidential Materials, Haig Special Files, National Archives, Washington, DC.

82 "fight such a limitation to the death": Haig to Kissinger, April 1, 1970, Washington, DC, "SUBJECT: Meeting with Secretary of Defense Laird and the President, 3/31/70," *FRUS* VI: Vietnam.

83 "Multiple unsolvable problems bearing in": April 15, 1970, entry in *Haldeman Diaries*.

83 "Set up political attack . . . Have to declare war": April 9, 1970, entry in ibid.

83 "an all-out hatchet job": March 10, 1970, entry in ibid.

83 "We have no intention" . . . "reap the whirlwind": Memorandum of conversation, Kissinger and Le Duc Tho, Paris, April 4, 1970, *FRUS* VI: Vietnam.

84 "the need for speed": McCain quoted in *History of the Joint Chiefs of Staff: The Joint Chiefs of Staff and the War in Vietnam, 1969–1970*, pp. 247–48.

84 "discussed possible cross-border attacks into Cambodia": Ibid.

85 "I think we need a bold move in Cambodia": President Nixon to Kissinger, April 22, 1970, Washington, DC, *FRUS* I: Foundations of Foreign Policy, 1969–1972.

86 "pussyfooting": Henry Kissinger, *White House Years* (New York: Little, Brown and Company, 1979), pp. 490–92.

86 "a political storm": Memorandum from Roger Morris, Winston Lord, and Anthony Lake of the National Security Council staff to Kissinger, April 22, 1970, Washington, DC, "SUBJECT: Cambodia," *FRUS* VI: Vietnam.

86 "P is moving too rashly": April 24, 1970, entry in *Haldeman Diaries*.

87 "There was no discussion": Memorandum of meeting among the president, secretary of state, secretary of defense, attorney general, April 28, 1970, Washington, DC, "SUBJECT: Cambodia/South Vietnam," *FRUS* VI: Vietnam.

87 "This is not an invasion of Cambodia": Nixon Address to the Nation on the Situation in Southeast Asia, April 30, 1970, Public Papers of Richard Nixon. The full text of the speech is online at http://www.presidency.ucsb.edu/ws/index.php?pid=2490.

87 "As Nixon concluded his maudlin remarks": Green oral history, FAOH.

9: "An unmitigated disaster"

88 "I made a very uncharacteristic": Nixon, *RN*, p. 454.

88 "P was really beat": May 1, 1970, entry in *Haldeman Diaries*.

88 "They're the greatest": Nixon, *RN*, p. 454.

89 "He's very disturbed": May 4 and 6, 1970, entries in *Haldeman Diaries*.

89 "We have to stand hard as a rock": Telephone conversation between Nixon and Kissinger, May 4, 1970, Box 363, Kissinger Papers.

89 "K. wants to just let the students go for a couple of weeks, then move in and clobber them": May 6, 1970, entry in *Haldeman Diaries*.

89 "The Cambodian incursion was an unmitigated disaster": Thomas R. Johnson, *American Cryptology During the Cold War, 1945–1989, Book II: Centralization Wins, 1960–1972*, Center for Cryptological History, National Security Agency, 1995, Top Secret Umbra, excised copy declassified 2013, pp. 572ff.

90 "By the time I had stopped laughing": Stearman oral history, FAOH.

90 "The press got hold" . . . "the advancing allies": Johnson, *Centralization Wins*, pp. 572ff.

91 "His instinct for the political jugular": Nixon, *RN*, p. 496.

91 "attack and counterattack": Exit interview with Charles W. Colson, conducted by Jack Nesbitt and Susan Yowell, Room 182 of the Executive Office Building, Jan. 12, 1973, Nixon Library.

91 "he'll do anything": May 16, 1972, NWHT, Oval Office.

92 "agitated and uneasy": Nixon, *RN*, p. 459.

92 "Four-thirty in the morning": Krogh Oral History Interview, Sept. 5, 2007, Nixon Library.

92 Lynn Schatzkin, Ronnie Kemper, and Joan Pelletier: Quoted in John Morthland,

"Nixon in Public," *Rolling Stone*, June 11, 1970, reprinted in Editors of Rolling Stone, *The Age of Paranoia* (New York: Pocket Books, 1972), pp. 306–9.

92 "flushed, drawn, exhausted": Krogh Oral History Interview, Sept. 5, 2007, Nixon Library.

93 "The weirdest day so far" and "The unwinding process is not succeeding": May 9 and May 15, 1970, entries in *Haldeman Diaries*.

94 "scooping up secret data": Sept. 30, 1969, entry in ibid.

94 "the President wants me to argue that he is as powerful a monarch as Louis XIV": James St. Clair, oral arguments before U.S. District Court judge John Sirica, May 1, 1974, *U.S. v. Nixon*.

95 "Marcos and his wife": Box 555, Symington Subcommittee, vol. 1, Nixon Presidential Materials, NSC Files, *FRUS* XX: Southeast Asia.

96 "democracy doesn't work": "Memorandum from the American Embassy in Thailand to the Department of State," Nov. 17, 1971, Bangkok, *FRUS* XX: Southeast Asia; see also "SUBJECT: Covert Support of the Thai Government Party in the Thai National Parliamentary Elections," Feb. 7, 1969, *FRUS* VI: Vietnam. "The Thai let us": Montgomery oral history, FAOH; Ambassador Unger's report on the Thai coup and Kissinger's analysis of the coup for Nixon are in *FRUS* XX: Southeast Asia.

96 "They had been content": James Marvin Montgomery oral history, FAOH.

97 "aware of our attacks": Nixon meeting with Souvanna Phouma, prime minister of Laos, and Kissinger, Oct. 7, 1969, "SUBJECT: The Public Position on US Activities in Laos," *FRUS* VI: Vietnam.

98 "The President chewed our butts": United States Senate Select Committee to Study Governmental Operations with Respect to Intelligence Activities, staff summary of Bennett testimony, undated but written in 1975. See also "Meeting with J. Edgar Hoover, Richard Helms, Lt. Gen. Bennett, and Adm. Gayler," June 5, 1970, Haldeman White House Files, Nixon Library.

98 "revolutionary terrorism" . . . "a plan which will enable": Presidential talking paper: Meeting with J. Edgar Hoover, Richard Helms, Lt. Gen. Bennett, and Adm. Gayler, June 5, 1970, Haldeman White House Files, Nixon Library.

98 "I'm not going to accept": Sullivan deposition, Nov. 1, 1975, United States Senate Select Committee to Study Governmental Operations with Respect to Intelligence Activities.

99 "in view of the crisis of terrorism": Nixon, *RN*, pp. 474–75.

99 "Haldeman basically gave him the portfolio": Huston oral history, Nixon Library, online at www.nixonlibrary.gov.

99 "we would continue our interdiction" . . . "it was worth taking risks": Minutes of Washington Special Actions Group meeting, June 15, 1970, 3:15 p.m., Washington, DC, "SUBJECT: Cambodia," Box H-114, "WSAG Minutes, Originals, 1970–1971, Cambodia 6/15/70," Nixon Presidential Materials, NSC Institutional Files (H-Files), NSC Files, National Archives, Washington, DC.

100 "I just hope they got it": Ibid. At 7:45 p.m. on July 15, the president called Kissinger to ask if he thought that the WSAG "got the message?" Nixon continued: "They said they were trying so I just hope they got it. No doubt about what we were going to do—we were going to take some gambles and risks."

100 "There were a great number of people": "Remarks by the President at WSAG Meeting," minutes of Washington Special Actions Group, Washington, June 19, 1970, Washington, DC, *FRUS* VI: Vietnam.

100 "We were instructed to receive him and take him to visit Lon Nol": Antippas oral history, FAOH.

100 "Phnom Penh did not need an Ambassador": Swank oral history, FAOH.

100 "The communists have overrun half of Cambodia": Special National Intelligence

Estimate SNIE 57–70, Aug. 6, 1970, Washington, DC, "SUBJECT: The Outlook for Cambodia," CIA.

101 "Listen, Henry, Cambodia won the war": Nixon to Kissinger, Oct. 7, 1970, Box 7, Chronological File, Kissinger Telephone Conversations.

10: "Only we have the power"

102 "Plan is for P": Oct. 14, 1970, entry in *Haldeman Diaries*.

103 "seeking to trap" . . . "We should bear in mind": Memorandum of conversation, Oct. 2, 1970, Madrid, *FRUS* XLI: Western Europe, NATO, 1969–1972.

103 "The differences between the United States": Background press briefing by President Nixon, Oct. 12, 1970, Hartford, CT, President's Daily Diary (declassified 2011), Nixon Presidential Materials, White House Central Files, National Archives, Washington, DC. Nixon also prepared a set of handwritten notes for the briefing. According to these notes, he planned to state that, in spite of differences in the Middle East, Latin America, and Europe, the United States and the Soviet Union shared a "vital" interest in communication to "avoid war," to "reduce armaments," and to "have trade." The president was neither "naive" nor "sentimental." The United States and the Soviet Union, allies in the Second World War, had become competitors in the Cold War. This competition would continue, even if the two countries agreed to hold a summit meeting. Rather than seek "quick victories," "sensational speeches," and "spectacular formulas," Nixon was determined to take the "long view" as he sought to build a "structure of peace" (notes from Oct. 12, 1970, Box 61: President's Speech File, President's Personal Files, Nixon Presidential Materials, National Archive, Washington, DC).

105 "unless the United States was willing": Memorandum of conversation, Oct. 22, 1970, 11:00 a.m.–1:30 p.m., Oval Office, participants included the president, Secretary of State Rogers, Kissinger, Gromyko, and Soviet ambassador Dobrynin, *FRUS* XIII: Soviet Union, October 1970–October 1971.

105 "P. obviously enjoyed the confrontation": Oct. 22, 1970, entry in *Haldeman Diaries*.

105 "a moment of unusual uncertainty": Memorandum from Kissinger to President Nixon, Oct. 19, 1970, Washington, DC, "SUBJECT: Your Meeting with Soviet Foreign Minister Gromyko, Oct. 22, 1970," *FRUS* XIII: Soviet Union.

105 "Put the past behind": Notes prepared by President Nixon for Oct. 22, 1970, meeting with Gromyko, undated, Washington, DC, President's Personal Files, Nixon Presidential Materials, Nixon Library.

105 "The US": Nixon to Kissinger, Oct. 12, 1970, 6:10 p.m., Washington, DC, Kissinger Telephone Conversations.

106 "Anyone who had lived in Chile": Phillips testimony, United States Senate Select Committee to Study Governmental Operations with Respect to Intelligence Activities, vol. VII, pp. 55ff., July 13, 1975, declassified 1994.

106 CONTACT THE MILITARY: The CIA's operations are fully documented in https://history .state.gov/historicaldocuments/frus1969-76v21 and Peter Kornbluh, *The Pinochet File* (New York: New Press, 2003).

107 A VIAUX COUP and OVERTHROWN: Ibid.

108 "come up with nothing": Sept. 15, 1970, entry in *Haldeman Diaries*.

108 "We wanted some confrontation": Oct. 29, 1970, entry in ibid.

108 "I could not resist showing them how little respect I had for their mindless ranting": Nixon, *RN*, pp. 492–93.

108 "a terrifying flying wedge of cops": Oct. 29, 1970, entry in *Haldeman Diaries*.

109 Larger government studies estimated: Lee N. Robins, "Lessons from the Vietnam

Heroin Experience," *Harvard Mental Health Letter*, Dec. 1994. See also Alfred W. McCoy with Cathleen B. Read and Leonard P. Adams II, *The Politics of Heroin in Southeast Asia* (New York: Harper and Row, 1972), pp. 223ff.

110 "a significant political failure" . . . "absolutely ruthless": Nixon, *RN*, pp. 495–97.

110 "amazing array of trivia" and "handling super fat cats and special assignments": Nov. 10 and 19, 1970, entries in *Haldeman Diaries*.

111 "John Dean asked me if I would set up a safe house" . . . He was also "quite dangerous": Miller oral history, FAOH.

112 "He started vying for favor on Nixon's dark side": Tim Weiner, "Charles Colson, Nixon's Political Enforcer, Dies at 80," *New York Times*, April 23, 2012.

11: "We're not going to lose this war"

113 "break the back of the enemy": CJCS Memo M-218-70, Dec. 23, 1970, Washington, DC, "SUBJECT: Conference with President Nixon," in Moorer Diary, July 1970–July 1974, Records of the Chairman.

114 "we've discovered that the enemy has our plan and is starting to mass their troops to counteract": Jan. 26, 1971, entry (declassified Nov. 2014) in *Haldeman Diaries*.

114 "we had received intercepts yesterday": Memorandum for the president's file by the president's deputy assistant for national security affairs Haig, Jan. 27, 1971, Washington, DC, "SUBJECT: Meeting of the President, Secretary of State Rogers, Secretary of Defense Laird, Director of CIA Helms, Chairman of JCS Moorer, Henry A. Kissinger and Alexander M. Haig in the Oval Office," *FRUS VII: Vietnam*.

114 "there could be no perception of defeat": *History of the Joint Chiefs of Staff: The Joint Chiefs of Staff and the War in Vietnam, 1971–1973*, Office of the Chairman of the Joint Chiefs of Staff, Washington, DC (declassified 2007), p. 5, Historical Division, Joint Secretariat, JCS.

114 "He did not agree with the connotation that the Laos operation was merely a raid": Memorandum for the president's file by Haig, Jan. 27, 1971, Washington, DC, "SUBJECT: Meeting of the President, Secretary of State Rogers, Secretary of Defense Laird, Director of CIA Helms, Chairman of JCS Moorer, Henry A. Kissinger and Alexander M. Haig in the Oval Office," *FRUS VII: Vietnam*.

115 "The pressure back here": *History of the Joint Chiefs of Staff: The Joint Chiefs of Staff and the War in Vietnam, 1971–73*, pp. 5–6.

115 "prodded remorselessly by Nixon and Kissinger": Alexander M. Haig, *Inner Circles* (New York: Warner Books, 1992), p. 273.

115 "The best legacy": Nixon to Kissinger, Jan. 24, 1971, Kissinger Telephone Conversations.

115 "our army's greatest concentration of combined-arms forces": *History of the Joint Chiefs of Staff: The Joint Chiefs of Staff and the War in Vietnam, 1971–73*, p. 9.

116 "Tchepone, a tiny town": Maj. Gen. Nguyen Duy Hinh, *Lam Son 719* (Washington, DC: U.S. Army Center of Military History, 1979), p. 90.

116 "We're not going to lose it": Feb. 18, 1971, NWHT, Oval Office.

117 "We can win in '72": Ibid.

117 "This is the moment of truth": *History of the Joint Chiefs of Staff: The Joint Chiefs of Staff and the War in Vietnam, 1971–73*, pp. 10–13.

117 THE PRESIDENT'S DECISION TO SUPPORT LAM SON 719: Kissinger to Bunker, March 1, 1971, Washington, DC, *FRUS VII: Vietnam*.

117 "the surface of the moon": Howland oral history, FAOH.

117 "Why is it that Hanoi": Minutes of a meeting of the 40 Committee, March 31, 1971, San Clemente, CA, *FRUS VII: Vietnam*.

117 "They've now fought for ten years against us": March 18, 1971, NWHT, Oval Office.

118 "It would be hard to exaggerate": Back-channel message from Kissinger to Ambassador Bunker, March 18, 1971, Washington, DC, *FRUS* VII: Vietnam.

118 "lost their stomach for Laos": *History of the Joint Chiefs of Staff: The Joint Chiefs of Staff and the War in Vietnam, 1971–73*, pp. 10–13.

118 "What has dramatically demoralized": *New York Times*, March 28, 1971.

118 "a bloody field exercise": Hinh, *Lam Son 719*, p. 163.

118 "a concrete demonstration": Military History Institute of Vietnam, *Victory in Vietnam: The Official History of the People's Army of Vietnam, 1954–1975*, trans. Merle L. Pribbenow (Lawrence: University Press of Kansas, 2002), p. 278.

118 "Tonight I can report": President Nixon, "Address to the Nation on the Situation in Southeast Asia," April 7, 1971, Public Papers of Richard Nixon, full text online at http://www.presidency.ucsb.edu/ws/index.php?pid=2972.

118 "The war has eroded America's confidence": April 21, 1971, NWHT, telephone tape.

119 "want to destroy you and they want us to lose in Vietnam": April 23, 1971, NWHT, Oval Office.

119 "All of this is a bunch of shit": Ibid.

119 "All that matters": May 10, 1971, NWHT, Oval Office.

119 "We'll bomb the goddamn North like it's never been bombed": April 6, 1971, NWHT, Old Executive Office Building.

120 "They relived": Statement by John Kerry to the Senate Committee of Foreign Relations, April 22, 1971, Cong. Rec. (92nd Cong., 1st Sess.), pp. 179–210.

120 "You'll find Kerry running for political office": April 23, 1971, NWHT, White House.

121 "Any military commander who is honest with himself": McNamara interview in *The Fog of War*, directed by Errol Morris (2003).

12: It's a conspiracy"

124 "This goddamn *New York Times* exposé": June 13, 1971, NWHT, telephone tape.

125 "It just shows massive mismanagement": June 13, 1971, NWHT, Oval Office.

125 "Goddamn it": June 15, 1971, NWHT, Oval Office.

125 "You can blackmail Johnson on this stuff": June 17, 1971, NWHT, Oval Office.

126 "Do you remember Huston's plan? Implement it": Ibid.

126 "You need a commander . . . It could be Colson": July 1, 1971, NWHT, Oval Office.

127 "We're up against an enemy" . . . "Is that clear?": Ibid.

127 "I just want to make that big play": June 29, 1971, NWHT, Oval Office.

127 "fears of what the President might do": Memorandum for the president's file, July 1, 1971, "China Trips, July 1971," Briefing Notebook, Kissinger Papers.

127 "We're not going to turn the country over": July 1, 1971, NWHT, Oval Office.

127 "You can say 'I cannot control him'": April 23, 1971, NWHT, Oval Office.

128 "I understand you are going to Beijing": Memorandum of conversation, Oct. 25, 1970, Washington, DC, "SUBJECT: Meeting Between the President and Pakistan President Yahya" (notes taken by Kissinger), *FRUS* E-7: Documents on South Asia, 1969–1972.

128 "The Chinese Government reaffirms its willingness": Memorandum of conversation, May 7, 1971, Palm Springs, CA, Participants: Joseph S. Farland, U.S. ambassador to Pakistan, Henry A. Kissinger, assistant to the president for national security affairs, *FRUS* E-13: Documents on China, 1969–1972.

128 "President Nixon was ambivalent": Lord oral history, FAOH.

128 "this was about as mysterious as you can get": Farland oral history, FAOH.

129 "'Do you know what I'm going to talk about'": Ibid.

129 "We were stepping into the infinite": Holdridge oral history, FAOH.

129 "As the sun came up": Lord oral history, FAOH.

130 "Kissinger and I and the others walked around": Ibid.

130 "as forthcoming as we could have hoped": Kissinger to President Nixon, July 14, 1971, San Clemente, CA., "SUBJECT: My Talks with Chou En-lai," *FRUS* XVII: China.

131 "repeatedly stressed—in an almost plaintive tone": Ibid.

132 "Krogh and his guys": July 20, 1971, NWHT, Oval Office.

132 "I listened intently": Egil Krogh, "The Break-in That History Forgot," *New York Times*, June 30, 2007.

132 "Where does Krogh stand now?": Sept. 8, 1971, NWHT, Oval Office.

133 "permanent tails": Ibid.

133 "On the IRS": Sept. 8, 1971, NWHT, Old Executive Office Building.

133 "We had one little operation" . . . "It may pay off": Sept. 8, 1971, NWHT, Oval Office.

13: "I can see the whole thing unravel"

134 "Our goal is clear": Conversation among President Nixon, Ambassador Bunker, and Kissinger, June 16, 1971, NWHT, Oval Office.

135 "There are no fair elections": Ibid.

135 "re-elect Nguyen Van Thieu": CIA memorandum for the 40 Committee, Feb. 3, 1971, Washington, DC, "SUBJECT: Covert Actions in Support of U.S. Objective in South Vietnam's 1971 Elections," *FRUS* VII: Vietnam.

136 "Turn on him? Never, never": Aug. 19, 1971, Washington, DC, Kissinger Telephone Conversations.

136 "Unless there is a real contest": Back-channel message from Ambassador Bunker in Saigon to Kissinger, Aug. 20, 1971, *FRUS* VII: Vietnam.

136 "For the hundredth [*sic*] and twentieth time": Kissinger, memorandum of conversation, Sept. 13, 1971, Paris, *FRUS* VII: Vietnam.

136 "The heart of the problem": Kissinger to Nixon, Sept. 18, 1971, Washington, DC, "SUBJECT: Vietnam," *FRUS* VII: Vietnam.

136 "A swift collapse": Ibid.

137 "I think we have to consider withdrawing the son-of-a-bitch": Sept. 14, 1971, Kissinger Telephone Conversations.

137 "Having been in the military" . . . "It was a grim picture": Lange oral history, FAOH.

137 "We have to keep in mind" . . . "not to overthrow Thieu": President Nixon's news conference, Sept. 16, 1971, online at http://www.presidency.ucsb.edu/ws/index .php?pid=3146.

138 "He started the damn thing!": April 7, 1971, NWHT, Oval Office.

139 "everything that flies" . . . "And with a victory": Sept. 17, 1971, NWHT, Oval Office.

139 "The behavior of the U.S.": NSC meeting on Vietnam, Sept. 20, 1971, Kissinger Papers.

139 WE ARE LAUNCHED ON A COURSE: Memorandum of conference with the president, Aug. 29, 1963, National Security file, JFKL. Richard Helms was at a White House meeting at noon on August 29, 1963, with the president, McNamara, and Rusk, among a dozen other top officials. The note taker recorded that Ambassador Lodge had already sent the message to the Vietnamese generals plotting to overthrow Diem that the United States would support them. "The President asked whether anyone had any reservations about the course of action we

were following," and Rusk and McNamara did. The president decided that "Ambassador Lodge is to have authority over all overt and covert operations" in Vietnam.

140 "We must bear a good deal of responsibility for it": Nov. 4, 1963, JFK Tapes, JFKL.

140 "the Kennedy Administration was deeply implicated": Neil Sheehan, "'Vietnam Hindsight' on the Kennedy Years," *New York Times*, Dec. 22, 1971.

140 "We have those tapes": Oct. 8, 1971, NWHT, White House.

141 "We've got to avoid the situation": Oct. 25, 1971, NWHT, White House.

141 "We will bomb the bejeezus" . . . "'Oh, horrible, horrible, horrible'": Nov. 20, 1971, NWHT, Oval Office.

14: "It is illegal, but . . ."

142 "These people are savages": Dec. 15, 1971, NWHT, Oval Office.

142 "a special feeling": Kissinger note attached to memorandum of conversation with ambassador to India Kenneth Keating and NSC aide Harold Saunders, June 21, 1971, National Security Council Files, Nixon Library.

143 "The Pakistani army was just murdering people": Veliotes oral history, FAOH.

143 "*Don't* squeeze Yahya": Nixon's handwritten note on Kissinger's memo, April 28, 1971, "SUBJECT: Policy Options Toward Pakistan," *FRUS* XI: South Asia Crisis, 1971.

143 "If they're going to choose to go with the Russians": Aug. 9, 1971, NWHT, Oval Office.

143 "She is a bitch": Nov. 5, 1971, NWHT, Oval Office.

143 "We will do everything we can": Nov. 15, 1971, NWHT, Oval Office.

144 "Yahya is beginning to feel cornered": Back-channel message from Ambassador Farland to Kissinger, Nov. 19, 1971, Islamabad, *FRUS* XI: South Asia Crisis.

144 "Is Yahya saying it's war?": Nov. 22, 1971, NWHT, Oval Office.

144 "didn't have any confirmation": Nov. 22, 1971, entry in *Haldeman Diaries*.

144 STRICTEST PRESIDENTIAL INSTRUCTIONS TO TILT TOWARD PAKISTAN: Back-channel message from Kissinger to Ambassador Farland, Nov. 24, 1971, Washington, DC, *FRUS* XI: South Asia Crisis.

144 "To the extent that we can tilt it toward Pakistan": Nov. 24, 1971, NWHT, Oval Office.

144 "Pakistan thing makes your heart sick": The president was in Key Biscayne, Florida; Kissinger in Washington, DC. Dec. 3, 1971, Kissinger Telephone Conversations.

144 "We have had an urgent appeal": Dec. 4, 1971, Kissinger Telephone Conversations.

145 Nixon authorized the arms transfers: Dec. 6, 1971, NWHT, Oval Office.

145 "The way we would do that is to tell the King": Dec. 9, 1971, NWHT, Oval Office.

145 "I was too easy on the goddamn woman": Dec. 6, 1971, NWHT, Oval Office.

145 "cold-bloodedly make the decision": Dec. 8, 1971, NWHT, Old Executive Office Building.

146 "I tell you, a movement of even some Chinese": Telephone conversation between Nixon and Kissinger, Dec. 8, 1971, NWHT, White House.

146 "What do we do if the Soviets move": Dec. 12, 1971, NWHT, Oval Office.

147 "Savages": Dec. 15, 1971, NWHT, Oval Office.

147 "only one place in the whole federal government" . . . "a federal offense of the highest order": Dec. 21, 1971, NWHT, Oval Office.

149 "the house detective": Memorandum for the record by David R. Young, "SUBJECT: Transcription of Tape Recorded Interview" of Admiral Welander by Ehrlichman and Young, Dec. 22, 1971, Nixon Library. This document, with handwritten annotations by Young on a hastily prepared typed transcript from the tape-recorded interview, was apparently purloined from Nixon's presidential records, then returned to the Nixon Presidential Library. Young's files remain almost

entirely sealed. A copy of the document can be accessed at http://nixontapes.org /welander.html.

149 "Your alter ego" . . . "Almost anything you name": Young, "SUBJECT: Transcription of Tape Recorded Interview," ibid.

150 "What we're doing here is, in effect, excusing a crime. . . . They had to": Dec. 22, 1971, NWHT, Oval Office.

151 "That's the question" . . . "Everyone else should go to jail!": Dec. 23, 1971, NWHT, Oval Office.

151 "Got any ideas?" . . . "That would do it": Dec. 24, 1971, NWHT, Old Executive Office Building.

151 "The main thing is to keep it under as close control as we can": Telephone conversation between Nixon and Mitchell, Dec. 24, 1971, NWHT.

151 warrantless wiretap on Radford: Memorandum for the president from David R. Young, undated, "SUBJECT: Record of Investigation into Disclosure of Classified Information in Jack Anderson Articles," Nixon Library.

151 "I don't care if Moorer is guilty": Dec. 24, 1971, NWHT, Old Executive Office Building.

151 "They can spy on him and spy on me and betray us!": Ehrlichman, *Witness to Power*, p. 307.

151 "The worst thing about it" . . . "But it's essential": Dec. 23, 1971, NWHT, Oval Office.

152 "it might partially explain their origin": Henry Kissinger, *Years of Upheaval* (New York: Simon and Schuster, 1982), p. 808.

15: "Night and Fog"

153 "immense opportunities and, of course, equally great dangers": Nixon, *RN*, p. 541.

153 "It isn't about China": Feb. 2, 1972, NWHT, Cabinet Room.

153 "Crack 'em, crack 'em, crack 'em": Ibid.

154 "Let's not have any illusions" . . . "they're suckers": May 4, 1972, NWHT, Oval Office.

155 "My order is to drop the Goddamned thing, you son of a bitch!": April 19, 1971, NWHT, telephone tape.

155 "Operation Sandwedge": The Operation Sandwedge plan is reproduced in the Final Report of the Senate Select Committee on Presidential Campaign Activities, better known as the Senate Watergate Committee or SSC, SSC Vol. 2, pp. 240–52. Caulfield's testimony on Sandwedge, its "covert intelligence-gathering capability," and his assignment to keep Don Nixon under surveillance is in SSC Vol. 21, pp. 9687–937. McCord's testimony on his role at CREEP and in the Watergate burglary is in SSC Vol. 1, pp. 125–248.

156 "From the campaign funds I need $800,000": Strachan talking memo for Haldeman, Oct. 28, 1971, House Judiciary Committee, better known as the Impeachment hearings, HJC Appendix IV, p. 45, Government Printing Office, Washington, DC, 1975.

157 "wheeler-dealers": Caulfield to Dean, Feb. 1, 1971, "SUBJECT: Hughes Retainer to Larry O'Brien," Senate Watergate Committee, SSC Vol. 21, p. 9755.

157 "Donald Nixon's son" . . . "a huge flap in Washington": Oakley oral history, FAOH.

159 "to move hard on Larry O'Brien": March 4, 1970, entry in *Haldeman Diaries*.

159 "making sensitive political inquiries at the IRS": To: H. R. Haldeman, From: Tom Charles Huston, July 16, 1970, Haldeman Papers, Nixon Library.

159 "As you probably remember there was a Hughes/Don Nixon loan controversy years ago": EYES ONLY: Higby to Dean, Aug. 10, 1970 (Higby was a White House aide known as Haldeman's Haldeman), Richard M. Nixon and Bruce Oudes, eds., *From: The President: Richard Nixon's Secret Files* (New York: Harper and Row, 1989), p. 151.

159 "Concerning Howard Hughes": Chapin to Colson, Dec. 12, 1970, in ibid., p. 186.
160 "The Secretary of Commerce came down": White oral history, FAOH.
161 "This Watergate thing kept coming back": Magruder oral history, Strober and Strober, *Nixon*, pp. 329–31.
162 "If this obsession . . . seems irrational": John W. Dean, *The Nixon Defense* (New York: Viking, 2014), p. 651.
162 "1972, as you know, was a very big year": Nixon interview on *Meet the Press*, broadcast April 10, 1988, NBC.

16: "From one extreme to another"

163 "It had a tremendous impact": Lord oral history, FAOH.
163 "the intangibles of your China visit": Kissinger to Nixon, Feb. 19, 1972, Washington, DC, "SUBJECT: Mao, Chou and the Chinese Litmus Test," *FRUS* XVII: China.
164 "We had no idea when they'd be back": Feb. 21, 1972, entry in *Haldeman Diaries*.
165 "I have read the Chairman's poems": Memorandum of conversation, Chairman Mao Tse-tung, Prime Minister Zhou En-lai, President Nixon, Henry A. Kissinger, Winston Lord, National Security Council staff, Feb. 21, 1972, Beijing, *FRUS* XVII: China.
167 "a different kind of communiqué": Lord oral history, FAOH.
167 "The conventional way": Memorandum of conversation, Nixon to Zhou, Feb. 21, 1972, Beijing, *FRUS* XVII: China.
167 "Why not give this up?": Memorandum of conversation, President Nixon and Prime Minister Zhou, Feb. 22, 1972, Beijing, *FRUS* XVII: China.
168 "the Taiwan question is the crucial question": Memorandum of conversation, President Nixon and Prime Minister Zhou, Feb. 24, 1972, Beijing, *FRUS* XVII: China.
168 "This would almost certainly be seized upon": Ambassador Marshall Green, FAOH oral history, privately published as *Evolution of US-China Policy 1956–1973: Memoirs of an Insider* (Arlington, VA: Association for Diplomatic Studies and Training, 1998).
168 "all hell had broken loose": Ibid.
169 "this communiqué was a disaster": Lord oral history, FAOH.
169 "Rogers arrived at the suite": Feb. 27, 1972, entry in *Haldeman Diaries*.
170 "The symbolism escaped no one": Green oral history, FAOH.
170 "Zhou En-lai handled the matter very skillfully": Lord oral history, FAOH.
170 "had very little to do with substance": March 21, 1972, NWHT, Oval Office.
170 "The network coverage" . . . "Shanghai at night": Feb. 22 and 27, 1972, entries in *Haldeman Diaries*.
171 "If the war in Vietnam": Memorandum of conversation, President Nixon and Prime Minister Zhou, Feb. 28, 1972, Shanghai, *FRUS* XVII: China.
171 "to negotiate an end to the war": Military History Institute of Vietnam, *Victory in Vietnam*, p. 289.
171 "We'll bomb the hell out of the bastards": March 14, 1972, NWHT, Oval Office.

17: "This is the supreme test"

172 "It looks as if they are attacking in Vietnam": March 30, 1972, NWHT, Oval Office.
172 "I don't know any more if I'm in northern South Vietnam or southern North Vietnam": Quoted in Sydney H. Schanberg, "'It's Everyone for Himself' as Troops Rampage in Hue," *New York Times*, May 4, 1972.
172 "We lose if the ARVN collapses": April 3, 1972, NWHT, Oval Office.

173 "For the President, battlefield success became paramount": Brown oral history, FAOH.

173 "There will be no consideration of restraints": April 4, 1972, entry in Moorer Diary.

173 "The P's massing a huge attack force": April 4, 1972, entry in *Haldeman Diaries*.

174 "God Almighty, there must be something": April 4, 1972, NWHT, Oval Office.

174 "An enormously potent ordeal": April 20, 1972, NWHT, Oval Office.

174 "I cannot impress upon you": Moorer to Admiral McCain and General Abrams, April 8, 1972. Nixon called Admiral Moorer into the White House the following week and told him, "American foreign policy is on the line, as I'm sure you know . . . and putting it in melodramatic terms, the honor of the armed services of this country. The United States with all of its power has had 50,000 dead. If we get run out of this place now, confidence in the armed services will be like a snake's belly. So we can't let it happen. . . . Don't lose. That's all. It's the only order you've got" (April 17, 1972, NWHT, Oval Office).

174 "The P called him and really laid it to him": April 6, 1972, entry in *Haldeman Diaries*.

174 "break the North Vietnamese": April 10, 1972, entry in *Haldeman Diaries*.

175 "When I showed the President Abrams' message": April 15, 1972, entry in Moorer Diary, *FRUS* VIII: Vietnam, January–October 1972.

175 "Any sign of weakness on our part": Nixon, *RN*, pp. 588–91 and 601.

175 "I have to leave this office": April 17, 1972, NWHT, Oval Office.

176 "I'll destroy the goddamn country": April 19, 1972, NWHT, Oval Office.

176 "Brezhnev is simple, direct, blunt and brutal": *FRUS* XIV: Soviet Union, October 1971–May 1972. Rose Mary Woods transcribed the memorandum from Nixon's taped dictation. Copies of the final version are on file in the Nixon Library. A stamped notation indicates that the White House Situation Room sent the message at 12:03 p.m. on April 20, 1972. Kissinger was on the plane heading for Moscow when the president's memorandum arrived.

176 "I put this brutally": April 20, 1972, NWHT, Oval Office.

177 "If they don't give anything": Ibid.

178 "All that is bullshit": Transcript of telephone conversation between President Nixon and Haig, April 21, 1972, *FRUS* XIV: Soviet Union.

178 "It was a tough speech": Nixon, *RN*, p. 593.

178 "There are to be no excuses and there is no appeal": Kissinger to Laird, April 28, 1972, *FRUS* VIII: Vietnam. The president had spent the day in the Bahamas and Key Biscayne. The full text of the message from Kissinger to Laird reads:

We have just received the following flash message from the President:
Immediate
From: The President
To: Henry Kissinger
1. The absolute maximum number of sorties must be flown from now thru Tuesday.
2. Abrams to determine targets.
3. If at all possible 1,000 sorties per day.
4. This will have maximum psychological effect.
5. Give me report soonest by message as to how this order is being specifically executed.
6. There are to be no excuses and there is no appeal.

179 "People didn't want to hear about it": Brown oral history, FAOH.

179 "I intend to cancel the Summit": Nixon to Kissinger, April 30, 1972, from Connally ranch in Texas, *FRUS* XIV: Soviet Union.

179 "As the pressure has mounted": Kissinger to Nixon, "SUBJECT: General Abrams' Assessment of the Situation in Vietnam," May 1, 1972, Washington, DC, *FRUS* VIII: Vietnam.

179 "The P kept telling him": May 1, 1972, entry in *Haldeman Diaries*.

179 "We will lose the country if we lose the war": May 4, 1972, entry in ibid.

180 "Hoover experienced loneliness": Mark Felt and John O'Connor, *A G-Man's Life* (New York: Public Affairs, 2006), p. 160.

180 "He died at the right time": June 2, 1972, NWHT, White House.

180 "Pat, I am going to appoint you": L. Patrick Gray III with Ed Gray, *In Nixon's Web: A Year in the Crosshairs of Watergate* (New York: Times Books, 2008), pp. 17–18.

180 "Never, never figure that anyone's your friend": May 4, 1972, NWHT, White House.

180 "We were now faced with three alternatives" . . . "The more the P thought about it": May 4, 1972, entry in *Haldeman Diaries*.

181 "Admiral, what I am going to say to you now is in total confidence": May 4, 1972, NWHT, Old Executive Office Building.

182 "The P very strongly put the thing": May 4, 1972, entry in *Haldeman Diaries*.

182 "We've had a damned good foreign policy": May 5, 1972, NWHT, Oval Office.

183 "I still think we ought to take the dikes out now": April 25, 1972, NWHT, Old Executive Office Building.

183 "The best way to assure that we could win was to pick our opponent": April 29, 1972, entry in *Haldeman Diaries*.

184 "The real question is whether the Americans give a damn anymore": Memorandum for the president's files, May 8, 1972, "SUBJECT: National Security Council Meeting," *FRUS* VIII: Vietnam.

184 "We now have a clear, hard choice": President's Address to the Nation on the Situation in Southeast Asia, May 8, 1972, Public Papers of Richard Nixon.

185 "I have determined that we should go for broke": Memorandum from Nixon to Kissinger, May 9, 1972, Washington, DC, *FRUS* VIII: Vietnam.

185 "the biggest dogfight since World War Two": Washington Special Actions Group meeting, May 10, 1972, Washington, DC, "SUBJECT: Vietnam," *FRUS* VIII: Vietnam.

186 "The record of World War II": Helms to Kissinger, Aug. 22, 1972, "An Assessment of the US Bombing and Mining Campaign in North Vietnam," *FRUS* VIII: Vietnam. The full text of the cover note Helm wrote on this assessment reads: "The record of World War II, the Korean War and Vietnam since 1965 strongly suggests that bombing alone is unlikely to transcend the realm of severe harassment and achieve true interdiction in the sense of stopping the movement of supplies a determined, resourceful enemy deems essential and is willing to pay almost any price to move."

186 "I want you to convey directly": Nixon to Kissinger and Haig, May 19, 1972, Washington, DC, HAK/President Memos, Top Secret/Eyes Only, NSC Files, Nixon Library.

18: "Palace intrigue"

187 "guide the course of history": Churchill quoted in Raymond A. Callahan, *Churchill: Retreat from Empire* (Wilmington, DE: SR Books, 1984), p. 185.

187 "The problem with the relationship": Toon oral history, FAOH.

188 "Pretty scary": May 11, 1969, entry in *Haldeman Diaries*.

189 "I read last night the whole SALT thing. . . . There's an awful lot still left to be worked out": May 19, 1972, NWHT, Oval Office.

189 "We have a few snags": May 19, 1972, Kissinger Telephone Conversations.

189 "indispensable": Conversation among President Nixon, the Joint Chiefs of Staff, Secretary of Defense Laird, and others, Aug. 10, 1971, Washington, DC, *FRUS* XXXII: SALT I, 1969–1972.

189 "there would be no limitations on MIRVs": Memorandum, July 31, 1970, Washington, DC, "Detailed Statement of the Provisions of U.S. SALT Position," *FRUS* XXXII: SALT I.

189 "Never before have nations limited the weapons on which their survival depends": Kissinger to Nixon, Tuesday, May 23, 1972, "SUBJECT: Your Moscow Discussions," *FRUS* XIV: Soviet Union.

189 "The fact that the two great adversaries could sit down": Garthoff oral history, FAOH.

190 "P was whisked off": May 22, 1972, entry in *Haldeman Diaries*.

190 "The war which the United States" . . . "a confidential talk": Memorandum of conversation, Brezhnev and Nixon, May 22, 1972, Moscow, *FRUS* XIV: Soviet Union.

191 "We are great powers": Box 75, President's Speech File, "May 22–29, 1972, Russia," President's Personal Files, White House Special Files, Nixon Library.

191 "We are both civilized men": Memorandum of conversation, Brezhnev and Nixon, transcribed from Kissinger's notes, *FRUS* XIV: Soviet Union.

192 "That the President of the United States": Gerald C. Smith, *Doubletalk: The Story of the First Strategic Arms Limitation Talks* (New York: Doubleday, 1980), p. 414.

192 "the single most emotional meeting": June 2, 1972, NWHT, Oval Office.

192 "Why don't we go see it right now?": Nixon, *RN*, p. 612.

192 "all of a sudden the P and Brezhnev": May 24, 1972, entry in *Haldeman Diaries*.

192 "Followed by Nixon's own car": Kissinger, *White House Years*, p. 1223.

193 "We certainly did not choose," "We want to sign important documents," and "Our people want peace": Memorandum of conversation, May 24, 1972, "SUBJECT: Vietnam," Moscow, *FRUS* XIV: Soviet Union.

194 "after the motorcade": Kissinger, *White House Years*, pp. 1228–29.

194 "The real problem": Back-channel message from Haig to Kissinger in Moscow, May 25, 1972, Washington, DC, *FRUS* XIV: Soviet Union.

195 "There is no room for additional compromise": Memorandum of conversations, May 25, 1972, 5:20–6:35 p.m. and 11:30 p.m.–12:32 a.m., Moscow, "SUBJECT: SALT," *FRUS* XXXII: SALT I.

Kissinger wrote in his memoirs that before the SALT discussions resumed at 5:20 p.m. (with, as usual, only a half hour's warning), he and his staff were "frantically analyzing various combinations of figures; the permutations seemed endless, but [they] had to ensure that the Soviets dismantled the maximum number of missiles. The numbers game of submarine baselines—how many could be traded in, and when they would reach different levels by various combinations of twelve-tube and sixteen-tube boats—forced us into numerous computations on long yellow pads, drawn up between sessions and then quickly scratched up and consumed during meetings." After the midnight meeting, Kissinger went to Nixon's Kremlin residence and reported that the talks had reached an impasse that only the Soviets could break. But he was "fairly confident" that the Soviets would accept the final U.S. proposal: "They could not permit a negotiation that lasted nearly three years to go down the drain" over the issues of silo dimensions and submarine missiles (*White House Years*, pp. 1236–40).

195 "There are two questions left open from yesterday": Memorandum of conversation, May 26, 1972, Moscow, "SUBJECTS: SALT; Communiqué," *FRUS* XIV: Soviet Union.

196 "In his compulsive need to control events, Kissinger had deceived everybody": Jaeger oral history, FAOH.

196 "Not one U.S. program was stopped by SALT": Minutes of a meeting of the Verification Panel, April 23, 1974, Washington, DC, *FRUS* XXXIII: SALT II, 1972–1980.

196 "The MIRV explosion": William G. Hyland, *Mortal Rivals: Superpower Relations from Nixon to Reagan* (New York: Random House, 1987), p. 54.

196 "I wish I had thought through the implications of a MIRVed world": Kissinger background briefing, Dec. 3, 1971, cited in Walter Isaacson, *Kissinger: A Biography* (New York: Simon and Schuster, 2005), p. 322.

197 "an explosive one": Memorandum of conversation, May 22, 1972, Moscow, *FRUS* XIV: Soviet Union.

197 "There are in the world today" . . . "whose are being cut": Memorandum of conversation, May 26, 1972, Moscow, *FRUS* XIV: Soviet Union.

197 "The Americans really are miracle workers!": Nixon, *RN*, p. 616.

197 "not for a summit of one summer": President Nixon's notes for an address to a Joint Session of the Congress on June 1, White House Special Files, Nixon Library, and President's address to a joint session of the Congress on return from Austria, the Soviet Union, Iran, and Poland, June 1, 1972, Public Papers of Richard Nixon.

198 "How would you see it" and "It would be very constructive": Memorandum of conversation among Brezhnev, Nixon, and Kissinger, May 29, 1972, Moscow, *FRUS* XIV: Soviet Union.

198 "the President agreed to furnish Iran with laser bombs and F-14s and F-15s": Memorandum of conversation, May 31, 1972, 10:30 a.m. to 12:00 p.m., Saadabad Palace, Tehran, Iran, Participants: Mohammad Reza Pahlavi, shah of Iran; the president; Dr. Henry A. Kissinger, *FRUS* E-4: Documents on Iran and Iraq, 1969–1972.

198 "all available sophisticated weapons short of the atomic bomb": Harold Saunders of the National Security Council staff to Kissinger, June 12, 1972, Washington, DC, *FRUS* E-4: Documents on Iran and Iraq.

199 "That was a fateful, disastrous step": Killgore oral history, FAOH.

199 "He wanted a conversation with His Imperial Majesty": Farland oral history, FAOH.

19: "We have produced a horrible tragedy"

203 "We got back into the Democratic break-in again": June 20, 1972, entry in *Haldeman Diaries*.

204 "What's the dope on the Watergate incident?": June 21, 1972, Nixon White House Tapes, Oval Office.

205 "Good deal!": June 23, 1972, NWHT, Oval Office.

205 "These should never see the light of day": Gray, *In Nixon's Web*, pp. 81–82. Dean corroborated Gray's account in his Watergate testimony.

206 "President Johnson told me": Haig to Kissinger, June 18, 1972, *FRUS* VIII: Vietnam.

206 "This arrogant son of a bitch is a traitor": Colson personal letter to Jay Lovestone, April 29, 1972. Lovestone, once a leader in the Communist Party of the United States, had become the fervently anticommunist director of the international division of the AFL/CIO; his office was jokingly called the AFL/CIA because Lovestone had worked closely with the Agency in the 1950s.

206 "Assault Book": Memorandum from Patrick Buchanan (with Ken Khachigian) for Nixon and Haldeman, June 8, 1972, Subject: "Assault Strategy," reprinted in

From: *The President: Richard Nixon's Secret Files*, edited by Bruce Oudes (New York: Harper and Row, 1989), pp. 463–74.

206 "It was a nightmare for me": McGovern oral history, Strober and Strober, *Nixon*, p. 264.

207 "We're sitting on a powder keg": Aug. 1, 1972, NWHT, Oval Office.

207 "if you stay ten points ahead" . . . "a settlement by Election Day": Aug. 2, 1972, NWHT, Oval Office.

208 "What in the name of God are we doing on this score?" . . . "We have all this power": Aug. 3, 1972, NWHT, Oval Office.

208 "All of our people are gun-shy": Aug. 3, 1972, entry in President's Daily Diary.

208 "My eyes burned from the lingering sting of tear gas": Nixon, *RN*, p. 678.

209 "Bad news": Ibid., pp. 679–80.

209 "Well, you had quite a day today, didn't you?": Sept. 15, 1972, NWHT, Oval Office.

210 "hurt all of us deeply": Bolz oral history, FBI.

210 "I knew somebody would break": Oct. 19, 1972, NWHT, Oval Office.

210 "He said: 'You have to tell us' ": Ibid.

211 "We set up dinner on the *Sequoia*": Sept. 28, 1972, entry in *Haldeman Diaries*.

211 "I know we have to end the war" . . . "He's made these tough decisions": Sept. 29, 1972, NWHT, Oval Office.

212 "We have a major crisis with Thieu" . . . "And cram it down his throat": Transcript of a telephone conversation between President Nixon and Kissinger, Oct. 4, 1972, Library of Congress, Kissinger Papers. The President's Daily Diary says Nixon was at Camp David when he placed the call, and Kissinger was in Washington.

212 "We must concentrate our efforts on doing whatever it takes to resolve our first objective": Doan Huyen, "Defeating the Americans: Fighting and Talking," in *The Diplomatic Front During the Paris Peace Talks on Vietnam*, edited by Vu Son Thuy, translated by Merle Pribbenow (Hanoi: National Political Publishing House, 2004), pp. 138–40.

213 "Well, you got three out of three, Mr. President": Oct. 12, 1972, NWHT, Old Executive Office Building.

215 "The P kept interrupting Henry": Oct. 12, 1972, entry in *Haldeman Diaries*.

215 "The Vietnam deal": Oct. 22, 1972, entry in ibid.

215 "Thieu has just rejected the entire plan": Back-channel message from Kissinger to Haig (Hakto 37/215), Oct. 22, 1972, Saigon.

215 "It is hard to exaggerate": Back-channel message from Kissinger to Haig (Hakto 41/219), Oct. 22, 1972, Saigon.

215 "The South Vietnamese people will assume that we have been sold out": Bunker to Haig, Oct. 22, 1972, Saigon.

216 "I knew immediately": Nixon, *RN*, p. 705.

216 "Peace is at hand": Kissinger, *White House Years*, p. 1400.

216 "The President regarded Kissinger's gaffe as a disaster": Haig, *Inner Circles*, p. 302.

217 "Your Government has managed to enrage the President": Memorandum of conversation: Henry A. Kissinger; Winston Lord; Tran Kim Phuong, ambassador of the Republic of Vietnam to the United States, Jan. 3, 1973, Washington, DC.

20: "A hell of a way to end the goddamn war"

218 "I am at a loss to explain": Nixon, *RN*, p. 717.

218 "We've got to really do something regarding a new government": Sept. 20, 1972, entry in *Haldeman Diaries*.

219 "It was done in an appallingly brutal way": Schultz oral history, Strober and Strober, *Nixon*, p. 272.

219 "it was a mistake": Nixon, *RN*, p. 769.

219 "ruin the Foreign Service": Nov. 13, 1972, NWHT, Oval Office.
219 "That goddamn Thieu": Nov. 15, 1972, Kissinger telephone conversations, Nixon Library.
219 "The list was so preposterous": Kissinger, *White House Years*, p. 1417.
220 I WOULD BE PREPARED TO AUTHORIZE A MASSIVE STRIKE: Back-channel message from Nixon to Kissinger in Paris (Tohak 78), Nov. 24, 1972.
220 "It's just a hell of a way to end the goddamn war": Nov. 30, 1972, NWHT, Oval Office.
220 "Above all" . . . "Start bombing the bejeezus": Haig memorandum, Nov. 30, 1972, "SUBJECT: The President's Meeting with the Joint Chiefs of Staff," *FRUS* IX: Vietnam, October 1972–January 1973.
220 "really agony" . . . "keep the hopes alive": Dec. 5–8, 1972, entries in *Haldeman Diaries*.
221 "only one viable realistic choice": Memo from Secretary of Defense Laird to President Nixon, Dec. 12, 1972, Washington, DC, "SUBJECT: Ceasefire Agreement."
221 "definitely on the front burner": Dec. 13 and 14, 1972, entries in Moorer Diary.
221 "They're shits" . . . "and never forget it": Dec. 14, 1972, NWHT, Oval Office.
222 "the P": Dec. 16, 1972, entry in *Haldeman Diaries*.
222 "The whole thing that counts": Dec. 17, 1972, Kissinger Telephone Conversations.
223 "He emphasized that 'the strikes must come off'" . . . "'damn certain everybody understood'": Dec. 17 and 18, 1972, entries in Moorer Diary.
223 "to stiffen his back" . . . "any more of this crap": Nixon, *RN*, pp. 734–35.
223 "You will be watched on a real-time basis": Dec. 18, 1972, entry in Moorer Diary.
223 "Now that we have crossed the bridge let's brutalize them": Telephone conversation between Moorer and Kissinger, Dec. 19, 1972, entry in Moorer Diary.
223 "The P kept coming back to the B-52 loss problem": Dec. 20, 1973, entry in *Haldeman Diaries*.
224 "He got kicked in the teeth": Dec. 20, 1972, NWHT, Oval Office.
224 "I just came from the President" . . . "This is a helluva way to run a war": Dec. 22–25, 1972, entries in Moorer Diary.
224 "Moorer is preparing a big strike": Dec. 23, 1972, Kissinger Telephone Conversations.
224 "This is December 24, 1972": Dec. 24, 1972, entry in President's Daily Diary.
225 "I've just lived through the most terrifying hour of my life": Dec. 27, 1972, NWHT, Oval Office.
225 "Never!" . . . "At great cost": Ibid.
225 "We gave them a hell of a good bang": Ibid.
225 "swallowed the hook": Dec. 28, 1972, entry in Moorer Diary.
226 "Colson could be in some real soup" . . . "undeniable specifics": Jan. 3, 1973, NWHT, Oval Office.
227 "Gordon Strachan": Smith oral history, FAOH.
227 "Colson told me": Nixon, *RN*, p. 745.
228 "I know it's tough for all of you": Jan. 8, 1973, NWHT, Old Executive Office Building.
228 "at an end" . . . "the way in which we use these years": Nixon, *RN*, pp. 746–51.

21: "You could get a million dollars"

229 "After the cease-fire": Jan. 23, 1973, entry in *Haldeman Diaries*.
229 "Whack the hell out of them": March 7, 1973, Kissinger Telephone Conversations.
229 "We have a stick and a carrot": Jan. 30, 1973, NWHT, Oval Office.
230 "Here's the judge saying I did this": Feb. 3, 1973, NWHT, Oval Office.
230 "all other illegal, improper, or unethical conduct": Senate Resolution 60, 93rd Cong. (1973–74), adopted unanimously, Feb. 7, 1973.
230 "We should play a hard game" . . . "not to let this thing run away with us": Feb. 9–11, 1973, entries in *Haldeman Diaries*.

230 "one that really had R.N. tattooed on him": Helms interview with Stanley I. Kutler, July 14, 1988, Box 15, Folder 16, Wisconsin Historical Archives, Wisconsin Historical Society, Madison, WI; cited with the kind permission of Professor Kutler.

231 "We would like to be able to put the DOD": Memorandum of conversation: President Nixon, Secretary of Defense Elliot Richardson, the Joint Chiefs of Staff, Feb. 15, 1973, *FRUS XXXV: National Security Policy, 1973–1976.*

231 "the most serious blunder": OPE Analysis, July 5, 1974, FBI Watergate Investigation.

232 "Would it hurt or help" . . . "We have got to get them": Feb. 16, 1973, NWHT, Oval Office.

233 "I must have scared him to death": Feb. 23, 1973, NWHT, Oval Office.

234 "This judge may go off the deep end": Feb. 28, 1973, NWHT, Oval Office.

235 "For Christ's sake": March 1, 1973, NWHT, Oval Office.

235 "Of course" said the president: Nixon press conference, March 2, 1973, Public Papers of Richard Nixon.

235 "morphed into a mini-Watergate" . . . "totally disenchanted": Dean, *The Nixon Defense*, p. 263.

236 "the continuing financial activity" . . . "No problem": March 2, 1973, NWHT, Oval Office.

236 "I am aware of what you're doing": March 7, 1973, NWHT, Oval Office. The presence of Pappas in the Oval Office is noted in the White House logs. But Nixon told his secretary, Rose Mary Woods, "I don't want to have anything indicating that I was thanking him for raising money for the Watergate defendants."

236 "I'll fire the whole goddamn Bureau": March 14, 1973, NWHT, Old Executive Office Building.

237 "Give them a lot of gobble-de-gook": March 14, 1973, NWHT, Oval Office.

237 "only if it's against the government": March 14, 1973, NWHT, Old Executive Office Building.

237 "Mr. Dean is Counsel to the White House" . . . "Members of the White House staff will not appear": The President's News Conference, March 15, 1973, Public Papers of Richard Nixon.

238 "There are some questions you can't answer": March 16, 1973, NWHT, Oval Office.

238 "Then you get into a real mess" . . . "We can't do it": Ibid.

238 "I realize the problems of being too specific": March 16, 1973, NWHT, telephone tapes.

239 "I think what you've got to do, John": March 17, 1973, NWHT, Oval Office.

239 "Is the Greek bearing gifts?": Dean repeated this conversational gem to Nixon during his "cancer on the presidency" soliloquy on March 21 and included it in his post-Watergate memoir *Blind Ambition: The White House Years* (New York: Simon and Schuster, 1976), p. 198.

240 "This is going to break this case": John J. Sirica, *To Set the Record Straight: The Break-in, the Tapes, the Conspirators, the Pardon* (New York: W. W. Norton, 1979), pp. 91–115.

240 "Future historians": Richard Kleindienst, *Justice: The Memoirs of an Attorney General* (Ottawa, IL: Jameson Books, 1985), p. 155.

240 "The only threat to the world's freedom" . . . "We are the force for peace": March 20, 1973, NWHT, Cabinet Room.

240 "I have the impression that you don't know everything" . . . "It's better to fight it out": March 21, 1973, NWHT, Oval Office.

242 "I would have to conclude that that probably is correct, yes, sir": *Hearings Before the Committee on the Judiciary on the Nomination of Louis Patrick Gray III*, 93rd Cong. (March 22, 1973).

243 "Gray is dead": March 22, 1973, NWHT, Oval Office.

243 "I don't give a shit what happens": March 22, 1973, NWHT, Oval Office.

243 "The courtroom exploded": Samuel Dash, *Chief Counsel* (New York: Random House, 1976), p. 30.

243 "The problem is" . . . "back to Washington": March 24–26, 1973, entries in *Haldeman Diaries*.

244 "A committee of Congress": March 27, 1973, NWHT, Old Executive Office Building.

244 "it isn't going to get any better": March 30, 1973, NWHT, Oval Office.

244 "Just remember" . . . "one foot outside it": Dean, *The Nixon Defense*, p. 363.

22: "Vietnam had found its successor"

246 *"Vietnam had found its successor"*: Nixon, *RN*, p. 783.

247 "that's the ball game": April 13, 1973, NWHT, Oval Office.

247 "Question: Is Hunt prepared to talk?": April 14, 1973, NWHT, Oval Office.

247 "I'm going to plead guilty": Magruder transcript, April 14, 1973, Book 4, Statement of Information, House Judiciary Committee, p. 709.

248 "The first one I talked to was your predecessor": Kleindienst, *Justice*, pp. 159–60. This is a verbatim transcript of a conversation tape-recorded by John Ehrlichman on April 14, 1973, and seized by the FBI and Watergate prosecutors roughly three weeks thereafter.

249 "It is a privilege to be here": Nixon remarks at the annual dinner of the White House Correspondents' Association, April 14, 1973, Public Papers of Richard Nixon.

249 "I didn't sleep but I did weep": Kleindienst, *Justice*, p. 161.

250 "What you have said, Mr. President": Nixon, *RN*, p. 827.

250 "Clearly he had been drinking": Dean, *The Nixon Defense*, pp. 415–16.

251 "What the hell am I going to do?": Gray, *In Nixon's Web*, p. 238.

251 "Everyone's in the middle of this, John": April 16, 1973, NWHT, Old Executive Office Building.

252 "The FBI has just served a subpoena": April 17, 1973, NWHT, Oval Office.

252 "intensive new inquiries": Nixon remarks announcing procedures and developments in connection with the Watergate investigations, April 17, 1973. Public Papers of Richard Nixon.

253 "throwing myself on the sword": Ibid.

253 "If matters are not handled adroitly": April 25, 1973, NWHT, Old Executive Office Building.

253 "I had never seen the President so agitated. . . . He was extremely bitter": William D. Ruckelshaus, "Remembering Watergate," speech before the National Association of Former U.S. Attorneys, Seattle, WA, Oct. 3, 2009.

254 "I don't think it should ever get out": April 26, 1973, NWHT, Oval Office.

255 "What the hell" . . . "get it done, done": April 28, 1973, NWHT, Camp David Study Table.

256 "respectable Republican cloth coat": The "Checkers Speech" transcript is among the Public Papers of Richard Nixon at http://www.presidency.ucsb.edu/ws/index.php?pid=24485.

257 "He looked small and drawn": Ehrlichman, *Witness to Power*, p. 390.

257 "The P was in terrible shape": April 29, 1973, entry in *Haldeman Diaries*.

257 "I followed my mother's custom": Nixon, *RN*, p. 847.

257 "an increasingly desperate search": Ibid., p. 850.

258 "Goddamn it": April 30, 1973, NWHT, telephone tapes.

258 *"You're* the Cabinet now, boy": Ibid.

258 "Still no cease-fire": NSC memorandum to Kissinger, May 9, 1973, "SUBJECT: Bunker Assessment of Vietnam Cease-Fire at X plus 90."

258 "Listen," she said: Lowenstein oral history, FAOH.

259 "Presidency had been so weakened": Stearman oral history, FAOH.

259 "It was the President's wish": Memorandum for the record, Vernon Walters, CIA, June 28, 1972.

259 "It will be very embarrassing": May 11, 1973, NWHT, Camp David.

260 "If you read the cold print": May 12, 1973, NWHT, Camp David Study Table.

260 "One of the things": Nixon, *RN*, p. 870.

260 "Henry ordered the whole goddamn thing": May 14, 1973, NWHT, Old Executive Office Building.

260 "Doesn't the President of the United States": May 11, 1973, NWHT, Camp David Study Table.

261 "Bullshit": May 11, 1973, NWHT, Camp David.

261 "a dangerous game we were playing": FBI special agent Nick Stames's interview with John N. Mitchell, May 11, 1973, FBI/FOIA.

261 "An FBI agent": Ruckelshaus speech to National Association of Former U.S. Attorneys, Oct. 3, 2009.

261 "Good god": May 12, 1973, NWHT, Camp David Study Table.

261 "the national security thing" . . . "son of a bitch": May 20, 1973, NWHT, Camp David Study Table.

261 "The bad thing is that the president approved burglaries": May 17, 1973, NWHT, Oval Office.

262 "If we allow ourselves": May 14, 1973, NWHT, Old Executive Office Building.

262 "He's thinking of you": Ibid.

23: "The President of the United States can *never* admit that"

264 "the grave, difficult and delicate issues": Nomination of Archibald Cox, Committee on the Judiciary, U.S. Senate, 93rd Cong., 1st Sess. (May 21, 1973), p. 143.

264 "the partisan viper": Nixon, *RN*, p. 929.

266 "The balance between the three branches": William Green Miller oral history, FAOH. Miller continued: "The balance in foreign affairs, defense and secret activities had tilted way over to a predominance by the Executive. This is the reason for war powers debate, and the War Powers Act, the struggle about treaty making, about who makes war, the efforts to limit the scope of executive orders, and deep inquiries into what actions require Senate ratification, the extent to which the legislature, the courts and the public should have access to information, including every aspect of intelligence. All of this ferment is from the same tapestry, the Gulf of Tonkin being the beginning, the first big lie that really bothered and shook the foundations of acceptable consensus between the White House and the legislature."

266 "Watergate is the bursting of the boil": Fulbright quoted in John W. Finney, "Cambodia: The House Gets Tough," *New York Times*, May 13, 1973. The financial trickery the Pentagon used to evade congressional restrictions on financing the war in Vietnam was extraordinary. "The Nixon Administration had utilized every possible way to keep things going," remembered Sen. Charles Mathias, a Maryland Republican. In 1972, "Mel Laird, who was then Secretary of Defense, exhumed a Food and Forage Act, which was a relic from the 19th century, which provided that when a cavalry commander got out beyond his normal source of supply, he could go to farmers and make a commitment that they would be paid for the hay that he would impound for his horses. Mel used the authority of the Food and Forage Act to get credit to keep going in Vietnam. . . . I think the mood developed in Congress that you just had to cut everything off because there were no halfway measures that would be effective" (Mathias oral history, FAOH).

266 "The Founding Fathers": *Senate Select Committee on Presidential Campaign Activities* (hereinafter Senate Watergate Committee), May 17, 1973.

266 "That could never happen here": Odle testimony, Senate Watergate Committee, May 17, 1973.

267 "The problem in Southeast Asia": Memorandum of conversation [notes by Maj. Gen. Brent Scowcroft, deputy assistant to the president for national security affairs], May 18, 1973, Washington, DC, *FRUS* XXXVIII: Part 1, Foundations of Foreign Policy, 1973–1976.

269 "he had a very important message": Caulfield testimony, Senate Watergate Committee, May 22, 1973.

271 "'I ordered that they use any means necessary'": May 23, 1973, NWHT, Oval Office.

271 "There's going to be a full-blown war": Joseph B. Treaster, "U.S. Forces Out of Vietnam; Hanoi Frees the Last P.O.W.," *New York Times*, March 29, 1973.

272 "There was no plan to end the war": May 24, 1973, Public Papers of Richard Nixon.

272 "Wouldn't it be better for the country": May 25, 1973, NWHT, telephone tapes.

273 "so that we can strategize": June 4, 1973, NWHT, Old Executive Office Building.

274 "a tape of a conversation": June 6, 1973, NWHT, Oval Office.

274 "I have no tapes": June 13, 1973, NWHT, Oval Office.

274 "It's almost a miracle": June 12, 1973, NWHT, Oval Office.

275 "We must recognize": June 18, 1973, NWHT, Oval Office.

275 "I think that I still have the record": Schlesinger Oral History Interview, Dec. 10, 2007, Nixon Presidential Library.

276 "we would never recover": Nixon, *RN*, p. 893.

277 "I thought to myself" . . . "'Nixon taped all of his conversations'": 2012 Chapman Law Review Symposium, 2012, "The 40th Anniversary of Watergate: A Commemoration of the Rule of Law," *Chapman Law Review* 16 (Spring 2012).

278 "Should have destroyed the tapes": Nixon, *RN*, pp. 901–4.

278 "The time has come to turn Watergate over to the courts" . . . "the conduct of this great office": Nixon address to the nation about the Watergate investigations, Aug. 15, 1973, Public Papers of Richard Nixon.

24: "The same enemies"

280 "Let others wallow in Watergate": Nixon remarks to members of the White House staff on returning from Bethesda Naval Hospital, White House Press Office, July 20, 1973, Public Papers of Richard Nixon.

280 "I'm going to hit them": June 13, 1973, NWHT, telephone tapes.

280 "We've been at this for four years": June 2, 1973, NWHT, Camp David Study Table.

281 "As you are well aware": June 3, 1973, NWHT, Camp David Study Table.

281 All testimony from Haldeman, Ehrlichman, and Mitchell quoted in this chapter is taken from the printed records of the Senate Watergate Committee.

284 "Now that we have disposed": Richardson affidavit, June 17, 1974, statement of information to House Judiciary Committee impeachment inquiry, Book XI.

285 "We've got an even worse problem than Agnew": Ruckelshaus, "Remembering Watergate."

286 "The President all along intended" . . . "the order discharging Cox": Ibid.

287 "I'm going to go home to read": These words were reported in newspapers around the world. "Whether we shall continue" and Doyle's remark are in James Doyle, *Not Above the Law* (New York: William Morrow, 1977), pp. 197–200.

288 "All our intelligence said": Minutes of a Cabinet meeting, Oct. 18, 1973, Washington, DC, in *FRUS* XXXVIII: Part 1, Foundations of Foreign Policy.

288 "The switchboard just got a call from 10 Downing Street": Transcript of telephone

conversation between Kissinger and Scowcroft, 7:55 p.m., Oct. 11, 1973, Washington, DC, in *FRUS* XXV: Arab-Israeli Crisis and War, 1973.

289 "If you don't do something": Armstrong oral history, FAOH.

290 "The Soviets were shipping warheads": Ransom oral history, FAOH.

290 "Nixon was in his family quarters": Sonnenfeldt oral history, FAOH.

290 "The Brezhnev letter" . . . "*what do we do?*": Moorer Diaries; CJCS Memo M-88-73, "SUBJ: NSC/JCS Meeting, Wednesday/Thursday, 24/25 October 1973," *FRUS* XXV: Arab-Israeli Crisis and War.

291 "One of the things that I recall": Eagleburger oral history, FAOH.

292 "A government of laws": Elliot Richardson, *The Creative Balance* (New York: Holt, Rinehart and Winston, 1976), pp. 46–47.

292 "to kill the President": Kissinger, *Years of Upheaval*, p. 581.

292 "You are absolutely free . . . ?": Hearings, Special Prosecutor, Committee on the Judiciary, U.S. Senate, 93rd Cong. 1st Sess., p. 570.

293 "a wild hare" and "Nixon lied to me": Saxbe oral history, Nixon Library.

294 "I for the first time realized": Jaworski oral history, Baylor University, Waco, TX. Online at http://digitalcollections.baylor.edu/cdm/ref/collection/buioh/id/1591.

294 "The answer—*fight*": Nixon, *RN*, p. 970.

25: *United States v. Richard Milhous Nixon*

295 "Above all else": Nixon, *RN*, p. 971.

295 "the so-called Watergate affair": State of the Union Address, Jan. 30, 1974.

296 "The biggest danger" . . . "the way he really feels": Nixon, *RN*, pp. 975–76.

297 "I meant that the whole transaction was wrong": The president's news conference, March 6, 1974.

298 "It is almost like we have a death wish": March 13, 1973, NWHT, Oval Office.

298 "all the additional evidence": The President's Address to the Nation, April 29, 1974.

299 "Deplorable, disgusting, shabby, immoral": Scott quoted in Christopher Lydon, "Senator Brands Conduct as 'Immoral,'" *New York Times*, May 8, 1974.

301 "The great tragedy": Nixon, *RN*, p. 1007.

301 "He came out to greet Chancellor Kreisky": White oral history, FAOH.

302 "The Egyptians, as I saw": Houghton oral history, FAOH.

303 "Wasn't that Nixon . . . ?": Nixon, *RN*, p. 1013.

304 "He stopped being the Secretary of State": Saunders oral history, FAOH.

304 "Who was going to be": Suddarth oral history, FAOH.

305 "a face carved out of wood": Goodby oral history, FAOH.

306 "My god, he really thinks": June 19, 1973, NWHT, telephone tapes.

306 "SALT—this is the most difficult": Memorandum of conversation, June 28, 1974, Moscow, *FRUS* XV: Soviet Union, June 1972–August 1974.

306 "We suggest that the U.S.": Memorandum of conversation, June 30, 1974, Oreanda, *FRUS* XV: Soviet Union.

307 "Sophisticates in the press": Memorandum of conversation, July 2, 1974, Moscow, *FRUS* XV: Soviet Union.

308 "For example, I am indicted": April 17, 1973, NWHT, Oval Office.

309 "I suppose it could be said": Nixon, *RN*, pp. 1050–51.

311 "*End career as a fighter*": Ibid., pp. 1056–57.

311 "Mr. President," Saxbe said: Saxbe interview with Stanley B. Kutler, May 15, 1987, cited in Kutler, *The Wars of Watergate* (New York: Alfred A. Knopf, 1990), p. 542.

313 "There was a hush as he went up to the podium": Ransom oral history, FAOH.

313 "I remember my old man": Nixon remarks on departure from the White House, Aug. 9, 1974, Public Papers of Richard Nixon.

Epilogue

316 "He just flat-lined": Steve Bull interview by Timothy Naftali for the Richard Nixon Presidential Oral History Project, June 25, 2007.

316 "Richard! Wake up, Richard!": This account of Nixon's brush with death is taken from the memoir of the physician who treated him, John C. Lungren, MD, *Healing Richard Nixon* (Lexington: University of Kentucky Press, 2003), pp. 83–89.

316 "What history says": Nixon/Frost interview, recorded May 4, 1977.

316 "As people look back on the Nixon administration": Nixon interview on NBC's *Meet the Press*, April 10, 1988.

317 "You have to, in some cases, sacrifice a lot of virtue": Ray Price interview by Timothy Naftali for the Richard Nixon Presidential Oral History Project, April 4, 2007.

Index

TIM WEINER is the author of five books. *Legacy of Ashes*, his history of the CIA, won the National Book Award. His journalism on secret government programs received the Pulitzer Prize for national reporting. As a correspondent for *The New York Times*, he covered war and terrorism in Afghanistan, Pakistan, Sudan, and other nations. He directs the Carey Institute's nonfiction residency program in upstate New York and teaches as an Anschutz Distinguished Fellow in American Studies at Princeton.